GENDE

YEAT

Irish
Studies

Richard Fallis, *Series Editor*

GENDER AND HISTORY IN YEATS'S LOVE POETRY

ELIZABETH BUTLER CULLINGFORD

SYRACUSE UNIVERSITY PRESS

82 Y£A

57242

Copyright © 1996 by Syracuse University Press
Syracuse, New York 13244-5160

First Syracuse University Press Edition 1996
96 97 98 99 00 01   6 5 4 3 2 1

Originally published in 1993. Reprinted by arrangement with
Cambridge University Press.

Extracts from W. B. Yeats's prose are reprinted with the permission
of Macmillan Publishing Company from *Essays and Introductions* by W. B. Yeats
© Mrs W. B. Yeats 1961.

Extracts from W. B. Yeats's prose are reprinted with the permission of Macmillan
Publishing Company from *The Variorum Edition of the Poems of W. B. Yeats,* edited by
Peter Allt and Russell K. Alspach. Copyright 1919, 1924, 1928, 1933, 1934 by
Macmillan Publishing Company, renewed 1947, 1952, 1956, 1961, 1962 by Bertha
Georgie Yeats. Copyright 1940 by George Yeats, Michael Butler Yeats,
and Anne Yeats.

Other W. B. Yeats selections are reprinted with permission of Macmillan Publishing
Company from *The Letters of W. B. Yeats,* edited by Allen Wade. Copyright 1953,
1954, and renewed 1982, by Anne Butler Yeats; from *Memoirs of W. B. Yeats,* edited
by Denis Donoghue. Copyright © 1972 by Michael Butler Yeats and Anne Yeats;
from *Explorations* by W. B. Yeats. © Mrs. W. B. Yeats 1962; from *A Vision* by W. B.
Yeats. Copyright 1937 by W. B. Yeats, renewed 1965 by Bertha Georgie Yeats and
Anne Butler Yeats; and from *Mythologies,* by W. B. Yeats. © Mrs. W. B. Yeats 1959.

The paper used in this publication meets the minimum requirements of American
National Standard for Information Sciences—Permanence of Paper for Printed
Library Materials, ANSI Z39.48-1984.∞™

Library of Congress Cataloging-in-Publication Data
Cullingford, Elizabeth Butler.
Gender and history in Yeat's love poetry / Elizabeth Butler
Cullingford. — 1st Syracuse University Press ed.
p. cm. — (Irish studies)
Originally published: Cambridge [England] ; New York : Cambridge
University Press, 1993.
Includes bibliographical references and index.
ISBN 0-8156-0331-2 (alk. paper)
1. Yeats, W. B. (William Butler), 1865-1939—Criticism and
interpretation. 2. Love poetry, English—Irish authors—History and
criticism. 3. Feminism and literature—Ireland—History.
4. Literature and history—Ireland—History. 5. Masculinity
(Psychology) in literature. 6. Women and literature—Ireland
History. 7. Sex role in literature. 8 Ireland—In literature.
I. Title. II. Series: Irish studies (Syracuse, N.Y.)
PR5908.L65C85   1996
821'.8–dc20   45-40268

Manufactured in the United States of America

For Alan and Daniel

WITH LOVE

From the dawn of time odes have been sung to love; wreaths heaped and roses; and if you asked nine people out of ten they would say they wanted nothing but this; while the women, judging from her own experience, would all the time be feeling, This is not what we want; there is nothing more tedious, puerile, and inhumane than love; yet it is also beautiful and necessary.

Virginia Woolf, *To the Lighthouse*

Read the *Agamemnon*, and see whether, in process of time, your sympathies are not almost entirely with Clytemnestra. Or consider the married life of the Carlyles and bewail the waste, the futility, for him and for her, of the horrible domestic tradition which made it seemly for a woman of genius to spend her time chasing beetles, scouring saucepans, instead of writing books. All human relations have shifted – those between masters and servants, husbands and wives, parents and children. And when human relations change there is at the same time a change in religion, conduct, politics, and literature. Let us agree to place one of those changes about the year 1910.

Virginia Woolf, *Mr. Bennett and Mrs. Brown*

Contents

Illustrations

Acknowledgments

In the making of this book I have incurred many debts of gratitude, both institutional and personal. The late Richard Ellmann was my first scholarly mentor, critic, and friend. Jane Marcus inspired my methodology, and was an unfailingly generous source of help and encouragement. In asking me to become his Associate Director at the Yeats International Summer School in Sligo, Declan Kiberd launched me into an experience without which the book would never have taken its present shape: it had its gestation during the six years of my tenure as Associate Director and then Director of the School. Many of my thoughts were first tried out on the stage of the Hawk's Well Theater and refined and polished in the pub afterwards. In Sligo I met people whose ideas and friendship were crucial to my work: George Bornstein, Angela Bourke, Carol Coulter, Terry Eagleton, Richard Finneran, Mary FitzGerald, Rob Garratt, Luke Gibbons, Marjorie Howes, Dillon Johnston, Karen Lawrence, David Lloyd, Lucy McDiarmid, Maureen Murphy, Edward Said, Ron Schuchard, Pat Sheeran, Mary Helen Thuente, Helen Vendler, Clair Wills and Katharine Worth. I am deeply grateful to Declan for introducing me to the stimulating mix of ideas, people, politics, and Irish culture that was and is the Yeats Summer School. I am indebted to all the members of the Yeats Society of Sligo, and to their secretary Georgie Wynne, for six years of support and hospitality.

At the University of Texas a group of friends and colleagues have provided intellectual stimulation, social relaxation, and shared childcare. Without Janis and Evan Carton, Betty Sue and John Flowers, Sue and Kurt Heinzelman, Chuck and Marcela Rossman, John Slatin and Anna Carroll, I might still have written the book, but life would have been harder and much duller. Janis Bergman Carton, Shelli Fowler, Kurt and Sue Heinzelman, Jane Marcus, Peter Middleton, Lionel Pilkington, and Ramón Saldívar generously read portions of the manuscript and suggested improvements. My colleague Barbara Harlow and graduate students Margot Backus, Tom Hofheinz, Katie Kane, Joe Kelly, Laura Lyons, Ed Madden, Rachel Jennings, and Karen Steele have made our Irish Interest Group an intellectually stimulating forum for discussion. Ivana Slavnic helped me to check references with exemplary patience and thoroughness.

The University of Texas itself has, in the persons of Vice-President William Livingston and Dean Robert King, given me much assistance with research and travel to Ireland. I have also benefited from a semester and two summers funded by Faculty Research Grants from the University Research Institute. At the inception of the project I spent a semester as Visiting Associate at Clare College, Cambridge; at its end I was awarded a National Endowment for the Humanities Fellowship (1991–92) to complete the manuscript. A Visiting Fellowship at University College Galway (1992) prompted a last crucial revision: to Dean Tom Boylan of the Galway Faculty of Arts, and to all those named above, my heartfelt thanks are due.

Saving the best wine for the last, I come to those who have read the manuscript in its entirety, and given me invaluable commentary, corrections, and suggestions. Without the labors of my husband Alan Friedman, an expert stylist, this book would be longer and less coherent than it is. Lyn Innes, a most generous reader to the Press, provided numerous valuable modifications to my argument. Deirdre Toomey and Warwick Gould solved textual problems, rectified errors, pointed out omissions, sent me articles, found references, and qualified my wilder assertions. No one could have been more thorough. To all four readers I dedicate whatever is good in this work. The errors are my own.

Portions of this work have already been published in a different form: Chapter 1 in *Gender and Irish Writing*, ed. David Cairns and Toni O'Brien Johnson (1991); Chapter 2 in *Yeats Annual* 9 (1992); part of Chapter 4 in *Textual Practice* 4.1 (1990); part of Chapter 5 in *Yeats: An Annual of Critical and Textual Studies* 9 (1991); part of Chapter 7 in *Yeats Annual* 4 (1985). My thanks are due to the editors for permission to reprint.

Abbreviations

Au   *Autobiographies*. London: Macmillan, 1955.
AV[A]   *A Critical Edition of Yeats's* A Vision (1925). Ed. George
            Mills Harper and Walter Kelly Hood. London: Mac-
            millan, 1978.
AV[B]   *A Vision*. 2nd ed. London: Macmillan, 1962.
AYF   *Always Your Friend: Letters between Maud Gonne and W. B.
            Yeats, 1893–1938*. Ed. Anna MacBride White and A.
            Norman Jeffares. London: Hutchinson, 1992.
CL1   *The Collected Letters: Volume 1, 1865–1895*. Ed. John
            Kelly. Oxford: Clarendon Press, 1986.
E&I   *Essays and Introductions*. London: Macmillan, 1961.
Ex   *Explorations*. Sel. Mrs. W. B. Yeats. New York: Collier,
            1962.
JS   *John Sherman and Dhoya*. Ed. Richard J. Finneran.
            Detroit: Wayne State University Press, 1969.
L   *The Letters*. Ed. Allan Wade. London: Hart Davis, 1954.
LDW   *Letters on Poetry to Dorothy Wellesley*. Ed. Dorothy
            Wellesley. London: Oxford University Press, 1964.
LMR   *Ah, Sweet Dancer: W. B. Yeats: Margot Ruddock: A Cor-
            respondence*. Ed. Roger McHugh. New York: Macmillan,
            1970.
LTSM   *W. B. Yeats and T. Sturge Moore: Their Correspondence,
            1901–1937*. Ed. Ursula Bridge. London: Routledge,
            1953.
Mem   *Memoirs: Autobiography–First Draft and Journal*. Ed. Denis
            Donoghue. London: Macmillan, 1972.
Myth   *Mythologies*. 1959. New York: Collier, 1969.
OBMV   *The Oxford Book of Modern Verse: 1892–1935*. Chosen by
            W. B. Yeats. New York: Oxford University Press, 1936.

SB   *The Speckled Bird.* Ed. W. H. O'Donnell. 2 vols. Dublin:
            Cuala Press, 1973.

SS   *The Senate Speeches.* Ed. Donald R. Pearse. London:
            Faber, 1961.

UP1–2   *Uncollected Prose.* Ed. John P. Frayne and Colton
            Johnson. 2 vols. New York: Columbia University Press,
            1970.

VP   *The Variorum Edition of the Poems.* Ed. Peter Allt and
            Russell Alspach. New York: Macmillan, 1957.

VPL   *The Variorum Edition of the Plays.* Ed. Russell Alspach,
            assisted by Catherine C. Alspach. New York: Mac-
            millan, 1966.

VSR   *The Secret Rose, Stories by W. B. Yeats: A Variorum Edition.*
            Ed. Philip L. Marcus, Warwick Gould, and Michael J.
            Sidnell. 2nd edn, London: Macmillan, 1992

YVP1–3   *Yeats's Vision Papers.* Ed. George Mills Harper, assisted
            by Mary Jane Harper. 3 vols. Iowa City: University of
            Iowa Press, 1992.

Note on texts

I have used the *Variorum Edition* of the poems in order to facilitate reference to earlier versions of Yeats's work. Where the difference between the first edition and the text used by the *Variorum* (the two-volume definitive edition of 1949) is significant, a matter of imagery, diction, or organization, I have quoted the earlier version, appending a "v" (for variant reading) to the page reference in the *Variorum*. Where variations are minor and do not affect the argument I have quoted directly from the *Variorum* text.

Introduction

When at the end of his poetic career Yeats self-mockingly numbers the female image among his circus animals, "Lion and woman and the Lord knows what" (*VP* 629), he demonstrates his sensitivity to the generic coerciveness of love poetry. The figure of "Maud Gonne" was a puppet controlled by the ringmaster, part of the "phantasmagoria" that allowed the famous "bundle of accident and incoherence" that was Yeats at breakfast to be reborn as a love poet, "something intended, complete" (*E&I* 509). To be a love poet one needs a Beloved to put "on show." Aware of the manipulation and objectification entailed by this procedure, Yeats knowingly juxtaposes "woman" and "lion" as animals that need taming. Yet "Maud Gonne" was also Maud Gonne, an individual who interpreted Yeats's poems as a personal tribute: "There is a danger of my growing very vain when I think of these beautiful things created for me – thank you" (*AYF* 294), she wrote when he sent her the "Raymond Lully" sequence. She, his first audience, saw his verse as unequivocally autobiographical: "To me you are too kind – You have often tried to defend & protect me with your art – & perhaps when we are dead I shall be known by those poems of yours" (*AYF* 356–57). Encouraging her reading practice by emphasizing correlations between the poems and the model, Yeats noted the "reference to your self in 'Among School Children'" (*AYF* 445). As late as 1925, when Gonne was no longer the Helen or Deirdre of his youth, he sent her the revised version of "The Sorrow of Love," commenting, "You may perhaps recognise the model for this particular portrait. I felt as I wrote that I had recalled the exact expression of that time & that I had seen it at last as I could not when I was young & dimmed the window glass with my hot breath" (*AYF* 431). Love poetry as portraiture becomes love poetry as circus act through the mediation of genre and audience: in the Big Top the poet must perform

I

the expected routines, and private intention is subsumed in public show.

In "Politics," which Yeats intended to stand at the end of his *Collected Poems*, the speaker attempts to separate public and private spheres. Thematically, the poem rejects politics in the interests of desire; generically, Yeats rejects public verse in the interests of love poetry, as the speaker turns away from the news report to gaze at a good-looking woman. Mann's statement, "In our time the destiny of man presents its meanings in political terms," is challenged by the semi-jocular ballad quatrains in which Yeats offers visual attraction as the individualist antidote to Mussolini, Stalin, and Franco:

> How can I, that girl standing there,
> My attention fix
> On Roman or on Russian
> Or on Spanish politics?

Written when the attention of the world had for a decade been anxiously fixed on just such topics, "Politics" sees love poetry as a distraction from history. In ironizing Mann it contests Jameson's assertion that the political perspective is "the absolute horizon of all reading and all interpretation."[1] Yet Adorno's suggestion that the lyric in its thematic withdrawal from the world bears the formal impress of intolerable political circumstances holds true for this poem. In naming rather than ignoring the dictatorships upon which he cannot concentrate, in mentioning the threat of war, if only to dismiss it, the speaker admits that his interlocutors may be right about the political turbulence of the 1930s:

> And maybe what they say is true
> Of war and war's alarms,
> But O that I were young again
> And held her in my arms!   (*VP* 631)

The title and epigraph impose themselves on our attention despite the poem's attempt to refute them. Love poetry cannot exclude itself from the processes of history.

Criticism is similarly bound to its political and historical moment: in constructing my Yeats, therefore, I have of necessity excluded many other Yeatses. My Yeats is more Irish than international modernist, less international modernist than traditionalist reviser of tradition. Topography, as Brian Friel suggests in *Translations*, is a political exercise. No literary map corresponds exactly to "the landscape of...fact," which is always irrecoverable, but every new map-maker emphasizes the revisionary value of her own "linguistic contour."[2] In reading Yeats's love poems through the lens of a genre-based feminist historicism, I am proposing a new map that is as partial (in both senses of that word) as those of my predecessors. I make no claim to comprehensiveness or exhaustive coverage: my choice of poems is shaped by my perspective. Although my focus is primarily the lyric verse, I do not consider all of Yeats's "love poems"; while I do discuss some of his "poems about love," not all of them lyrics. Yeats made the distinction himself: "The poems in 'Words for Music Perhaps' describe first wild loves, then the normal love of boy & girl, then follow poems about love but not love poems, then poems of impersonal ecstasy, & all have certain themes in common."[3] To pursue his distinction too rigorously is to risk an unproductive argument about categories; but for Yeats, love poems were direct emotional utterances, by "Yeats" or some other fictive persona, written to or about the beloved or about the lover's state of mind. "Poems about love" might be narrative rather than lyric, or reflective and philosophical rather than passionate.

Feminist critics are often characterized as humorless and pre-scriptive: "If the poet is lucky, he will be let off with a caution, and advised not to compose while under the influence of *fin-de-siècle* images of women."[4] To counter this negative stereotype I have tried to articulate a feminist approach to Yeats that relates ideology to aesthetics, and situates both in their cultural context. Yeats described himself as "a man of my time, through my poetical faculty living its history" (*OBMV* xxxiv). Through his love poetry he lived the history of the changing social relations between men and women, a history that modified the formal conventions he inherited from his pre-decessors in the genre. In "Lyric Poetry and Society"[5] Adorno suggests ways in which the supposedly private, subjective, and individualistic lyric mode registers social pressures for change, while Jameson has argued that "form is immanently and intrinsically an ideology in its own right."[6] When a new genre emerges, its formal conventions embody a symbolic social message, but later prac-titioners infuse the generic meanings of the original form with new and sometimes contradictory meanings produced by different his-torical conditions. The male love lyric, which is formally structured upon the figurative relations of power between lover and mistress, necessarily reflects changes in the actual balance of power between men and women.

The sexual politics of love poetry require analysis because the genre helps to create and sustain the various ideologies of love, which is not a natural force, but a socially created phenomenon with its roots in historical and material circumstances. La Rochefoucauld said that, "There are people who would never have fallen in love, had they not heard love talked about":[7] lust may be biological, but love is cultural. If we investigate the relations of power sustained by the discourse of romantic love, we discover that, despite the abjection of the lover before his goddess, most male-authored Western love poetry sustains the cultural superiority of men. Its canonical works deny to the beloved woman a voice and a subjectivity of her own: she is imaged as flower, star, Madonna, but seldom as a speaking subject. Representing women as beautiful, mysterious, and romantic, but also as silent and incapable of agency or of logical thought, "courtly" love poets like Dante, Petrarch, and their successors reinforce gender stereotypes even as they worship the Eternal Feminine.[8]

Yeats saw the importance of love in the production of gender identity: "Each divines the secret self of the other, and refusing to believe in the mere daily self, creates a mirror where the lover or the beloved sees an image to copy in daily life" (*Au* 464). Love poetry too functions as a mirror in which women see themselves, but the image represented there is mediated by the male gaze: as Berger puts it, "Men look at women. Women watch themselves being looked at."[9] In giving women an "image to copy in daily life," love poets claim to divine the "secret self" that is the essence of femininity. The anthropologist Jane Harrison wondered why "women never want to write poetry about Man as a sex – why is Woman a dream and a terror to man and not the other way around?"[10] Meditating on Harrison's question, Adrienne Rich describes her experience as a female reader of the male canon:

And there were all those poems about women, written by men: it seemed to be a given that men wrote poems and women frequently inhabited them. These women were almost always beautiful, but threatened with the loss of beauty, the loss of youth – the fate worse than death. Or, they were beautiful and died young, like Lucy and Lenore. Or, the woman was like Maud Gonne, cruel and disastrously mistaken, and the poem reproached her because she had refused to become a luxury for the poet.[11]

Speaking of the loss of youth and the transience of beauty, Rich evokes the *carpe diem* tradition, which is neither courtly nor romantic, and treats the beautiful woman as an object of lust rather than as an aesthetic inspiration. Neither as Madonna/Muse nor as sexual toy, however, can a woman voice her own desire or exist as a speaking subject. The tradition of women's love poetry provides some exceptions; but in its deployment of conventional tropes (woman as rose; love as hunting, war, or death; the blazon) and fixed linguistic and spatial relations (the abject but loquacious male lover, the elevated but silent female Beloved) most variants of the genre have been conservative, successfully naturalizing and universalizing their socially constructed ideological premises.

Yeats may appear vulnerable to feminist criticism on two grounds: as a love poet in a tradition that has stereotyped and silenced its female object, and as a modernist. Feminist critics of modernism have both re-evaluated neglected women writers and challenged the canons of modernist form established by misogynist writers like Eliot and Pound. Eliot and Pound were not, at least after World War One, much interested in love poetry – perhaps because it was a popular, accessible genre; perhaps because, according to Woolf, "on or about December, 1910, human character changed," and the shift in relations between men and women modified the forms of literary expression.[12] Modernist love poems are few: "The Love Song of J. Alfred Prufrock" thematizes the difficulty of the genre for a modern male sensibility terrorized by vampiric women who keep the subject "pinned and wriggling on the wall."[13] If "To be a modern writer and to write generically is a contradiction in terms,"[14] then Yeats, who bends and hybridizes, but does not ultimately abandon the traditional molds of love poetry, cannot be easily assimilated to modernism. Yeats's earliest work, moreover, is interesting precisely because of those qualities that have led male critics to denigrate it as insufficiently modern: its adoption of a feminine subject position and its "effeminate" style and form. Yeats's tenuous and intermittent identification with traditional models of masculinity resulted in an oblique relationship to the canonical genre of the love lyric. To paraphrase Simone de Beauvoir, one is not born a man, one becomes one; and Yeats had considerable trouble becoming a man.

Cixous argues that male poets can sometimes fracture or at least complicate the cultural and generic hegemonies within which they write. The hierarchical ideology in which the male element of the

binary opposition always defeats and destroys the female has not
been monolithic; gaps and inconsistencies always occur:

Sometimes I find where to put the many-lifed being that I am. Into
elsewheres opened by men who are capable of becoming woman. For the
huge machine that ticks and repeats its "truth" for all these centuries has
had failures, or I wouldn't be writing. There have been poets who let
something different from tradition get through at any price – men able to
love love; therefore, to love others, to want them; men able to think the
woman who would resist destruction and constitute herself as a superb,
equal, "impossible" subject, hence intolerable in the real social context.
Only by breaking the codes denying her could the poet have desired that
woman. Her appearance causing, if not a revolution, harrowing explosions
... (Only for poets, not for novelists who stick with representation. Poets
because poetry exists only by taking strength from the unconscious, and the
unconscious, the other country without boundaries, is where the repressed
survive – women or, as Hoffmann would say, fairies.)[15]

Yeats's relationship to the discourse of patriarchy was always fissured
by contradictions. As a white, male, middle-class, Protestant citizen
of the British Empire, with an acknowledged debt to canonical
English writers (*L* 872), he belonged to the dominant literary
tradition. As a colonized Irishman, however, he was acutely conscious
of repression and exclusion. His commitment to the occult tradition,
which represents centuries of opposition to the ruling discourses of
patriarchal religion and male science, marginalized him further. The
perceived irrationality of occult investigation marks its practitioners
as "feminine"; and many of Yeats's theosophical colleagues were
women seeking new sources of power in a religious organization that
did not bar them from office because of their sex.

   Yeats inherited the male-dominated literary tradition of poetic
love at a moment of crisis and change in gender relations. When he
began to write in the 1880s, women had made significant legal
advances: for example, the first Married Women's Property Act was
passed in 1870. Women were demanding, and beginning to achieve,
access to higher education. The birth rate was declining as middle
and upper-class women began to use contraception, a weapon that
equalled the franchise in its enabling potential. Women were not
given the vote until 1918, but between 1905 and 1914 suffrage
demands became increasingly vocal and difficult to ignore. The
"Woman Question" and the concomitant exploration of sexual
identity were among the major cultural issues of the time. Each small

advance triggered a violent resistance based both on male self-interest and on an ancient, largely unconscious fear of female sexuality. Woolf wrote:

No age can ever have been as stridently sex-conscious as our own; those innumerable books by men about women in the British Museum are a proof of it. The Suffrage campaign was no doubt to blame. It must have roused in men an extraordinary desire for self-assertion ... when one is challenged, even by a few women in black bonnets, one retaliates, if one has never been challenged before, rather excessively.[16]

Although the figure of La Belle Dame Sans Merci is archetypal, the extraordinary proliferation of *fin de siècle* representations of women as vampires, monsters, Medusas, and Salomés can be partly explained as the product of male apprehension that women, long subordinated, would in the course of their liberation exact a terrible revenge upon their oppressors.[17] The male modernists' obsession with masculine impotence and female power may be similarly explained.[18]

Yeats, however, moved in circles sympathetic to emancipation. His father was a disciple of John Stuart Mill, an early champion of women's rights. Although he disliked the theatrical techniques of Shaw and Ibsen, Yeats responded positively to their dramatic analyses of the "Woman Question." Through his early involvement with the socialist group that gathered around William Morris[19] and his friendship with actresses like Florence Farr, Yeats met many "New Women."[20] Although Gonne was primarily an Irish nationalist, she acted on feminist principles, founding her women's association, Inghinidhe na hEireann, on behalf of "all the girls who, like myself resented being excluded, as women, from National Organisations."[21] The contradiction between the politics of Yeats's historical situation and the generic conventions of nineteenth-century love poetry brought form and social context into productive tension. Yeats could see that "the heroines of all the neo romantic London poets namely, Swinburn, Morris, Rossetti – and their sattelites ... are essentially men's heroines with no seperate life of their own" (*CL*1 30; Yeats's spelling). Only with difficulty, however, could he elude the generic constraints of neo-romanticism and create an autonomous poetic beloved.

Yeats's social contexts were multiple: moving between London, Dublin, and Sligo he encountered widely different attitudes towards sexuality and the emancipation of women. His figuration of the Muse as Ireland, however, gave a nationalist resonance to many poems that were ostensibly about love. The Rose of his early work focuses patriotic as well as personal desire: the desire for a free nation, represented in Irish tradition as a beautiful woman. Lyons suggests that the publication of Douglas Hyde's *Love Songs of Connacht* signalled the coming of a new power into Irish literature:[22] Yeats's positive response to Hyde's book reflected his nationalist delight in an anonymous popular love tradition separate from the conscious, individual artistry of the European courtly genre: "Sheer hope and fear, joy and sorrow, made the poems, and not any mortal man or woman, and the veritable genius of Ireland dictated the quaint and lovely prose" (*UP*1 293).

In "Adam's Curse" (1902) Yeats directly challenged the tenets of courtliness by characterizing "the old high way of love" as "hollow" (*VP* 206). He simultaneously denigrated his own early poetics as "unmanly," the "feminine" products of "a womanish introspection" (*L* 434). His reading of Nietzsche and his work in the theater caused him to seek "more of manful energy" (*VP* 849) in his writing. Paradoxically, this "manful energy" came to inform his poetic representation of the Beloved. As women advanced towards social power, Yeats acknowledged that power in verses like "No Second Troy," where overt and thematic disapproval of Gonne's politics is countered by the forcefulness of the poetic form in which she is represented.

As Yeats's attitudes towards nationalism changed, so too did his representation of the romantic heroine. The "terrible beauty" of "Easter 1916" is, among other things, that of a political woman whose heart has been turned to stone. A revision of his poetics accompanied Yeats's re-evaluation of romance. After the Treaty of 1922, his identification between woman and Ireland was ruptured, and he began to use female speakers like Crazy Jane to protest the social policies of the Catholic Free State. Although he was attracted to the aesthetic Mariolatry of Lionel Johnson, to the beliefs and practices of the Catholic peasantry, and to many of the symbols and rituals of the Church, anti-clericalism was always latent in Yeats.[23] It must be emphasized, however, that Yeats was hostile only to what he called "an ignorant form of Catholicism" (*L* 873). When Partition confirmed the dominance of Rome in the South by segregating the Protestants in the North, Yeats constructed the erotic in opposition to the Catholic sexual ethic, and to censorship, which he feared would exclude from Ireland "all great love poetry" (*SS* 177). Warning against such a strategy, Foucault claims that the arena of sexuality is always saturated by the power of the State. But the peculiar nature of post-Independence Irish culture, controlled to a great extent by the Catholic Church rather than by secular bureaucracies, made sexual protest both legitimate and necessary. Yeats's choice of women young and old to voice this protest represents both a return to his identification with femininity and a realization of who would suffer most from the regressive social policies of the new State. The radicalism of Yeats's later work, however, was complicated by his intensifying interest in eugenic theory, which defines sexuality as instrumental to racial improvement and replaces personal relationships with the impersonality of the stud farm. The tension between eugenic theory and the genre of love poetry was among the few unproductive contradictions of Yeats's poetic career.

Yeats loved, liked, collaborated with, and respected women – most of the time. He encouraged their intellectual and creative work, assumed their professional competence, chose them as allies. His best friends were all women. Gonne wrote to him, "I want to thank you my own for being generous with me *as you have always been*. I have brought suffering to you so often, & you never reproach me" (*AYF* 271–72). Although these biographical facts condition his lyric representation of the feminine, the distance between poet and speaker, autobiography and creative fiction, differs from poem to poem. Michael Robartes forbids the Dancer to put herself to school, but Yeats tried to keep Iseult Gonne at her Sanscrit studies. The father of "A Prayer for my Daughter" urges a quiet life and a good marriage, but Yeats was delighted when Anne Yeats started designing sets for the Abbey Theater. Yeats claims that "A poet writes always of his personal life" (*E&I* 509), but he observes that "all that is personal soon rots: it must be packed in ice or salt." Yeats's ice and salt were the conventions of the love lyric and the traditional meters and stanza forms of the English poetic tradition: "If I wrote of personal love or sorrow in free verse, or in any rhythm that left it unchanged, amid all its accidence, I would be full of self-contempt because of my egotism and indiscretion, and foresee the boredom of my reader. I must choose a traditional stanza, even what I alter must seem traditional" (*E&I* 522). His love poetry demonstrates the tension between personal experience, inherited formal conventions, and the histories of the emancipation of women and the decolonization of Ireland. Whatever the limitations of his sexual politics, they do not vitiate the power of his love poetry to fascinate feminist readers. His complex position in history and culture, his long obsession with a "New Woman," his indeterminate gender identity, his oblique relationship to the canonical tradition, and his constant remaking of his poetics, render simple judgments impossible. Yeats thought that "All propositions... which set all the truth upon one side can only enter rich minds to dislocate and strain... and sooner or later the mind expels them by instinct" (*Mem* 151). A critic who would do justice to the insights of feminism while engaging fully with Yeats's poetry must entertain the recuperative as well as the suspicious critical impulses, and accept contradiction as inevitable. My aim is not to set all the truth upon one side, but to take a different path through the familiar landscape.

CHAPTER I

The anxiety of masculinity

Love poetry, the discourse of sexuality in verse, is inflected by the gender of the subject position adopted by its author. In this respect Yeats's work is problematic. As an Irish nationalist poet he was expected to produce "manly" verse in order to counteract the colonial stereotype of the Irish as effeminate and childish.[1] Yet he conceived of his poetic vocation as demanding a "feminine" receptivity and passivity, and as inheritor of an organic romantic poetic he saw the production of verse as analogous to the female labor of producing a child. "Man is a woman to his work, and it begets his thought," he wrote in 1909 (*Mem* 232). Gilbert and Gubar argue that in the nineteenth century literary creativity was metaphorically defined as a male generative activity: pen as penis, author as father;[2] but Mary Ellmann notes an equally strong association between "childbirth and the male mind."[3] The organic childbirth metaphor, discarded by neo-classical poets, was revivified by the Romantics.[4] In 1911 Gonne, employing a bold gender-role reversal, deplored Yeats's absorption in theater to the detriment of love poetry:

> Our children were your poems of which I was the Father sowing the unrest & storm which made them possible & you the mother who brought them forth in suffering & in the highest beauty & our children had wings –
>
> You & Lady Gregory have a child also *the theatre company* & Lady Gregory is the Father who holds you to your duty of motherhood in true marriage style. That child requires much feeding & looking after. I am sometimes jealous for my children. (*AYF* 302)

"That the Night Come" shows that Yeats accepted both Gonne's masculine self-definition and her metaphors: in the "storm and strife" of her existence she resembles "a king" (*VP* 317). Susan Friedman argues, however, that male poets who adopt the female model of pregnancy are indulging in "a form of literary *couvade*, male appropriation of procreative labor to which women have been confined":[5] the comparison between poetic and physical creativity, which masks women's inability to participate in cultural labor, keeps them at the work of producing babies. Nevertheless, Gonne's version of the trope, with its confident adoption of the active, stormy, and paternal role, and its comic depiction of Yeats as the submissive wife of a dominating Gregory, suggests that the use of this metaphor during the period of women's emancipation may signify a shift in power rather than an appropriative strategy. Yeats's encouragement and promotion of women artists such as Katharine Tynan, Florence Farr, Althea Gyles, Augusta Gregory, Dorothy Wellesley, and Margot Ruddock, moreover, allow us to interpret his use of the childbirth metaphor as sympathetic identification rather than usurpation. As a comrade he exhorted Wellesley: "Write verse, my dear, go on writing, that is the only thing that matters" (*L* 860).

Yeats was fascinated by William Sharp's attempt to reinvent himself as the Celtic poetess Fiona MacLeod; and Freudian and Jungian critics concur in describing him as female identified.[6] While the Freudians regard this identification as a problem, a neurosis caused by his unsatisfactory relationship with his mother,[7] Kiberd uses the Jungian model to argue that, although in his youth Yeats was "an unconscious slave to his *anima*," he later accepted and expressed the woman within.[8] His insistence on the androgyny of the male artist is characteristic of the Decadence,[9] a period during which, Jane Marcus argues, the concept of androgyny "extends the range of male sexuality into the feminine, but continues to regard the extension of female sexuality into the historical masculine as perverse."[10] Womanly men were more acceptable than mannish women. Androgyny has been condemned by feminists on the grounds that to celebrate the combination of stereotypically "masculine" and "feminine" qualities is to presume that aggression is naturally male, and passivity naturally female, and to advocate with Jung that men seek an eternal woman, women an eternal man, within themselves. Jungian formulations superimpose two essentialist stereotypes rather than revealing gender identity as a social construction. Diana Fuss, however, claims convincingly that essentialism is neither good nor bad in itself, but as it is deployed,[11] while Carolyn Heilbrun insists that androgyny means the deconstruction of stereotypes, "a movement away from sexual polarization and the prison of gender."[12] If we grant that for some writers the goal of androgyny was the freedom to be active or passive or a mixture of the two regardless of biology,

Heilbrun's contention may be acceptable. Ashis Nandy claims that in India the denigration of *klibatva*, or femininity-in-masculinity, as the "final negation of a man's political identity, a pathology more dangerous than femininity itself," was part of the disastrous legacy of colonialism. Indians became convinced that to fight the aggressive, controlling, and powerful oppressor it was necessary to adopt his standards of "masculinity," and thus created an absolute sexual polarization not native to Hindu culture.[13] Contemporary objections to Jung and to the concept of androgyny should not lead to the dismissal of an idea that challenged the dominant constructions of gender during Yeats's lifetime. Yeats once argued that, "In judging any moment of past time we should leave out what has since happened" (*Ex* 359). We cannot do that, but as historicists we should balance contemporary theoretical questions with the solutions that were intellectually possible and politically useful at a specific moment in history.

Like many Romantic poets, Yeats was unable to identify with the norms of masculinity dominant in the late nineteenth century. He exalted emotion over reason. He loathed the Victorian myth of science and progress; and his early desire to cast out of his verse "those energetic rhythms, as of a man running" and replace them by "wavering, meditative, organic rhythms" (*E&I* 163) demonstrates his rejection of masculine form. He espoused an organic, Keatsian, consciously essentialist "feminine" poetics in which "words are as subtle, as complex, as full of mysterious life, as the body of a flower or of a woman" (*E&I* 164). His horoscope showed him to be a man dominated by the moon,[14] and in his later years he developed a philosophy based upon a lunar myth that privileged traditionally feminine symbolism: moon over sun, night over day. Although his father praised active men, Yeats was timid and passive, dependent upon reverie and dreams for his inspiration. While the autonomous, unified phallic self of patriarchal tradition claims sole authorship both of history and literary texts, Yeats, whose most aggressively phallic symbol, the tower, is "Half dead at the top" (*VP* 482), subverted the potency of this imperial maleness; despite his post-1903 Nietzschean posturings, it was always an ironic mask. He described himself as "one that ruffled in a manly pose / For all his timid heart" (*VP* 489). His dialogical theory of the gyres, in which opposites alternately increase and decrease in strength but contain and never obliterate each other, reveals his rejection of a unitary position.

At the beginning of his career Yeats was metaphorically ravished by a Muse who displayed the traditionally masculine qualities of aggression and initiation. Laura Armstrong, whom he described as a "wild creature" (*Au* 76), "woke me from the metallic sleep of science and set me writing my first play" (*L* 117). Although Armstrong played a conventionally feminine role in rescuing Yeats from the "metallic" sterility of rational and scientific thought and turning him toward the intuitive world of poetry, Yeats's portrait of himself as a Sleeping Prince awakened by an energetic Princess reverses gender stereotypes. His account of their first meeting emphasizes his passivity:

I was climbing up a hill at Howth when I heard wheels behind me and a pony-carriage drew up beside me. A pretty girl was driving alone and without a hat. She told me her name and said we had friends in common and asked me to ride beside her. After that I saw a great deal of her and was soon in love. I did not tell her I was in love, however, because she was engaged. She had chosen me for her confidant and I learned all about her quarrels with her lover. (*Au* 76)

Armstrong, unconventionally hatless and driving alone, literally carried off the poet, who became the passive listener to her tales of love.

The Island of Statues, written for Armstrong, explores numerous ambiguities of gender. An Enchantress lives on an island, guarding the flower of immortality within a "brazen-gated glade" (*VP* 667). Penetration of this symbolically feminine enclosure is archetypally dangerous: male questers in search of the flower must be certain to choose correctly; if they fail, the Medusan Enchantress will turn them to stone. The plucking of a flower is an ancient metaphor for the taking of virginity, and we hardly need Freud's interpretation of the Medusa as the castrating female genitals surrounded by snaky hair to see in *The Island of Statues* a thinly veiled expression of Yeats's doubts about his ability to conform to traditional standards of masculine behavior. Indeed, the impotence of all the male characters in the play is striking. The lovers of the shepherdess Naschina, Thernot and Colin, are the first of Yeats's passive poets mesmerized by inaccessible and courageous females: Aillil in early versions of *The Shadowy Waters*, Septimus in the drafts of *The Player Queen*, Aleel in *The Countess Cathleen*. (Aleel was a Yeatsian self-portrait written to be played by a woman, Farr.) Naschina favors Almintor, an ostensibly more heroic type. Yeats, however, could not yet create a successful masculine male: Almintor chooses the wrong flower and is duly turned to stone. The resourceful Naschina assumes a male disguise and confronts the Enchantress. In a Shakespearian denouement, the Enchantress falls in love with the disguised shepherdess; but her infatuation destroys her, and Naschina restores the statues to life. Like Rosalind, Portia, and Viola, the androgynous female in male clothing unites the best qualities of both sexes. Yet while Shakespeare's transvestite heroines are reincorporated into conventional patriarchal society at the close of the action, Naschina's success transforms her into a figure of the excluded Eternal Feminine: at the end of the play, unlike her lover, she casts no shadow. A resourceful woman becomes Symbolic Woman. To add to the indeterminacy of effect, Yeats presents the Enchantress's unconsciously lesbian passion for the shepherdess with sympathy: a sympathy that Gonne endorsed in favoring the Enchantress and hating Naschina (*CL*1 134).

"The Wanderings of Oisin" (completed before Yeats met Gonne, but substantially revised thereafter) also has a heroine who, like Armstrong, takes the sexual initiative. Niamh "a child of the mighty Shee" (*VP* 5v) comes from the land of the young to claim Oisin as her lover. As Yeats climbed into Armstrong's pony cart, Oisin mounts Niamh's steed and is captured by her: "she bound me / In triumph with her arms around me" (*VP* 9v). Marital status, however, changes the "amorous demon" (*VP* 2v) to "a frightened bird" (*VP* 25). Once "The gentle Niamh [is] my wife" (*VP* 24), she is made timid by fear of losing Oisin. Each time an object from Ireland reminds him of the human world he has left behind, Niamh, "white with sudden cares" (*VP* 44v), tries to distract him by moving on. When he finally goes back she is left lamenting like Calypso or Dido: "I would die like a small withered leaf in the autumn, for breast unto breast / We shall mingle no more" (*VP* 56). The epic form, unlike the lyric, gave Yeats a traditional model of masculinity: the epic hero leaves his women behind. Although Yeats later mockingly represented Oisin as "led by the nose / Through three enchanted islands" (*VP* 629), he was retrospectively projecting the masterful, rejecting Gonne into the timid and devoted figure of Niamh:

> But what cared I that set him on to ride,
> I, starved for the bosom of his faery bride? (*VP* 629)

At the time of the original composition he could not have been starved for her bosom, since he had not yet encountered her.

Nevertheless, the lines describing Niamh, which were minimally changed during Yeats's numerous revisions, employ many of the images later associated with Gonne:

> A pearl-pale, high-born lady, who rode
> On a horse with a bridle of findrinny;
> And like a sunset were her lips,
> A stormy sunset o'er doomed ships.   (*VP* 3v)

A Rossettian iconography was waiting for its incarnation.[15]

Yeats attempted no more epics. Aware that an audience accustomed to the "manly" patriotic ballad verse of *The Spirit of the Nation* might not appreciate his lyrics,[16] he attempted in "To Ireland in the Coming Times" (1892) to establish himself as a masculine writer in a political context:

> *Know, that I would accounted be*
> *True brother of a company*
> *That sang, to sweeten Ireland's wrong,*
> *Ballad and story, rann and song.*

This poem subsumes the erotic longings focused on the symbol of the Rose under a political agenda: like many Irish poets before him Yeats writes love poetry to his country under the guise of a woman. One who must insist that he is the "true brother" of Davis, Mangan, and Ferguson, however, obviously expects his audience (explicitly constructed as male, as "*him who ponders well*") to doubt his gender identification, and suspect the femininity of his subject matter:

> *Nor be I any less of them*, [the true brothers]
> *Because the red-rose-bordered hem*
> *Of her, whose history began*
> *Before God made the angelic clan,*
> *Trails all about the written page.*

Yeats knows that his pursuit of "*faeries, dancing under the moon*" (*VP* 137–39) situates him on the margins of acceptable discourse. The lyric writer embraces a poetics that is already culturally gendered: as Parker suggests, "much of the history of lyric associates it with the female or the effeminate."[17] Its characteristics of emotion, brevity, and intimacy can be negatively coded as hysteria, triviality, and embarrassing self-revelation. The lyric writer may exploit the feminine, but he is also contaminated by it.

"The Madness of King Goll" (1887), for example, depicts the renunciation of political authority and prowess in war for the metaphorically feminine domain of nature, poetry, and madness. Abandoning his defense of Ireland against the Viking invaders, Goll becomes a crazed wanderer in the woods, a celebrant of the nature goddess Orchil. Only his harp affords him relief: poetry justifies his madness and alienation from masculine pursuits. The poem ends disastrously, however, with the instrument broken and the poet still exiled from the male world of political action: "My singing fades, the strings are torn, / I must away by wood and sea" (*VP* 86v). Yeats's identification with this sexual and poetic impasse is suggested by his father's portrait of him as the mad king holding the broken harp.[18]

Goll's pattern is repeated by Fergus, who in the *Tain* is a figure of great potency, the lover of the insatiable Queen Maeve. Yeats's Fergus seeks to exchange the public responsibilities of manhood for "the dreaming wisdom" of the Druid. The Druid warns of the loss of power and diminution of masculinity inherent in the choice of wisdom, dreams, and poetry:

> Look on my thin grey hair and hollow cheeks
> And on these hands that may not lift the sword,
> This body trembling like a wind-blown reed.
> No woman's loved me, no man sought my help.　　(*VP* 103)

Allen Grossman argues that in Yeats's early poetry the wind, symbol of vague desires and hopes, also represents the shifting and unstable libido.[19] The image of the Druid's body "trembling like a wind-blown reed" suggests that, in choosing dreams, the Druid and Fergus open themselves to the sorrow of infinite and unsatisfied desire.

Desire, in "The Man who Dreamed of Faeryland," destroys what society has defined as masculinity. The dreamer is on the threshold of manhood – as lover, as money-maker, as perpetrator of violence – but he is immobilized by the image of a timeless, feminine Faeryland where "Danaan fruitage makes a shower of moons" (*VP* 127v). He is ruined by his inability to adapt to the patriarchal order, and by his impossible desire for a maternal paradise. Yeats seldom wrote about his mother. When he did, he associated her with Ireland and with the oral tradition, emphasizing her fondness for exchanging stories about fairies and supernatural events with the fishermen's wives at Howth (*Au* 61; *Myth* 15–21). As a collector of Irish fairy stories he associated himself with the only happiness he ever saw his mother enjoy. In 1887 the unhappily married Susan Yeats suffered a stroke, and became mentally impaired. Yeats describes people who have withdrawn from the world into total or partial insanity as "away" or absent in fairyland (*VP* 801). His account of his mother's stroke as a liberation into "perfect happiness" (*Au* 62) suggests that he saw her too, in her twelve-year absence, as an inhabitant of fairyland. Yeats's vision of fairyland as the place of the mother, a psychic retreat from the problems and challenges of the world, was ambivalent: the cost of feminine wisdom might be insanity. Of the fairies he wrote:

It is natural, too, that there should be a queen to every household of them, and that one should hear little of their kings, for women come more easily than men to that wisdom which ancient peoples, and all wild peoples even now, think the only wisdom. The self, which is the foundation of our knowledge, is broken in pieces by foolishness, and is forgotten in the sudden emotions of women, and therefore fools may get, and women do get of a certainty, glimpses of much that sanctity finds at the end of its painful journey. (*Myth* 115)

Women, fairies, primitives, lunatics, and saints fracture the phallic, unified Cartesian self, foundation of the Law of the Father. Yeats felt his selfhood dispersed and threatened but his poetry enabled by his identification with these marginal figures.

Male selfhood and its constitution in language are central to "The Song of the Happy Shepherd" and "The Sad Shepherd." The Happy Shepherd rejects war, philosophy, and science, but, believing that "Words alone are certain good," he clings to the masculine Logos, to the constitutive importance of language: "The wandering earth herself may be / Only a sudden flaming word." He solipsistically affirms the self and its speech as the only "truth," but male identity is sustained by an Other:

> Go gather by the humming sea
> Some twisted, echo-harbouring shell,
> And to its lips thy story tell,
> And they thy comforters will be,
> Rewording in melodious guile
> Thy fretful words a little while,
> Till they shall singing fade in ruth
> And die a pearly brotherhood.   (*VP* 65–66)

In "The Sad Shepherd" the "twisted, echo-harbouring shell" is characterized as female by "her wildering whirls." As in the myth of the nymph Echo, woman is a melodious hollow chamber, a sounding-board for male complaint. The Ovidian reference, however, also ironizes the speaker by identifying him with Narcissus. The happy shepherd, a verbal narcissist, suggests that the male find a sympathetic female who will repeat his words in her own way. She will add nothing original, nor will she speak of herself: man provides the lyrics, woman the melody. This hierarchical opposition, however, is complicated by the fact that in rewording Logos the "echo-harbouring shell" also transforms it into poetry: for Yeats the supremely important act. The masculine "brotherhood" of words will take a "pearly" color from the vessel through which it has passed.

"The Song of the Happy Shepherd," moreover, is answered by its companion poem, "The Sad Shepherd," in which the sea-shell retakes the initiative. When the protagonist attempts to communicate with the stars, the sea, and the dewdrops, those archetypally "feminine" natural presences are busy talking to themselves. He therefore

> Sought once again the shore, and found a shell,
> And thought, *I will my heavy story tell*
> *Till my own words, re-echoing, shall send*
> *Their sadness through a hollow, pearly heart*;
> *And my own tale again for me shall sing,*
> *And my own whispering words be comforting,*
> *And lo! my ancient burden may depart.*

The words "*I*," "*my*," and "*me*" dominate this passage. The egotistical shepherd discovers, however, that the "wildering whirls" of the female sea-shell dissipate the imperial self:

> Then he sang softly nigh the pearly rim;
> But the sad dweller by the sea-ways lone
> Changed all he sang to inarticulate moan
> Among her wildering whirls, forgetting him.

The world is not a single male word, Logos, comprehensible to all, but many female voices singing "inarticulate" melodies among themselves. In Kristevan terms, one who speaks the language of the father, the language of lack and desire, confronts but cannot understand the semiotic language of the mother, the "wildering whirls" of the onomatopoeic song of self-containment: he

Cried all his story to the dewdrops glistening.
But naught they heard, for they are always listening,
The dewdrops, for the sound of their own dropping. (*VP* 68–69)

In these two poems Yeats questions the relation of gender to poetry. Femininity is figured as oceanic, the origin both of being and of verse; but Yeats complicates this familiar representation by making the female archetypes impervious to the male who seeks to use them for his own expressive ends. They sing their own song. In Cixous's words, Yeats is one of those poets who frequently, though not always, "let something different from tradition get through."[20] As a man who loves women and respects their difference while he identifies with them, and as a writer aware that the anxiety of masculinity is also the anxiety of modernity, he remakes inherited forms and tropes while remaining deeply conscious of his poetic precursors.

In early poems that are explicitly addressed to a mistress, and therefore formally located in the love tradition, Yeats accepts certain conventions: the woman as goddess, as Muse, as aesthetic object. His revisions of the genre, however, are demonstrated in his handling of the *carpe diem* formula. Poems in the *carpe diem* tradition, modelled on the works of Horace, Catullus, and Ovid, urge immediate sexual enjoyment in terms that devalue the object of desire. Although he wrote several poems within the tradition, Yeats could not muster the masculine bravado required by a genre that blatantly proffers male sexuality. In assuming the existence of female sexual pleasures, the *carpe diem* poets sometimes arrive at a cheerfully lascivious mutuality: Marvell enjoins his Coy Mistress to "roll all our strength, and all / Our sweetness, up into one ball."[21] Behind the impatient energy lies a threat, however. In *Twelfth Night* Shakespeare's Orsino voices the master metaphor of the genre: "For women are as roses whose fair flower / Being once displayed, doth fall that very hour."[22] Innumerable manipulators of the formula use the rosebud cliché to insist that the woman who refuses to yield her chastity will wither on the branch, her essential biological purpose unfulfilled. Edmund Waller's "Go, Lovely Rose" epitomizes a tradition in which the perennial conflation of woman with nature emphasizes the passivity of the female,[23] whose function is to display herself for male "commendation" and consumption:

Bid her come forth,
Suffer herself to be desired,
And not blush so to be admired.

Even the syntax is passive. The comparison becomes overtly coercive in the final stanza, where the rose is instructed to:

> die! that she
> The common fate of all things rare
> May read in thee;
> How small a part of time they share
> That are so wondrous sweet and fair![24]

Instead of concluding that the cruel mistress feared pregnancy, objected to his character or looks, or preferred someone else, the *carpe diem* poet arrogantly insisted that the woman's virginity was like uninvested capital: unless "used" by him it was "wasted." Waller implies that he is the young woman's only chance: if she refuses him she will never find another. In "To the Virgins, to Make Much of Time" Herrick also deploys withering rosebuds to claim that a woman sexually unused is a woman dead:

> Then be not coy, but use your time;
> And while you may, goe marry:
> For having lost but once your prime,
> You may for ever tarry.[25]

Herrick is specific about the social implications of his economic and horticultural metaphors: if a woman "spends" time without "using" it to service a man, she will become a superfluous old maid. The message is repeated in poem after poem: woman's only function is to please physically and to procreate. She needs to make the most of her brief bloom: once it has gone she is worthless. Poets admit that men die too, but their useful and natural lives more nearly coincide. Loss of manly beauty does not mean loss of manly function.

Yeats did not present Gonne with Marvell's grotesque choice: yield your virginity to me or to the worms. His rejection of this convention may be demonstrated by comparing "When You are Old" with Ronsard's "Quand Vous Serez Bien Vielle," from which it derives:[26]

> Quand vous serez bien vielle, au soir, à la chandelle,
> Assise aupres du feu, devidant & filant,
> Direz chantant mes vers, en vous esmerveillant,
> Ronsard me celebroit du temps que j'estois belle.[27]

Ronsard uses the conventional theme of mutability as an "erotic threat."[28] If his mistress fails to satisfy him, "Vous serez au fouyer

une vielle acroupie, / Regrettant mon amour et vostre fier desdain."
She will be lonely and regretful because she has missed her chance
with him, and he enjoys imagining her unhappiness. Yeats does not
resort to such sexual bullying. His beloved is not admonished:
"Vivez, si m'en croyez, n'attendez a demain: / Cueillez des
aujourd'huy les roses de la vie." Yeats makes no mention of those
perennially transient roses, nor is his poem an attempt at seduction.
The woman will age whether or not she requites his love: he offers her
the poem as a source of melancholy pleasure during the sleepy
twilight of old age, a reminder that

> many loved your moments of glad grace,
> And loved your beauty with love false or true,
> But one man loved the pilgrim soul in you,
> And loved the sorrows of your changing face.   (*VP* 121)

Although his verses recall her lost youth they do not accuse her of
cruelty towards her celebrant: love has "fled"; she has not repelled
him by her "fier desdain." The deterioration caused by aging is not
used as a weapon against her; instead the poet lovingly details her
present charm: her "soft look" and her "moments of glad grace."
Ronsard's object of desire has no specific characteristics; she is,
simply and unoriginally, "belle." Yeats values particular beauties of
her body, but is even more attracted by beauty of soul: unlike other
suitors he loved "the pilgrim soul in you / And loved the sorrows of
your changing face." In his Introduction to *The Penguin Book of Love
Poetry* Stallworthy notes with pained surprise that throughout the
entire amatory tradition, "We look in vain for the features,
lineaments of a living woman."[29] It is Stallworthy's surprise that is
remarkable: women in this tradition are objects, not individuals.
Yeats's "pilgrim soul," however, a phrase we associate with Gonne's
courage and determination, provides an exception to this rule. It
associates her, moreover, with the journeying quester of male
mythology rather than with the passive maiden of the courtly
tradition. Nor can a pilgrim soul wither like a youthful body: Yeats
subverts the *carpe diem* genre even as he employs it. His refusal to
imitate Ronsard's sonnet form (his poem has twelve lines instead of
fourteen) may even suggest a stylistic disengagement from that most
traditional vehicle of the love tradition.

   Instead of using mutability as a coercive strategy, Yeats promises
to love his mistress even when she has lost the bloom of youth, and

whether or not she yields to him. While others may desert her, he will remain faithful:

> Time's bitter flood will rise,
> Your beauty perish and be lost
> For all eyes but these eyes.   (*VP* 173)

In assuring her that what he values is a beauty that he will always see, no matter what her outward appearance, Yeats abandons the crude assumption that a woman's worth is coterminous with her beauty. "The Folly of Being Comforted" enacts his rejection of that assumption:

> One that is ever kind said yesterday:
> "Your well-belovèd's hair has threads of grey,
> And little shadows come about her eyes;
> Time can but make it easier to be wise
> Though now it seems impossible, and so
> All that you need is patience."
>   Heart cries, "No,
> I have not a crumb of comfort, not a grain.
> Time can but make her beauty over again."

The beauty of Yeats's beloved, which consists in energy rather than passivity, in "nobility" rather than in freshness of the flesh, can only increase with the passage of time. Here Yeats employs a modified, couplet form of the Shakespearian sonnet, but his claim that "Time can but make her beauty over again" challenges Shakespeare's basic premise, which is that nothing but art or procreation can withstand the depredations of "Devouring Time" (Sonnet 19).[30] Despite his emotional use of the concluding couplet, "if she'd but turn her head, / You'd know the folly of being comforted," Yeats refuses to claim, as Shakespeare does, that "in black ink my love may still shine bright" (Sonnet 65):[31] a claim that witnesses more to the poet's desire for personal immortality than to the qualities of the beloved. In "The Folly of Being Comforted" the older woman inspires a devotion unlinked to the flawless skin and auburn hair of the young beauty:

> Because of that great nobleness of hers
> The fire that stirs about her, when she stirs,
> Burns but more clearly. O she had not these ways
> When all the wild summer was in her gaze.   (*VP* 199–200)

Yeats's insecure masculinity prevented him from employing the sexually cynical poetics of the *carpe diem* mode. His use of the woman-as-rose metaphor, as we shall see, reflected his opinion that, "The only two powers that trouble the deeps are religion and love" (*UP*2 133). His Rose is not a reminder of falling petals, but a Dantesque sacred symbol and an eternally desirable image of Ireland.

CHAPTER 2

At the feet of the goddess: the feminist occult

Yeats's early poetry consistently deploys the traditional romance structure of elevation and abasement: the mistress is above and the lover is at her feet. "He wishes for the Cloths of Heaven" is a classic of the courtly genre:

> Had I the heavens' embroidered cloths,
> Enwrought with golden and silver light,
> The blue and the dim and the dark cloths
> Of night and light and the half-light,
> I would spread the cloths under your feet:
> But I, being poor, have only my dreams;
> I have spread my dreams under your feet;
> Tread softly because you tread on my dreams.　　(*VP* 176)

Elaborate repetition and consonantal patterning establish the cloths of heaven as both the starry skies and the costly blue vestments of a priest dedicated to the Virgin Mary. Expensive formal and imagistic embroidery, however, is beyond the means of the "poor" poet, who resorts to chivalric gesture, spreading his dreams under the feet of his goddess as Raleigh spread his cloak over the puddle for Queen Elizabeth.[1] The spare, impoverished diction of "But I, being poor, have only my dreams" demands sympathy for the indigent male. Yeats was penniless while Gonne was economically independent, but his love service also follows tradition in reversing the normal distribution of sexual power.

The history of the genre intersected with the history of nineteenth-century gender relations when Rossetti revived the medieval courtly lyric. Rossetti's influence on Yeats was mediated by the latter's occultism and interest in Irish politics; but common to all of his interests was the trope of the woman as goddess: a rhetorical form that in the time of the troubadours referred to actual relations of

25

power. Changed social conditions emptied it of its original meaning but it was capable of being recharged by historical events: the accession of Queen Elizabeth to the English throne, for example, or the nineteenth-century movement for women's rights.

C. S. Lewis argues that courtly love, characterized by religious worship of the female and by male self-abasement, began "quite suddenly at the end of the eleventh century in Languedoc," with the lyrics of the troubadours.[2] Although the term "courtly love" has been declared useless,[3] or dismissed as a nineteenth-century invention,[4] Lewis's assertion of the cultural construction of the sentiments remains valuable. Aspects of the courtly ethos can be discovered in other cultures and periods, and troubadour poetry is less homogeneous and more dependent upon pose and artifice than Lewis suggests,[5] but a love convention in which the suitor is ennobled by his devotion to the wife of another man is without historical precedent. Catullus and Propertius described the pains of unrequited passion, but they never pretended, as did Arnaut Daniel, to be improved by it:

> Each day I am a better man and purer,
> for I serve the noblest lady in the world,
> and I worship her, I tell you this in the open.
> I belong to her from my foot to the top of my head.[6]

Nor can Catullus' disgusted enslavement to Lesbia be compared with Bernart de Ventadorn's freely entered vassalage:

> Good lady, I ask you for nothing
> but to take me for your servant,
> for I will serve you as my good lord,
> whatever wages come my way.[7]

In the first version of *A Vision* Yeats, anticipating Lewis's description of the change in sensibility that produced romance, used his occult system to explain his own devotion to Gonne:

When the tide changed and God no longer sufficed, something must have happened in the courts and castles of which history has perhaps no record, for with the first vague dawn of the ultimate *antithetical* revelation man, under the eyes of the Virgin, or upon the breast of his mistress, became but a fragment. Instead of that old alternation, brute or ascetic, came something obscure or uncertain that could not find its full explanation for a thousand years.

Comparing the different responses to female bodily beauty offered by ascetic Byzantine Christianity and the *Arabian Nights*, Yeats traced the influence of the latter on courtly love:

The Bishop saw a beauty that would be sanctified but the Caliph that which was its own sanctity, and it was this latter sanctity, come back from the first Crusade or up from Arabian Spain or half Asiatic Provence and Sicily, that created romance.

As Warwick Gould points out, Yeats idealizes the *Arabian Nights*: the beauty that is its own sanctity belongs in the original to a member of the Caliph's harem, not to an unattainable mistress.[8]

Yeats's misinterpretation supports his definition of romance as a turning away from the Church and its Bishops towards a self-delighting bodily beauty that needs no religious transfiguration:

Throughout the German "Parsifal" there is no ceremony of the Church, neither Marriage nor Mass nor Baptism, but instead we discover that strangest creation of romance or of life, "the love trance." Parsifal in such a trance, seeing nothing before his eyes but the image of his absent love, overcame knight after knight, and awakening at last looked amazed upon his dinted sword and shield; and it is to his lady and not to God or the Virgin that Parsifal prayed upon the day of battle. (*AV*[*A*] 196–98)

In old age Yeats claimed that "My mediaeval knees lack health until they bend" (*VP* 603);[9] in youth he played Parsifal, offering his lady a chaste, exalted, and infinitely extended poetic service. Feeling himself to be a fragment beside his beloved (*Mem* 63), he worshipped her completeness as if she were a replacement for the God who no longer sufficed:

> my heart will bow, when dew
> Is dropping sleep, until God burn time,
> Before the unlabouring stars and you.   (*VP* 164)

Long before he met Gonne he had adopted the generic literary framework into which she would fit: "Perhaps I should never marry in church, but I would love one woman all my life" (*Mem* 32). Like his promise to serve his lady "until God burn time," his solemn embrace of lifelong fidelity demonstrates none of the playful artifice that tempered the seriousness of Provençal poets. Although it was significantly altered by its later interpreters, however, the troubadour code has had a vast effect on the social framing of sexual desire in post-medieval Western Europe. Frederick Goldin claims that "from that brief moment and that small circle came the customary language of devotion in our world ever since, down to the present moment."[10] The rejection of the Church for a feudal ideal of vassalage or service based upon courtly hierarchies became the paradigm not only for Yeats's love poetry, but for his social attitudes in general. Insofar as the Church's negative view of women has been a major factor in their oppression, especially in Ireland, Yeats's feudalism has progressive as well as reactionary aspects.

The lyrics of the twelfth-century troubadours reflected an anomalous historical situation. Aristocratic women in the South of France had for a brief time real social power: they could inherit and hold property in their own right, and vassals could swear fealty to a female overlord. Since many noblemen were absent on the crusades, the *domina* was often the effective head of her household. The relationship between sex, money, and cultural production helped to make possible a poetry in which the aristocratic woman played goddess, and the lover expected to be enriched by his elaborate cult of passion, to acquire "pretz," "valors," and "ricors" in his lady's service. The language, without ceasing to be erotic, also suggests material ambition.

Medieval marriage was usually a dynastic and patriarchal property arrangement.[11] Explicitly rejecting marriage as the vehicle of eroticism, this small privileged group imagined a world in which sexual passion is mutual and women have humble lovers rather than tyrannical husbands.[12] The genre was enthusiastically adopted by women poets[13] and promoted by female patrons.[14] Beatrice of Die wrote to her lover:

> I'd give almost anything
> to have you in my husband's place,
> but only under the condition
> that you swear to do my bidding.[15]

The frank expression of female desire is made possible by the Lady's possession of poetic power. While courtly lyrics and romances caused little improvement in the social position of women,[16] and the lady's erotic dominance never seriously threatened the status quo, much troubadour poetry formulated an imaginative opposition to patriarchy that was made possible by specific historical and social conditions: conditions that disappeared as feudal society gave way to the hierarchical, centralized order of the Church and the monarchy.[17] The goddess addressed by the last troubadours was the Virgin Mary.[18] According to Kelly, medieval courtesy shaped the man to please the lady. In the Renaissance reformulation of manners the lady was shaped to please the man: "The relation of the sexes here assumed its modern form, and nowhere is this made more visible than in the love relation."[19]

The representative cultural text in this transition is *La Vita Nuova*, which chilled the warmth of Provence with what Joyce's Stephen called "the spiritual-heroic refrigerating apparatus, invented and patented in all countries by Dante Alighieri."[20] Many troubadour poets had lamented the unavailability of their married ladies, but Dante fetishized the inaccessible by transporting his beloved to heaven.[21] *La Vita Nuova* is a record of his love for a dead woman, one whose power is entirely spiritual and whose chastity is assured. Male desire is therefore both frustrated and infinitely sustained.

> My lady is desired in the high Heaven...
> Love saith concerning her: "How chanceth it
> That flesh, which is of dust, should be thus pure?"

> She hath that paleness of the pearl that's fit
> In a fair woman, so much and not more;
> She is as high as Nature's skill can soar.[22]

No lady could go "higher." In "Ego Dominus Tuus," Yeats defined Dante's desire as "A hunger for the apple on the bough / Most out of reach." The worldly womanizer "mocked by Guido for his lecherous life" seeks psychological compensation in becoming the platonic lover of "The most exalted lady loved by a man" (*VP* 368–69). Yet this exaltation masks a powerful imaginative coercion of the female symbol. In *La Vita Nuova* the words "Ego Dominus Tuus" are spoken by Love, as he forces the reluctant Beatrice, naked except for a blood-colored cloth, to eat Dante's flaming heart.[23] In adopting the role of the passive victim "devoured" by the female, Dante abdicates sexual responsibility: the woman controlled by Love controls him.[24] The paradigm of male abjection derives from the courtly tradition, but the historical shift from material to spiritual female power, from Eleanor of Aquitaine to the Virgin Mary, helped to internalize the convention. Instead of suggesting the relations between the lover and some Other, however faintly realized, it now becomes the vehicle for obsessive exploration of the male self. Beatrice's exaltation is her exclusion: Dante speaks less of her than of the feelings she arouses in him. Her death is the symbolic acknowledgment of what was always already the case: she exists only as a textual mechanism, a projection of Dante's literary ambitions. When some practical young women ask him, "To what end lovest thou this lady, seeing that thou canst not support her presence?" he replies that, since she refuses to salute him, he now places his satisfaction entirely "In those words that do praise my lady."[25] Dante's true love-object is his own text, a text enabled by the absence of his beloved. Yeats's poem "Words" self-consciously examines the relation between loss and poetic achievement established by Dante as the foundation of the love tradition: had Gonne accepted him, he "might have thrown poor words away / And been content to live" (*VP* 256).

Dante's influence upon the Pre-Raphaelites, who adopted his imagery and sensibility without sharing his religious beliefs, was crucial. Despite the pervasive medievalism of nineteenth-century culture[26] troubadour poetry was not widely known in England, and the lyric model of *amour courtois* was provided by Rossetti's translations of Dante and his predecessors:[27] a refrigerated version of the tradition that came to suit late Victorian taste. Rossetti attempted to play Dante to Elizabeth Siddal's Beatrice. Their long and painful relationship, which ended with her suicide, provided him with an authentic dead beloved and an inexhaustible fund of guilty remorse. He buried the manuscript of his unpublished poems between her cheek and her hair: later he regretted the gesture and had the coffin dug up in order to retrieve it. This gothic vignette literalizes the ascendancy of the text over the female body. As in *La Vita Nuova*, the poet's words take life from the woman's corpse.

Yeats was introduced to Rossetti's poems and paintings in his sixteenth year, and became "in all things Pre-Raphaelite." When he saw *Dante's Dream at the Time of the Death of Beatrice*, "its colour, its people, its romantic architecture had blotted all other pictures away" (*Au* 114–15). After Rossetti's death in 1882 numerous retrospective exhibitions and publications dealt with the Pre-Raphaelites,[28] and Yeats immersed himself in the most important "subconscious influence" on his early work (*Au* 302). In adopting Rossetti as a model, Yeats embraced a vision of woman as priestess, Sibyl, or goddess:

Figure 1 Dante Gabriel Rossetti, *Proserpine*.

Woman herself was still in our eyes... romantic and mysterious, still the priestess of her shrine, our emotions remembering the *Lilith* and the *Sibylla Palmifera* of Rossetti...Johnson's favourite phrase, that life is ritual, expressed something that was in some degree in all our thoughts, and how could life be ritual if woman had not her symbolical place? (*Au* 302)

That symbolical place was not, however, in the home. The mid-Victorian idealization of the bourgeois married woman as the comfort, inspiration, and moral conscience of her husband, his refuge from the competitive values of the marketplace, the madonna-like mother of his almost immaculately conceived children,[29] had no place in Rossetti's iconography. Courtly lovers had argued that love was impossible in marriage, and Dante's angel never entered his house. Rossetti's brooding *Proserpine* (Fig. 1),[30] his towering *Astarte Syriaca* (Fig. 2), which Yeats took Gonne to see,[31] and his sultry *Pandora*, are all solid, sombre depictions of thwarted and threatening female energy. Nina Auerbach accurately describes them as "sinister."[32] If Dante had spiritualized the troubadour image of woman, his namesake returned her to the world of sense without stripping her of her power. Even dead heroines like the Blessed Damozel retain their corporeality in Rossetti's negotiation of the intersection between spirit and sense. In his story "Hand and Soul" a woman tells the painter Chiaro dell'Erma that she is an image "of thine own soul within thee."[33] Like many male love poets, Chiaro in painting the woman represents himself. Hunt complains, however, that in depicting his soul Rossetti, unlike Dante, neglected to obliterate the female body: "He insists so much upon the woman's actual physical existence that she fails to suggest any spiritual meaning."[34] Although Rossetti subordinated the features of his sitters to his conception of the ideal female type, that type in its aggressive and substantial fleshliness challenges the myth of saintly domestic compliance fostered by Victorian patriarchy. Auerbach suggests that we re-appropriate these images of powerful women even if they indicate their creator's fear of the female sex. She argues that

Elizabeth Siddal/Beata Beatrix breaks free of creating male divinity to orchestrate her own beatitude. Rossetti's painting... presents a grand woman as both object and source of worship, a Beatrice in the act of consecrating herself with no need of a controlling Dante, of Rossetti, or of God.[35]

Siddal, taken over by the Pre-Raphaelites as a girl of sixteen, acquired an education with Rossetti's help, and became a poet and

Figure 2 Dante Gabriel Rossetti, *Astarte Syriaca*.

painter.[36] Both she and Rossetti were friends of Barbara Leigh-Smith, the prominent feminist who supported higher education for women and helped to found Girton College at Cambridge. John Ruskin, who admired and bought Siddal's paintings, nicknamed her "Ida" after Tennyson's feminist princess, who also founds a college exclusively for women.[37]

If literature is a socio-symbolic act, a genre structured upon sexual relations must be affected by changes in the balance of power between men and women. Troubadours worshipped a social superior, but in the nineteenth century the generic gesture of male self-abasement before the woman, inverting as it did existing power and class positions, had multiple ideological meanings. We might read the Pre-Raphaelite reinvention of the idea of courtly love as a ruse designed to persuade non-aristocratic women that it is better to be adored than emancipated. Courtly sentiment, adulterous in origin, helped to palliate unromantic Victorian patriarchal marriage, obfuscating the facts of male power and female subservience.[38] "Woman" is granted immense textual and symbolic significance in order to disguise (or to maintain against increasingly vehement feminist demands) her lack of social significance.

Readings of Rossetti's icon, however, may be inflected in different ways. To depict woman as Pandora or Lilith suggests the old misogynistic idea "of the perilous principle in the world being female from the first."[39] The political consequences are obvious: the devil incarnate has no right to vote. Nevertheless, to worship a threatening Astarte or Proserpine may be to acknowledge, if not to welcome, her increasing social and erotic power. In his representations of women Rossetti alternated between the voluptuous whore and the inaccessible virgin who reminded him of his mother. Fanny Cornforth, model for *Lilith* and the prostitute of *Found*, stands opposed to Siddal, figured as *Beata Beatrix*. Elementary psychologizing, however, does not exhaust the social significance of Rossetti's woman-worship. Jane Morris was pleased by the reverence she evoked from Rossetti and his circle: "I never saw such men … it was being in a new world to be with them. I sat to them and was there with them, and they were different to everyone else I ever saw. And I was a holy thing to them – I was a holy thing to them."[40] If woman is the priestess of her shrine she is not a chaste and dependent Victorian child-wife and mother. She is not to be denied the vote because of post-Darwinian arguments about her evolutionary inferiority to the male of the species. If it was like "being in a new world" for a working-class girl to share the lives of the later Pre-Raphaelites, it may be because the site of their difference from and resistance to Victorian patriarchy, however compromised that resistance, was precisely the woman as goddess.

Rossetti's influence is especially apparent in the verses of *The Wind Among the Reeds*. John Harwood has identified a number of these as "'Olivia Shakespear' poems," and reads them in the light of Yeats's first experience of physical love. He admits, however, the difficulty of distinguishing between a poem written to Shakespear and a poem written to Gonne, and accepts the fact that "the poems are not literal autobiography."[41] These love lyrics, indeed, demonstrate the power of generic conventions to transform personal circumstance. In "He gives his Beloved certain Rhymes" the lover abases himself according to courtly formula, but his goddess resembles neither Gonne, whose "small hands were not beautiful" (*VP* 356), nor Shakespear, whose skin was dark. She has the pallor, the sorrowful face, the long heavy hair, and the totemic hands of a Rossetti icon:

> Fasten your hair with a golden pin,
> And bind up every wandering tress;
> I bade my heart build these poor rhymes:
> It worked at them, day out, day in,
> Building a sorrowful loveliness
> Out of the battles of old times.
>
> You need but lift a pearl-pale hand,
> And bind up your long hair and sigh;
> And all men's hearts must burn and beat;
> And candle-like foam on the dim sand,
> And stars climbing the dew-dropping sky,
> Live but to light your passing feet. (*VP* 157–58)

The "poor" poet of "He wishes for the Cloths of Heaven" here labors at his "poor" rhymes. His appropriation of the foam and the stars to light his beloved's feet suggests that he is ready to spread himself, as well as his dreams, beneath them. A similar fetishization of the woman's feet, or of the hem of her garment, appears in many of Yeats's early poems: he kisses "the quiet feet" of Cathleen ni Houlihan (*VP* 207) and follows "*the red-rose-bordered hem*" of Eternal Beauty (*VP* 137). This abasement or bending of "mediaeval knees" (*VP* 603) also bears an inverted relation to Christian iconography, in which the prostitute Mary Magdalene washes the feet of Christ with her tears and dries them with her hair; the woman troubled with the flux touches the hem of Christ's garment; and the weeping Virgin stands at the foot of the Cross. In adopting the abjection of the outcast, unclean, and sorrowing women, Yeats identifies politically with the downtrodden, as Christ himself did when he washed the feet of his apostles in token of humility. Yeats's divinity, however, is female. In "A Poet to his Beloved" his verses are religious offerings laid "reverently" before his goddess in elaborately interwoven lines:

> I bring you with reverent hands
> The books of my numberless dreams,
> White woman that passion has worn
> As the tide wears the dove-grey sands,
> And with heart more old than the horn
> That is brimmed from the pale fire of time:
> White woman with numberless dreams,
> I bring you my passionate rhyme.   (*VP* 157)

Grossman argues that Yeats's "white woman" with the ancient heart is a figure for the gnostic Sophia or Wisdom, who is either the bride of God or the bride of the dead, but never the bride of the poet. He claims that "The symbolist attitude toward the white woman ... was a perverse transfiguration of the courtly convention."[42]

The occult significance of the white goddess of *The Wind Among the Reeds* reflects the fact that the generic messages encoded in the courtly form that Yeats inherited from Rossetti were complicated and modified by the historical and social forces of the last two decades of the century. Theosophy, romantic socialism, and Irish nationalism, as represented by Helena Petrovna Blavatsky, William Morris, and Maud Gonne, all claimed his allegiance. The points of contact between these apparently unrelated philosophies and people were in fact numerous; and all in their different ways deployed the symbol of the goddess in order to liberate previously occluded sources of religious and political power. As a love poet whose most indispensable inherited formal gesture was to kiss, metaphorically, the feet of his queen, Yeats filled a rhetorical and ideological structure that is potentially empty or even actually delusive with a content that was, in his case, revolutionary.

Radical lesbian advocates of female difference such as Mary Daly, Adrienne Rich, and Audre Lorde, have celebrated goddesses as offering powerfully enabling images for women deprived of participation in the divine by the masculine Christian Trinity. Daly claims that "the symbol of the Great Goddess ... is the key to salvation from servitude to structures that obstruct human becoming."[43] Feminists opposed to the essentialization of female difference, however, argue that worship of the goddess simply valorizes the previously inferior partner in the masculine/feminine hierarchy instead of deconstructing that opposition altogether.[44] The celebration of biological womanhood, and women's difference from men as it has been socially constructed by a patriarchal culture, leads to women's re-imprisonment in reductive stereotypes of the Eternal Feminine.[45] The task is the creation of a culture in which polarized sexual difference will disappear in the play of multiple differences. Anti-essentialists wish to disengage from metaphor and myth, even from myths that present the female principle triumphant. Arguing that it is largely a product of the male imagination, they reject the concept of a female principle altogether.

As each new theory is unmasked as covertly essentialist, it becomes apparent that the question of essentialism must be reinserted into history and into material practice. Felski notes that "the dividing line between a repressive stereotype and an empowering symbol of cultural identity is often a very narrow one."[46] As a strategy and an enabling mythology, the metaphorical revalorization of the previously repressed and occluded female principle has had, and may still have, distinct political advantages.[47] Since, as Moi argues, "our necessary utopian wish to deconstruct sexual identities always runs up against the fact that patriarchy itself persists in oppressing women *as women*,"[48] the initial site of resistance may legitimately be female difference, symbolized by the figure of the goddess.

It was so for Madame Blavatsky, a powerful and unconventional woman whose mother, Helena von Hahn, known as the George Sand of Russia,[49] wrote feminist novels about women's imprisonment in marriage. Acting on her mother's principles, Blavatsky ran away from her elderly first husband and divorced her second. During her stay in America she wrote articles on feminism for the Russian press.[50] Her first major work, *Isis Unveiled* (1877), blends material from Buddhist, Hindu, Tantric, Hermetic, neo-Platonic, Kabbalistic, and Rosicrucian traditions to argue that, as Blake proclaimed and Yeats believed, "All Religions Are One." While Blavatsky was writing the book she felt herself to be in the presence of the goddess:

I am solely occupied, not with writing *Isis*, but with Isis herself. I live in a kind of permanent enchantment, a life of visions and sights, with open eyes, and no chance whatever to deceive my senses! I sit and watch the fair good goddess constantly. And as she displays before me the secret meaning of her long-lost *secrets*...the veil, becoming with every hour thinner and more transparent, gradually falls off before my eyes.[51]

Isis reveals in her visionary striptease the secrets of an ancient tradition in which the Absolute was ineffable, and therefore without gender, while female emanations of divinity were equal or even superior to male ones.

Scholars have investigated Yeats's occult studies,[52] but many regard his esoteric interests as an embarrassing or politically sinister aberration. Deane asserts that for Yeats, "fascism was the political form of occultism."[53] Tuchman, explaining why the theosophical content of so many modernist paintings (by Kandinsky, Munch, Kupka, Malevich, Mondrian, and Duchamp among others) has until recently been ignored by art historians, argues that mystical beliefs became suspect in the thirties because of Hitler's interest in the occult.[54] Theosophy, like the political theory of nationalism, the philosophy of Nietzsche, and the music of Wagner, was open to fascist appropriation. Despite Hitler's interest in magical power, however, Yeats's Order of the Golden Dawn was on the Gestapo's list of proscribed organizations.[55]

Theosophists also opposed British imperialism. When Blavatsky and Olcott visited Ceylon and accepted Buddhism, they protested the attacks on that faith by imperialist Christian missionaries.[56] A Hindu writer in the *Indian Chronicle* called the Theosophical Society "the only foreign movement which appeals to the national feeling of India."[57] Gandhi writes that it was the Theosophists who first introduced him to the *Bhagavad Gita*. After visiting Blavatsky in London he read her *Key to Theosophy*, which "stimulated in me the desire to read books on Hinduism, and disabused me of the notion fostered by the missionaries that Hinduism was rife with super-stition."[58] Hinduism became to Gandhi a spiritual focus for nationalist resistance. Theosophy was initially linked with socialism, feminism,[59] and the politics of national liberation.

Yeats became a founding member and first President of the Dublin Hermetic Society in 1885.[60] When Blavatsky settled in London in 1887 he visited her regularly: in 1888 he joined the Esoteric Section of the Theosophical Society, the membership of which "was restricted to a few favoured individuals who were in her Blavatsky Lodge or otherwise close to her."[61] The central contradiction of Theosophy is apparent here. Although Blavatsky insisted that the first aim of the movement was "to form a nucleus of the Universal Brotherhood of Humanity without distinction of race, colour, sex, caste or creed,"[62] she also argued that this spiritually democratic work could be furthered by esoteric groups. Nevertheless, Theosophy theorized itself as a Utopian and meliorist organization. From 1887 to 1890, the period of his greatest closeness to Blavatsky, Yeats also frequented William Morris's socialist Sunday evenings, and he saw no contradiction between his two allegiances: he frequently linked Blavatsky and Morris in laudatory reminiscences (*Mem* 24).[63] Theosophists and socialists shared an earnestness about social improvement:

I was much among the Theosophists, having drifted there from the Dublin Hermetic Society. Like the Socialists, they thought little of those who did not share their belief, and talked much of what they called Materialism. All good work, whether practical or in the arts, had been done, they held, with the conscious aim of improving mankind, and they were very conscious themselves of possessing that aim. (*Mem* 23)

The anti-materialist philosophy of the Theosophists appeared similar to the anti-materialism (or anti-capitalism) of the socialists. Yeats was deeply hostile to "modern civilization": Victorian capitalism, scientific rationalism, and bourgeois sexual morality. He saw collectivists, anarchists, occultists, and nationalists as natural allies in the struggle.

Although Blavatsky and Morris may seem an unlikely couple, numerous socialists like Robert Dale Owen were interested in occultism. In America experimental socialist communities – Fourierists and Owenites – were hospitable to spiritualism,[64] while spiritualist publications defended the rights of American Indians, women, and organized labor.[65] Andrew Jackson Davis, the "Poughkeepsie Seer" about whom Yeats wrote in "Swedenborg, Mediums, and the Desolate Places," was attracted to Fourier's egalitarian and Utopian ideas.[66] The English socialist Edward Carpenter, inspired equally by Whitman and the *Bhagavad Gita*, wrote a long poem called *Towards Democracy*.[67] Annie Besant, advocate of birth control, socialist organizer of the successful match-girls' strike at Bryant and May, and a supporter of women's suffrage,[68] converted to Theosophy in 1889. She did not abandon her political radicalism: she later became an opponent of British Imperialism in India and first President of the National Congress Party.[69] She was one of the secretaries of the Esoteric section during the time that Yeats, who thought her "a very courteous and charming woman" (*L* 137), attended its meetings.

Together they experimented in clairvoyance. Besant, who was of Irish origin and supported Home Rule,[70] later lectured in Dublin on "Theosophy and Ireland," explaining her conviction (shared by Yeats) that "Ireland was ultimately to emerge as the spiritual mentor of Europe."[71] After Blavatsky's death in 1891 Besant succeeded her as head of the Theosophical Society in Europe and India.

Annie Besant was not the only advanced woman to embrace Theosophy. Eva Gore-Booth, the friend of Yeats's youth who dedicated her life to the cause of suffrage and trades unionism among working-class women in Manchester, was a Theosophist.[72] So was Gonne's socialist friend Charlotte Despard, the President of the Women's Freedom League, who lectured on the connections between Theosophy and the women's movement.[73] These connections were vigorously asserted by the Irish suffragist and medium Margaret Cousins, at whose house Yeats and Gonne attended a seance. She wrote that "amongst the Theosophists, suffragettes and vegetarians we felt on the terra firma of the present, with its insistence on work to be done today."[74]

When in 1890 Yeats was ejected from the Esoteric section of the Theosophists, he joined the Hermetic Society of the Golden Dawn, which drew on the Western rather than the Eastern occult tradition. Many of the early Golden Dawn members, particularly women, were drawn from the Theosophical Society. Although the Golden Dawn was founded by Freemasons, it admitted women on equal terms with men: of the 189 members initiated during 1888–96, 84 were female.[75] Yeats's friend, the actress Florence Farr, who was radically opposed to Victorian sexual and domestic morals, and his theatrical patron Annie Horniman, liberated woman but sexual prude,[76] were both senior to him in the Order. His protégée Pamela Coleman Smith, whom he introduced to the Golden Dawn, collaborated with one of its founding members, A. E. Waite, in the production of the Rider Tarot pack.[77] She was also a member of the Suffrage Atelier and designed feminist political posters.[78] Gonne, rejected by Irish nationalist societies because of her sex, was accepted into the Golden Dawn, although she later resigned because of its Masonic affiliations.

The attraction of occult societies for rebellious women is obvious. Patriarchal religion offered them no role except that of humble worshipper, no model except the virgin mother; and access to the masculine Deity was controlled by an exclusively male priesthood. Explaining Besant's conversion, Shaw suggested that "She 'saw herself' as a priestess above all. That was how Theosophy held her to the end."[79] Shaw's tone is mocking, but some occult societies offered women the power denied them by orthodoxy. In the Isis-Urania Temple of the Golden Dawn, which was symbolically under the protection of Venus, a woman could progress toward magical Adeptship through the inspiration of the goddess, could become indeed "the priestess of her shrine."

The centrality of the feminine symbol in occult theory is reflected in Yeats's poem "The Rose of the World," where the "red lips" and "mournful pride" of the Rossetti beauty modulate into the loneliness of Eternal Beauty: Helen, Deirdre, and Gonne in her role as the embodiment of Ireland:

> We and the labouring world are passing by:
> Amid men's souls, that waver and give place
> Like the pale waters in their wintry race,
> Under the passing stars, foam of the sky,
> Lives on this lonely face.
>
> Bow down, archangels, in your dim abode:
> Before you were, or any hearts to beat,
> Weary and kind one lingered by His seat;
> He made the world to be a grassy road
> Before her wandering feet. (*VP* 112)

The Rose of the World is a version of Ennoia, the Wisdom figure of the Gnostics,[80] who is the first emanation of the Deity, existing with God before the creation. The love poet lays himself and the world at her feet.

Elaine Pagels has documented Gnostic speculations about the female elements of divinity, rigorously suppressed by the orthodox fathers of the early Church. She argues for a correlation between religious theory and social practice: Gnostic sects allowed women to preach, prophesy, and baptize, while the orthodox community subordinated the female sex.[81] Yeats had no access to the facts about Gnosticism uncovered by recent scholarship, but the Gnostic tradition passed on to him by Blavatsky and Mathers agrees with the original in its reverence for the female principle. Introducing the *Kabbalah Unveiled*, Mathers wrote:

I wish particularly ... to direct the readers' attention to the stress laid by the Qabalah on the Feminine aspects of the deity and to the shameful way in which any allusions to these in the ordinary translations of the Bible have been suppressed.[82]

In Kabbalism, the Shekinah, or Divine principle, is identified with the vagina.[83] Anthropomorphizing the Torah as female, Theodor Reik says: "*She* is considered older than the world and is assigned a cosmic role... Even in this diluted form we recognise the primal female goddess."[84] The rituals of the Golden Dawn represent the *sephiroth*, symbols of deity, as feminine; and Yeats's Rose, the presiding deity of his early love poems, is also an avatar of the goddess. She symbolizes his rejection of Victorian rationalism and his desire for an alternative to the masculine Trinity.

The search for a goddess of origins was also part of a Victorian social revolution against patriarchy that theorized matriarchy as the origin of civilization. The discipline of anthropology was founded upon the speculations of such men as Bachofen, McLennan, and Morgan about the primacy of mother-right.[85] Whether they were feminists is as irrelevant as whether they were correct: what is important is their questioning of the patriarchal family as the essential and immutable model for social relations. Drawing on Morgan's *Ancient Society*, Marx and Engels posited the matriarchal *gens* as the original, pre-capitalist form of social organization, and argued that this primitive communist grouping was destroyed by the twin institutions of slavery and private property, embodied in the authoritarian paternal household. In *The Origin of the Family, Private Property, and the State* (1884), Engels described this transition as the "*world historical defeat of the female sex.*" He also argued that, although the patriarchal family was well established among the classical Greeks, "the position of the goddesses in their mythology, as Marx points out, refers to an earlier period, when the position of women was freer and more respected."[86] Feminist classical scholars may question the historical basis of this judgment,[87] but I wish to establish only that Yeats, disciple of William Morris, would have seen the poetic recovery of the goddess as a project compatible with advanced socialist and feminist thought.

CHAPTER 3

The Liebestod

One of the central tropes of romance is the *Liebestod*, which conflates sexuality with death. De Sade, Baudelaire, Freud, Bataille, and Yeats regard this association as an essential aspect of human nature. De Sade claims that "There is no better way to know death than to link it with some licentious image,"[1] while in *Beyond the Pleasure Principle* Freud argues that the death drive and the erotic drive are inextricable. Lacan, developing Freud's suggestion that "something in the nature of the sexual instinct itself is unfavourable to the realisation of complete satisfaction,"[2] defines desire as created and determined by absence. Yeats similarly declares that "the desire that is satisfied is not a great desire" (*Myth* 337), and that while love may end, desire is infinite (*AV* [*B*] 40). As Socrates points out in Plato's *The Symposium*, we cannot desire what we already possess.[3] Desire, therefore, is always displaced into the beyond: death is the ultimate object of all desire. Freud claims that "*the aim of all life is death*"[4] and Yeats explicitly connects the longing for annihilation with sexual passion:

All our lives long, as da Vinci says, we long, thinking it is but the moon that we long [for], for our destruction, and how, when we meet [it] in the shape of a most fair woman, can we do less than leave all others for her? Do we not seek our dissolution upon her lips? (*Mem* 88)

Bataille suggests that fantasies of dissolution inevitably stimulate erotic feelings because nature's wastefulness demands the extinction of the individual as the price of the continuation of the species. In copulation and in death man surrenders himself to nature's process, lets go of his unique identity, and becomes a part of the whole.[5]

All of these explanations, including Freud's, are speculative. All depend on reasoning by analogy, and all assume the male subject position. While for Yeats the idea of dissolution was connected with spiritual alchemy,[6] it also evokes the economic metaphor of "spend-ing": the Renaissance idea that every act of love brings a man closer to his death. "Spending" is tied to the miserly mechanics of the male orgasm: women's capacity for sexual pleasure is not disabled by satisfaction. The explanation of the association between love and death as man's vision of his penis as erect before sex and moribund afterwards reveals the masculine premise upon which the analogy stands, and falls.

Though questionable and gender-specific, the link between Eros and Thanatos pervades Western love poetry. It takes several related literary forms: the poet loves a dead woman or a deadly woman destroys the poet; lovers die in each other's arms or their love is consummated after death. The sexual act may be conventionally troped as the "little death," or associated with the murder of one partner by the other. Sexual violence, the experience of pain as erotic, depends upon the same cultural constructions as the *Liebestod*.

The *Liebestod*, however, represents itself as consensual: partners seek love in death together. The mainstream pornographic tradition, in which representations of pain and death stimulate male eroticism, depends on an imbalance of power: the victim is usually female. Freud defines sadism as primarily masculine,[7] and Bataille concurs: "the female partner in eroticism was seen as the victim, the male as the sacrificer."[8] A lesbian sado-masochist might challenge this definition, however, and Freud himself paradoxically asserted that the cold, narcissistic, and predatory female was the "truest" type of womanhood.[9] Western culture sanctions not only the idea of woman as masochistic erotic victim, but also its opposite: the woman as whip-wielding goddess of pain (Swinburne's Dolores and Faustine) or Gorgon who turns men to stone. For Mary Ellmann the "effect of alternation, the sheer coexistence of irreconcilable opinions ... breeds dissent,"[10] but there is an uncanny logic at work here: the desire to humiliate is linked to the fear of being humiliated.

The masochistic victim and La Belle Dame Sans Merci are contradictory stereotypes that were exaggerated, though they did not originate, in a society convulsed by the early feminist challenge to male hegemony. The cultural and historical processes that form these stereotypes, however, are mediated through the unconscious. Fear of women and the concomitant desire to brutalize them are internalized by men as terrible or abject female images. Jacqueline Rose sees the unconscious, the medium by which ideology creates the gendered subject, as "the distorted effect of an oppressive social world."[11] The intersection of culture with the psyche creates unstable and un-predictable personality structures: for example, women may find their sexual arousal bound to images of male violence even as they consciously reject the association; and the example of *Wuthering Heights* is sufficient to demonstrate that women writers participate in the love-and-death tradition.

Benoîte Groult, however, dismisses the unconscious, seeing the eroticizing of female victimage as the result of male sexism:

"The unique and supreme sensual pleasure of love lies in the certainty of causing pain," wrote Baudelaire, as could have Sade, Lautréamont, Masoch, Bataille, Leiris, and a thousand others as well ... Desire is reduced to the taste for that which is dirty, degrading, and destructive, which is to say, for death. This idea moves us onto familiar ground, the one ruled by the "Divine Marquis" who, to his credit, at least openly displayed "the most monstrous disdain for woman upon which a philosophy has ever been built." [12]

Attacking the opposite stereotype of the terrible Medusa, Cixous also elides the unconscious, implying that sexual violence answers a male need, and can be evaded simply by absenting oneself: "Men say that there are two unrepresentable things: death and the feminine sex. That's because they need femininity to be associated with death; it's the jitters that give them a hard-on! for themselves! They need to be afraid of us ... Let's get out of here."[13] Rose, however, refuses to surrender the territory of the unconscious entirely to cultural forces. Seeing human sexuality as intractably violent, and accepting Freud's analysis of the death drive, she insists that "as feminism turns to questions of censorship, violence and sado-masochism, psychoanalysis hands back to it a fundamental violence of the psychic realm – hands back to it, therefore, nothing less than the difficulty of sexuality itself."[14] Rose does not deny that socialization, although incomplete and precarious, produces personality structures shaped by ideology; but she argues that the "fundamental violence" of the psychic realm is reinforced, not created, by the violence that issues from socially produced inequalities of gender. For Rose the difficulty of sexuality is therefore intimately linked with that of politics;[15] her position mediates between social constructionism and psychoanalytic essentialism.

The association between love and death in Yeats's verse, then, can

be read as overdetermined: an inherited generic trope reanimated by
the rise of feminism intersects with Yeats's private pathology, and is
intensified by the unavailability of Gonne. As we have seen, in the
love poetry of the troubadours, Dante, and Petrarch, and medieval
romances like *Tristan*, the absence or unobtainability of the beloved
is indispensable. The Lady of the troubadours is married; Beatrice is
dead; Isolde is King Mark's queen. De Rougemont notes that
Tristan and Isolde never miss a chance of getting parted, and defines
this passion as narcissism: the male poet's preoccupation with a
figment of his own imagination. Contact with a material woman
destroys it. "She is the woman-from-whom-one-is-parted: to possess
her is to lose her." De Rougemont attacks the cult of passion as
justifying serial adultery, since it attaches supreme value to an
experience that consumes itself in the achievement: "How patent the
degradation of a Tristan who has *several* Iseults."[16] In "Ephemera"
Yeats's lovers, on the brink of parting because their passion is
exhausted, console themselves with the thought that:

> other loves await us;
> Hate on and love through unrepining hours.
> Before us lies eternity; our souls
> Are love, and a continual farewell.   (*VP* 80–81)

De Rougemont, a conservative apologist for Catholic marriage,
seems an unlikely ally for feminists, but his critique of the love and
death cult can be separated from his religious moralism. He argues
that passion needs to be stimulated by barriers, and that death is the
definitive barrier: the most satisfactory women, therefore, expire
before possession can render them worthless. The dead woman,
unlike the living one, can be imaginatively possessed forever: she is
incapable of change or self-assertion. Love poetry, like elegy,
frequently feeds on the obliterated subjectivity of the person who
occasions it, whether woman or corpse. The literary convention of
the dead beloved, which encodes hostile male wishes toward living
women, also models the realities of social and sexual power. In
marriage, the early Victorian woman died as an autonomous legal
subject: man and wife became one person and that person was the
husband. The wife was entombed and sanctified as the "angel in the
house." The worship of the dead woman has long been a stock
property of the poetic tradition, but the irruption of live women with
destabilizing demands for suffrage, education, financial and legal

autonomy, and equality in the love relationship, recharged the trope with the power of male fear and desire to maintain the status quo. Apparently without considering his argument discreditable to men, Bataille claims that "the idea of death is linked with the urge to possess. If the lover cannot possess the beloved he will sometimes think of killing her; often he would rather kill her than lose her."[17] When numerous women openly declare their dissatisfaction with their bondage, the individual lover's need to possess has a political resonance.

Yeats's poem "A Dream of Death" was prompted by the rumor that Gonne was about to confirm her unavailability by dying in the South of France. Ramazani calls Yeats's proleptic epitaph "a miniature of the epitaphic process of much love poetry";[18] and the poem takes melancholy satisfaction in prematurely enclosing Gonne in a box:

> And they had nailed the boards above her face
> The peasants of that land,
> And wondering planted by her solitude
> A cypress and a yew.   (*VP* 123v)

Along with the rumor of Gonne's illness had come reports of her friendship with a Frenchman (*Mem* 44): Yeats's emphasis on the "solitude" of the corpse encodes his wish that none but himself or death should possess her. His epitaph, "She was more beautiful than thy first love" (*VP* 123v), defines her as primarily an agent in his own affective life. No wonder that Gonne herself, convalescing in St. Raphael with her lover Millevoye, "was greatly amused when Willie Yeats sent me a poem, my epitaph he had written with much feeling."[19]

Yeats's epigraph to *The Secret Rose* (1897), "As for living, our servants will do that for us" (*Myth* 144), was borrowed from Villiers de L'Isle Adam's play *Axel*, which he saw in Paris with Gonne. Like the "peasants" of "A Dream of Death," the servants in *Axel* take up the vulgar burdens of existence that the aristocrats cast away: the *Liebestod* is a class privilege. The independent-minded heroine Sara flamboyantly escapes the prison of her convent only to find herself re-immured with the hero Axel in his family tomb. Yeats describes Sara as a "Medusa," quoting her assertion that "flowers and children have died in my shadow" (*UP*1 324), but it is Axel who tries to kill her and then, after they fall in love, insists that she join him in suicide.

Life, which cannot equal the perfect existence together they have imagined, will become "a barren exercise, my Sara, and an unworthy sequel to this miraculous wedding night whereon, still virgins, we have yet possessed each other for all time."[20] Sara pleads for one night of love, but Axel seems to fear that after such talk of perfection his sexual performance will prove disappointing. (Yeats implied as much in *A Vision*: wondering at his "absurd" choice of death over sex, Denise de L'Isle Adam declares that Axel "was just shy" [*AV*[*B*] 42–43].) Axel and Sara drink poison: then "Clasped in each other's arms, they lie on the sand of the burial corridor, exchanging the last breath on one another's lips."[21] Presumably the idea that death is preferable to consummation consoled the frustrated Yeats.

Axel informs "He wishes his Beloved were Dead," where Yeats's dream of his beloved as a corpse has become conscious desire for her death:

> Were you but lying cold and dead,
> And lights were paling out of the West,
> You would come hither, and bend your head,
> And I would lay my head on your breast;
> And you would murmur tender words,
> Forgiving me, because you were dead.

This last line has a peculiar resonance. For what must the woman forgive the speaker? Have they quarreled? Has he murdered her? Clearly he wishes to imprison her:

> Nor would you rise and hasten away,
> Though you have the will of the wild birds,
> But know your hair was bound and wound
> About the stars and moon and sun:
> O would, beloved, that you lay
> Under the dock-leaves in the ground,
> While lights were paling one by one.   (*VP* 175–76)

The speaker longs for the beloved's demise because in death she will forgive him, maternally caress him, and not abandon him for political meetings or holidays with her other lover. This lyric of the posthumous embrace requires the bondage of the autonomous woman: she must exchange "the will of the wild birds" for the prison of her own hair, even if that prison seems to span the cosmos. Necrophilia is a common fantasy of the rejected male. In Swinburne's "The Leper" a poor scribe, despised by his proud mistress, tends her when she succumbs to leprosy. After her death he joyfully embraces her corpse, asserting that he is

> glad to have her dead
> Here in this wretched wattled house
> Where I can kiss her eyes and head.[22]

Swinburne's poem is more overtly ghoulish than Yeats's. The scribe delights in the destruction of his mistress's beauty and jealously preserves the corpse; both writers, however, celebrate the superior malleability and availability of the deceased woman.

In "The Blessed Damozel" Rossetti creates a dead beloved who actively looks forward to sexual reunion with her lover: she expects:

> to live as once on earth
> With Love, – only to be,
> As then awhile, for ever now
> Together, I and he.[23]

In Rossetti's Heaven desire is not quenched by satisfaction: two lovers become eternally one. Rossetti fantasizes a return to the symbiotic bond between infant and mother, which Freud in *Beyond the Pleasure Principle* identifies as the source of the death wish. The subject wishes to reduce the tension that causes sensations of unpleasure; the state in which the organism experienced least tension was the womb; the grave is a retreat to the womb.[24] Since the child in the mother's body is an image of perfect union, the lover seeks the womb through the grave, love in eternity. The maternal image becomes explicit in "He wishes his Beloved were Dead" when the speaker wishes to "lay my head on your breast" (*VP* 175); and in "He thinks of his Past Greatness,"

> his head
> May not lie on the breast nor his lips on the hair
> Of the woman that he loves, until he dies.   (*VP* 177)

Yeats's autobiographical novel *The Speckled Bird* contains a passage, written during his affair with Shakespear, that exposes the psychological basis of this fantasy. His hero's adoration

was not for a woman, who would have bound his soul to definite hopes and dreams, but for that absolute of emotions, as it is in eternity, and which [we] seek and find for a moment in the paintings of the old [and] modern Pre-Raphaelites... and which we seek and do not find in the bed of love. (*SB* 139)

A real woman in a real bed inevitably disappoints: the material presence of the Other destroys the poet's love affair with the lost mother. The unattainable woman leaves undisturbed the contemplation of absolutes.

Yeats's fantasies about the female as corpse are supplemented by a masochistic fascination with images of men murdered by women. As a Romantic and a Pre-Raphaelite he absorbed the literary and pictorial tradition of La Belle Dame Sans Merci: the inaccessible woman who lures and then destroys her admirers.[25] Pater imposed upon Leonardo's Mona Lisa his own lurid vision of the *femme fatale*, which Yeats reprinted as poetry in his *Oxford Book of Modern Verse*: "Like the Vampire, / She has been dead many times, / And learned the secrets of the grave" (*OBMV* 1). The oldest incarnation of this vampire is Adam's rebellious first wife, Lilith, a succubus popularly blamed for nocturnal emissions. Yeats, who described the fairies as the "children of Lilith" (*Myth* 15), knew Rossetti's narcissistic and sanguinary depiction of the witch, who,

> subtly of herself contemplative,
> Draws men to watch the bright net she can weave,
> Till heart and body and life are in its hold.

> Lo! as that youth's eyes burned at thine, so went
> Thy spell through him, and left his straight neck bent
> And round his heart one strangling golden hair.[26]

Erotic strangling becomes decapitation in the decadent cult of Salomé, which helped to shape Yeats's image of the dancer with the inexpressive face.[27] Yeats also admired Swinburne's erotic tragedy *Chastelard*, whose hero spends most of the play contriving to have his head cut off in the presence of his "passionate and gorgious [*sic*]" beloved, Mary Queen of Scots (*CL*1 29).

The Medusa, who turns men to stone until she is decapitated by Perseus, embodies both aspects of the identification between femininity and death. Pater was obsessed with Leonardo's painting of the Medusa's head: "Leonardo alone cuts to its centre; he alone realises it as the head of a corpse, exercising its powers through all the circumstances of death. What may be called the fascination of corruption penetrates in every touch its exquisitely finished beauty."[28] In his early story "The Binding of the Hair" Yeats uses the severed head, a motif that pervades ancient Irish art and myth as well as decadent erotica, to suggest the symbolic castration of the

unsuccessful lover: the head of the poet Aodh sings to his Queen the
love poem "He gives his Beloved certain Rhymes" (*VSR* 180–81).
Despite his admiration for Pater, however, Yeats in his simple story
and gentle poem eschews the latter's fascination with corruption and
obsession with the malignancy of women; not until his late plays did
he exploit the full erotic potential of the trope of the severed male
head.

The violence of passionate sexuality, however, was theorized by
Yeats long before he experienced it. In *John Sherman* (1891) he wrote:
"Perfect love and perfect friendship are indeed incompatible; for the
one is a battlefield where shadows war beside the combatants, and
the other a placid country where Consultation has her dwelling" (*JS*
54–55). When he attempted to embark upon an affair with
Shakespear, he found confirmation for his suspicion that desire was
created and sustained only by opposition. Although her patience
with his hesitations and nervous impotence finally freed him from the
burden of his virginity, her kindness, sensitivity, and tact failed to
enkindle the fires of passion. "It will always be a grief to me that I
could not give the love that was her beauty's right, but she was too
near my soul, too salutary and wholesome to my inmost being," he
wrote (*Mem* 88). In *On Baile's Strand* Cuchulain claims that love is but
"a kiss / In the mid-battle … A brief forgiveness between opposites"
(*VPL* 489).

In one of Yeats's most decadent works, "The Travail of Passion,"
written in 1895 just before his affair with Shakespear, sexuality
becomes crucifixion. Believing that "The only two powers that
trouble the deeps are religion and love" (*UP*2 133), Yeats gives the
word "passion" a triple force: erotic desire, acute suffering, and the
death of Christ on the Cross:

> When the flaming lute-thronged angelic door is wide;
> When an immortal passion breathes in mortal clay;
> Our hearts endure the scourge, the plaited thorns, the way
> Crowded with bitter faces, the wounds in palm and side,
> The vinegar-heavy sponge, the flowers by Kedron stream;
> We will bend down and loosen our hair over you,
> That it may drop faint perfume, and be heavy with dew,
> Lilies of death-pale hope, roses of passionate dream.   (*VP* 172)

The "flaming … door" that is "wide" is at once the door of heaven
and the gateway of occult initiation. The Golden Dawn, like other
occult societies, used its religious rites as displaced vehicles for the

frustrated eroticism of its members:[29] at his initiation into the 6/5 grade Yeats's hands were tied behind his back, a chain was hung round his neck, he was bound to a cross, and he received the symbolic stigmata.[30] The poem's female speakers pity the man's "Travail" and offer to cover him with Yeats's habitual symbol of female sexuality: long, scented hair. The collocation of hair and perfume suggests Mary Magdalene, one of the three Maries who remained faithful to Christ. The phallic lilies are "death-pale," their only "hope" the Resurrection, while the feminine roses remain enduringly "passionate."

From his masculinist point of view Bataille speculates that all eroticism has a sacramental character, and posits a fundamental identity between the act of religious sacrifice and the act of love: both reveal the flesh in its paroxysms, both temporarily destroy the powers of reason and will, and both enact union with the divine.[31] Although for Bataille sexual victims are always female, "The Travail of Passion" describes a male sexual martyrdom, and the psychological state it records suggests why in his insecure youth Yeats found "the old association of love and death" (*L* 828) attractive. Although he explored the tropes of the dead beloved, the dying poet-lover, and the sexual apocalypse, however, most of his early love poetry is wistful rather than perverse; it also self-reflexively foregrounds the dubious motives of the tradition in which it participates.[32] Yeats, the most traditional of modernists, the most modern of traditionalists, cannot exploit a genre without exposing its structures. Even "He wishes his Beloved were Dead" disarms by the frankness of its title.

The young queen in "The Cap and Bells" is often read as a Fatal Woman who accepts her lover's suit only at the price of his manhood: when she disdains the jester's offer of his heart and soul he metaphorically castrates himself, like Attis the devotee of Cybele: "'I have cap and bells,' he pondered, / 'I will send them to her and die'" (*VP* 160).[33] Yeats, however, remarked that while "He wishes for the Cloths of Heaven" presaged erotic defeat, "The Cap and Bells" offered a prescription for erotic success.[34] His comment suggests that a woman is won not by courtly abjection, but by ironic deployment of the jester's professional mask, his cap and bells. The problem, for Yeats as for the speaker of "Never Give all the Heart," is that recognition of the erotic power of the mask long precedes the ability to assume it. "Play" is impossible if one is enslaved by genre: "deaf and dumb and blind with love" (*VP* 202).

Yeats lacked confidence in his masculinity, and being repeatedly refused weakened his self-esteem; but he liked and respected women too much to represent them as devouring monsters or rotting corpses. Compared to Rossetti, Swinburne, and Pater, he is warily self-conscious, brooding over his own failures rather than hostile to female demands. In "He mourns for the Change that has come upon him and his Beloved, and longs for the End of the World," the poet's desire for the Last Day is motivated by weariness and frustration. "He hears the Cry of the Sedge," Yeats's apocalyptic version of "La Belle Dame Sans Merci," which signals its Keatsian derivation through the word "sedge," laments the absence rather than the malignancy of the beloved:

> I wander by the edge
> Of this desolate lake
> Where wind cries in the sedge:
> *Until the axle break*
> *That keeps the stars in their round,*
> *And hands hurl in the deep*
> *The banners of East and West,*
> *And the girdle of light is unbound,*
> *Your breast will not lie by the breast*
> *Of your beloved in sleep.*   (*VP* 165)

Esoteric symbols from the Golden Dawn and fashionable *fin de siècle* apocalyptic ideas converge to project personal despair onto a cosmic canvas. Armageddon becomes a metaphor for the impossibility of consummation. Or, the poem hints, consummation might precipitate the end of the world. The deliberate and reiterated choice of an unattainable woman reveals an Axel-like unwillingness to approach the bed,[35] but Yeats's fears about potency translate into self-defeat, not into vicious accusation.

Although the Decadence gave new currency and special perversity to the cult of La Belle Dame Sans Merci, Yeats also found the stereotype in Irish tradition: Mary Hynes; the Cailleac; or the "malignant" Irish Muse, the Leanahaun Shee, whose "lovers, the Gaelic poets, died young. She grew restless, and carried them away to other worlds, for death does not destroy her power."[36] Yeats noted that

love was held to be a fatal sickness in ancient Ireland, and there is a love-poem in the *Love Songs of Connacht* that is like a death-cry: "My love, O she is my love, the woman who is most for destroying me, dearer is she for making me ill than the woman who would be for making me well." (*E&I* 180)

Yeats's Rose goddess lacks the decadent perfume of the *fleurs du mal* because she breathes the fresh air of Connacht. "The Rose of the World," for whom "Troy passed away in one high funeral gleam, / And Usna's children died" (*VP* 111), is an Irish Medusa, not sensual but mystical. The idea of apocalypse is political as much as sexual: in a note on "The Valley of the Black Pig" Yeats identifies "the darkness that will at last destroy the gods and the world" with "the coming rout of the enemies of Ireland" (*VP* 808–09). "The Secret Rose" combines erotic desire with what Thuente calls the "millenial note common in Irish folklore,"[37] in which the end of the world represents not orgasm but the desired end of English rule:

> When shall the stars be blown about the sky,
> Like the sparks blown out of a smithy, and die?
> Surely thine hour has come, thy great wind blows,
> Far-off, most secret, and inviolate Rose?   (*VP* 170)

Yeats's "inviolate Rose" fuses the courtly worship of the sexually unavailable goddess with the representation of Ireland as a beautiful woman. The culture of Irish nationalism offered a publicly and politically acceptable form for a private obsession with male martyrdom.

CHAPTER 4

Thinking of her as Ireland

The allegorical identification of Ireland with a woman, variously personified as the Shan Van Vocht, Cathleen Ni Houlihan, and Mother Ireland, is, like all political deployments of the female symbol, strategic and constructed. The sexual politics that identify land as Woman in Ireland, however, are contradictory and make little sense out of their historical context. The current debate about the symbolic value of Mother Ireland engages feminists hostile to a system of representation that occludes the presence of non-mythical females; Irish revisionist historians who consider Cathleen ni Houlihan an essential Republican icon and denigrate her accordingly; Republican women who affirm that Mother Ireland means everything to them; and psychoanalytic critics who are unwilling to dismiss the positive affective power of the maternal image.[1] Although the image has been primarily the creation of men, Loftus reminds us that women too have produced representations of Mother Ireland, and that her significance is not unitary, but multiple.[2] A feminist critique of the figure should not be interpreted as complicity with the revisionist impulse, nor as a blanket rejection of Irish nationalism. Nationalism, as Said and Lloyd insist, had its progressive decolonizing historical moment:[3] the repressive, anti-feminist Free State created by bourgeois nationalists was not the inevitable consequence of the Republican ideals of 1916.

The legendary power, energy, and freedom of pre-Christian mythical heroines like Brigid and Maeve, who was a goddess of the land, may have reflected the greater social autonomy of aristocratic women in ancient Ireland: the Brehon laws demonstrate unusual concern for the rights and even the happiness of women in marriage.[4] The figure of the goddess can be read as a celebration of the energies of women and the Utopian politics of matriarchy; and in the nineteenth and twentieth centuries she inspired women to nationalist

55

action. The recovery of Irish myth offered Yeats female images that, whatever their relation to pre-Christian social life, intersected fruitfully with the icons of the contemporary suffrage campaign and informed the self-representations of women like Gonne and Marki-evicz.

Clark argues, however, that while ancient Irish literature contains numerous powerful and dangerous women, the culture remained patriarchal.[5] Negatively interpreted, goddesses may reflect male fear and envy of the mother, mediated in Christian times through the structure and iconography of Catholicism. Devotion to the Mother of God has often coincided with misogyny. Mary's maternal role reinforces a biologistic insistence on woman as reproducer and nurturer; while adoration of her virginity masks a hatred of the unclean female body and a denial of female desire.[6] Mariolatry in Ireland was the identification of a conquered people with a cult that was anathema to their Protestant oppressors, yet its effects on Irish women have been repressive. From a structuralist point of view the identification of the land as female reflects the patriarchal opposition between male Culture and female Nature, which defines women as the passive and silent embodiments of matter. Politically, the land is seen as an object to be possessed, or repossessed: to gender it as female is to confirm and reproduce the social arrangements that construct women as material objects, not as speaking subjects. When the myth of the goddess is used by men as a political instrument, it is often ascribed to an essential feminine principle rather than to the male imagination that has created and manipulated it. Images of women that originated as the projections of male anxieties and aggression are used to validate the need to control and subordinate the female sex. Heaney draws an analogy between the preserved bodies of human sacrifices in the peatbogs of Denmark and the corpses on the streets of contemporary Belfast: both, he suggests, are victims of the goddess:

You have a religion centring on the territory, on a goddess of the ground and of the land and associated with sacrifice. Now in many ways the fury of Irish Republicanism is associated with a religion like this, with a female goddess who has appeared in various guises. She appears as Caithleen Ni Houlihan in Yeats's play; she appears as Mother Ireland, she appears you know playing her harp. I think that the kind of republican ethos is a feminine religion in a way.[7]

Heaney vacillates between the positions of detached anthropological observer and dismayed devotee of the goddess. His volume *North* is saturated with the myth of the devouring female: in "Kinship" she is both "Insatiable bride" and "Our mother ground / ... sour with the blood / of her faithful."[8]

While Heaney poetically reproduces the myth that he intellectually deplores, Conor Cruise O'Brien, opposing all deployment of mythology for political ends, describes the intersection between literature and politics as unhealthy.[9] He blames the confusion between symbol and reality in the North of Ireland on the contemporary IRA, "people who are seeking in history for an immortality promised in literature." He argues that "the conception of history as a series of blood sacrifices enacted in every generation ... is most essentially a literary invention. The great propagandist of this notion, as far as Ireland is concerned, was the poet Yeats."[10] O'Brien attacks the contamination of literary discourse by political statements, as if it were possible to write verse devoid of ideological reference. Edna Longley agrees that in Northern Ireland, "poetry and politics, like church and state, should be separated."[11] It is, however, possible to criticize the political implications of specific myths without rejecting the notion of political poetry altogether;[12] and to note a connection between the iconography of 1916 and that of the IRA without feeling compelled to repudiate the former.

Yeats is indeed one of the great modern propagandists of the notion of blood sacrifice, and the influences on *Cathleen ni Houlihan* and the related love poem "Red Hanrahan's Song about Ireland" are ancient and complex. Although Yeats modified his mythical sources considerably, he sustained the identification of woman with the land. He also reached back into prehistory to resurrect the tradition of human sacrifice to the goddess, in which sexuality is conflated with violent death as the blood of the young male victim sinks into the receiving earth.[13] When the generic tropes of death-obsessed nineteenth-century love poetry intersect with the darker recesses of Irish myth and the historical forces of Irish nationalism the result is explosive.

Writing on women in Irish mythology, Proinsias MacCana argues that "it would be hard to exaggerate the importance of this idea of the land and its sovereignty conceived in the form of a woman." The rightful king must copulate with the goddess before he can claim the throne: the essence of the myth is sexual, and the woman is not a mother but a seductress. Queen Maeve, who had nine husbands and claimed that "she was never 'without one man in the shadow of

another,'" is not simply promiscuous: she is a humanized version of
the goddess of sovereignty.[14] In "The Old Age of Queen Maeve"
(1903), a narrative poem framed by two frank declarations of love for
Gonne, Yeats fuses the Irish goddess with his own Beloved:

> And she'd had lucky eyes and a high heart,
> And wisdom that caught fire like the dried flax,
> At need, and made her beautiful and fierce,
> Sudden and laughing.
>   O unquiet heart,
> Why do you praise another, praising her,
> As if there were no tale but your own tale
> Worth knitting to a measure of sweet sound?   (*VP* 181)

Maeve's cairn on Knocknarea was one of Yeats's sacred places, a
geographical and physical reminder of the union of his love for the
land and his love for Gonne.

When unable to find her proper mate, the goddess becomes old,
ugly, and crazed, but she is miraculously restored to youth and
beauty when she persuades some intrepid male to make love to her.
His reward is kingship. The magically powerful old hag, or Cailleac,
as she is called, appears under many guises in Irish folklore and
literature. A famous early Gaelic poem, the "Cailleac Bheara,"
identifies her with the physical contours of the island itself:

> The sea grows smaller, smaller now.
> Farther, farther it goes
> Leaving me here where the foam dries
> On the deserted land,
> Dry as my shrunken thighs,
> As the tongue that presses my lips,
> As the veins that break through my hands.[15]

Yeats, who corrupts her name to Clooth-na-Bare, describes the
Cailleac both as the ancient mother of the gods and as a beautiful
fairy who beckons to men from pools and drowns them (*VP* 801–02).[16]
He imagines her in contradictory guises: young and old, beautiful
and ugly, fatal mistress and primal mother.

As the colonization of Ireland progressed, the myth changed: the
idea of miraculous renewal became increasingly improbable. By the
eighteenth century the Cailleac as a figure for sovereignty dis-
appeared.[17] Although poets of the dying Gaelic civilization like

O'Rathaille and Owen Roe O'Sullivan still picture Ireland as a woman, she no longer issues shameless sexual invitations. In their *aislingi*, or vision poems, a beautiful maiden, the *spéirbhean*, waits passively for an exiled Jacobite prince to return and end her oppression. The *aisling* is a courtly form, but its heroine derives from the older myths. In O'Sullivan's "A Magic Mist" the speaker asks if she is Helen of Troy and she replies that she is not: she is the goddess of sovereignty:

> "I am none of those women you speak of,
>   and I see that you don't know my clan.
> I'm the bride wed in bliss for a season
>   – under right royal rule – to the King
> Over Caiseal of Conn and of Eoghan
>   who ruled undisputed o'er Fodla."[18]

Despite her royal origins, however, oppression has begun to extinguish the *spéirbhean*'s sexual energies. She is still a sexual object, for the poet describes her physical charms, and occasionally she is raped by the invader. Colonization, however, has destroyed native masculinity along with political independence, and no true Irishman remains to mate with her. The post-Famine intensification of the Catholic vision of woman as a creature of purity and innocence may also have influenced the depiction of the *spéirbhean* as desirable but chaste.[19]

Yeats adopted the *aisling* form in "The Song of Wandering Aengus," in which a "glimmering girl" inspires the speaker to undertake a love-quest (*VP* 149–50).[20] The "apple blossom in her hair" imagistically evokes Yeats's first meeting with Gonne, at which he noted her "complexion like the blossom of apples" (*Mem* 40). He memorialized this moment in the first version of "The Arrow": "Blossom pale, she pulled down the pale blossom / At the moth hour and hid it in her bosom" (*VP* 199v). Aengus also sees his *spéirbhean* at the moth hour; but Yeats revised the line "And stars like moths were shining out" (*VP* 149v) in order to change the time from dusk to dawn, the proper moment for an *aisling* vision: "And moth-like stars were flickering out" (*VP* 149). The reference to apple blossom merges Gonne as Yeats's Beloved with Gonne as an image of Ireland. Sigerson's *Bards of the Gael and Gall*, which Yeats reviewed in 1897, claims that it was "a favourite figure of recent [i.e. Jacobite] Irish bards to describe a maiden as a 'blossom of the Apple-tree.'"[21] "The

Song of Wandering Aengus" is thus both love poem and national allegory. Yeats admired the *aisling* poets for their patriotism:

The political poetry of these men was no light matter in its day. Because of it they were hated and pursued by the powerful and the rich, and loved by the poor. They disguised their meaning in metaphor and symbol. The poet goes out in the morning and meets a beautiful spirit weeping and lamenting, a "banshee" with "a mien of unearthly mildness." On her he lavishes all his power of description, and then calls her Ireland. Or else he evades the law by hiding his sedition under the guise of a love-song. Then Ireland becomes his Kathleen, Ny-Houlahan, or else his Roisin Dubh, or some other name of Gaelic endearment. To her he sings:

> "*Oh! the Erne shall run red*
> *With redundance of blood,*
> *The earth shall rock beneath our tread,*
> *And flames wrap hill and wood,*
> *And gun peal and slogan cry*
> *Wake many a glen serene,*
> *Ere you shall fade, ere you shall die,*
> *My dark Rosaleen!*
> *My own Rosaleen!*
> *The judgement hour must first be nigh,*
> *Ere you can fade, ere you can die,*
> *My dark Rosaleen!*"   (*UP*1 149–50)

"Roisin Dubh" was not in fact an *aisling* poem,[22] but an anonymous Gaelic ballad from the early seventeenth century. Yeats quotes Mangan's translation, which renders the vaguely apocalyptic line "The world [will] be in crimson battle on the ridges of the hills"[23] as the militaristic and contemporary "gun peal and slogan cry." Mangan clearly agreed with the nineteenth-century editor James Hardiman that "Roisin Dubh" was "an allegorical ballad, in which strong political feelings are conveyed, as a personal address from a lover to his fair one."[24] Yeats also assumes that the love poem disguises political sentiments. O'Sullivan, however, inverts the relation of passion to patriotism: he claims that the patriotic ballads originated generically as love poems. The name of the girl in an existing love song was retained to indicate the tune, and then applied allegorically to Ireland.[25] Although the Rose as a figure for Ireland comes not from Celtic antiquity, as Yeats once speculated (*VP* 812), but from the nineteenth century,[26] the imbrication of love and patriotism in the tradition of Irish popular verse, ballads and *aislingi* alike, underwrites his invocations of the "*Red Rose, proud Rose, sad Rose of all my days*" (*VP* 101), the "Rose of all Roses, Rose of all the World!" (*VP* 113), and the "Far-off, most secret, and inviolate Rose" (*VP* 169).

The ancient native tradition of identifying both the physical reality and the political identity of the land as female was ironically congruent with imperial strategies of representation that used the language of familial power relations to describe the colonial context. In the nineteenth century, the new racist pseudo-science of ethnography characterized the Irish as a feminine people. According to Ernest Renan: "If it be permitted us to assign sex to nations as to individuals, we should have to say without hesitance that the Celtic race ... is an essentially feminine race."[27] Arnold developed Renan's views in "On the Study of Celtic Literature":

No doubt the sensibility of the Celtic nature, its nervous exaltation, have something feminine in them, and the Celt is thus peculiarly disposed to feel the spell of the feminine idiosyncrasy; he has an affinity to it; he is not far from its secret.[28]

Despite his endorsement of the Celt's poetic melancholy and natural magic, Arnold saw the passivity, excitability, and inefficiency manifested by this conquered people as evidence of their need for a firm "masculine" ruler: a circular argument that served the ends of imperialism. The nationalist response to this caricature was to invert it, and insist on Irish masculinity: to attempt to become, in Ashis Nandy's formulation, "hyper-masculine."[29] The man who is trying to prove his hyper-masculinity naturally demands that his woman be hyper-feminine: which in the post-Famine Irish Catholic context meant an intensification of the already heavy emphasis on virginity and motherhood, and a denial of autonomous female desire. Kearney, who notes a change in the image of Ireland from the passive daughter-figure of the eighteenth-century *aisling* tradition to the more militant mother goddess of the nineteenth and twentieth centuries, suggests that both images are related to the "social stereotypes of the Irish woman as pure virgin or equally pure son-obsessed mother."[30]

In *The Celtic Twilight* Yeats recounts a folktale that demonstrates the defeat of the old myths of sequential sexuality by the new puritanism of the Catholic Church. The Sidhe tell a young mother that her baby girl will marry a fairy prince, and instruct her to bury a log from the fire to ensure her daughter's longevity. Like Queen Maeve, the girl outlasts not one but seven fairy princes, until,

At last one day the priest of the parish called upon her, and told her that she was a scandal to the whole neighbourhood with her seven husbands and her long life. She was very sorry, she said, but she was not to blame, and then she told him about the log, and he went straight out and dug until he found it, and then they burned it, and she died, and was buried like a Christian, and everybody was pleased. (*Myth* 78–79)

Yeats's tone indicates that he saw the humorous side of this story, but in youth he was a prisoner of the Irish cultural stereotype of purity that it mocks. Although, as we have seen, he identified Queen Maeve with Gonne, he refused to allow that there might be sexual similarities between them. He had learned in 1898 about Gonne's affair with Lucien Millevoye,[31] but in "The Old Age of Queen Maeve" he explicitly denied that she had Maeve's "wandering heart" (*VP* 186). Emphasizing instead Gonne's eugenic suitability for motherhood, he described her as "great-bodied and great-limbed, / Fashioned to be the mother of strong children" (*VP* 181). In an ambiguous metaphor he represented her as at once the symbolic mother of the Irish treason felony prisoners and the daughter of Mother Ireland: "They had brought to light the woman in her, for instead of 'Mother Ireland with the crown of stars upon her head' she had these seven and twenty prisoners to brood over her" (*Mem* 107).

Yeats allegorized both his sexual difficulties with Gonne and his traditional inheritance as an Irish love poet in the story "Red Hanrahan," on which he collaborated with Gregory. It derives from two sources: the old myths of sovereignty and the eighteenth-century *aisling*. Red Hanrahan was originally called O'Sullivan the Red (*VSR* 197) after the famous *aisling* poet Owen Roe O'Sullivan (1748–84). The formulaic "vision" proper to an *aisling* occurs after an old man transforms a pack of cards into a hare and hounds, and sends Hanrahan on a magical hunt. The hunt occurs frequently in the ancient myths of royal initiation: Niall of the Nine Hostages is hunting when he meets the hag whose embrace will guarantee him the kingship.[32] Hanrahan enters a "big shining house," where he sees "a woman, the most beautiful the world ever saw, having a long pale face and flowers about it, but she had the tired look of one that had been long waiting" (*VSR* 91). The woman, Echtge, offers a sexual encounter that will endow the protagonist with Pleasure, Power,

Courage, and Knowledge: in this she resembles the Cailleac. From the *aisling* tradition comes the notion that Echtge is young and passive, a sleeping beauty who, unlike the mythological "man-pickers" Maeve, Grania, or Deirdre, makes no direct overtures to the man of her choice. Like her colonized country, she has been "long waiting." Echtge is identified with the land through the mountain range, Slieve Echtge, in which the story takes place.

Yeats represents Hanrahan as a failed Grail knight unable to rise to the challenge offered by the magical woman. He is too intimidated by her beauty to ask the meaning of the symbols – the cauldron, the stone, the spear, and the sword – with which she is surrounded. Her status as the immutable poetic image of his desire precludes his acting to secure her for himself. Like Dante speechless before Beatrice, or Petrarch content to worship Laura at a distance, the poet intuits that possession would destroy his image: his imaginative projection cannot survive contact with a real woman. His weakness causes him to lose not only the queen, but also his mortal sweetheart, Mary Lavelle, who has disappeared by the time he awakens from his trance. "Red Hanrahan," first printed ten months after Gonne's marriage in February 1903, is the thinly disguised account of Yeats's failure either to win her or to succeed with another. His affair with Shakespear in 1896 had been short lived: sabotaged by his continuing obsession with the "image" of Gonne, just as Hanrahan's relationship with Mary Lavelle was ended by his encounter with the goddess of the land. In "The Lover mourns for the Loss of Love" the speaker acknowledges that his affair with the "beautiful friend" has failed to "end in love" because female reality cannot compete with male fantasy:

> She looked in my heart one day
> And saw your image was there;
> She has gone weeping away.   (*VP* 152)

Toomey suggests that when in 1898 Gonne finally revealed the truth about Millevoye and kissed Yeats for the first time she was making "pathetically plain sexual overtures."[33] His failure to take prompt advantage of what he called her "temporary passionate impulse" (*Mem* 134) suggests his inability to accommodate her transmutation from the untouchable "image" of his own courtly love poetry into someone else's discarded mistress.

Yet Yeats's interrogation of the love poet's professional investment in an inhuman image of the female, and the patriot's instrumental

vision of his country as a pure woman, preceded his sexual failures
with Shakespear and Gonne. In his 1892 story "The Devil's Book,"
an early version of "Red Hanrahan," the poet-protagonist fails to
accept the goddess he has worshipped when she descends from her
iconic niche.[34] Cleona, Queen of the Munster Fairies, takes on
humanity in order to woo him, but she is cruelly rejected: "I tell you
that it was not you, but the Fairy woman that I loved. She had no
sorrows... she would not grow old and git [*sic*] grey hairs" (*VSR*
193). Revising his story in 1897 Yeats imagistically connects the fairy
woman with his country: "dressed in saffron, like the women of
ancient Ireland," she is identified with the symbolic Rose of "To
Ireland in the Coming Times" by "the border of little embroidered
roses that went round and about the edge of her robe." Yeats used
these stories to represent the difference between Woman as poetic
icon of Ireland and a living woman "full of the tender substance of
mortality" (*VSR* 190, 192). Generically self-conscious as always, he
was aware of the icon's occlusion of women who were neither pure,
young, nor exempt from sorrow.

In the middle section of "The Tower" (1926) Yeats returns after
twenty years to the failure of Red Hanrahan, but when he arrives at
the painful moment of his hero's encounter with the queenly women,
he breaks off abruptly: Hanrahan follows the hounds "O towards I
have forgotten what – enough!" Had Yeats really forgotten he could
have looked it up. He has summoned Hanrahan to ask him a question
about Echtge:

> Does the imagination dwell the most
> Upon a woman won or woman lost?
> If on the lost, admit you turned aside
> From a great labyrinth out of pride,
> Cowardice, some silly over-subtle thought
> Or anything called conscience once;
> And that if memory recur, the sun's
> Under eclipse and the day blotted out.   (*VP* 412–14)

Although his tone is admiring rather than gynephobic, the speaker's
avoidance of the "great labyrinth," an intricate subterranean hole
suggestive of the female genitals, hints at Yeats's sexual anxieties.[35]
Incapable of direct reference to the queenly Echtge, the woman lost
through his own cowardice, Yeats substitutes two other female
figures who embody aspects of the male-created goddess. The cruelly
autocratic Mrs. French, whose servant "Clipped an insolent farmer's

ears / And brought them in a little covered dish" (*VP* 410), enacts her capacity to mutilate. Mary Hynes, the peasant Helen celebrated in the nineteenth century by the blind Gaelic poet Antony Raftery, is a more attractive figure, but no less deadly: one of her drunken admirers "was drowned in the great bog of Cloone" (*VP* 411). She is, however, deadly to herself as well as to men: like Gonne she represents "the sorrow of beauty," and like many lovely women she dies young (*Myth* 300). The motif of drunkenness suggests Mary Hynes's origin in the myths of royal initiation: Maeve's name means "she who intoxicates" and the goddess "presents the draught of sovereignty to one king and husband 'in the shadow of another.'"[36] In *The Celtic Twilight* Yeats quotes Raftery's poem about Mary Hynes:

> The table was laid with glasses and a quart measure,
> She had fair hair, and she sitting beside me;
> And she said, 'Drink, Raftery, and a hundred welcomes,
> There is a strong cellar in Ballylee.' (*Myth* 24)

Mary Hynes has Maeve's sexual forwardness and generosity: it is she who invites Raftery to Ballylee and offers to intoxicate him.

The second Hanrahan story, "Hanrahan and Cathleen, the Daughter of Houlihan," contains Yeats's first literary use of the figure with which, in nationalist eyes, he was to become identified. Hanrahan spends his time composing "poems disguising a passionate patriotism under the form of a love-song addressed to the Little Black Rose or Kathleen the Daughter of Hoolihan or some other personification of Ireland" (*VSR* 207). Cathleen ni Houlihan, probably the name of the girl in an earlier love song, was first used as a figure for Ireland in the late eighteenth century, when the blind Gaelic poet Heffernan wrote a rousing ballad that promises Irish freedom "When the Prince is seen with Cathaleen Ni Houlihan!"[37] Yeats, who was commissioned to write an article on Heffernan for the *Dictionary of National Biography*, identified him as having written "the origonal [*sic*] of Mangan's 'Kathleen Ni Houlahan'" (*CL1* 117).[38]

Hanrahan's song establishes Cathleen as a character quite different from the implacable hag familiar to us from Yeats's play. The refrain denominates her as a daughter rather than a mother: a *spéirbhean*, not a Cailleac. Yeats, playing with the stereotypical idea that all women are either virgins or whores, locates Hanrahan in the disreputable dwelling of "his middle-aged sweetheart" Margaret

Rooney, a former vagrant who has set up house with her crony Mary
Gillis: "They had both some dilapidated remnants of tolerably good
looks, and had outlived jealousy and made good girdle-cakes" (*VSR*
206–07). In this sexually compromising setting, Hanrahan evokes the
purity of Cathleen, looking as he does so like "a king of the poets of
the Gael and a ruler of the dreams of men," and weeping over
"Ireland and her sorrows" (*VSR* 207–08):

> O tattered clouds of the world, call from the high Cairn of Maive,
> And shake down thunder on the stones because the Red Winds rave!
> Like tattered clouds of the world, passions call and our hearts beat:
> But we have all bent low and low and kissed the quiet feet
>   Of Kathleen the Daughter of Hoolihan.

Love poem and patriotic poem are blended. Yeats's lines are
"fourteeners," seven-stress couplets that can be resolved into 4/3
ballad measure.[39] Meter and refrain identify the poem with the
traditional nationalist ballad. The image of Cathleen with "flame"
in her eyes, "purer than a tall candle before the Blessed Rood"
suggests the effusions of Irish Catholic Mariolatry: the chaste lover
kisses the feet, not the lips, of his beloved. Yeats's crossing of the *aisling*
with the Marian hymn is puritanical: the image of Kathleen stills the
beating of worldly, passionate hearts, and purifies bodies that are like
"heavy swollen waters" (*VSR* 208–09).

    In "The Death of Hanrahan the Red" the Cailleac Beare figures
prominently as Whinny Byrne of the Crossroads, a crazy old woman
who wanders the woods crying aloud that she is beautiful and ageless.
Her metamorphosis into a young girl, however, occurs not during
copulation with the hero, but at the moment of his death:

He saw the withered earthen face and withered earthen arms, and for all his
weakness shrank farther towards the wall; and then faint white arms,
wrought as of glistening cloud, came out of the mud-stiffened tatters and
were clasped about his body; and a voice ... whispered in his ears: "You will
seek me no longer upon the breasts of women ... Look, they have lighted our
wedding tapers!" (*VSR* 226)

Yeats connects the myth of sovereignty with the myth of blood
sacrifice: wedding and grave are conflated. This manoevre is
paradigmatic. Ireland's long history of ineffective rebellion, com-
bined with the Arnoldian imperialist rhetoric that insisted that
failure was an essential part of the Irish character, caused many Irish
writers to insist that defeat was more desirable than success. Yeats,

who used Arnold's most famous Ossianic tag, "They went forth to the Battle, / but they always fell" as the variant title of "The Rose of Battle" (*VP* 113), was one of those who displaced the cheerful copulations of Maeve and Mor by the blood sacrifice of the anxious male.

Describing the origin of the play he wrote in close collaboration with Gregory, Yeats associated himself with the *aisling* tradition: "I had a very vivid dream one night, and I made *Cathleen ni Houlihan* out of this dream" (*Ex* 116). Yeats's unconscious was saturated with national politics, ancient myth, and the conventions of love poetry: he created Cathleen, while Gregory provided the peasant characters and the Kiltartan dialogue.[40] In 1798 an apparently crazed old peasant woman enters the cottage where Michael Gillane is preparing for his wedding. Yeats distinguishes her from the passive woman of the *aisling* tradition by her class, her age, and her history of wandering the country to incite the people to revolution: "when the trouble is on me I must be talking to my friends" (*VPL* 222).[41] Claiming that "many a man has died for love of me" (*VPL* 224), Cathleen persuades Michael to abandon his bride and join the ranks of patriotic martyrs. As they leave, Michael's father asks, "Did you see an old woman going down the path?" and receives the now-immortal reply, "I did not, but I saw a young girl, and she had the walk of a queen" (*VPL* 231). Nuala Ní Dhomhnaill praises Yeats for having recovered the figure of the Cailleac, abandoned by the *aisling* poets, when he incorporates the transformation from ancient hag to young queen into his allegory of Ireland. Like Whinny Byrne, however, this version of the Cailleac demands not sex but death: she is an avatar of the sacrificial goddess of prehistory. Mother Ireland may have had many suitors, but she never satisfied them physically: "With all the lovers that brought me their love I never set out the bed for any" (*VPL* 226). Like the Queen of Heaven she is a Virgin Mother and demands virgin martyrs; like the woman of the courtly tradition she is unobtainable. Just as Hanrahan abandons marriage to Mary Lavelle in pursuit of the immortal Echtge, Michael Gillane sacrifices his marriage to Delia for the sake of a spiritual and political ideal. Although the old woman is metamorphosed into the springtime bride, it is the shedding of blood, not the emission of semen, which does the trick. Yeats distinguishes carefully between the terrible claims of Mother Ireland and the protective response of a biological mother: unwilling to sacrifice her son for her country, Bridget Gillane urges her husband to "Tell him not to go" (*VPL* 230). Yet *Cathleen ni Houlihan* unambiguously endorses patriotic sacrifice as the highest sublimation of sexual love. To die for one's country is to translate the *Liebestod* into political terms.

The male myth of woman as pure mother demanding sacrifice of her sons suggests an unconscious fear of the all-powerful mother of infancy, and implies that in the political as well as the sexual sphere the mother will demand the death of her lover as the price of his gratification. Adoration and abhorrence are fused in a symbol that ignores women's own desire. As we have seen, that apparently indestructible poetic formula, "the old association of love and death" (*L* 828), also functions in history. An uncritical acceptance of the connection between female sexuality and death as "essential" or archetypal permits ideological manipulation of the sacrificial mother as a mobilizing image in times of national crisis. Jane Marcus argues that "the inimical concepts of life and death, motherhood and war ... have no natural affinity but are coupled anew for every war to glamorize destruction and keep women producing cannon fodder for the next."[42] Women's sexuality is extinguished as they assume the roles of mothers, nurses, and mourners of dead male heroes.

Yeats is commonly linked with Pearse as the chief popularizer of the discourse of male self-sacrifice for the motherland, which, it is claimed, still has currency in the Maze prison and the Catholic ghettos of Belfast.[43] Pearse's role in the development of Irish nationalism is problematic and contested;[44] but to criticize the anti-feminist tendency of his literary works is not to repudiate 1916.[45] Despite the endorsement of female suffrage in the Proclamation of the Republic, Pearse's representation of women was deeply conventional. "I Am Ireland" evokes the maternal figure:

> I am Ireland:
> I am older than the Old Woman of Beare.
>
> Great my glory:
> I that bore Cuchulainn the valiant.[46]

Deliberately desexualizing the Gaelic myth, Pearse claims that Mother Ireland is older and lonelier than that shameless hag, the Cailleac. Instead of dallying with numerous lovers, she has borne valiant sons like Cuchulain. How she got pregnant is tactfully shrouded in mystery. Pearse endorsed Yeats's vision of Ireland as a pure woman. "When I was a child," he wrote,

I believed that there was actually a woman called Erin, and had Mr. Yeats's *Kathleen ni Houlihan* been then written and had I seen it, I should have taken it not as an allegory, but as a representation of a thing that might happen any day in any house.[47]

In his play *The Singer* Pearse rewrote *Cathleen ni Houlihan*, combining the dramatic functions of the Poor Old Woman and the sacrificial victim in his male hero, MacDara. The removal of Cathleen displaces all the significance of Mother Ireland onto the real mother, Maire, whom MacDara compares to the Virgin. Her religious elevation confines the mother to the role of watcher and mourner:

'Tis a pity of the women of the world. Too good they are for us, and too full of care. I'm afraid that there was many a woman on this mountain that sat up last night. Aye, and many a woman in Ireland. 'Tis women that keep all the great vigils.

The claim that "to be a woman and to serve and suffer as women do is to be the highest thing" ensures that women keep on serving and suffering. By collapsing Cathleen into Mary, Pearse demands that actual mothers behave like symbolic ones, that they say with Maire "I am his mother, and I do not grudge him,"[48] rather than protesting with Bridget Gillane, "Tell him not to go." Pearse's ultimate betrayal of women, and of mothers, is his appropriation of the maternal voice:

> I do not grudge them: Lord, I do not grudge
> My two strong sons that I have seen go out
> To break their strength and die, they and a few,
> In bloody protest for a glorious thing.[49]

Women are venerated only to be marginalized as producers of sons for slaughter, ungrudgingly offering men to death for the cause. Although extreme, Pearse's rhetoric was not exceptional: his attitude to women and to war was commonplace in the first half of the century.[50]

Yeats gradually became aware of the dubious nature of the myth of male sacrifice, and of his own complicity in giving it artistic currency. After the Rising he wrote: "Now I began running through the years from my youth up & measure[d] my responsibility for an event that has been a great grief to me & many mother[s]."[51] He associates himself with the humanly bereft rather than the triumphantly sacrificial maternal figure: with Bridget rather than Cathleen. In "Modern Ireland" (1932) he argued that, with the Rising, "something new and terrible had come in Ireland, the mood of the mystic victim." Although he never ceased to celebrate the heroes' contribution to Irish freedom, Yeats felt that the experience of civil war cast doubt upon their ethic, for "it is not wholesome for a people to think much of exceptional acts of faith or sacrifice, least of all to make them the sole test of [a] man's worth."[52] The author of *Cathleen ni Houlihan* had certainly done some rethinking.

Contemporary Irish feminists and political activists are still divided on the utility of Mother Ireland. Some ask with MacNeice:

> Kathaleen ni Houlihan! Why
> Must a country, like a ship or a car, be always female,
> Mother or sweetheart?[53]

In the television program *Mother Ireland*[54] Mairead Farrell, the IRA volunteer assassinated in 1988 by the SAS in Gibraltar, recalled how in Armagh jail, "It became a standard joke in there you know, this mother image ... our joke was, 'Mother Ireland get off our back' ... it didn't reflect what we believed in, and it just doesn't reflect Ireland." Bernadette Devlin, however, still claimed allegiance to Mother Ireland:

I just grew up very conscious of Mother Ireland before I was aware of a social and political and economic system that went with it, and I would still hold very strongly to it for all her strengths and weaknesses and contradictions and areas of reaction ... I would still very much see myself as a child of Mother Ireland.

The image, then, offers a source of emotional strength and a confirmation of political identity to women like Devlin. Farrell concedes that: "Maybe at one time people could relate to it."

Mother Ireland, indeed, has many faces: one looks towards Rome; another towards the warrior women of Irish myth; another draws its power from the emotional bonds of childhood. Gonne, motherless at an early age, saw Ireland as "the all-protecting mother," but opened her autobiography *A Servant of the Queen* with a goddess who is less maternal than Amazonic:

I saw a tall, beautiful woman with dark hair blown on the wind and I knew it was Cathleen ni Houlihan. She was crossing the bog towards the hills, springing from stone to stone over the treacherous surface, and the little white stones shone, marking a path behind her, then faded into the darkness. I heard a voice say: "You are one of the little stones on which the feet of the Queen have rested on her way to Freedom."

The goddess certainly empowered Gonne both as a patriot and as a woman: she accepted the peasants' identification of her as the "woman of the Sidhe," the "Triumphant One," the "woman of the prophecy."[55] "Red Hanrahan's Song about Ireland" was her favorite Yeats poem, and she identified with her role as Cathleen ni Houlihan: excluded from the fraternity of the nationalists she confirmed her political identity in myth. In old age she often signed her letters "the Shan Van Vocht" or "old Maedhe."[56] Yeats thought of her as "in a sense Ireland ... the romantic political Ireland of my youth" (*Mem* 247), and she did nothing to disabuse him of his illusion that she was the land personified. For many other nationalists she became the living embodiment of the Spirit of Erin. In letters from prison Constance Markievicz, an admirer of Gonne's, quoted Cathleen's lines and claimed: "That play of W. B.'s was a sort of gospel to me."[57]

The intersection of nationalism and sexuality was exemplified in Yeats's collaboration with Gonne on their projected "Castle of the Heroes." Together they sought to make connection with the spirit of the land in order to release its political energies. Gonne wrote:

We were both held by the mysterious power of the land. To me Ireland was the all-protecting mother, who had to be released from the bondage of the foreigner, to be free and able to protect her children; to Willie, less aware of the People than of the Land, Ireland was the beauty of unattainable perfection, and he had to strive to express that beauty so that all should worship.[58]

While Gonne saw her country in terms of the family, Yeats adopted the structures of courtly romance, with Ireland as the unattainable beloved.

The agency and power with which the Irish tradition of the woman warrior invested the courtly figure of the goddess and the love poets' formulaic Rose infuse "To Ireland in the Coming Times," in which Yeats seeks "*to sweeten Ireland's wrong*" through an evocation of her divine feminine origin in

> *the red-rose-bordered hem*
> *Of her, whose history began*
> *Before God made the angelic clan.*

The rose-decked goddess shares the creative power of the Gnostic Sophia. Older than "*the angelic clan*," it is she who brings Ireland to life: "*The measure of her flying feet / Made Ireland's heart begin to beat.*" It is not enough for the courtly lover to spread his dreams under those feet, for they mark a historical path he must follow, the path of nationalist action. As the brother of "*Davis, Mangan, Ferguson*" he must follow "*After the red-rose-bordered hem*" (*VP* 137–39). The poet of Ireland situates himself on the margins, the borders, of the hegemonic political and lyrical traditions. Woven into the hem of the Irish Rose is the narrative of the oppressed: its cloth is not the cloth of heaven, but of history.

CHAPTER 5

Venus or Mrs. Pankhurst: from love to friendship

Adorno claims that the historical relation of individual to society in the lyric poem "will be the more perfect, the more the poem eschews the relation of self to society as an explicit theme and the more it allows this relation to crystallize involuntarily from within the poem."[1] Arthur Symons's painfully explicit poem, "On Reading of Women Rioting for their Rights" (1907), overtly addresses social changes caused by the prospective social empowerment of women. It is not a love poem, but in using the sonnet form, that most traditional vehicle of the genre, Symons suggests the impossibility of love poetry when the paradigm of female elevation and male abasement no longer obtains:

> What is this unimaginable desire
> In women's heads? Would you come down again
> From where you are, to be no more than men?
> Why is it that you call it getting higher
> To slip with each step deeper into the mire?
> You would be even as men are? Is it then
> So clean a thing to be a citizen
> And take a dirty daily wage for hire?
>
> Man has long since laid up his soul in pawn,
> And lent his body out for a machine;
> He has long since forgot that he has been
> The master, not the servant of the dawn:
> But now the woman fights for leave to ply
> A friendly muckrake with him in his sty.[2]

Symons may be aiming to persuade women not to compete with him in the marketplace, but we should credit his critique of alienated wage-labor under capitalism. Man, the "servant" of the system, contrives a fantasy escape by pretending to be the servant of a woman, whom he sees as outside the normal relations of exchange,

73

unalienated, other, above. This nineteenth-century ideological fic-
tion is congruent with the dominant structural convention of the love
lyric, in which the positions of lover and beloved reverse the relations
of power between the sexes. Thus women's fight to rise is described by
Symons, whose mental instability seems to have been connected with
his fear of the suffrage movement,[3] as a battle for the muckrake, a
descent into the mire.[4] The muckrake, significantly, is coded as
"friendly": friendship is all that remains when romantic illusion has
been destroyed.

Yeats had read Symons's poem: he marked up the proofs of the
collection in which it appeared, *Knave of Hearts* (1913). He cannot,
however, have approved of its sentiments. He was sympathetic to
suffrage demands, and "friendly" with actresses, socialists, national-
ist activists, and "New Women": overlapping categories that
included Katharine Tynan,[5] Annie Besant, Florence Farr, Constance
and Eva Gore-Booth, Edith Craig, Pamela Coleman Smith, Evelyn
Sharp, Sarojini Naidu,[6] and Maud Gonne. The London and Dublin
milieux in which he moved, as poet, playwright, occultist, and
romantic socialist, were saturated with suffrage sentiment. Even
before the suffrage campaign began to acquire wide publicity the
theater was a fertile breeding ground for activism. Farr, though not
a suffrage campaigner, was an Ibsenite New Woman who identified
with *Rosmersholm*'s Rebecca West, the part she created on the London
stage.[7] May Whitty, the first Countess Cathleen, later became a
prominent member of the Actresses Franchise League. In 1902
Yeats's friendship with Edith Craig, lesbian and committed suffra-
gist,[8] blossomed with her espousal of his most anarchistic play, *Where
There Is Nothing*: "She says it is the only play for the last fifteen years
she has cared about" (*L* 383). Pamela Coleman Smith, who was later
a member of the Suffrage Atelier,[9] helped Craig produce designs for
the play, which was eventually produced by the Stage Society at the
Royal Court under the direction of Harley Granville-Barker, a
sympathizer with women's political demands.

Both for Gonne and for Yeats himself, however, the suffrage issue
was secondary to Irish nationalism. When Gonne went into the
House of Commons to offer her services to Michael Davitt, "An
elderly woman standing near me asked me if I was interested in the
Suffrage movement, and gave me leaflets. I knew little about it but
quite agreed women should vote."[10] Irish suffragists were constantly
exhorted to work for a free Ireland, in which women would resume

the ancient rights and privileges accorded to them under the Brehon laws, rather than accept the vote from an Imperial parliament.[11] In 1900, however, Gonne founded her separate women's association, Inghinidhe na hEireann (the daughters of Erin). They addressed each other as "sister" and adopted Brigid as their patron: speaking on "the Goddess Brigid" at their first ceilidh, Gonne returned the saint to her place in the ancient Celtic pantheon.[12] Although their primary dedication was to nationalism, Inghinidhe demanded "Freedom for Our Nation and the complete removal of all disabilities to our sex."[13]

Those disabilities were brought home to Gonne when in February 1905 she sought a divorce from her husband John MacBride, whom she had married partly as a "sacrifice to convention."[14] In court she accused him of drunkenness, brutality, and adultery with her sixteen-year-old step-sister Eileen. In private she used his alleged indecent assault upon the ten-year old Iseult Gonne as a bargaining weapon (*AYF* 203, 215–19).[15] During the summer of 1905 Yeats speculated to John Quinn that Gonne's unhappy experience might turn her towards more active feminist agitation:

The woman's [*sic*] question is in a worse state in Dublin than in any place I know, and she seems naturally chosen out by events to stir up rebellion in what will be for her a new way. I am always hearing stories of women who are bound in a worse way where the clerical conception of life is less strong than in Dublin to drunken husbands.[16]

Although Gonne's closest friend in Paris was Madame Avril de Sainte-Croix, a prominent feminist (*AYF* 461), Cassandra Laity suggests that she was not "enough the New Woman for Yeats" where sex was concerned.[17] The literary associations of the New Woman as she was represented by male authors (Ibsen's Nora, Hedda Gabler, and Rebecca West; Hardy's Tess and Sue; Synge's Nora and Pegeen) were sexual in nature: debates about her often centered on questions of free love, female libidinal fulfillment, and divorce; issues in which men also had vested interests. Yeats's own concern for the liberation of women centered primarily on lifting sexual repression and challenging the tyranny of domesticity: child of a miserable marriage himself, he idealized "lawless women without homes and without children" (*Au* 64). Some constitutional suffragists like Mrs. Fawcett, however, disliked the implication that female political and sexual emancipation were inextricably intertwined: free-love feminists like Emma Goldman and Margaret Sanger were in the minority.[18] Christabel Pankhurst, whose book *The Great Scourge and How to End It* identified venereal disease as the cause of modern degeneracy, preached sexual restraint: her slogan was "Votes for Women and Chastity for Men."[19]

Gonne, who told Yeats in 1898 that she had "a horror and terror of physical love" (*Mem* 134), was not, despite her two illegitimate children, a sexual rebel: conscious of the prejudices of Irish nationalists, she sought to conceal Iseult's identity. Her experience with John MacBride, however, did help to strengthen her interest in women's rights: although Inghinidhe na hEireann was officially silent, she sent messages of support to suffragist meetings protesting the Cat and Mouse Act and the exclusion of women from the Home Rule Bill.[20] Yeats too committed himself publicly to the cause of militant women. When Mrs. Pankhurst spoke in Dublin in October 1910, Hanna Sheehy Skeffington associated the Irish Women's Franchise League with "the militant policy of the advanced English suffragists." She then announced that "sympathetic messages" had been received from Tim Healey, Councillor Nannetti, and W. B. Yeats.[21]

The militant phase of the suffrage campaign began in 1905, when Christabel Pankhurst and Annie Kenney were arrested after interrupting a speech by Sir Edward Grey with the repeated question, "Will the Liberal Government give votes to women?" Christabel Pankhurst wrote that, after this incident, "the long, long newspaper silence as to woman suffrage was broken":[22] suffragists and suffragettes (as the militants of the Women's Social and Political Union were christened by the *Daily Mail*) began to appear in news photographs and cartoons, on posters and postcards, in the theater and the music hall. Their deliberately theatrical and spectacular tactics (mass meetings, processions, pageants, and pilgrimages) gained them a prominent place in the popular culture of the day: according to Tickner, "the development of photographic reproduction in the daily press and the development of suffrage spectacle go hand in hand."[23] This spectacle can be read as an attempt by women to reject the passivity and lyrical stasis of the aesthetic object imposed by the proprietary male gaze, and to orchestrate themselves as a collective, public, and self-moving theatrical experience. At the two huge marches of June 1908 and the Coronation Procession of June 1911, vividly embroidered banners bearing the names of famous women or the mottoes of local suffrage societies provided the indispensable elements of structure and spectacle. This agitation by symbol was reported approvingly even by those newspapers that opposed the cause.[24] Although the excitement did not spread to Ireland until the foundation of the Irish Women's Franchise League in 1908, Irish suffragists adopted the same symbolic strategies as their English counterparts. Hanna Sheehy Skeffington, one of the founders of the League, wrote that

We had colours (orange and green), a Votes for Women badge, slogans; we made use, with feminine ingenuity, of many good publicity devices and stunts, and became a picturesque element in Irish life, the Irish being always glad of any new element, especially one that challenged and took sides. We held parades, processions, pageants (a Pageant of Great Women which went back to Irish history for heroines).[25]

Joan of Arc was a popular focus for militant pageantry: at the women's Coronation procession she appeared in armor on a white horse. Gonne, who united nationalism with feminism, was commonly referred to in the press as "the Irish Joan of Arc." The visual image of the strong and politically committed woman received different inflections according to the politics of those who wielded it: while to the anti-suffrage cartoonists the suffragettes were shrieking harridans, bitter spinsters, or man-hating Amazons, they identified themselves with heroines, queens, and martyrs.

The love poems that Yeats wrote for Gonne after the turn of the century bear the impress of women's self-representations. Unlike Symons, Yeats was not afraid of female enfranchisement. Saturated as he was in the Irish tradition, he readily accepted the Amazonic and queenly women of suffrage propaganda as types of Maeve, Aoife, Scathach, and Emer; and he welcomed the "wild," autonomously desiring, and sexually emancipated personae of certain "New Women," reminiscent as they were of Grania and Deirdre, or, to invoke a different tradition, of Shelley's Cythna. Even before the suffrage campaign attracted wide attention he had begun to characterize Gonne as Amazonic. His poem "The Arrow," written before 1903, radically transforms the poetic cliché of the lover transfixed by Cupid's dart: the "arrow" of the title, made out of a "wild" thought, seems to be the woman's weapon rather than the stock property of the love poet (*VP* 199). Gonne's chosen code name in Inghinidhe na hEireann was Maeve, and in "The Old Age of

Queen Maeve" (1903) Yeats aligns her with Celtic women warriors: "For there is no high story about queens / In any ancient book but tells of you" (*VP* 186). Like Maeve she is beautiful, fierce, courageous, and high-hearted, and the repeated adjectives "high" and "great" establish her lofty physical and moral stature. In *On Baile's Strand* Cuchulain attacks Conchobar's negative characterization of Aoife:

> You call her a "fierce woman of the camp",
> For, having lived among the spinning-wheels,
> You'd have no woman near that would not say,
> "Ah! how wise!" "What will you have for supper?"
> "What shall I wear that I shall please you, sir?" (*VPL* 487)

To valorize the "wild" and warlike Aoife he derides her opposite, the subservient, domestic wife who flatters and serves her husband.

In earlier love poems Gonne had figured as Helen, Deirdre, the Gnostic Sophia, the Rose of oppressed Ireland; and the poet had knelt at her feet in approved courtly fashion. His absorption in the work of Nietzsche, however, which began in 1902, caused Yeats to re-evaluate his lyrical poetics as well as his philosophy. Nietzsche's insistence upon hardness and "virility"[26] suggested to Yeats that the failings of his own early poetry could be analyzed in terms of gender:

In my *Land of Heart's Desire*, and in some of my lyric verse of that time, there is an exaggeration of sentiment and sentimental beauty which I have come to think unmanly ... it is sentiment and sentimental sadness, a womanish introspection ... [instead of] the energy of the will out of which epic and dramatic poetry comes there is a region of brooding emotions full of fleshly waters and vapours which kill the spirit and the will, ecstasy and joy equally ... I cannot probably be quite just to any poetry that speaks to me with the sweet insinuating feminine voice of the dwellers in that country of shadows and hollow images. I have dwelt there too long not to dread all that comes out of it. (*L* 434).

He insisted continually upon the effeminacy of lyric (*Ex* 220), and wrote little lyric poetry between 1903 and 1908. His turn to the drama was a search for what he called "more of manful energy" (*VP* 849). When he returned to lyric he brought with him a commitment to "epic" values: his beloved is "A Woman Homer Sung" (1910), "heroic," "proud," and "fiery" (*VP* 255).

Conventional as were his definitions of poetic "manliness" (elliptical condensation of syntax, the replacement of parataxis by subordination, stress-packed lines, colloquial diction, consonantal rather than vocalic emphasis, dissonant rhyme, ironic and witty tone), Yeats paradoxically employed his new poetics to increase the energy of his lyric heroines. Like the New Woman herself, his beloved casts off the stereotypes of Victorian femininity together with the rhythms of Victorian verse. "No Second Troy," written December 1908, reflects the poet's awe at her energy and stature. Although the poem celebrates her as unique, her beauty "solitary" in a banal age, her power individual rather than collective, the representation of femininity in the poem draws energy from women who have adopted mass protest, offering the spectacle of a world turned upside down, the little streets hurled upon the great. Two huge suffrage processions occurred in the summer of 1908. Yeats was in London at the time of the National Union of Women's Suffrage Societies march on June 13, and in Paris with Gonne just after the even larger Women's Social and Political Union demonstration (estimated at between a quarter and a half a million people) on June 21. Caroline Watts's poster, *The Bugler Girl*, which depicts a young woman in "medieval" armor with helmet, sword, and banner "blowing an inspiriting call to the women of Great Britain to come out and stand by their sisters in this fight" (Fig. 3),[27] was displayed all over the country in the weeks before the NUWSS procession. "No Second Troy" revises the traditional love poem in order to accommodate this actively heroic female type:

> Why should I blame her that she filled my days
> With misery, or that she would of late
> Have taught to ignorant men most violent ways,
> Or hurled the little streets upon the great,
> Had they but courage equal to desire?
> What could have made her peaceful with a mind
> That nobleness made simple as a fire,
> With beauty like a tightened bow, a kind
> That is not natural in an age like this,
> Being high and solitary and most stern?
> Why, what could she have done, being what she is?
> Was there another Troy for her to burn?   (*VP* 256–57)

The poetic elevation of the original sonnet heroines, Beatrice and Laura, reflected no social power. The Helen of "No Second Troy," however, has taken power into her own hands: if she is "high" above the poet it is because she has placed herself there. The insistently interrogatory syntax demonstrates Yeats's anxiety about the type of

Figure 3 Caroline Watts, *The Bugler Girl*.

womanhood represented by Gonne. Although she sometimes used her beauty to persuade men to adopt her causes, she rejected conventional romance. The poem's heroine transgresses all the stereotypes of femininity: she is violent, courageous, noble, fiery, solitary, and stern; her beauty is a weapon – "a tightened bow" – rather than a lure. "Reconciliation," written a few months earlier, similarly identifies her with masculinity: with "Kings" and medieval weaponry, "Helmets, and swords, and half-forgotten things / That were like memories of you" (*VP* 257). In figuring her as Helen, Yeats radically modifies the archetype: Homer's passive queen, the sex object over whom men fight their battles, becomes a warrior, identified by the simile of the bow as an Amazon. Yeats's active syntax attributes to her the agency of a subject: instead of causing Troy to be destroyed, she burns it herself. The classical tradition has been crossed with the ancient Irish one in which Cuchulain is trained to fight by the female warrior Scathach, meets his most formidable opponent in the queen Aoife, and marries "Great-bladdered Emer" (*VP* 628).

"No Second Troy" is nevertheless an ambiguous poem for the feminist reader, who may suspect that the cult of the exceptional woman has little relevance to the predicament of her non-exceptional counterparts, and that the individual woman can do little without the kind of collective action favored by the suffragists. In the early years of their acquaintance Yeats had described Gonne as the heroic ideal manifested in female form: "She is very Irish, a kind of 'Diana of the Crossways'" (*CL*1 137). Meredith's feminist heroine, Diana Merion, was modelled on the famous nineteenth-century campaigner for women's rights, Caroline Norton.[28] In representing Diana, Meredith attempts to give "blood, brains to the veiled virginal doll, the heroine." He warns male fiction writers to

teach your imagination of the feminine image you have set up to bend your civilised knees to, that it must temper its fastidiousness, shun the grossness of the over-dainty ... You must turn on *yourself*, resolutely track and seize that burrower, and scrub and cleanse him; by which process ... you will arrive at the conception of the right heroical woman for *you* to worship: and, if you prove to be of some spiritual stature, you may reach to an ideal of the heroical feminine type for the worship of mankind.[29]

Meredith's awareness that images of femininity are the creation of men, together with his depiction of a heroine beleaguered by a patriarchal legal system and committed to votes for women, made him a hero of the suffragists.[30] In *Diana of the Crossways* he addresses the question of the political utility and concomitant danger of depictions of exceptional women: "For, when the fictitious creature has performed that service of helping to civilise the world, it becomes the most dangerous of delusions, causing first the individual to despise the mass, and then to join the mass in crushing the individual."[31] Meredith, however, mistakenly assumed that the exceptional heroine would soon be rendered obsolete by social advances. The recovery by early feminists of queens, saints, and goddesses was historically timely and politically useful. The suffragist reanimation of the militant allegorical female figures of Justice and Liberty reclaimed male representations of women for feminist purposes. We cannot yet dispense with the resources of myth, the power of the Amazon or Queen Maeve, the imaginative liberation offered by the exceptional heroine of poetry or fiction.

Our positive response to the celebration of female agency and power in "No Second Troy" is qualified, however, by the poet's restrictions on the exercise of that power. Gonne lives in an age that, according to Yeats, affords no fitting outlet for the energy of the heroic woman. Revolution is not an appropriate activity for a Helen. Thus the poem takes back with one hand what it gives with the other: the exceptional woman is acknowledged, but her freedom to constitute herself as a subject through political action is denied, and her frustrated power is defined as destructive. When in old age Yeats lamented the fact that he had known "A Helen of social welfare dream, / Climb on a wagonette to scream" (*VP* 626), he abandoned the ambivalence that makes reading "No Second Troy" an interesting experience, and drew instead on anti-suffrage propaganda, which commonly deployed the nineteenth-century stereotype of the hysterical woman.

Although Yeats in 1908 found no political space for the Amazon, he had to listen – as men everywhere were forced to listen – to women's voices. According to Jane Marcus, "*Interruption of male political discourse*, as invented by Christabel Pankhurst, practiced for a decade at by-elections and in storming the houses of Parliament and taught to thousands of women of every class and social background, is the real key to the genius of militant suffrage in giving the women of England a political voice."[32] Although lyric discourse traditionally privileges the monologic meditations of the male speaker, Yeats's theater experience enabled several love poems in dialogue: "The Folly of Being Comforted" (1902), "Adam's Curse" (1902), and "The Mask" (1910). Not until 1915, however, just after the close of the militant suffrage campaign on the declaration of war, does the female voice in Yeats's verse mount a direct political challenge to the male lyric consciousness.

"The People," written in 1915 and published in *The Wild Swans at Coole* (1919), shows Yeats initially resisting the impulse to write a love poem: it begins with a self-pitying and disgruntled tirade about the squandering of his talent in Dublin theater politics. He claims the right of the lyric poet to retreat from the social world of his time and class, from "The daily spite of this unmannerly town" that renders his "trade" uneconomic: "'What have I earned for all that work,' I said, / 'For all that I have done at my own charge?'" (*VP* 351). The aristocratic, timeless spaces to which he wishes to retire are the ancient cities of Ferrara, rendered pastoral by the Marvellian "green shadow" of its wall, and Urbino, dignified by the patrician presences of the Duchess Elizabetta Gonzaga and her courtiers. Disgusted by bourgeois Dublin, in which his "trade" produces the negative return of spite and infamy, Yeats embraces the aristocratic world of Castiglione's etiquette book *The Courtier*. Reflecting the restrictions on female behavior that accompanied the rise of classical humanism in the Renaissance, Castiglione calls upon the Lady to give up unbecoming pursuits like riding and handling weapons.[33] This reduction in activity was accompanied by a corresponding renunciation of voice. Yeats wrote in his 1909 Journal: "Perhaps we may find in the spectacle of some beautiful woman our Ferrara, our Urbino. Perhaps that is why we have no longer any poetry but the poetry of love" (*Mem* 156). This definition of the female object of a love poem as topographical spectacle, radically distinct from the active spectacle of the suffragists, is one with which the speech-maker Gonne, who was often careless of her beauty, had no sympathy; and the poem's dialogic movement is completed by her vocal reproof to the poet for his snobbery and lyric exclusivity. The interruption is couched in her own words: the poet imitates rather than appropriates Gonne's voice.

Recalling "After nine years" (actually eight) an exchange of letters with Gonne in 1907, while he was in Italy with Gregory, Yeats recaptures his first appreciation of Ferrara and Urbino as aristocratic antitheses to "unmannerly" Dublin. In the 1915 poem his bitterness

towards the town "Where who has served the most is most defamed"
(*VP* 351) is overdetermined, occasioned both by the events of 1907
(the dispute over the *Playboy* and the attack on Gonne by nationalists
loyal to her husband) and by the 1913 dissensions over Hugh Lane,
"a man / Of your own passionate serving kind" (*VP* 292), whose
plans for a Dublin gallery were sabotaged by what Yeats came to call
"the mob."

   Yeats's contempt for ill-breeding, reinforced by Gregory, Castig-
lione, Nietzschean philosophy, and his irritation about theatrical
politics, had been violently stimulated when in 1903 Gonne married
her social inferior, a man whose family kept a public house in
Westport. "You are going to marry one of the people," he warned in
a letter that expresses both his personal anguish and the snobbery it
elicited. Her conversion to Catholicism, "a lower order of faith is
thrusting you down socially, is thrusting you down to the people."
The love poet maps his lyric worship of his goddess onto the structure
of social class, and codes her marriage as a poetic and political
descent from "the proud solitary haughty life which made [you]
seem like one of the Golden Gods" (*AYF* 165). In reply, Gonne
insisted on the difference between his individualist and spatial poetic
model and her experience of herself as an impersonal collective voice:
"You say I leave the few to mix myself with the crowd while Willie
I have always told you I am the voice, the soul of the *crowd*" (*AYF*
166). Thereafter, although he stood loyally by her during her
controversial and painful divorce proceedings, they carried on a
running epistolary dispute about the failings of the Dublin crowd,
with Gonne maintaining that despite the personal vileness of
MacBride and the calumnies of his partisans, "there is more good
than you admit in the unconscious thought of the masses of the
people" (*AYF* 221).[34] In an unpublished quatrain Yeats unfairly
blames her for his own quasi-eugenic preoccupation with mis-
cegenation:

> My dear is angry that of late
> I cry all base blood down
> As though she had not taught me hate
> By kisses to a clown.   (*Mem* 145)

These unpleasant lines resonate through "A Prayer for my Daugh-
ter" and *Purgatory*, in both of which "fine women eat / A crazy salad
with their meat" (*VP* 404). Reviled in some Irish newspapers after

her separation from MacBride, and hissed by MacBride's supporters when in 1906 she attended an Abbey performance with Yeats, Gonne nevertheless dispassionately defended the motives of those who had attacked her, and rebuked Yeats for his injustice towards the people. She allowed that the *Playboy* dispute had thrown up old enemies,

who profit of moments such as these to attack you bitterly & even treacherously, as in my case, the frauds who I had exposed, the publicans & drunkards I had driven out the cowards who I had made own their cowardice all join MacBride's party & whisper calumny against me – but in neither of our cases were the people generally to blame & even from a national point I think their action is a healthy sign. (*AYF* 241)

Was Yeats rereading old letters when he wrote the poem? He reproduces Gonne's breathless syntax in the sentence suspended over seven lines:

> "The drunkards, pilferers of public funds,
> All the dishonest crowd I had driven away,
> When my luck changed and they dared meet my face,
> Crawled from obscurity and set upon me
> Those I had served and some that I had fed;
> Yet never have I, now nor any time,
> Complained of the people."   (*VP* 352)

If a male poet cannot produce an "authentic" female voice, he can adopt a female subject position that contests and in this case defeats his own prejudices. The male speaker offers a stumbling apology for his intellectualism and confesses its inadequacy in the face of her purity of intention. She is the Phoenix, self-renewing symbol of the Fenian cause, as well as the champion of the socially downtrodden whom he in his snobbish anger has derided. Her interruption, which appeals directly to his heart, reduces him once more to the abject position of the unsuccessful lover, and deprives him even of his verbal polish: the poem ends with movingly awkward repetition:

> And yet, because my heart leaped at her words,
> I was abashed, and now they come to mind
> After nine years, I sink my head abashed.   (*VP* 353)

Thanking Yeats for "The People" Gonne wrote, "To me you are too kind – You have often tried to defend & protect me with your art –

& perhaps when we are dead I shall be known by those poems of yours" (*AYF* 356–57). In giving his beloved an authentic, powerful, and conclusive voice within the poem, a voice that ultimately silences his own, Yeats makes a political statement on the level of form that contains and amplifies the thematic politics of a commitment to "the people" rather than to the aristocratic withdrawal of the traditional lyric. Ironically it is not woman as spectacle but woman as speaker who turns "The People" into a love poem.

If "The People" transforms an argument into a love poem, "Michael Robartes and the Dancer" does the opposite by demonstrating how the introduction of the female perspective reinflects the genre. The woman who ceases to be silent makes it impossible to impose the traditionally uninterrupted homage of the male gaze. In "A Woman Homer Sung" (1910) Yeats had wanted to "[shadow] in a glass / What thing her body was" (*VP* 255). The Dancer, however, sabotages his project by engaging his persona Michael Robartes in argument, replacing viewing by voicing. Her six brief interjections range in tone through the deflatingly ironic ("You mean they argued"), the *faux naïf* ("And must no beautiful woman be / Learned like a man?"), and the prudish ("I have heard said / There is great danger in the body"). She has the last word, but her concluding line is ambiguous: she is "perplexed" by but not necessarily acquiescent to Robartes's arguments for the primacy of the flesh: "They say such different things at school" (*VP* 385–87). "Michael Robartes and the Dancer" mimes the debate in the popular press between suffragists and anti-suffragists, and the feminist debate between women who saw the body as a source of danger and those few like Victoria Woodhull and Emma Goldman who advanced the riskier proposition that bodies were made for pleasure.

Robartes's obsessions are visual and pictorial: he is "an uncompromising Pre-Raphaelite," and in the introduction to *A Vision* Yeats locates him in the National Gallery of London, gazing at "the story of Griselda pictured in a number of episodes" (*AV*[*A*] xv). Chaucer's tale of a submissive woman bullied by her sadistic husband is an appropriate model for Robartes, who denigrates women's struggle for power and voice. In the poem he adopts the role of docent, lecturing the Dancer on the proper interpretation of a potent image of male strength and feminine victimage: St. George and the Dragon. Numerous nineteenth-century painters, among them Burne-

Jones,[35] reinforced the lesson of this myth by depicting naked and helpless female flesh rescued by clothed and impermeable male chivalry. Robartes, who has been away in the desert for twenty years, is horrified by the changes in the relations between men and women that have occurred since 1898. In his view the Lady has disrupted the chivalric formula and made the traditional position of lover untenable: instead of being properly grateful to her rescuer she identifies with the wounded Dragon. The line, "the half-dead dragon was her thought," metaphorically equates the "dragon" with female intellectual powers. It also has a suffragette persona: it "shrieked and fought." Robartes's picture of the woman of ideas derives from hostile caricatures of the suffragists, who were so often reviled as "the shrieking sisterhood" (in Eliza Lynn Linton's phrase) that Emmeline Pethick Lawrence decided to appropriate the abusive term:

> Now you know we have been called "The Shrieking Sisterhood", but you see how much need there is for our "shrieking". It is the duty of every woman here to come and help us shriek. Perhaps you say, you don't know how to shriek. Come and join the Women's Social and Political Union. We will teach you.[36]

The dragon's apparently unquenchable appetite for the fight also owes much to the newspaper photographs of women physically embroiled with policemen that accompanied the later stages of the campaign, and were editorialized as evidence of hysteria.

Robartes's opposing ideal, appropriate for such an inveterate frequenter of galleries, is that familiar image from high art, the beautiful woman with a looking glass:

> She would have time to turn her eyes,
> Her lover thought, upon the glass
> And on the instant would grow wise.

This mirror-wisdom concerns the capitalist economics of the visual: "your lover's wage / Is what your looking-glass can show"; her "beating breast" and "vigorous thigh" are payment for the lover's heroic feats as dragon-killer (*VP* 385–86). As in "Peace," the woman's body exists to "show what Homer's age / Bred to be a hero's wage" (*VP* 258). The man's wage is the woman's show. "A Thought from Propertius" (1915), a less complicated but more disturbing poem than "Michael Robartes and the Dancer," assesses the exchange value of the female anatomy even more brutally. The "noble" woman with "great shapely knees" is first presented as accompanying Pallas Athena to the altar, and then, in an abrupt reversal of this classical image of virginity and purity, as a suitable candidate for rape: "fit spoil for a centaur / Drunk with the unmixed wine" (*VP* 355). Yeats alludes to the wedding feast of Pirithous depicted upon the Olympia pediment, at which the drunken centaur Eurytion abducted the bride.[37]

Biographically, the juxtaposition or interchangeability of goddess and rape victim reflects Yeats's agonizing double experience of Gonne. Sexually unattainable (except for a brief period) to him, the "great stone Minerva" of his visions (*Mem* 134) and the Eternal Rose of his early verse was also mistress of Lucien Millevoye, mother of his two illegitimate children, and later the battered and betrayed wife of the drunken and possibly adulterous John MacBride. Read in its contemporary historical context, however, the poem hints that it is precisely in her resemblance to Athena, the virgin war-goddess, patroness of independent and learned women, and indeed of the Suffrage Atelier, that the woman invites her own violation. The hero and the lover earn their wages while the drunken and unlicensed centaur steals his, but the word "fit" troublingly implies the speaker's approval of the theft.[38] In "Michael Robartes and the Dancer" the dancer is urged to reject Athena, and forbidden to attend college: the only knowledge Robartes would allow her is carnal knowledge. Women are permitted "thought" only if

> The lineaments that please their view
> When the long looking-glass is full,
> Even from the foot-sole think it too.   (*VP* 387)

In his classic discussion of the female nude John Berger argues that "Men look at women. Women watch themselves being looked at. This determines not only most relations between men and women but also the relation of women to themselves. The surveyor of woman in herself is male: the surveyed female. Thus she turns herself into an object – and most particularly an object of vision." Analyzing the pictorial trope of the nude woman with the looking glass he claims that the function of the mirror was "to make the woman connive in treating herself as, first and foremost, a sight."[39] Michael Robartes has exactly these designs upon the Dancer: she should find her reflected image pleasing because it will feed the scopophilic hunger of her lover.

For Yeats the representation of women had generic implications: ideal beauties belonged to tragedy; realistically depicted women to comedy. In his famous *Essay on Comedy* Meredith had argued that the full flowering of the comic spirit depended upon equality between the sexes.[40] Yeats regretfully agreed, noting that "our new art of comedy" was displacing the stylized beauty of Pre-Raphaelite women. Modern art offered him no asylum for his affections, "no man I could have wished to be, no woman I could have loved" (*E&I* 242). He sought not character but the expression of "personal emotion through ideal form":

And when we love ... do we not also, that the flood may find no stone to convulse, no wall to narrow it, exclude character or the signs of it by choosing that beauty which seems unearthly because the individual woman is lost amid the labyrinth of its lines ... When we choose a wife, as when we go to the gymnasium to be shaped for woman's eyes, we remember academic form. (*E&I* 243–44)

Desire, then, is canonical. Although written in 1910, this passage anticipates in its eugenic preoccupations the Yeats of "The Statues" and *On the Boiler*. In hinting at the mutuality of the gaze, however, Yeats complicates the definition of woman as visual object: men too must be "shaped for woman's eyes."

Yeats's conception of ideal or academic form was constructed out of Greek statuary, Renaissance paintings, and the Pre-Raphaelites. When that canon was challenged by Manet's *Olympia* (Fig. 4), however, Yeats was attentive to the generic implications of the disruption.[41] Manet's parody of Titian's *Venus of Urbino* both fascinated and puzzled him:

I saw the *Olympia* of Manet at the Luxembourg and watched it without hostility indeed, but as I might some incomparable talker whose precision of gesture gave me pleasure, though I did not understand his language. I returned to it again and again at intervals of years, saying to myself, "Some day I will understand"; and yet it was not until Sir Hugh Lane brought the *Eva Gonzales* to Dublin, and I had said to myself, "How perfectly that woman is realised as distinct from all other women that have lived or shall live," that I understood I was carrying on in my own mind [the] quarrel between a tragedian and a comedian. (*E&I* 242)

Yeats associates the individuality of Manet's prostitute, who directly and disconcertingly returns the gaze of the viewer and whose hand

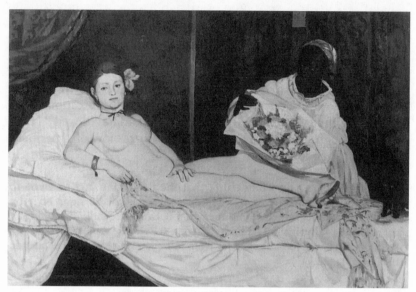

Figure 4 Edouard Manet, *Olympia.*

denies visual access to her genitals, with the new spirit of comedy, which destroys the impersonal canonical mask of beauty and replaces it with a particular female character. Yeats equates comedy with resistance to the construction and appropriation of the female body by male systems of representation; and despite his own formal adherence to those systems, the gesture pleases him. When he recast *The Player Queen* as comedy he symbolically valorized Decima's feminist refusal to play the canonical but subservient role of the battered wife of Noah (*VPL* 735). In the lyric his late turn to comedy enabled the creation of his female speakers Crazy Jane and the Woman Young and Old.

In engaging with the suffrage position on the dangerous potential of bodily pleasure, "Michael Robartes and the Dancer" situates itself within the larger framework of women's history. But why does Yeats focus so intensely upon the image of the woman with a looking glass in his presentation of the debate between an old-fashioned lover and a feminist in search of an education? Among the many possible answers to this question is a historical one: a specific event now nearly forgotten, but at the time notorious and much publicized. On 10 March 1914 the militant suffragist Mary Richardson took an axe to

Figure 5 Diego Velásquez, *Venus at Her Mirror* (*The Rokeby Venus*).

Velázquez's *Venus at Her Mirror* (Fig. 5), which depicts the goddess reclining naked, inspecting herself in a mirror. Richardson did not pick this nude by accident:

I had to draw the parallel between the public's indifference to Mrs. Pankhurst's slow destruction and the destruction of some financially valuable object.

A painting came to my mind. Yes, yes – the Venus Velásquez had painted, hanging in the National Gallery. It was highly prized for its worth in cash. If I could damage it, I reasoned, I could draw my parallel. The fact that I had disliked the painting would make it easier for me to do what was in my mind.

Richardson was not hostile to all images of women painted by men: only to this particular one. As she walked nervously around the gallery, waiting for an opportunity to strike, "I found I was staring at an almond-eyed madonna whose beauty it was far beyond my powers to reproduce. Her smile, however, impressed itself sufficiently upon my senses to bring me a certain calmness of mind."[42] The pure and clothed madonna gave her the courage to strike at the naked woman displayed for male consumption. Richardson's narrative unconsciously mimes the rhetoric of the suffragist chastity crusade, which emphasized the horrors of prostitution, and would have placed *Olympia* in the same category as the *Venus of Urbino*, the *Venus at Her Mirror*, and the voluptuous paintings of "Paul Veronese / And all his sacred company," who

> Imagined bodies all their days
> By the lagoon you love so much,
> For proud, soft, ceremonious proof
> That all must come to sight and touch.   (*VP* 386)

Like the Dancer, Richardson felt that "there is great danger in the body" because the female body is the classic site of male exploitation. She took up her axe against the power of the proprietary male gaze. She wrote that she had "tried to destroy the picture of the most beautiful woman in mythological history as a protest against the Government for destroying Mrs. Pankhurst who is the most beautiful character in modern history."[43] She wanted to replace woman as object by woman as moral agent: to substitute for the fantasies of male mythology the revolutionary activities of historical women. Unlike Yeats, she considered character more important than beauty.

Velázquez is not Veronese, but Mary Richardson's attack upon Venus in defense of Mrs. Pankhurst surely alerted Yeats to the fact that women increasingly considered representation, in the artistic as well as the political sense, to be a contentious issue. Harwood thinks that, despite biographical evidence that shows Yeats attempting to persuade Iseult Gonne to become, if not "learned like a man," at least a reasonable translator of Bengali, "Michael Robartes and the Dancer" "remains a chauvinist *poem*";[44] but it is rather a poem about an increasingly embattled chauvinism. Although considerable distance exists between himself and the pompous and dictatorial Robartes, Yeats uses the character to test both his own prejudices and the inherited generic norms of love poetry against feminist objections and demands. His dislike of "opinion" and abstract thought in women, his love of the physical coherence of the Dancer, his celebration of the pleasures of the body as against the exactions of the intellect and the suffragist defense of chastity, are all called into question by the woman's voice. She may not win the argument, but she refuses to be silenced. In "Michael Robartes and the Dancer" Yeats uses the lyric form to stage a social quarrel about the effect of changing sexual roles; but it is also that quarrel with himself out of which, he insisted, poetry is made.

The suffragists demanded civil equality: the right to vote on exactly the same terms as men. In his anti-suffrage poem Symons derided this sexual egalitarianism because, in removing women from their position on the pedestal, it disturbed the spatial relations that inform what Yeats called "the old high way of love" (*VP* 206). Symons therefore mocked women's unromantic desire to ply a "friendly" muckrake with their male co-workers in the sty. Aristotle declared friendship between the sexes impossible because friendship is founded upon equality, and women are inferior to men. In youth Yeats believed that friendship precludes the possibility of romantic love, that passion and equality are incompatible; but he never thought with Aristotle that men and women could not be friends and collaborators. Of John Sherman and Mary Carton he wrote:

Nothing had ever come to break in on their quiet companionship and give obscurity as a dwelling-place for the needed illusions. Had one been weak and the other strong, one plain and the other handsome, one guide and the other guided, one wise and the other foolish, love might have found them out in a moment, for love is based on inequality as friendship is on equality. (*JS* 55)

Despite his clear-headed analysis of love as the product of "illusions," the thirty-one-year-old Yeats still needed his fantasies. Only the stimulus of inequality could generate the desire whose frustration produced poetry. He was unable to overcome the fact that he found Shakespear too sympathetic to inspire passion: "she was too near my soul, too salutary and wholesome to my inmost being" (*Mem* 88). The ideal image therefore took precedence over the "beautiful friend" (*VP* 152). As he entered middle age, however, he became dissatisfied with both the personal and the poetic dimensions of romantic idealization, and the inequality that sustained it. As the political equality of women became the crucial social issue of the time, Yeats began to develop a definition of love that privileged mutual friendship and erotic equality rather than the passionate disequilibrium of the lyric mode.

From 1898 to 1903 and again from 1908 to 1909 he endured the tensions of the "spiritual marriage" in which he and Gonne shared erotic symbolic meditations and attempted to meet on the astral plane. Her letters demonstrate that she took their occult relationship as seriously as he did, and was the more successful of the two at disembodied communication. The "spiritual marriage" modelled on the chaste relationship of the alchemists Nicolas Flamel and his wife

Pernella should not be dismissed as their bizarre private invention: in the early years of the century Margaret and James Cousins, W. T. Horton and Audrey Locke, Moina and McGregor Mathers, and Virginia and Leonard Woolf, were among those who preferred platonic comradeship to a sexual relation. The problem with Yeats's "marriage" was not so much its "spiritual" nature as the unequal distribution of power between the protagonists. Yeats's obsession was sustained because he desired Gonne more than she desired him: despite his own early failures of nerve, the sisterly platonic friendship she continued to offer gradually became in his eyes an inadequate substitute for sexuality. In "All Souls' Night" (1920) Yeats described the spiritual marriage between Horton and Locke in ambiguously oxymoronic terms as a "sweet extremity of pride / That's called platonic love" (*VP* 471); while in his prose he called it "a most needless trampling of the grapes of life" (*AV[A]* x). About himself and Gonne he was less tentative: in 1914 he condemned the spiritual marriage as a "*barren passion*" (*VP* 270), while in 1915 it became "that monstrous thing / Returned and yet unrequited love" ("Presences," *VP* 358). Her letters to him confirm that his love was returned; but repeatedly insist on the need to keep it "pure": in 1910 she wrote in religious terms, "what you have written for me will live because our love has always been high & pure – You have loved generously and unselfishly as few men have loved – It is what remains to me out of the wreck of life, what I can take with me into the peace of the Sanctuary" (*AYF* 294).

As early as "Baile and Aillinn" (1901) Yeats had begun to appreciate that his absorption in this barren passion might have cost him "*all this life can give us*": "*A child's laughter, a woman's kiss*" (*VP* 190). Although the narrative presents a mythical *Liebestod* in entirely positive terms, the italicized commentary hints at the "folly" of such tales, which prevent the achievement of mundane sexual satisfaction: in comparison with their glamour,

> *No common love is to our mind,*
> *And our poor Kate or Nan is less*
> *Than any whose unhappiness*
> *Awoke the harp-strings long ago.*   (*VP* 190)

The new sexual theories of Havelock Ellis (who used Yeats as a guinea-pig for mescal experiments) challenged Victorian medical assumptions about the connection between health and sexual purity, as well as romantic notions about the virtues of sublimation. As always, passion and poetics were intertwined in Yeats's imagination: if " all arts are an expression of desire,"[45] desire is given shape by art. In "Adam's Curse" (1902) he reflected on the textual convention that had mediated and frustrated his own desires: the "Precedents out of beautiful old books" that constituted the poetics of courtly love (*VP* 205).[46]

Adam's curse is work: so the poet laments the labor of poetic creation. His female interlocutor reminds him that Eve too is cursed: she must bring forth children in sorrow and be subject to her husband and his desires.[47] To fulfill both these injunctions she must actively fashion herself as aesthetic spectacle, poem of the flesh:

> "There is one thing that all we women know
> Although we never heard of it at school –
> That we must labour to be beautiful."   (*VP* 205v)

The woman's laborious self-fashioning compels the "heartache" of a lover; the lover's fulfilled desire compels her to labor in childbirth. The division between cultural and reproductive functions, between male work and female childbearing, is as old as the biblical curses to which Yeats alludes; but he complicates the gendered binary by using women's work, "stitching and unstitching," as a metaphor for his own poetic labor. Eve's poem, like Adam's, is despised by the "schoolmasters" (*VP* 204–05): both are implicitly condemned for frivolity. The lyric poet allies himself with the beautiful woman against the masculine worlds of finance, education, and institutional religion.

In a post-lapsarian world the social mediation of desire is hard work; the labor of love is neither "blossoming" nor "dancing" (*VP* 445). Pedantic courtly lovers are controlled by their difficult, if beautiful, texts:

> There have been lovers who thought love should be
> So much compounded of high courtesy
> That they would sigh and quote with learned looks
> Precedents out of beautiful old books.

Yeats, however, is tired of the genre. In the triangulated structure of the poem, the "beautiful mild woman" is destined for reproductive fulfillment, but the silent "you" who provides the emotional focus of the closing stanzas has chosen, and imposed, a different labor. Although he "strove / To love you in the old high way of love," both have grown "As weary-hearted as that hollow moon." Their failure is as much the fault of the text as of the world: in sustaining the inequality of the lover on his knees before the idealized beloved, courtly love, "an idle trade enough," prevents the achievement of sexual union or emotional equality. The two women are "close friend[s]" but the man and his beloved are not (*VP* 204–06). Yeats's moon, a worn and hollow shell, has verbal and imagistic affinities with Shelley's "companionless" moon, the "dying lady, lean and pale" whose pallor is the result of "weariness."[48] The Romantic metaphor, like the lovers, is literally exhausted. The "old high way of love," although recalled in later poems when Yeats represents himself as "some last courtier at a gypsy camping-place / Babbling of fallen majesty" (*VP* 314), is never again presented without irony.

Yeats's interrogation of the courtly inequality that precludes friendship and mutuality can be traced through the numerous drafts of *The Shadowy Waters*, a long poem about love conceived in 1883 but not completed until 1906. The hero Forgael, like Axel or the poet of Shelley's *Alastor* (or like Yeats himself in his symbolic meditations with Gonne), seeks union in eternity with the woman of his dreams, because human love is unsatisfactory. An ordinary man, he argues,

> Loves in brief longing and deceiving hope
> And bodily tenderness, and finds that even
> The bed of love, that in the imagination
> Had seemed to be the giver of all peace,
> Is no more than a wine-cup in the tasting,
> And as soon finished.

In later drafts Yeats introduced a powerful spokesman against the romantic point of view, the sailor Aibric, who counsels acceptance of mortal life. Earthly love may be disappointing, but it is all we have. When Forgael insists that all true lovers believe in something less ephemeral, even if they must go to the country of the dead to find it, Aibric retorts:

> When they have twenty years; in middle life
> They take a kiss for what a kiss is worth,
> And let the dream go by.   (*VP* 228–29)

Romantic passion is now defined as an adolescent complaint.

Yeats records his partial awakening from the romantic dream in the development of the heroine, Dectora. At first she is merely a figment of the solipsistic male imagination: in the courtly code the

Other has no existence independent of the poet's mind. Forgael longs for "a refuge ... for an hour / from myself," for another autonomous and equal human being to love, but cannot escape from the prison of narcissism: "He is like a man living in a tower of polished black stones which each reflect his face."[49] In describing Forgael's predicament Yeats analyzes the inability of most love poets to render the beloved except as a reflection of the self: it is to his credit that, like Shelley in *Alastor*, he sees this lack as a problem. The dream woman who visits the poet of *Alastor* speaks with "the voice of his own soul,"[50] while Forgael initially rejects Dectora because "Your eyes are but / my eyes, your voice is but my voice."[51] Yeats anticipates Woolf's observation that "Women have served all these centuries as looking-glasses possessing the magic and delicious power of reflecting the figure of man at twice its natural size."[52] The superlative qualities of the Beloved validate the taste, virtue, and power of the lover, despite his protestations of unworthiness. Like the suffragists who were attaining independent voice as Yeats was revising his poem, however, Dectora gradually acquires a separate identity and a will of her own. She changes from a passive, Rossettian symbol of Forgael's soul to a passionate individual, and her speaking role is increased from draft to draft until she comes to dominate the conclusion of the poem. Unlike the devoted Arab maiden ignored and abandoned by the poet of *Alastor*, Dectora claims the right to join Forgael on his journey: to replace the solitary male quester of courtly and Shelleyan tradition with a united couple. In the final version she triumphs: "We are alone for ever, and I laugh, / Forgael, because you cannot put me from you." Instead of rejecting the offer of human love for the delusions of romantic dream, as does the poet of *Alastor*, Forgael and Dectora "grow immortal" through accepting their mutual passion (*VP* 251–52).

Despite its increasing maturity, however, *The Shadowy Waters* does not entirely escape the spell of *Axel*. Aengus, the god of love, hates "Peaceable men that shut the wind away, / And keep to the one weary marriage-bed" (*VP* 224), so Forgael and Dectora must abandon the world to sail away together over the horizon: their love still mimics the *Liebestod*. "King and No King" (1909), however, an explicit rejection of the idea of satisfaction in or after death, celebrates the state that the *Liebestod* would avoid: the friendship achieved by satisfied lovers who are no longer controlled by passion. Written after his brief physical involvement with Gonne in 1908, and her renunciation of sexuality in favor of a resumption of their "spiritual marriage," the poem questions the Catholic justification for self-denial: the promise of satisfaction in the hereafter:

> And I that have not your faith, how shall I know
> That in the blinding light beyond the grave
> We'll find so good a thing as that we have lost?
> The hourly kindness, the day's common speech,
> The habitual content of each with each
> When neither soul nor body has been crossed.   (*VP* 258)

These moving lines, with their anticipation of the last stanza of "Among School Children," where "The body is not bruised to pleasure soul" (*VP* 445), plead for the life that continues this side of the grave after romance has died. While the young Yeats had been torn between the desire to possess and the fear that possession destroys desire, the unmarried man of forty-four envisages passion's demise in terms redolent of middle-aged routine. The romantic death-wish evinced in his early verse is now ascribed to his beloved, who in "That the Night Come" rejects "The common good of life" in favor of "what proud death may bring" (*VP* 317).

In the narrative poem "The Two Kings" (1912)[53] Yeats manipulates his mythic source, "The Wooing of Etain," to recuperate "the one weary marriage-bed" through a woman who does not dream of fairyland. In the legend Etain, wife of Eochaid the King of Ireland, self-abnegatingly resolves to sleep with his brother, Ailill, who is dying for love of her. When she goes to their tryst, however, she finds not Ailill but Midir, her former fairy husband, who wants her back. She refuses to abandon her earthly mate; Ailill is cured of his love; and Eochaid is grateful for Etain's kindness to his brother. Everyone behaves exquisitely. Yeats ignores the less edifying mythic sequel, in which a persistent Midir finally succeeds in carrying off a passive Etain, in order to develop his own Edain as an apologist for human passion. Yeats gives Edain the controlling voice: the story is her self-justification to Eochaid, and a fervent testament of her love for him. She tells how Midir disparaged earthly love because it ends at the grave, and wooed her with a copy of "The Man who Dreamed of Faeryland" in his pocket, offering her an eternal life where:

> Pleasure itself can bring no weariness,
> Nor can time waste the cheek, nor is there foot
> That has grown weary of the wandering dance. (*VP* 284–85)

The legendary Etain had rejected Midir in prosaic terms: "I will not exchange the king of all Ireland for thee; for a man whose kindred and whose lineage is unknown."[54] Yeats's Edain, repeating the words she spoke to Midir, is passionately eloquent:

> "How should I love," I answered,
> "Were it not that when the dawn has lit my bed
> And shown my husband sleeping there, I have sighed,
> 'Your strength and nobleness will pass away.'?
> Or how should love be worth its pains were it not
> That when he has fallen asleep within my arms,
> Being wearied out, I love in man the child?
> What can they know of love that do not know
> She builds her nest upon a narrow ledge
> Above a windy precipice?"   (*VP* 285)

No subscriber to the *carpe diem* mode, Edain defines human love as sustained rather than destroyed by the threat of mortality. Her use of the maternal metaphor, however, suggests her conventional definition of women's role in marriage: she loves the child in her husband, and she tells Eochaid's brother:

> That our sufficient portion of the world
> Is that we give, although it be brief giving,
> Happiness to children and to men.   (*VP* 282)

Edain is a man's woman. As if obliquely reproving Gonne for her treatment of Yeats, she proposes to send out troops to capture the unknown woman who has spurned Eochaid's brother, and to force her to requite his love. When she discovers that this woman is herself, she is ready to "give" her body for his cure, as Gonne was not.

Yet "Friends" (1911) allows that even Yeats's troubled relationship with Gonne deserves the name of friendship. In admitting the importance of relations between the sexes that depend on mutuality as well as sexuality it offers a redefinition of love. Jeffares identifies the first "friend" as Shakespear and the second as Gregory;[55] but Toomey and Harwood reverse the ascriptions.[56] Pethica attributes the biographical difficulty to Yeats's "confusion" of his creative debt to Gregory with his sexual debt to Shakespear.[57] Yeats originally wrote of the first woman that despite the "unpassing cares" of "fifteen / Many times troubled years," nothing "Could ever come between / Heart and delighted heart" (*VP* 315v). In changing the line to "Mind and delighted mind" his first consideration may have been rhyme, but he also blurred the distinction between passion and intellect. He praises his second friend in overtly sexual terms:

> her hand
> Had strength that could unbind
> What none can understand,
> What none can have and thrive,
> Youth's dreamy load, till she
> So changed me that I live
> Labouring in ecstasy.   (*VP* 315)

While the power of a woman's "hand" to relieve her friend of "youth's dreamy load" suggests his liberation from virginity, however, the change enables ecstatic "labour." The implications of the "confusion" between Gregory and Shakespear noted by Pethica are both social and generic: "Friends" celebrates neither the equably asexual comradeship of John Sherman and Mary Carton nor the unequal passion of Yeats for Gonne, but the possibility, so emphatically rejected by Symons, of loving a friend and feeling friendly towards a lover, and working together with both.

   "Friends" registers Yeats's initial resistance to including Gonne in the same category as Gregory and Shakespear:

> And what of her that took
> All till my youth was gone
> With scarce a pitying look?
> How could I praise that one?

The poet hesitates to bestow the appellation "friend" on the object of his passionate adoration and the cause of his greatest emotional defeat. Yet the rhetorical resistance intensifies his subsequent tribute:

> When day begins to break
> I count my good and bad,
> Being wakeful for her sake,
> Remembering what she had,
> What eagle look still shows,
> While up from my heart's root
> So great a sweetness flows
> I shake from head to foot.   (*VP* 315–16)

"Friends" climaxes with an image of orgasm. Yeats is able to overcome the self-pity of the disappointed passionate lover without losing the emotional intensity that links him with Gonne, who used to sign her letters to him "Always your friend."

The failure of his early affair with Shakespear did not end their relationship, which, after a second physical interlude in 1910, lasted until her death.[58] "After Long Silence" (1929) defines friendship retrospectively as love:

> Speech after long silence; it is right,
> All other lovers being estranged or dead,
> Unfriendly lamplight hid under its shade,
> The curtains drawn upon unfriendly night,
> That we descant and yet again descant
> Upon the supreme theme of Art and Song:
> Bodily decrepitude is wisdom; young
> We loved each other and were ignorant.   (*VP* 523)

Banishing "unfriendly lamplight" and "unfriendly night," the extremes of glare and darkness, the old but still connected lovers can inhabit a moderately illuminated room that stands as a paradigm for the quiet space of friendship; but they talk of love, "the supreme theme of Art and Song."[59] The "wisdom" of maturity is bought at the price of bodily decrepitude, and there is pathetic irony in the disjunction between the intellectual elaborations implied by "descant" and the ignorant simplicity of past performance; but the poem does moving justice to a relationship that has survived the absence of passion. One of Yeats's greatest love poems, "After Long Silence" is also one of his finest poems on friendship. A poet who used his art to celebrate his friendship with so many women implicitly acknowledges the equality between the sexes claimed by the suffrage movement. Although he keeps the idea of friendship in dialogue with his nostalgia for romantic conflict, Yeats continually affirms "friendly" collaborative labor rather than associating it, as Symons does, with the muckrake and the pigsty.

CHAPTER 6

The occult epithalamium

Theorists of the lyric frequently equate the thematic concerns of love poems with lyric form itself. Northrop Frye claims that "the private poem" derives from an emotional block, "something a poet has to write poetry about instead of carrying on with ordinary experience. This block has traditionally been frustrated love."[1] Although Yeats wrote numerous lyrics that have nothing to do with love, he shared Frye's estimation of its generic importance. In the frame story of *A Vision*, the magus Michael Robartes decides to entrust his occult papers to the ascetic Owen Aherne. Aherne, however, proves unsuitable because he is too Christian, so Robartes proposes to give them to Yeats. Aherne protests: "'You will give them to a man,' I said, 'who has thought more of the love of woman than of the love of God.' 'Yes,' he replied, 'I want a lyric poet'" (*AV*[*A*] xxi). Speaking through Robartes, Yeats connects the love of woman as subject and lyric poetry as formal expression. His early poems demonstrate that he found his most fruitful inspiration in love frustrated, and sought to erect frustration into a poetic and philosophical principle. In *A Vision* the man of Phase Seventeen, Yeats's phase, "selects some object of desire ... some woman perhaps," and Fate snatches her away. Then the imagination "must substitute some new image of desire" (*AV*[*A*] 76). Absence is the precondition for poetic inspiration. Just before his marriage he wrote: "The poet finds and makes his mask in disappointment, the hero in defeat. The desire that is satisfied is not a great desire, nor has the shoulder used all its might that an unbreakable gate has never strained" (*Myth* 337).

What happens to the lyric genre when desire is satisfied, and when the love of a woman brings with it not only physical release but also the gift of occult wisdom? Yeats's marriage to George Hyde-Lees in October 1917, and their spiritualist collaboration, which lasted until 1923 and resulted in *A Vision*, deeply affected both Yeats's love poetry and his philosophy. The publication of the automatic writing reveals that, despite its forbidding abstraction, *A Vision* was initially Yeats's attempt to make sense of his sex life. He frequently suggested that the frustration of his love for Gonne had produced his most powerful poetry (*AV*[*A*] xxiii), a view that she shared: "you make beautiful poetry out of what you call your unhappiness and you are happy in that … The world should thank me for not marrying you."[2] We might therefore wonder about the poetic consequences of marriage to another woman.

The sexual foundations of *A Vision*, although occluded in the published versions, help to render Yeats's relation to the "high" modernism of the twenties oblique and problematic. Feminist re-readings of modernism, most notably those by Gilbert and Gubar, emphasize the war between the sexes as a governing trope of male modernist writing.[3] In the case of *A Vision*, collaboration between the sexes was the enabling precondition of Yeats's achievement, and the topic of sexual love dominated his conversation with the spirits. High modernists were not particularly occupied with the popular genre of love poetry; perhaps because of the sex "war," or perhaps because romance was difficult to reconcile with the change in human character posited by Woolf, who argued that the alteration of the power relations between men and women must also alter literary expression.[4] The title of "The Love Song of J. Alfred Prufrock" is a conscious irony on Eliot's part: alternately cowed and disgusted by the women of the salons, Prufrock cannot bring himself to speak, let alone sing a love song. Yeats's occult system, on the other hand, enabled some remarkable love poems to his wife. If modernism and genre are antithetical terms then Yeats, who bends but does not abandon the generic norms, cannot be satisfactorily classed with the misogynist modernists.

Marriage has traditionally been the occasion of a particular kind of lyric, the epithalamium. In this ceremonial genre the community, in the person of the poet, awakes the bride, supervises the wedding ceremony, laments the tedious length of the wedding feast, brings the newly-weds to bed, and anticipates, sometimes with considerable prurience, the deflowering of the virgin. The social message of the epithalamium is clear: it celebrates the sexual conquest of the passive and voiceless bride-object by the heroic male bridegroom, and upholds the institution of patriarchal marriage in which the woman's sexual identity and desire are denied in favor of her essential role as breeder.[5] Donne reaches the nadir of generic bad taste in his "Epithalamium Made at Lincoln's Inne" when he describes the bride awaiting the bridegroom:

> Like an appointed lambe, when tenderly
> The priest comes on his knees t'embowell her.[6]

The soon-to-be-embowelled bride, it is assumed, wishes to abandon the virgin state not for any physical pleasure the procedure may afford her, but in order to become a mother. Carew figures male sexual pleasure as military conquest:

> Then boldly to the fight of Love proceed,
> 'Tis mercy not to pitty though she bleed,
> Wee'le strew no nuts, but change that ancient forme,
> For till tomorrow Wee'le prorogue this storme,
> Which shall confound with its loude whistling noyse
> Her pleasing shreekes, and fan thy panting joyes.[7]

The woman's opinion of this sanguinary battle is never canvassed. Yet everyone, so the fiction goes, is "pleased" by her shrieks, and by the union, which reclaims the loneliness of the individual into the harmony of community.[8]

Unlike the epithalamium, the love lyric is often theorized as a retreat from the world of politics, economics, and social pressures. According to Adorno, however, it is precisely in its articulation of the need for such a retreat that the lyric registers the difficulty of social relations.[9] The pervasive romantic construction of love as anti-social (as in Yeats's early poems "The Lover tells of the Rose in his Heart" and "The White Birds") posits an authentic "private" self opposed to:

> the noisy set
> Of bankers, schoolmasters, and clergymen
> The martyrs call the world.   (*VP* 205)

The courtly lyric draws its energy from the premise of unattainability: if the lady should prove kind, the imaginative promise of an unworldly private space would have to be exchanged for the sanction of a society that the romantic lover despises. When the lyric re-enters the community, as in the epithalamium, it displays the economic, political, and social implications of love institutionalized as marriage. Such overtness may account for the paucity of Romantic epithalamia: it may also explain Yeats's oblique relationship to the form.

Yeats adopted classical models for the writing of elegy, but shunned the most obvious formal conventions of epithalamia for his marriage poems, despite thinking Spenser's *Epithalamion* "the most beautiful of all his poems" (*E&I* 362). Yeats's avoidance of such a public and ceremonial form may be explained biographically: his marriage to George Hyde-Lees took place while his imagination was still dominated by Gonne's daughter Iseult. The disturbed and disturbing poem "Owen Aherne and his Dancers," written in the week after the wedding, reveals both his continuing obsession with Iseult, and his anxiety about his wife: "O but her heart would break to learn my thoughts are far away" (*VP* 450). George Yeats apparently thought that Yeats had long wanted to marry her, and the dispelling of this illusion led her to consider leaving him during their honeymoon.[10] The situation, therefore, was far from epithalamic. In "Under Saturn" (1918) and "An Image from a Past Life" (1919) the speaker reassures his companion that she need fear no competition from past lovers:

> Do not because this day I have grown saturnine
> Imagine that some lost love, unassailable
> Being a portion of my youth, can make me pine;
> And so forget the comfort that no words can tell
> Your coming brought.   (*VP* 390–91v)

That the poems had to be written, however, suggests the continuing threat posed by "some lost love." In a note to "An Image from a Past Life," Yeats fears that preoccupation with the ideal, the "sweetheart from another life" (*VP* 390) who is transparently Gonne, may destroy the possibility of happiness. The Arab sage Kusta-ben-Luki, after dreaming of a woman loved in former existence, finds her resemblance both in a Persian painting and in a living woman. "He made a long journey to purchase the painting which was, he said, the better likeness, and found on his return that his mistress had left him in a fit of jealousy" (*VP* 821). Yeats had lost Shakespear in a similar manner, and now risked losing his wife.

George Yeats rescued the marriage by successfully attempting automatic writing. She admitted that she had intended to fake it:[11] well attuned to her husband's sensibility, she knew that a message from the spirits validating their marriage would carry more weight than human persuasion. She testified, however, that her hand was seized by a superior power; and so began an arduous joint enterprise in spirit communication. In *A Vision* Yeats placed George Yeats at

Phase Eighteen (*AV*[*A*], Notes 23), the phase where love begins to be possible:

Its object of desire is no longer a single image of passion, for it must relate all to social life; the man seeks to become not a sage, but a wise king, no longer Ahasuerus, and seeks a woman who looks the wise mother of children. Perhaps now, and for the first time, the love of a living woman ... is an admitted aim. (*AV*[*A*] 80)

In keeping with the *Arabian Nights* pastiche of *A Vision*'s frame narration, Yeats wrote several oriental love poems celebrating matrimony: the Solomon and Sheba series and "The Gift of Harun Al-Rashid." He had once hoped that his spiritual marriage with Gonne would resemble that of the magician Nicholas Flamel and his wife Pernella (*Mem* 49): now his real marriage seemed about to fulfill his desire. Emphasizing the importance, even the primacy, of his wife's role in the collaboration, Margaret Mills Harper claims that "many – perhaps most – seminal ideas of *A Vision* originated in the mind of George Yeats,"[12] and argues that the communal genesis of *A Vision* subverts the concept of individual control over the text.[13]

Yeats's private joy in this occult dissolution of identity, however, must be set within the sombre public context of the First World War. The automatic writing has its historical place within the resurgence of spiritualism caused by the terrible losses at the front. After the "classic" period of English spiritualism in the 1860s and 70s interest in the subject had declined.[14] Yeats, however, had always been fascinated by spiritualist phenomena, even though his fellow-occultists thought seances were compromised by fraud and manipulation.[15] When mass bereavement combined with the decay of religious faith sent thousands of grieving relatives to mediums in quest of proof that their loved ones had survived death, Yeats shared their experiences:

To-day while the great battle in Northern France is still undecided, should I climb to the top of that old house in Soho where a medium is sitting among servant girls, some one would, it may be, ask for news of Gordon Highlander or Munster Fusilier, and the fat old woman would tell in Cockney language how the dead do not yet know they are dead, but stumble on amid visionary smoke and noise, and how angelic spirits seek to awaken them but still in vain. (*Ex* 51)

Three months after Yeats's marriage Robert Gregory was shot down on the Italian front; and Yeats leaned heavily on spiritualist beliefs and practices in writing his elegies. "Shepherd and Goatherd" is formally a traditional pastoral lament, but it rehearses the unorthodox ideas about the spirit's life after death that he and George Yeats were evoking through the automatic script (*YVP*1 318). Emphasizing the generic rather than the unconventional, Yeats wrote to Gregory that he was "trying a poem in manner like one that Spenser wrote for Sir Philip Sidney" (*L* 646). The second of his two poems upon the occasion, "In Memory of Major Robert Gregory," appears at first to conform more strictly to generic expectations, especially in its use of the Cowley stanza. Beneath the formality, however, and tying the poem to its historical moment, is an echo of Yeats's fat old medium in Soho evoking for Cockney servant girls the spirits of dead soldiers. As in the overtly occult poem "All Souls' Night," the poet enacts a summoning ritual in which he offers to bring his dead friends, including and culminating with the recently deceased airman, to meet his mediumistic bride.

The Spenserian model underlies the description of the dead hero as "Our Sidney and our perfect man" (*VP* 325). Spenser the elegist was also the poet of marriage, however, and in this poem his two roles are conflated. The opening stanza both enacts and cancels the traditional ceremony of welcoming the bride to her new house: the old, cold, and damp Thoor Ballylee:

> Now that we're almost settled in our house
> I'll name the friends that cannot sup with us
> Beside a fire of turf in th' ancient tower,
>
> All, all are in my thoughts to-night being dead. (*VP* 323–24)

Vendler, suggesting that we read this elegy as a displaced epithalamium, reconstructs its poetic genesis thus:

The poet, newly married, wishes to write an epithalamium as a wedding gift to his wife. However, no inspiration comes for a song (or lyric) so he decides to prime the pump by naming those he would have liked to have her meet, had he been able to write a symposium-with-living-friends poem on the occasion of his marriage.[16]

The fact that everyone he thinks of is dead, however, turns the poem into a group-elegy that modulates into an elegy for the son of his noble patron. His insistence that none of the dead friends he now proposes to summon to his seance-cum-dinner-party "can set us quarrelling" suggests that there may have been quarrels about living friends at Coole, where the couple had stayed while waiting to move into the tower: "Always we'd have the new friend meet the old / And we are hurt if either friend seem cold."[17] The poem tactfully focuses on the lack of welcome to the bride not from Gregory but from her dead son, who being absent can cause no dissension between the newly-weds. Yet Yeats apparently fails to consider that to replace the dominating mother by her deceased offspring might not seem much of an improvement to a youthful bride looking for a welcome to her new house. The fact that the "companions of [his] youth" (*VP* 324) are all in the grave offers a stark reminder to the young woman that she has married a man of fifty-two. The cast-list of characters includes two confirmed bachelors, Lionel Johnson and George Pollexfen, and one, John Synge, who died before his wedding. Only Gregory, married himself, and lovingly familiar with the local landscape, could have provided the sort of hospitality a woman might desire: "He might have been your heartiest welcomer." Yeats takes seven stanzas to get to the traditional elegiac evocation of the dead man's virtues, the subject announced by his title. Once the poem has established its uncertain generic grip he still retains sight of its originating occasion: the newly-wed couple (their union unobtrusively but intimately signalled by the pronoun "us") and their occupation of the crumbling tower, which Gregory, who "could so well have counselled us / In all lovely intricacies of a house" (*VP* 327), might have helped to restore. At the conclusion he returns to his conception of a reunion of dead friends around the living bride: he intended to mask his inability to write an epithalamium by summoning them

> Until imagination brought
> A fitter welcome; but a thought
> Of that late death took all my heart for speech.   (*VP* 328)

It is perhaps fortunate, since he planned to call up "all" his past friends, that the thought of Gregory interrupts the dismal catalogue, and puts an end to this epithalamium so mournfully hybridized by elegy. Only in the parenthetical lines "Until imagination brought / A fitter welcome" does he admit that the welcome he has contrived is *un*fit, that he has failed to produce an appropriate nuptial poem, and that the bridal introduction has turned into a lament for the death of youth.

After five years of married life, during which he incessantly consulted the spirit world through George Yeats's automatic writing and talking in her sleep, Yeats wrote a poem that, despite its hybrid affinities with the dramatic monologue and the verse epistle, is also "a long epithalamium."[18] "The Gift of Harun Al-Rashid" (1923) seeks to invest his marriage with the sexual glamour of the *Arabian Nights*, which, like Yeats's *Vision*, is structured and sustained by the love, wisdom, and ingenuity of a female raconteur. George Yeats plays Scheherazade, compelling Yeats's interest for a thousand and one nights not by stories, but by spirit communications.[19] The poem takes the form of a letter from the sage Kusta Ben Luka, which describes the genesis of his philosophy in the marriage arranged for him by the Caliph Harun Al-Rashid, and in the words spoken in her sleep by his young bride. Unlike the traditional epithalamium it celebrates not a wedding (the ceremony itself is never mentioned) but a marriage; yet the opening of the poem contains a covert reference to the epithalamic form. Kusta, instructing his friend to preserve his letter in the Caliph's library, hesitates about whether it should be hidden inside the pages of Sappho or Parmenides:

> And pause at last, I was about to say,
> At the great book of Sappho's song; but no,
> For should you leave my letter there, a boy's
> Love-lorn, indifferent hands might come upon it
> And let it fall unnoticed to the floor.
> Pause at the Treatise of Parmenides
> And hide it there, for Caliphs to world's end
> Must keep that perfect, as they keep her song,
> So great its fame.   (*VP* 461)

Sappho's are the first extant epithalamia: the genre as we know it began with her.[20] Although she wrote one triumphalist and possibly parodic celebration of the groom's virility, she composed no less than three laments for lost maidenhood:

> Like a hyacinth in
> the mountains, trampled
> by shepherds until
> only a purple stain
> remains on the ground.[21]

It is not surprising that Yeats chose to invoke the world's most famous female lyricist in an autobiographical poetic account of his marriage: his neglect of patriarchal epithalamic conventions was partly a function of his sexual timidity.[22] He was psychologically and poetically unable to convert his habitual stance of abject lover into that of sexually successful bridegroom. Kusta stresses not his potency but the fact that he is "falling into years" (*VP* 463). His agency in the matter of the marriage is also in doubt. The idea comes from the Caliph, and at first it appears that the girl does too. The match could thus be represented as the passing of the bride-object from one man to another, a structural reflection of the arranged political marriages for which many earlier epithalamia were composed,[23] except that Yeats introduces the generically revolutionary concepts of the woman's choice and satisfaction in love. In his notes to the poem he offers two possible versions of the story:

According to one tradition of the desert, she had, to the great surprise of her friends, fallen in love with the elderly philosopher, but according to another, Harun bought her from a passing merchant. (*VP* 828)

The poem itself, however, presents only the first version: although the Caliph "gives" the girl to Kusta, she is in love with him already; and in defiance of convention the marriage is presented as the result of the bride's dream and wish:

> A girl
> Perched in some window of her mother's house
> Had watched my daily passage to and fro;
> Had heard impossible history of my past;
> Imagined some impossible history
> Lived at my side.   (*VP* 466)

When George Yeats's mother wrote asking Gregory to convince Yeats of "the entire undesirability" of his engagement to her daughter, she confided that "I was very much afraid that Mr Yeats meant to propose to my daughter in Nov. [19]15 ... But it was only a mutual interest in astrology which they shared, which is, so Mr Yeats tells me 'a very flirtatious business'!"[24] Yeats and George Hyde-Lees had been engaged in very flirtatious business even earlier than 1915: Harwood suggests that her attachment to him may have begun in 1911, and that "Yeats's sponsoring her for admission to the Golden Dawn in 1914 may have been, on her side, an event of considerable emotional significance."[25] When the Caliph is advertising the suitability of the girl he has found for Kusta Ben Luka he claims that she "shares / Your thirst for those old crabbed mysteries" (*VP* 465). Mrs. Tucker wrote that George Yeats "thinks he has wanted her since the time of the astrological experiments,"[26] and for both partners sexual and occult interests had always been indistinguishable.

In the 1925 version of *A Vision* Yeats lamented that Parmenidean abstraction had displaced the concerns that occupy 75 percent of the automatic script:[27] "I have not even dealt with the whole of my subject, perhaps not even with what is most important, writing nothing about the Beatific Vision, little of sexual love" (*AV[A]* xii). The *Vision* papers reveal that the script was sexual both in its content – pages of questions and answers concern Yeats's relationships with Maud Gonne, Iseult Gonne, Mabel Dickinson, Olivia Shakespear, and George Yeats – and in the conditions of its reception. The power with which the spirits were able to communicate depended on the quantity and quality of Yeats's sexual relations with his wife. Although in September 1919 the controls praised him as a "good husband – good lover" (*YVP2* 414), he subsequently fell short, and two months later Ameritus complained bitterly, "I cant be left for so long again without force," and insisted "After next Martha [their code name for George's period] without fail on these dates … write the dates down" (*YVP2* 482). Ameritus informed Yeats that "What is important is … that both the desire of the medium and her desire for your desire should be satisfied" (*YVP2* 487), and asserted the necessity for female orgasm. When Yeats asked why is "the finish essential to give you force," Ameritus explained that "at End woman becomes male, man becomes female." In orgasm the woman experiences "a climax not a hollowing out" (*YVP2* 484). Rejecting the passive "hollowing out" of the conventional female role in intercourse, and actively pursuing orgasmic satisfaction, the sexually modern woman George Yeats had to suggest to her husband that he was not too old to come twice. Ameritus advised Yeats to practice making love more than once a night, lest his powers decline: "it is like not taking enough exercise & a long walk exhausts you." The connection between frequent intercourse and healthy exercise has little to do with romance, much to do with the modern sexual theories of Havelock Ellis. "You mean," queried Yeats anxiously, "by only doing it once I will lose power of doing it twice." Yes, warned Ameritus darkly, "& then of doing it once" (*YVP2* 349). Lest Yeats should abandon sex in his enthusiasm for automatic writing, he was reminded that "Mediumship in this case arises because of certain sexual emotions – When those lack there is no mediumship" (*YVP2* 487). George Yeats's desire for sexual satisfaction accorded with the latest in psychical research: Dr. Hereward Carrington argued that orgasm and manifestation were coincident in mediums like the famous Eusapia Palladino.[28]

While George Yeats was prepared to spend hours helping her husband work through his obsessions with other women, she obviously had her own agenda. No one has suggested that the spirit communication was entirely a product of the faking with which George Yeats, by her own admission, began; but Margaret Mills Harper's comment that "a young woman was giving a subtle lesson in who she was and how to conduct wedded life to her new husband" suggests the purposeful quality of much of the script.[29] When the control Thomas tells Yeats: "The more you keep this medium emotionally and intellectually happy the more will script be possible now" (*YVP2* 119), the instructions are certainly coming from wife to husband. Ameritus told Yeats that the "script depends on the love of medium for you – all intensity comes from that" (*YVP2* 323), and his poetic translation of these words lies at the heart both of the poem and of the system:

> The voice has drawn
> A quality of wisdom from her love's
> Particular quality.   (*VP* 469)

"The Gift of Harun Al-Rashid" manifests his continuing concern with the relationship between revelation and love. He represents the bride as initially obsessed with his occult books:

> Yet was it love of me, or was it love
> Of the stark mystery that has dazed my sight,
> Perplexed her fantasy and planned her care?   (*VP* 466)

The poem was written after the abandonment of automatic writing in favor of the "sleeps," as they were called,[30] and the mediumistic bride is ignorant of her wisdom, as George Yeats was not. Kusta Ben Luka fears what may happen if she learns what is really going on in their bedroom:

> What if she lose her ignorance and so
> Dream that I love her only for the voice,
>
> Were she to lose her love, because she had lost
> Her confidence in mine, or even lose
> Its first simplicity, love, voice and all,
> All my fine feathers would be plucked away
> And I left shivering.   (*VP* 468–69)

Kusta's fear of losing the woman's "voice" if he loses her love reflects a radical reconception of the silent heroines of the epithalamium, and of love poetry in general. This woman is valuable because she speaks; not because she can be looked at. Yeats's fear may also reflect the fact that by 1922 George Yeats had became bored by her task as medium. Perhaps she felt trapped by the nuptial stratagem she had herself initiated; certainly she wanted Yeats to get *A Vision* out of the way by writing it down (though she opposed publication) and return to his poetry. In the poem Kusta adopts a tone of avuncular understanding: "nor has she now / That first unnatural interest in my books" (*VP* 468), though he fears that his own undiminished obsession with the spirit world may make his wife feel that she is loved only for her occult abilities. "The Gift of Harun Al-Rashid" emphasizes the constant vigilance needed to maintain complementarity between husband and wife, and the delicacy of the balance between erotic and occult sympathies.

When Yeats chooses between Sappho and Parmenides as the repository of the story of *A Vision*, he is choosing between the hidden meanings of the script, which are erotic and personal, and its overt significance, which is philosophical and historical in content, and geometrical in mode. Sappho's love poetry is rejected as too potent: a lovesick youth absorbed in her "great book" might let the letter "fall unnoticed to the floor." Sappho's work speaks directly to the lover; Yeats's text addresses him obliquely. Sappho operates in the poem as one voice in a dialogue between eroticism and philosophy:

> All those abstractions that you fancied were
> From the great Treatise of Parmenides;
> All, all those gyres and cubes and midnight things
> Are but a new expression of her body
> Drunk with the bitter sweetness of her youth.   (*VP* 469)

As a complement to Parmenides' abstract geometry, the love-lorn boy absorbed in Sappho's book is replaced by the woman's body in the act of love. In response to George Yeats's quest for orgasmic fulfillment, Yeats replaces the fertility that the traditional epithalamium offers the virgin in recompense for her defloration with a revolutionary emphasis on her bodily pleasure: "Drunk with the bitter sweetness of her youth." Out of a woman's sexual satisfaction the "gyres and cubes and midnight things" are born: "desert geometry" depends on the lyric poet not as permanently frustrated

Petrarchan, nor as the bullish bridegroom of the Renaissance epithalamium, but as good husband and good lover.

When Yeats wrote his poem in the 1920s the ideology of patriarchal marriage embodied in the form of the epithalamium was under serious threat. While Yeats and his wife were collaborating on *A Vision*, women, who during the war had entered the workforce in enormous numbers, and whose contributions to victory could not be overlooked, were granted the franchise in England and Ireland. Yeats's sensitivity to changes in the balance of power between men and women is registered poetically in his distortions of the epithalamium. Like the Solomon and Sheba poems, "The Gift of Harun Al-Rashid" focuses on the woman's desire, rejects the triumphalist perspective of the bridegroom, insists on complementarity in love, and depicts the woman as a channel for wisdom rather than offspring. The *Arabian Nights* are voiced by a woman to whose wisdom the whole structure bears monumental witness; and "The Gift of Harun Al-Rashid" also challenges gender positions as the woman speaks: "She seemed the learned man and I the child." To underline the anti-patriarchal nature of the communication Yeats describes her words as "Truths without father." In these respects his poem challenges the traditional ideology of matrimony. In other ways, however, Yeats remained enslaved to the stereotype. Despite the wisdom of her nights the child-bride, providing "a woman's care" (*VP* 466) to the aging sage, spends her days in mindless domestic routine: she "swept the house and sang about her work / In childish ignorance of all that passed" (*VP* 468). Yeats's emphasis on the gap in years between himself and his wife infantilizes her poetically.

A more serious problem, common both to the automatic script and the poem, to Yeats's life and art, concerns his use of a woman as medium: as transmitter rather than originator of arcane knowledge. During the period of automatic writing George Yeats never sank into a mediumistic trance, and she eventually abandoned the convention of running the letters together when her pen was moved.[31] After the birth of Anne Yeats her title was changed from "medium" to "Interpreter" (*YVP2* 200), a change that reflects her intelligent contribution to their joint quest for knowledge. Yet in "The Gift of Harun Al-Rashid" Yeats makes only oblique reference to George Yeats the active and conscious writer, teacher of both sexual and philosophical truths. Although he had two contrasting models of mediumship on which to draw, he set aside the powerful, collaborative, and perhaps even controlling "Interpreter" in favor of the passive and unconscious receptacle of the Djinn's voice: "Or was it she that spoke or some great Djinn? / I say that a Djinn spoke" (*VP* 467).

If we position George Yeats within the cultural history of women and spiritualism, we can appreciate the paradoxes of power and passivity, voicing and silence, that she represents. Claiming that "Victorian spiritualism was another of the hidden or forgotten factors in women's long struggle for increased effectiveness, status, and autonomy," Alex Owen documents the connections between spiritualism and feminism. As we have already seen, spiritualists tended to be social progressives: "Many women became involved in spiritualism via their participation in women's rights agitation and the anti-slavery crusades, and there was a strong feminist presence amongst American mediums and believers." In an era of few outlets for female talent or opportunities for female display, the role of the medium, like that of the actress, permitted some women to make lucrative and spectacular careers for themselves. Seances allowed female mediums to violate gender norms, both in assuming male personae and in speaking as a proper Victorian lady could never have spoken. Owen stresses the transgressive function of mediumship, but she also demonstrates how the seance tended to reinscribe the woman into the stereotype of passivity and receptivity:

Passivity became, in the spiritualist vocabulary, synonymous with power … the very quality which supposedly made women such excellent mediums was equally construed as undermining their ability to function in the outside world. Female passivity, the leit-motif of powerful mediumship, also positioned women as individuals without social power.

Similarly, the voice of the medium broke the Victorian prescription against women's speech but, as Owen argues, "Having claimed the right to be heard, the medium went to great lengths to dissociate herself from her words."[32] Spiritualism was haunted by questions of fraudulence, and the medium's speech could be considered authentic only in so far as it was not her own. This is why Kusta Ben Luka must claim that the "voice" belongs to the Djinn and not to his wife. Yeats's seance play *The Words upon the Window Pane* authenticates the voice of Jonathan Swift, not that of Mrs. Henderson the medium. After she has articulated the exchange between Swift and Vanessa, the Swift scholar John Corbet congratulates her in terms often used to damn spiritualist women as frauds: "When I say I am satisfied I do not mean that I am convinced it was the work of spirits. I prefer to think that you created it all, that you are an accomplished actress and scholar" (*VPL* 955). But the medium knows nothing about Swift, and is not learned enough to be an impostor: her main preoccupation is making a living. Paradoxically, Yeats must downplay her active intelligence in order to validate her communications. The more "genuine" the spiritual manifestations, the less conscious the participation of the woman through whom they come. Mrs. Henderson, left alone on stage to recuperate after the seance, makes herself a cup of tea. Her prosaic activities are twice interrupted by the voice of Swift, whose spirit still lingers in the room long after any motive for fraud has disappeared along with the seance participants. With the crash of the breaking saucer and Swift's final words, "Perish the day on which I was born!" (*VPL* 956), Mrs. Henderson both authenticates herself as a medium and obliterates herself as a woman.

The figure of the medium is therefore politically and historically ambivalent. For Yeats it was related to the problematic figure of the witch, paradoxical symbol both of transgressive power and abject victimage. In describing a seance he compared the two: "The witch, going beyond the medium, offered to the slowly animating phantom certain drops of her blood" (*Myth* 350). He claimed that the modern seance returned him to medieval systems of belief: "When I saw at Mrs. Crandon's objects moved and words spoken from some aerial centre, where there was nothing human, I rejected England and France and accepted Europe. Europe belongs to Dante and the witches' sabbath, not to Newton" (*L* 807). Yeats favors the passionate credulity that persecutes over the rationalist skepticism that refuses either to believe or to interrogate. Yet his sympathy is almost always with the witch, who appears in his verse more often as a figure of beauty and power than of evil.

Yeats also invests Irish witches with political and patriotic significance. They may have their flaws, but they are to be excused because they are "countrywomen of ours" (*UP*1 171). They are more agreeable than witches of other nationalities because "never being burnt or persecuted has lessened the bitterness of their war against mankind" (*UP*1 131). He insists that the Irish are morally superior to the English and Scots because they have refrained from burning witches: "In Ireland we have left them alone. To be sure, the 'loyal minority' knocked out the eye of one with a cabbage-stump on the 31st of March 1711, in the town of Carrickfergus. But then the 'loyal minority' is half Scottish" (*Myth* 107). Sexism and Unionism are neatly equated. When in 1895 a Tipperary peasant gave the lie to Yeats by burning his wife, whom he suspected of being a changeling, Yeats was horrified: "The country people seldom do more than threaten the dead person put in the living person's place, and it is, I am convinced, a sin against the traditional wisdom to really ill-treat the dead person" (*UP2* 277).[33]

When Yeats figures women as witches, therefore, the association is usually positive, although stereotypical. He said of Gonne after a political arrest, "She had to choose (perhaps all women must) between broomstick and distaff and she has chosen the broomstick – I mean the witches' hats" (*L* 697). Powerful women are set against domestic ones, broomstick against distaff. In "Lines Written in Dejection," composed before his marriage, he laments that he has been abandoned by the witches, who represent lunar energy, power, and creativity:

> All the wild witches, those most noble ladies,
> For all their broom-sticks and their tears,
> Their angry tears, are gone.
> The holy centaurs of the hills are vanished;
> I have nothing but the embittered sun;
> Banished heroic mother moon and vanished,
> And now that I have come to fifty years
> I must endure the timid sun.   (*VP* 343–44)

Celebrating witches as representative of "heroic mother moon," Yeats ratifies essentialist stereotypes of the feminine. This poem, however, was written in 1915, just after the suspension of militant suffrage activity on the declaration of war. Yeats's lament for the departure of the "noble ladies" has political as well as personal resonance.

In George Yeats he found himself possessed of a miraculous combination of distaff and broomstick. His most famous marriage lyric casts himself as King Solomon and his wife as the Queen of Sheba, but the title is "Solomon and the Witch." Yeats interpreted their story to represent fidelity as well as passion: "the love of Solomon and Sheba must have lasted, for all the silence of the Scriptures" (*Au* 464). The Sheba of the post-nuptial "Solomon and the Witch," however, differs radically from the Sheba of "On Woman" (1914). This earlier Sheba also offers wisdom and sexual

pleasure, but she drives the speaker "mad," and his fidelity consists
in waiting for her to lead him another dance in his next incarnation.
"On Woman" proposes two different models of femininity: the non-
competitive, "friendly" woman (the distaff); and then the "perverse
creature of chance" who both makes men "wise" and drives them
crazy (the broomstick).[34] The poem opens with praise for the distaff:

> May God be praised for woman
> That gives up all her mind,
> A man may find in no man
> A friendship of her kind
> That covers all he has brought
> As with her flesh and bone,
> Nor quarrels with a thought
> Because it is not her own.

In these lines (typographically broken off from the rest of the poem)
the traditional union of masculine "mind" or "thought" with
feminine "flesh and bone" enables friendship, but not passion. The
non-opinionated woman who "gives up all her mind" is passed over
by the speaker: he wishes to re-live his relationship with a Sheba who
is intellectual, difficult, and aggressive in bed: "She the iron
wrought." Despite the high emotional cost, he prefers to "live like
Solomon / That Sheba led a dance" (*VP* 345–46).

The Sheba of "Solomon and the Witch," however, modelled on
George Yeats rather than on Gonne, is sensual without being
"perverse." She is a "witch" because her sexual and her occult
powers, like those of Yeats's wife, are indissolubly linked. Reading the
poem against the grain of the typical epithalamium, we see that its
presentation of the wedding night is formally subversive. The
"pleasing shrieks" of the bride that traditionally announce the
militaristic sexual triumph of the bridegroom are displaced by
Sheba's mediumistic cry of sensual pleasure, reported directly to the
audience by herself:

> And thus declared that Arab lady:
> "Last night, where under the wild moon
> On grassy mattress I had laid me,
> Within my arms great Solomon,
> I suddenly cried out in a strange tongue
> Not his, not mine."

Yeats replaces the male poet/voyeur listening at the bedroom door
with the woman's voice testifying openly about her sexual and occult

experience: unlike the bride of Kusta Ben Luka Sheba is both mediumistic and conscious of it. The increased number of female speakers in Yeats's love poetry after 1914 parallels the public assumption of voice by the suffragettes; but it is also a result of his dialogue with George Yeats. "Solomon and the Witch" dates from the period before the automatic writing was replaced by the "sleeps": Sheba's role is an active one in both a formal and a thematic sense. As the title of the poem suggests, she is more witch than medium, and she speaks more than she is spoken through: Solomon's role is merely that of translator. The perfect love of Solomon and Sheba unites fate with desire, Chance with Choice. This union of Chance and Choice is extremely rare, because love

> tests a lover
> With cruelties of Choice and Chance;
> And when at last that murder's over
> Maybe the bride-bed brings despair,
> For each an imagined image brings
> And finds a real image there.

Indeed, the despair that Yeats imagines haunting many bride-beds nearly haunted his own. George Yeats did not get what she had expected. Having brought to the marriage her "imagined image" of the distinguished poet, magus, and lover, she found there an aging man obsessed with his sexual failures and images of his past loves. The public machinery of the epithalamium, which congratulates the couple on the excellence of their Chance no matter what their Choice might have been, must have served to disguise and palliate many politically expedient personal calamities. Conversely, "Solomon and the Witch" celebrates the occult and sexual initiative with which Yeats's young wife averted disaster. It reveals that the satisfaction of desire need not entail the silencing of the poet's voice, though it may prompt inclusion of the woman's speech.

The sexual apocalypse of Yeats's early love poetry is here reframed as comedy. The perfection of a love-making in which both partners embrace in reality the "imagined image" they have desired is supposed to cause the end of the world:

> "Yet the world ends when these two things,
> Though several, are a single light,
> When oil and wick are burned in one;
> Therefore a blessed moon last night
> Gave Sheba to her Solomon."

Since Solomon and Sheba are still there in the morning, however, the conjunction of male wick and female oil obviously leaves something still to desire; and Sheba, piqued that their simultaneous orgasm was not spectacular enough to destroy the world, insists that they have another go: "And the moon is wilder every minute. / O! Solomon! let us try again" (*VP* 387–89). A poem that began with the woman's voice reporting candidly on last night's sexual experience ends with her humorous urging that it be repeated tonight, under the light of the witches' wild moon, sign of female power and heroism. The sexual comedy that in classical fescennine verses took the form of ribald male joking at the expense of the bride is appropriated by Yeats's Sheba. The wedding night frozen into the hieratic formal structure of the epithalamium is, through her provocative and teasing initiative, here opened up and prolonged into a succession of nights dedicated to sexual and occult exploration. Desire satisfied is not desire quenched, but desire continually reborn.

CHAPTER 7

Shrill voices, accursed opinions

"Easter 1916," a political elegy, is also a poem about love: the martyrs' love of Ireland, and Yeats's devotion to Gonne as the symbol of Ireland. Praising his countrymen for being good lovers, Yeats claimed they "had never served any abstract cause, except the one, and that we personified by a woman" (*Au* 545). "Easter 1916" evokes the personified "terrible beauty" or sacrificial queen while it examines the emotional costs of a political *Liebestod*. Yeats thought the patriot O'Leary "was like some man who serves a woman all his life without asking whether she be good or bad, wise or foolish" (*Au* 215), but he himself was ready to interrogate his images. "Easter 1916" was written before his marriage separated him from Gonne and enabled his hostile analysis of her in "A Prayer for my Daughter" (1919), where the "terrible beauty" is far more terrible than beautiful. The two poems, though written three years apart, are connected by more than their proximity in *Michael Robartes and the Dancer*: both thematize the destruction of "sweetness" by women's "shrill" devotion to "opinions." Both are related to Yeats's poem about the incarceration of Constance Markievicz, "On a Political Prisoner," and, like "Michael Robartes and the Dancer," both question the effect of participation in public and intellectual life upon the woman's role in love poetry as the aesthetic object of male contemplation, and in history as the inspiration of male political action.

Markievicz stands in for Gonne in "Easter 1916."[1] The Countess, condemned to death for her part in the Rising but reprieved because of her sex, offered a mirror image of Gonne's devotion to her country and of what might have been her fate had she stayed in Dublin. Yeats claimed that he had been the first to tell Markievicz about Gonne, "in imitation of whom, perhaps, she was to earn the life-sentence she is now serving" (*Mem* 78). Gonne herself, who wrote after the Rising that "Constance Markievicz was like a sister to me,"[2] must have strengthened Yeats's identification of the two women. Once the very embodiment of "romantic political Ireland" (*Mem* 247), Gonne is mentioned in "Easter 1916" only as the victim of John MacBride, who had "done most bitter wrong / To some who are near my heart," but his ambivalence about their relationship informs the poem's hesitant judgments about the politics of love for one's country. The fact that not just one, but two beautiful women who could have moved in Ascendancy and Garrison circles had chosen to dedicate themselves to nationalist politics convinced Yeats that he was observing not an aberration, but a historical trend. The lines describing Markievicz are suggestively juxtaposed with the first articulation of the refrain, "A terrible beauty is born," so she appears as a concrete realization of that abstract oxymoron: her beauty in the distant past; her terrible fanaticism in the immediate past; her "change," in which both terms of the opposition are retained but transvalued, eternally present. Yeats was originally more generous in his assessment of her character:

> That woman at while would be shrill
> In aimless argument;
> Had ignorant good will,
> All that she got she spent,
> Her charity had no bounds.   (*VP* 392v)

Although the last two lines are weakly non-specific, reading like a pious obituary for some Lady Bountiful, in omitting them as he revised Yeats showed artistic judgment rather than tact. He kept the rhyme word "spent," but changed the nature of the Countess's spending from economic beneficence to ignorant time-wasting. Omitting the archaic phrase "at while," Yeats tightened the diction, but its absence suggests that Markievicz was not occasionally but always shrill. The loosely articulated "Had ignorant good will," is integrated into the syntax but strengthens the negative tone; "ignorant good-will" becomes her defining characteristic. In introducing the aesthetically pleasing verbal balance between "days" and "nights," Yeats improves the rhetorical frame around his picture; but the increased temporal precision leaves Markievicz no time for anything but ignorance and argument:

> That woman's days were spent
> In ignorant good-will,
> Her nights in argument
> Until her voice grew shrill.   (*VP* 392)

In excising the reference to her generosity Yeats casts doubts upon his own. Did he sacrifice Markievicz's historical specificity to the exigencies of poetic economy, rhythmic balance, and formal closure; or did his view of her harden as, staying with Gonne in Normandy while he wrote the poem, he watched her uncompromising reaction to the Rising?

Markievicz was a prominent supporter of labor and a leading member of Connolly's socialist Citizen Army. Her work feeding hungry school children and striking workers hardly merits Yeats's patronizing dismissal of her "ignorant good-will."[3] As we have seen, the shrill-voiced woman was associated in popular culture with suffrage agitation, and Markievicz was a suffragist, though Republicanism and socialism dominated her political agenda. In 1896 she had asserted the need for militant women to be "shrill":

John Stuart Mill said thirty years ago that the only forcible argument against giving women the suffrage was "that they did not demand it with sufficient force and noise". Now, one of the many sneers I have been accustomed to hear against women is that they make too much noise; and yet we are told the principal argument against our having votes is that we don't make noise enough.[4]

Yeats, however, declares that Markievicz's argumentativeness and social concern have destroyed both her youthful beauty and her "sweet" voice. She is no longer a pleasing object of aesthetic contemplation. Though she is not in fact dead, he elegizes her, as he was to do again in "On a Political Prisoner," through the class-specific image of the Anglo-Irish huntswoman:

> What voice more sweet than hers
> When, young and beautiful,
> She rode to harriers? (*VP* 392)

Much love poetry that celebrates the beloved as a (dead) aesthetic object adopts an elegiac tone. "In Memory of Eva Gore-Booth and Con Markievicz" (1927) elegizes not two sisters in the fullness of their intellectual and political commitment, one working with her companion Esther Roper for suffrage and the rights of trade unionists, the other a nationalist revolutionary, Minister for Labor in the first Dáil, and President of Cumann na mBan; but the apolitical Ascendancy "girls" they once were, both beautiful, one a "gazelle" (*VP* 475). Yeats could have been thinking of either of the sisters when he later wrote dismissively that he had known "A Helen of social welfare dream / Climb on a wagonette to scream" ("Why should not Old Men be Mad?" *VP* 626). Non-Helens may occupy themselves with social welfare, but the beautiful have their work cut out guarding their good looks.

The static, aesthetically attractive image of the two lovely young women, framed in their exotic silk kimonos by the great windows of the Big House,[5] is disfigured by the women's assumption of public voice: "a raving autumn shears / Blossom from the summer's wreath." (The word "wreath" ambiguously evokes both the garlands of a summer wedding and the metaphorical flowers brought to a grave by the writer of elegy: both love and death.) As Yeats searched for an image appropriate to his sense of loss, he returned to the identification of Ireland as a woman who resembles the sisters in their politicized old age. "Ireland is a hag," he wrote. Although the line was canceled, it fits with Stallworthy's reading of the "great gazebo" as Yeats's "early vision, more romantic than realistic, of a resurgent Ireland."[6] Ireland is a hag in *Cathleen ni Houlihan* and, as we have seen, Markievicz regarded Yeats's play as a gospel. Yeats deplored his own influence on her: the line originally read "*I* the great gazebo built."[7]

Aesthetics intersect with class snobbery as the former Ascendancy belle "drags out lonely years / Conspiring among the ignorant": the loss of beauty is accompanied by social descent. A canceled line in the drafts disparages her socialism as "Contagion of the popular breath,"[8] recalling his earlier condemnation of the "popular enmity" that governed her thought (*VP* 397). In asserting "the folly of a fight / With a common wrong or right," Yeats devalues the sisters' interventions in politics in favor of their status as "Pictures of the mind": his mind. To claim that "The innocent and the beautiful / Have no enemy but time" (*VP* 475–76) is to echo the *carpe diem* mode and to dismiss the facts of history with a willful blindness that Yeats seldom shows elsewhere. Under the guise of elegy Yeats revivifies the clichés of the love genre (obsession with the visual, the beautiful object framed in a window, emphasis on fine clothing, depiction of women as female deer or fragile blossoms, aristocratic pretensions, concern with the passing of time) in a vain attempt to cancel or reverse the processes of history.

"Easter 1916" does not question the right of male patriots to engage in argument: since men are not defined as aesthetic objects, their beauty cannot be spoiled by opinions. Yeats made the distinction clear when he wrote of Gonne in 1909:

I fear for her any renewed devotion to an opinion. Women, because the main event of their lives has been a giving of themselves, give themselves to an opinion as if [it] were some terrible stone doll. We [men] take up an opinion lightly and are easily false to it, and when faithful keep the habit of many interests ... the opinion becomes so much a part of them [women] that it is as though a part of their flesh becomes, as it were, stone. (*Mem* 192)

Although Yeats can see that the difference between the sexes is socially constructed by the fact that men have "many interests" while for women "the main event of their life has been a giving of themselves," he accepts this disparity as natural law.

The idea that a political woman's flesh turns to stone, however, is degendered in "Easter 1916." "September 1913" had explicitly linked the "delirium" of Irish male nationalist martyrs with sexual passion:

> "Some woman's yellow hair
> Has maddened every mother's son":
> They weighed so lightly what they gave.   (*VP* 290)

Here the trope is used approvingly: for men in the Irish national tradition, sexuality and politics are properly fused. "Easter 1916," however, while it celebrates the *hieros gamos* between the martyrs and their motherland, asks whether the sacrifice of change occasioned by obsessive love of country may not give political men as well as political women hearts of stone.

Yeats admitted after the Rising that "'Romantic Ireland's dead and gone' sounds old-fashioned now" (*VP* 820). His reflections on the romantic gesture of the martyrs led him back to the Romantic model of his youth, Shelley, whose poem *Alastor* had helped to shape his approach to the subject of love.[9] In *Alastor* a young poet sees a dream-vision of ideal feminine perfection, before which "His strong heart sunk and sickened with excess / Of love." This "excess of love" drives him on a desperate search for the dream-woman, a search that can only end in death:

> Lost, lost, forever lost,
> In the wide pathless desert of dim sleep,
> That beautiful shape! Does the dark gate of death
> Conduct to thy mysterious paradise,
> O Sleep?

Worn out by his failure to find his dream-beloved, the poet descends "to an untimely grave." Shelley acknowledges the destructiveness of the poet's fatal passion, but he is contemptuous of those who have never felt the power of the dream:

They ... deluded by no generous error, instigated by no sacred thirst of doubtful knowledge, duped by no illustrious superstition, loving nothing on this earth ... are morally dead. They are neither friends, nor lovers, nor fathers, nor citizens of the world, nor benefactors of their country.[10]

The same ambivalence about the passion that leads to death informs "Easter 1916," which affirms the political *Liebestod* only after numerous qualifications. Meditating on the dubious practical efficacy of the rebellion, Yeats remembers Shelley's Poet, whose heart "sickened with excess of love," who was deluded by a generous error, and who sought his vision of love first in dreams and then in the grave:

> Was it needless death after all?
> For England may keep faith
> For all that is done and said.
> We know their dream; enough
> To know they dreamed and are dead;
> And what if excess of love
> Bewildered them till they died?   (*VP* 394)

"Excess of love" gives birth to a "terrible beauty": the romantic sacrifice and the woman for whom it is offered are dangerously fused. Dalton has suggested a source for Yeats's "terrible beauty" in Sheridan Le Fanu's long poem *The Legend of the Glaive*, where the sorceress Fionula, whom Dalton identifies with Eire, is described as "the Cruel, the brightest, the worst, / With a terrible beauty." She exemplifies her cruelty by sending a young man to die for her in battle.[11] Here the "terrible beauty" is not an ideal image of the miraculous transformation wrought by sacrifice, but an actual woman, a witch.

In "On the Medusa of Leonardo da Vinci in the Florentine Gallery," Shelley represents the Medusa's head as both alluring and repellent. He is fascinated by the fusion of female beauty, male violence, and pain; by

> Loveliness like a shadow, from which shine,
> Fiery and lurid, struggling underneath,
> The agonies of anguish and of death.

Throughout the poem Shelley repeatedly juxtaposes terror and beauty: "Its horror and its beauty are divine"; "'Tis the tempestuous loveliness of terror"; "all the beauty and the terror there." Shelley's contention, that "it is less the horror than the grace / Which turns the gazer's spirit into stone,"[12] explains why Yeats's poem balances the beauty of a generous love against the terrible consequences of single-minded devotion:

> Hearts with one purpose alone
> Through summer and winter seem
> Enchanted to a stone
> To trouble the living stream.   (*VP* 393)

"Too long a sacrifice" has the same effect as the glance of the Medusa: it makes a stone of the heart. Yeats criticizes the rebels for their singlemindedness, but if they have loved their country to excess, he has loved a female image of that country with the same persistency. Toomey has noted the sexual connotations of the word "trouble" in Yeats's work;[13] and the imagery of water in motion that represents the world of change in "Easter 1916" is linked with sexual fulfillment rather than sublimation, as Yeats's juxtaposition of male and female birds indicates:

> The long-legged moor-hens dive,
> And hens to moor-cocks call;
> Minute by minute they live:
> The stone's in the midst of all.   (*VP* 393)

Gonne recorded that, as Yeats recited "Easter 1916" to her on the beach in Normandy, he made the connection between stifled sexuality and patriotic dedication explicit, begging her to "forget the stone and its inner fire for the flashing, changing joy of life." Adopting his metaphor, however, she said that her mind was "dull with the stone of the fixed idea of getting back to Ireland."[14] When he later sent her a completed draft she commented tartly, "No I don't like your poem ... you who have studied philosophy & know something of history know quite well that sacrifice has never yet turned a heart to stone though it has immortalised many" (*AYF* 384).

Composed at the same time as "Easter 1916," "Men improve with the Years" uses the same images of stone and stream, and in so doing constructs an intertexual analogy between love and patriotism. Yeats

claims that his romantic "dreams," like the dreams of Ireland shared
by the political martyrs, have also turned him into stone:

> But I grow old among dreams,
> A weather-worn, marble triton
> Among the streams.   (*VP* 329)

The triton, like the patriots, troubles the living stream: "enchanted"
to a stone by the terrible beauty, he cannot respond to "The Living
Beauty" or "pay its tribute of wild tears" (*VP* 334). In "The Laugh
of the Medusa" Cixous has pointed out that the "terrible beauty" is
in the eye of the male beholder. Women did not create the figure of
the deadly woman or the mother who demands the blood of her
children. Eire as a pre-Christian earth-goddess who demands human
sacrifice[15] is an avatar of the "Great Mother," the feminine figured
in tripartite form as life-giving womb, pleasure-giving vagina, and
devouring grave. Yeats found anthropological authority in Frazer for
the fertility myth that he called "the old ritual of the year...the
mother goddess and the slain god" (*VP* 857), but the male creator of
culture imposes upon himself this archetypal story of his infan-
tilization and destruction by the mother. His incapacities as bearer
and inadequacies as nurturer combine with childhood memories of
total dependence to produce a figure of terror. Although she certainly
needed and depended on him, and later even teasingly warned him
against matrimony (*AYF* 320), Gonne did not compel Yeats's
sacrifice; indeed she warned him against making it. She insisted that
if the "absolutely *platonic friendship*" she offered "unsettles you &
spoils your work then you must have the strength & courage at once
to give up meeting me" (*AYF* 85). Though wanting him on her
terms, she reminded him that he was always free to reject them. In
1899 she wrote, "my dear Friend I do not want you to make up your
mind to sacrifice yourself for me. I know that just now, perhaps, it is
useless my saying to you 'love some other woman'. All I want of you
is not to make up your mind *not* to" (*AYF* 130). The sacrifice, like the
Medusa complex, was self-imposed.[16]

   "Easter 1916" does not challenge the poetic stereotype of the
"terrible beauty," but presents it in both its negative and positive
aspects. When Yeats wishes to claim bardic authority in immor-
talizing the dead heroes of 1916 he figures them as children, with
himself and his audience as surrogates for Mother Ireland in her
nurturing rather than destructive embodiment:

> our part
> To murmur name upon name,
> As a mother names her child
> When sleep at last has come
> On limbs that had run wild.   (*VP* 394)

Even this move has been challenged: Kiberd argues that Yeats, in employing the old colonialist metaphor of parent and child, "has infantilized the fallen rebels in much the same way as they obligingly, if unconsciously, infantilized themselves in the opening sentence of their proclamation."[17] This judgment, however, neglects the psychological empowerment that the rebels must have felt in naming themselves the "children" of Mother Ireland, and that Yeats reflects in mourning them as such. So powerful, indeed, is the metaphor of the mother and the sleeping child that Yeats is forced to remind himself in a heavily stressed, grimly alliterative, and unmusical monosyllabic line that it is only a figure: "No, no, not night but death" (*VP* 394). The image of the mother is evoked only to be canceled: unlike Pearse, Yeats distinguishes biological mothers from symbolic, sacrificial ones.

During the composition of "On a Political Prisoner" in late 1918,[18] Yeats admitted that he was writing about Markievicz in order to avoid writing about Gonne, which must mark a new generic departure: the prophylactic love poem.[19] The two women were in Holloway Jail with Kathleen Clarke, widow of Tom Clarke, who like them had been interned in May 1918 as a political suspect in the fictional "German Plot."[20] Yet Yeats, writing of Markievicz as if she were alone, describes her taming of a seagull when she was in solitary confinement in Mountjoy after the Rising. She wrote to her sister Eva of "sea-gulls and pigeons, which I had quite tame."[21] The tame seagull that represents Markievicz's patience in confinement is contrasted with the wild bird springing out of its nest, "Upon some lofty rock to stare / Upon the cloudy canopy." Unlike the modest and unobtrusive linnet of "A Prayer for my Daughter," the seagull with its "storm-beaten breast" is an image of freedom, energy, and risk (*VP* 397). The impatient horsewoman Yeats remembers is similarly celebrated for "wildness" and physical courage on the apolitical hunting field. At the time he had written to her after reports of a hunting accident, "Sligo is always full of rumours & the slightest one about its wild huntswoman naturally & properly echoes from mountain to mountain" (*CL*1 462). Twenty-five years later he remembered how,

> When long ago I saw her ride
> Under Ben Bulben to the meet,
> The beauty of her country-side
> With all youth's lonely wildness stirred,
> She seemed to have grown clean and sweet
> Like any rock-bred, sea-borne bird.   (*VP* 397)

Gonne wrote to Yeats that, "The poem I like best in the new book is the one to the prisoner, I like all the part about the seabird. Poor Con, she must indeed be patient & endure these long months of imprisonment" (*AYF* 422). In selecting the seabird for approval, Gonne fails to note that its cleanliness, loneliness, and sweetness have been polluted by Markievicz's prominent role in politics, which is imaged as "drinking the foul ditch" in the company of the blind. As in "No Second Troy," aristocratic individualism is contaminated by leadership of the crowd. Between the admiring evocation of the solitary and patient prisoner, and the nostalgic depiction of the wild young huntress, lies the portrait of an agitator: "Her thought some popular enmity" (*VP* 397). In his 1932 broadcast "Poems about Women," Yeats asserts that, "In the lines of the poem which condemn her politics I was not thinking of her part in two rebellions but of other matters of quarrel."[22] The problem was not her nationalism, which Yeats shared, but his perception that in pursuing it "her mind / Became a bitter, an abstract thing" (*VP* 397). Yeats deplored abstraction wherever he found it, especially in himself, but in women it was inexcusable because unaesthetic. O'Casey, not an unbiased observer, but certainly no fan of Gonne's, wrote that "Countess Markievicz lagged far behind Maud Gonne in dignity, character, and grace, and couldn't hold a candle to her as a speaker. Her passionate speeches always appeared to be strained, and rarely had any sense in them; and they always threatened to soar into a still-born scream."[23]

Markievicz's "popular enmity," however, mirrors Gonne's "intellectual hatred" in "A Prayer for my Daughter" (*VP* 405). Yeats's fear of what appears in the drafts as "a popular tempest" and "some demagogue's song / To level all things"[24] was increased by the Bolshevik revolution of 1917, which was initially supported by both Gonne and Markievicz.[25] Yeats associated women with "levelling" and socialism because many of the women he knew were interested in social welfare (*AV[B]* 263). One of the things that is falling apart at the beginning of "The Second Coming," the drafts of which reveal a similar preoccupation with "the mob" and the death of innocence,[26] is the traditional hierarchy of the family, in which women remain at home rather than participating with "passionate intensity" in the destruction of the old order (*VP* 402).

At the time of the poem's composition in early 1919 Yeats's personal relations with Gonne were strained. During her prison term in Holloway Yeats and George Yeats, then pregnant with Anne, had borrowed her Dublin house. After her release in October 1918 she defied an order banning her return to Dublin, and arrived on her own doorstep, only to be turned away by Yeats, who feared the effect of military searches on the health of his wife. George Yeats was indeed suffering from severe pneumonia, but Gonne was understandably outraged, and the result was a spectacular, though short-lived, public quarrel. Metaphorically protecting his wife and child against the stormy incursions of his former Aphrodite, Yeats based his prayer on an attempted rejection of all that Gonne represented: having once "praised her body and her mind / Till pride had made her eyes grow bright" ("A Memory of Youth," *VP* 314), he now abandoned praise for vituperation,

> because the minds that I have loved,
> The sort of beauty that I have approved,
> Prosper but little. (*VP* 405)

The image of the terrible beauty haunts this poem as a negative example. The birth of his daughter leads Yeats to reconsider his models of femininity: he proleptically prescribes the sexual identity of one who at the poem's inception was, according to the drafts, no more than a month-old child. The baby in the cradle of the first two stanzas becomes the marriageable girl in front of her looking-glass in stanza three: the intervening years of childhood are elided. In three canceled stanzas the poet addresses his daughter as a young woman of twenty-four or twenty-five.[27] George Yeats was twenty-seven when she married Yeats; he was fifty-one. Chesler suggests that "patriarchal marriage, prostitution, and mass 'romantic' love are psychologically predicated on sexual union between Daughter and Father figures."[28] Imagining Anne at the age of twenty-five, Yeats also celebrates her mother. His prayer for his daughter is subtextually a love poem to his

wife, a tribute to the woman won that praises her by disparaging the
"woman lost"; but which, as Perloff has argued, still gives pride of
poetic place to the "terrible beauty" he is attempting to exorcise.[29]
Despite the fact that Yeats's emotional preoccupation at the inception
of his marriage was with Iseult Gonne,[30] it is with the "Maud
Gonne" who has dominated his love poetry that Yeats engages in "A
Prayer for my Daughter."

At the opening of the poem the storm is "howling," the wind is
"levelling," the sea-wind "screams" on the tower and "screams" as
it assaults the elms. "Gregory's wood" offers an inadequate
protection (*VP* 403). When Yeats asks why "Maud Gonne," the sort
of beauty that he has celebrated in his love poems, has failed to
prosper, his metaphor connects her with the images of storm and
voice: she has rejected the virtues prized by "quiet natures" for "an
old bellows full of angry wind" that will both "howl" and "burst,"
but ultimately fail to "tear the linnet" from the protecting leaf (*VP*
405). What threatens the future identity of the baby Anne, therefore,
is not only the postwar political chaos evoked in the drafts of the
poem,[31] but also the model of femininity offered by the type of
woman who raises her voice in the service of "opinions": who like
Markievicz in "Easter 1916" spends her nights in argument until her
voice grows "shrill." Yeats's use of the legal phrase "Assault and
battery of the wind" suggests that he is drawing on the anti-feminist
rhetoric frequently employed by those who opposed the "shrieking
sisterhood" of the suffragettes, who not only raised their voices in
public, but were frequently arrested for attacking policemen. Even
the suffragist Eva Gore-Booth had reservations about "educated and
upper class women who kick, shriek, bite and spit."[32] At the
beginning of World War One Gonne had written to Yeats that
women would soon be "in a terrible majority... I always felt the
wave of the woman's power was rising, the men are destroying
themselves & we are looking on" (*AYF* 348). Although she herself
hoped that female ascendancy might bring peace rather than
slaughter, her metaphor of women's power as a rising "wave" may
have prompted Yeats's vision of the future issuing "Out of the
murderous innocence of the sea" (*VP* 403).

Gonne had been "the loveliest woman born / Out of the mouth of
Plenty's horn," but her mind, according to Yeats, was "opinionated"
and "choked with hate," a hate not only private and emotional but
abstract and public: "An intellectual hatred is the worst" (*VP* 405).

Yeats saw hatred as a positive motivating force for himself,[33] but not for women.[34] Gonne's political opinions were not wrong in themselves, but damaging because as a female she was unable to take them lightly: they had made a stone of her heart. In *A Vision* Yeats categorizes her as a woman of Phase Sixteen whose False Creative Mind is "Opinionated Will," and in whom "all the cruelty and narrowness of that intellect are displayed in service of preposterous purpose after purpose till there is nothing left but the fixed idea and some hysterical hatred" (*AV*[*A*] 71–72). From its inception the Western philosophical tradition has conceived of intellect and reason as "transcendence of the feminine."[35] Yeats argues that the woman who encroaches with passionate intensity on the male preserve of abstract ratiocination is unnatural: he figures her, conventionally, as a hysteric.

His poetic condemnation of female hatred, however, was not merely the fruit of the quarrel with Gonne, which was soon resolved as Yeats tried to salvage Iseult Gonne's marriage. "A Prayer" is the culmination of a long discussion about her character. In 1909 Gonne had told him that political considerations determined her decision to marry John MacBride. Taking all the blame for "the forgetfulness of that spiritual marriage long ago, which if we had obeyed would have saved us both from the long weariness of separation," she insisted that "all the crushing sorrow that came on me *I have earned.*" In marrying MacBride, "I was carried away on the wave of hate which I thought righteous, I sought a wild revenge which because impersonal I thought noble. I forgot that those who would distribute life or death must be purer than the angels & that I was full of human passion & weakness" (*AYF* 272). Her allusion to distributing life or death suggests the abortive plan to assassinate Edward VII in Gibraltar, for which her honeymoon trip to Spain was the cover (*AYF* 168). In "King and No King" (1909) Yeats accepted her version of events, claiming to have "been defeated by that pledge you gave / In momentary anger long ago" (*VP* 258). Anger and hatred had always been problematic for Gonne: Yeats later reminded her of an early vision in which a spirit had told her that "your third and lowest Hell was revenge (labour from hatred)" while her highest Heaven was "labour from devine [*sic*] love" (*AYF* 443–44). The early poem "The Two Trees" derives from this opposing vision of love and hate. The blossoming, fruit-bearing, "merry" tree of love, whose "hidden root / Has planted quiet in the night" (*VP* 134), is a precursor of the "rooted" "flourishing hidden tree" and the "merriment" of its occupant the linnet, and anticipates the "quiet natures" of "A Prayer for my Daughter" (*VP* 404–05). The storm that models the wrong kind of femininity in the later poem reflects the "stormy night" of "The Two Trees," in which the "Broken boughs and blackened leaves" of the tree of hatred are reflected "in the dim glass the demons hold" (*VP* 135). Adopting Yeats's poetic and occult terminology Gonne wrote in 1910: "Of all my work & all my effort little will remain because I worked on the ray of Hate, I think, & the Demons of hate which possessed me are not eternal – what you have written for me will live because our love has always been high & pure" (*AYF* 294). Ironically, Yeats's most passionate condemnation of hatred in women was originally voiced by Gonne herself.

The anxious father, therefore, prays that Anne may become like her mother rather than like the "terrible beauties" who were driven by opinionated hatred into disastrous marriage choices:

> May she be granted beauty and yet not
> Beauty to make a stranger's eye distraught,
> Or hers before a looking-glass, for such,
> Being made beautiful overmuch,
> Consider beauty a sufficient end,
> Lose natural kindness and maybe
> The heart-revealing intimacy
> That chooses right, and never find a friend.   (*VP* 403–04)

Kindness and the capacity for intimate friendship are not the stuff of romance. Yeats turns from the image of the woman for whom men would die, and implicitly from the image of Ireland as a woman who asks for sacrifice. That traditional male symbol of female narcissism, the lovely woman with a looking-glass, is less appealing than the courtesy and "glad kindness" of a woman friend. Undermining the romantic idea of love at first sight, Yeats now values the woman he had not initially desired:

> In courtesy I'd have her chiefly learned;
> Hearts are not had as a gift but hearts are earned
> By those that are not entirely beautiful;
> Yet many, that have played the fool
> For beauty's very self, has charm made wise,
> And many a poor man that has roved,
> Loved and thought himself beloved,
> From a glad kindness cannot take his eyes.   (*VP* 404)

In "A Drinking Song" Yeats had said that "love comes in at the eye" (*VP* 261), but here he challenges the visual metaphor that dominates traditional love poetry. The lover's gaze is held by non-visual qualities: by kindness and courtesy rather than perfect features.

The revision of romance is accompanied by a revaluation of Helen and Aphrodite, the legendary symbols of beauty and destructive sexuality. In *A Vision*, Helen of Troy, like Iseult Gonne, is a woman of Phase Fourteen:

> Is it not because she desires so little and gives so little that men will die and murder in her service? One thinks of THE ETERNAL IDOL of Rodin: that kneeling man with hands clasped behind his back in humble adoration, kissing a young girl a little below the breast, while she gazes down, without comprehending, under her half-closed eyelids. (*AV[A]* 68)

The connection between beautiful women and violence was, for Yeats, a given: "Aphrodite rises from a stormy sea ... Helen could not be Helen but for beleaguered Troy" (*AV[B]* 267–68). Although the trope is a poetic commonplace, Irish events in the aftermath of the rising confirmed the association between women and extreme politics. The widows and bereft mothers of the revolution (Mrs. Pearse, Kathleen Clarke, Grace Plunkett, Hanna Sheehy Skeffington), and the women of Cumann na mBan like Kathleen Lynn and Winifred Carney who had been "out" in Easter Week, played a large symbolic and practical role in the electoral recrudescence of Sinn Fein. In February 1918 the franchise was granted to women over thirty, and women stood for Parliament for the first time. In December 1918 Markievicz, still in jail in Holloway, united Republican, suffragist, and labor support to win a seat in the House of Commons. The wave of women's power indeed seemed to be rising.

Seeking to protect his daughter from the violence that these beautiful women seemed to foment or attract, and from disastrous personal relationships like that of Gonne and the soldier John MacBride, Yeats warns her that:

> Helen being chosen found life flat and dull
> And later had much trouble from a fool,
> While that great Queen, that rose out of the spray,
> Being fatherless could have her way
> Yet chose a bandy-leggèd smith for man. (*VP* 404)

Both the passive and the active beauties – Helen who was chosen and Aphrodite who was free to choose – find inappropriate mates. Thus the Horn of Plenty is undone, and women's natural fertility dried up. Aphrodite's birth in the sea spray connects her with the "murderous" instability of changing winds and tides rather than with "rooted" peace. Yeats's stress on the goddess as "fatherless" recalls the legend of her origin. The Titan Cronos castrated and killed the original Father Uranos while he was copulating with Gaia, the Earth. He threw his father's genitals into the ocean: the goddess was born out of the blood and semen that spread onto the surface of the water. Aphrodite is thus the original "terrible beauty," a daughter who takes life from her father's castration, and who exemplifies the union of blood and seed, sexuality and violent death. Yeats explains her marriage to Vulcan the armorer: "perhaps if the body have great perfection, there is always something imperfect in the mind ... Venus out of phase chose lame Vulcan" (*AV*[*A*] 74). Perfect beauties, charged with sexual desire, are dismissed from Anne Yeats's world, just as Prospero, in supervising and manipulating his daughter's marriage, banished Venus and Cupid from the courtly Masque. The birth of Yeats's daughter spurred a re-evaluation of his Muse.

This re-evaluation is both positive and negative. It is refreshing to be offered the "not entirely beautiful" woman as an ideal, and to see courtly frustration replaced by kindness and friendship as the model of male/female relations. Pleasing, too, is the notion of love as a gradual development rather than a thunderbolt. In its depiction of George Yeats and what she meant to him the poem evokes a mature and sympathetic relationship. The rejection of the "screaming" woman of ideas, however, is itself shrill in tone and unjust to Gonne's public activities: it marks a regression in Yeats's acceptance of changing gender roles. His wishes for his daughter, understandable in the immediate historical context of war and political instability, nevertheless purchase safety at the price of sequestration. Instead of standing for Parliament or getting herself locked up in Holloway, Anne is to

> become a flourishing hidden tree
> That all her thoughts may like the linnet be,
> ... ...
> O may she live like some green laurel
> Rooted in one dear perpetual place.   (*VP* 404–05)

Like Wordsworth's Lucy, the child in the cradle was "half" hidden; his grown daughter is to be hidden entirely, to dwell amidst untrodden ways. Something of Prospero's proprietary interest in the preservation of Miranda's chastity is evident in Yeats's allusion to the rape narrative of Apollo and Daphne. Daphne, fleeing from the lustful Apollo, prayed to her father, the river god Peneus, that she might remain forever a virgin rather than be forced by the god. Peneus responded by turning her into a laurel tree, thus preserving her chastity at the expense of her humanity. The idea of a single life is reinforced by the allusion to Wordsworth's "The Green Linnet," a bird that is "Too blest with any one to pair; / Thyself thy own enjoyment."[36]

Joyce Carol Oates is so enraged by the implications of the Daphne allusion that she ignores the linnet altogether:

This celebrated poet would have his daughter an object in nature for others' – which is to say male–delectation. She is not even an animal or a bird in his imagination, but a vegetable: immobile, unthinking, placid, "hidden" ... the poet's daughter is to be brainless and voiceless, *rooted*.[37]

While some male critics allude to the poem's chauvinism,[38] Oates excoriates Yeats's "crushingly conventional" imagination. Yet Yeats nowhere says that the "hidden tree" is to be an object for male delectation. His identification of his daughter with the virgin Daphne and the tuneful linnet suggests the opposite: that he sequesters her in the cloister to protect her imaginatively from rape. Iseult Gonne was supposedly molested by John MacBride (*AYF* 231–32), and in *A Vision* Yeats noted that women of her Phase "are subject to violence ... here are women carried off by robbers and ravished by clowns" (*AV[A]* 69). To keep his women pure the father will defend them against other males, but protection against rape entails the loss of women's humanity. In conjunction with Yeats's rejection of intellectual hatred in women, his identification of his daughter with the linnet and the rooted tree implies her subordinate relationship to male culture.

Between the polar opposites of the screaming witch and the tuneful virgin, the wind and the bird in the tree, the poem briefly constitutes the woman as a subject whose soul is "self-delighting, / Self-appeasing, self-affrighting." These lines appear to offer her not only "radical innocence" but spiritual independence: her "own sweet will is Heaven's will" (*VP* 405). This independence, however, is immediately curtailed by the appearance of a bridegroom who reinscribes her into the structures of patriarchy. As late in the process of composition as the typed fair copy Yeats wrote, "And may she marry into some old house."[39] The hypothetical son-in-law is chosen because of his aristocratic social status and ownership of landed property rather than because of his sexuality. Before the bride enters the Big House of the Anglo-Irish aristocracy the "rich horn" and the "spreading laurel tree" must be translated into the symbolic abstractions "custom" and "ceremony": nature gives way to a culture. The bride, although recovering "radical innocence," remains linguistically "rooted" (in the original sense of *radical*) within a social milieu that endorses passive rather than active women. Assaulted by wind and bellows, she is nevertheless "happy still" – both continually happy and happy in abstention from movement. Implicit in the famous rhetorical question "How but in custom and in ceremony / Are innocence and beauty born?" (*VP* 405–06) is the idea of woman as the reproducer of the ideals and values of a patriarchal society. Only within the protective, paternalistic structures of tradition can the vulnerability of innocence and beauty be "borne," be endured; and out of the daughter's body are "born" the generations that will sustain and continue those traditions. The baby in her cradle is imagined as a future wife and mother whose happy stillness and quiet nature act as a barrier against the destructive forces of arrogance and hatred unleashed by the storm of female revolt. If the Horn of Plenty, symbol of eugenically correct fertility, is not to be undone, women must mate according to their birth, must cease to "eat / A crazy salad with their meat" (*VP* 404). Although in his youth Yeats idealized women who, like Shelley's proto-feminist Cythna, "accompanied their lovers through all manner of wild places, lawless women without homes and without children" (*Au* 64), now he envisages his young wife and daughter as angels in the house.

The incestuous structure of patriarchal marriage is suggested by the privileging of the laurel tree as the last image of the poem. In the social context of which Yeats approves, a daughter can achieve freedom from paternal incest-wishes only when her father publicly relinquishes her to another man during the marriage ritual.[40] The wedding "ceremony" implicit in the epithalamic last stanza of the poem should dissolve paternal ownership of the daughter, but in consigning her to a bridegroom who exists only as a reflection of his own prejudices and desires, Yeats subverts the exogamous intention of the paternal gift. Although formally he releases his daughter to the bridegroom, covertly he invites her to return to him and to the imprisonment of the laurel tree.

"A Prayer for my Daughter" is the product of its historical moment: the year 1919, in which Yeats's anxieties about the future were intense. The poem's relation to the apocalyptic "The Second Coming" is a commonplace. Ireland was beginning its struggle against England, and post-war Europe was menaced, Yeats thought, by Bolshevism. Women with leftist political opinions, newly enfranchised, represent the "future years" that come "Dancing to a frenzied drum, / Out of the murderous innocence of the sea" (*VP* 403). Mapping his longing for political stability onto gender relations Yeats, who was constantly demanding that his wife's spirits explicate his troubled relationships with Iseult and Maud Gonne, imagined the re-establishment of social order as analogous to the restoration of sexual hierarchy. This position was not one he could long sustain.

CHAPTER 8

Swans on the cesspool: Leda and rape

The representation (or non-representation) of bodies and sexuality in
Irish culture is conditioned by the social power of the Catholic
Church. St. Paul's anti-feminism and valorization of the spiritual
over the physical were especially influential in Ireland.[1] Penitential
Catholicism intensified by residual Victorian prudery, however, is
only part of the story.[2] Nancy Scheper-Hughes explores the social
and economic etiology of rural schizophrenia to explain why the
"Irish body image unconsciously reflects and reinforces sexual
repression."[3] Economic conditions resulting from colonial exploi-
tation and the Great Famine played a major part in producing late
marriages and a high rate of celibacy in the Irish countryside.[4]
Sexuality was subordinated to the need to pass on the meager
landholding undivided to the male heir. Surplus sons and daughters
could emigrate, enter the convent or the priesthood, or try to marry
for money. Erotic pleasure was not high on the agenda: the survival
of the family in perilous economic circumstances dictated sexual
choice. A nineteenth-century street-ballad laments this state of
affairs: a young wooer is dismayed to learn that his beloved's family
will "force my own colleen to wed / An old man for his gold." He
identifies this social practice as peculiarly Irish:

> Why is it in our dear land,
> Full of warm hearts and true
> They wed for money not for love,
> As other nations do.[5]

The answer is that small farmers clinging desperately to their land
did not speak the cultural language of romance: eroticism is a luxury
for the well-off or a reckless consolation for those who have nothing
to lose. When the small farmers moved to town, they brought their
ethic with them despite the fact that it was no longer economically

140

relevant, and their sexual conservatism was reinforced by a celibate clergy.

The establishment of an Irish nation transformed the politically rebellious but virginal Cathleen ni Houlihan into a home-bound pious housewife, as the conservative and petty-bourgeois Free State Government perfected its version of Irish identity as Gaelic, Catholic, and sexually pure. Although women played a major part in the fight for Independence, the state they got was not the state for which they had struggled: it failed to cherish the children of the nation equally. All of the six women deputies in the Dáil voted against the Treaty. As they refused to take the Oath and were excluded from the political process, Yeats correctly prophesied that the loss of the "emotional ladies" might "unbalance things for a time on to the side of hard-headedness & the man of business."[6] The social policies of the twenties and thirties erased the revolutionary achievements and silenced the voices of Irish women.

The dominance of Catholicism in the South was reinforced by the colonial legacy of Partition, which reified existing religious divisions. Because decolonization failed to change the way Southern Ireland was administered, the new government, backed by the clergy, emphasized the Irish language and the Catholic ethical code as the defining marks of independence.[7] Mary Douglas argues that fetishization of purity is characteristic of threatened minorities, whose concern with political boundaries is displaced into an obsession with bodily orifices and secretions.[8] Although the Catholics were a majority in the South, Ireland's boundaries were compromised from without by continued British presence in the Treaty Ports, and from within by Partition and the bitter legacy of civil war: the revolution was unfinished. Consolidating their power in uncertain times, the Catholic authorities displaced their anxiety about political unity and identity into an obsession with sexuality, defined as "dirt" and identified as "foreign" in origin.[9] Lee also suggests that this obsession "permitted a blind eye to be turned towards the social scars that disfigured the face of Ireland": rural and urban poverty, emigration, and mental disease.[10] In their 1924 Lenten Pastorals, which Yeats condemned as "rancid, course [*sic*] and vague" (*UP*2 438), the Bishops lambasted "women's immodest fashions in dress, indecent dances, unwholesome theatrical performances and cinema exhibitions, evil literature and drink."[11] Their condemnations of licentious behavior suggest that Ireland was experiencing a watered-down version of the sexual revolution of the Twenties, not roaring but squeaking: "The pity of it, that our Catholic girls ... should follow the mode of pagan England by appearing in public semi-nude."[12] Was it for this, runs the subtext of many such effusions, that all that blood was shed?

In response to the perceived threat of national demoralization, Catholic morality was enacted into law. Film censorship was instituted in 1923; the censorship of literature and the press, preceded by the establishment of a Committee on Evil Literature in 1926, became law in 1929. In 1925 the Bishops forced Cosgrave to revoke the legal right to divorce inherited by the Free State from the English Parliament.[13] Although the importation and sale of contraceptives was not formally outlawed until 1935, advertisements for or explanations of birth control devices were banned by the Censors. At the same time, illegitimacy carried an overwhelming social and legal stigma. Both the main political parties and the majority of the population accepted the sexual purity legislation, since it accorded with their own prejudices, and the only systematic opposition to the policy of giving Catholic moral standards the backing of the State came from Yeats and his allies.[14]

Yeats began by opposing the Censorship of Films Bill (1923). He did not take refuge in the Audenesque claim that poetry makes nothing happen, but argued that the appeal of the arts to "our imitative faculties" was counterbalanced by their good effects (*SS* 52).[15] The Bill, however, passed, and cleanliness was legally established as next to godliness. As Douglas points out, "holiness requires that different classes of things shall not be confused," so "Hybrids and other confusions are abominated."[16] The horror inspired by the hybrid underlies the reaction to Yeats's "Leda and the Swan," a poem representing the violent rape of a woman by a god in ornithological disguise. Yeats sited the poem in the public arena to arouse controversy and flout censorship. In the context of its publication in the monthly paper *To-morrow* (August 1924), its transgressive intent is apparent.

According to Yeats, the poem was inspired by a meditation on the Irish situation in relation to world politics. The first version was finished at Coole in September 1923 in the atmosphere of political instability resulting from the Civil War. Yeats told Gregory of "his long belief that the reign of democracy is over for the present, and in reaction there will be violent government from above, as now in

Russia, and is beginning here. It is the thought of this force coming into the world that he is expressing in his Leda poem."[17] The swan-god, it seems, originated as another rough beast, an unlikely amalgam of Lenin and President Cosgrave, subduing the anarchic masses in the person of Leda; but Yeats insisted that "as I wrote, bird and lady took such possession of the scene that all politics went out of it, and my friend tells me that his 'conservative readers would misunderstand the poem'" (*VP* 828). All politics did not evaporate in the alchemy of the creative process, however: class politics were overshadowed though not effaced by the politics of sexuality.

The poem, first titled "Annunciation,"[18] was too hot for AE's *Irish Statesman* to handle, but when a group of young intellectuals – Iseult and Francis Stuart, Cecil Salkeld, Liam O'Flaherty, and F. R. Higgins – started a radical monthly paper, Yeats gave them "Leda and the Swan" for the first number. The other contributions included a short story by Lennox Robinson, "The Madonna of Slieve Dun," about a peasant girl who is raped by a tramp while she is unconscious. She comes to believe that she is pregnant with the Messiah, but dies while giving birth to a girl. *To-morrow* thus offered its readership not one but two rapes. Yeats's "violent annunciation" from above (*VP* 828) was paired with a parody annunciation from below: both the brutish tramp and the bestial swan-god can be read as blasphemous stand-ins for the Holy Spirit. Like "Leda," Robinson's story had been refused by another Irish periodical "because it was indecent and dealt with rape,"[19] although it had been previously published in America.[20] The topic, however indirectly treated, was taboo. "The Madonna of Slieve Dun" is not explicit: the rape, unlike Leda's, takes place in the white space between paragraphs. In positing a naturalistic explanation for the girl's pregnancy, however, the story suggests that there may also be one for the Virgin Mary's; it casts doubt upon the Virgin Birth.[21] So the printers reasoned, for, operating their own extra-legal censorship, they refused to produce the paper. Mary's reproductive and sexual body was systematically erased by Irish Catholic devotion to the Virgin: the Christian Brothers would have been scandalized by those medieval Madonnas who offer a bare breast to the nursing Christ child.[22]

The printers provided Yeats with an opportunity to engage the forces of Catholic public opinion head on. "I am in high spirits this morning, seeing my way to a most admirable row," he wrote (*L* 705). Since *The Countess Cathleen* Yeats had been regularly abused by

Catholic newspapers; during the twenties, with his accession to national prominence as Senator and Nobel Prize recipient, the attacks increased in number and venom.[23] Although he claimed "I never see the popular Catholic press," he knew what it said: "George Russell and I and the head of the Education Board are accused ... of being in a conspiracy to destroy the Catholic faith through free education. At least I am told so" (*L* 705). O'Casey brought copies of *The Irish Rosary*, *The Leader*, and *The Catholic Bulletin* to the attention of Gregory,[24] so Yeats knew that his name had become a byword for paganism, anti-Catholicism, opposition to Gaelic culture, and snobbery. He was part of what *The Catholic Bulletin* called "The New Ascendancy."

Keogh characterizes the *Bulletin* as "an anti-Cosgrave journal pulsating with confessional prejudices."[25] Kearney locates it in the long if not particularly honorable Irish tradition of political journals organized on sectarian lines.[26] O'Callaghan correctly points out, however, that the *Bulletin*, frequently cited to demonstrate the intemperance of the Catholic attitude toward Anglo-Ireland, was an extreme example of the genre.[27] Animus against Yeats saturates its editorials, probably written by the influential Jesuit, Father T. J. Corcoran, Professor of Education at University College Dublin.[28] Corcoran was a supporter of de Valera,[29] while Yeats was a Cosgrave man. The *Bulletin* continually vilified Freemasons, while Yeats had celebrated his uncle's Masonic funeral in "In Memory of Alfred Pollexfen" (*VP* 360). Corcoran formulated the Government's plans for making Irish the medium of instruction in the schools;[30] Yeats, while desiring to see Ireland speak Gaelic, protested against reading the prayers in the Senate in a language most of the Senators did not know and objected to railway signs in a language few Irishmen spoke (*SS* 57–58, 79).[31] The *Bulletin* had been founded in 1911 to warn against the dangers of immoral literature;[32] Yeats vocally opposed censorship. The *Bulletin* kept a close eye on the Official Reports of the Senate, and frequently quoted Yeats's speeches verbatim:[33] it also monitored the columns of *The Irish Statesman*.

Although the Dublin printers objected to Lennox Robinson's story and not to Yeats's poem, he had chosen "Leda" as the most provocative work he could offer the editors of *To-morrow*. In this political context the poem differs from the "Leda and the Swan" published in the exclusive (and expensive) Cuala Press edition of *The Cat and the Moon and Certain Poems* (May 1924), in the avant-garde

American *Dial* (June 1924), and later as epigraph to the historical section of *A Vision*, "Dove or Swan?" (1925).[34] It also differs from the poem that appears in later collected editions. The context provided by the other material in the paper, the hostile Catholic audience, and the desire to create public scandal, produces a text that rhetorically intervenes in cultural politics via the representation of a female body and the enactment of a male desire for power.

George Yeats told Gregory that "Leda," "now it is known it goes into *Tomorrow*, [is] being spoken of as something horribly indecent."[35] Yeats composed a polemical editorial, signed by Stuart and Salkeld, which sought to by-pass the provincial Irish clergy and redefine indecency by appealing to the more tolerant artistic standards of the Renaissance papacy: "We are Catholics, but of the school of Pope Julius the Second and of the Medician Popes, who ordered Michaelangelo and Raphael to paint upon the walls of the Vatican." Michaelangelo, creator of a celebrated version of Leda and the Swan, is praised as "the most orthodox of men" because he depicts "the lust of the goat, the whole handiwork of God, even the abounding horn." If the representation of sexuality is orthodox, the Irish bishops are heretics. A valid poetics must incorporate "the whole handiwork of God," so "we count among atheists bad writers and Bishops of all denominations" (*UP2* 438). Yeats, himself no atheist, fused his provocative politics with religious belief: "My dream is a wild paper of the young which will make enemies everywhere and suffer suppression, I hope a number of times, with the logical assertion, with all fitting deductions, of the immortality of the soul" (*L* 706). Gregory remarked primly that "it would be hardly necessary to display the immorality of the body as an argument for the immortality of the soul,"[36] but Yeats was establishing his political strategy for the next decade: in defense of the body as part of "the whole handiwork of God" he would be holier than the Pope.

Yeats's anti-purity crusade inevitably encompassed the work of James Joyce. In May 1924 Yeats had thought Pound's plan to import *Ulysses* into Ireland imprudent: "no one dare wake an ecclesiastical terrier, which is at present only hunting in its dreams ... *Ulysses* – that would wake the terrier in earnest" (*L* 705). The *To-morrow* controversy, however, emboldened him. In August, judging the literary competition at the Tailteann Games, Yeats endorsed *Ulysses* in a prestigious cultural forum:

It is our duty to say that Mr. James Joyce's book, though as obscene as *Rabelais*, and, therefore, forbidden by law in England and the United States, is more indubitably a work of genius than any prose written by an Irishman since the death of Synge.[37]

His defense of a banned book provoked an attack from a non-ecclesiastical Protestant source, Professor Wilbraham Trench of Trinity College, who wrote to the *Irish Statesman*:

J. Joyce rakes hell, and the sewers, for dirt to throw at the fair face of life, and for poison to make beauty shrivel and die ... and Dr. Yeats undertakes that no citizen of Dublin shall fail to know his name. In season and out of season he has proclaimed him a genius... But there have been geniuses who wallowed in the mire before, though whether any quite equally foul-minded, who shall say?[38]

The diction of this letter set the terms for the debate that followed: sewers, dirt, mire, and foulness were the linguistic counters taken up by *The Catholic Bulletin*, and applied interchangeably to the authors of *Ulysses* and "Leda and the Swan." By rhetorical contamination, Joyce's interest in defecation was associated with Yeats's interest in rape. Yeats and his friends were subsequently and repeatedly abused as "the Sewage School"[39] and "the Cloacal Combine."[40]

Joyce really did have a cloacal obsession: Brenda Maddox's account of the humiliations to which he subjected his wife makes unpleasant reading.[41] Literary evidence for Joyce's interest appears in the episode of Bloom's defecation, which occurs early in *Ulysses* and is written in plain language: of the many readers (including Yeats)[42] who gave up before reaching the end of the book, most would have encountered Leopold on the jakes. Joyce had anticipated his detractors in "The Holy Office" (1904), which satirized the Dublin of the Celtic Twilight:

> all these men of whom I speak
> Make me the sewer of their clique.
> That they may dream their dreamy dreams
> I carry off their filthy streams.[43]

The Catholic Bulletin, developing the cloacal metaphor with prurient relish, reprinted Trench's letter and announced that in *To-morrow* "the Dublin aesthetes... have provided themselves with a new literary cesspool."[44] The language of the would-be censors became complicit with the excrement that they sought to exclude from the social body.

The Irish Statesman[45] welcomed *To-morrow* with a paternalistic pat on the head, doubting whether it was "impish enough to arouse violent antagonisms. It really requires a great deal of art to stick a needle into the national being so that it sits up and howls."[46] *To-morrow* did not have a sufficiently large circulation to stick needles very far into the national being, but it certainly lacerated Corcoran, who sat up and howled. The ecclesiastical terrier was hunting in its dreams no longer. In the November issue of the *Bulletin*, though Lennox Robinson is granted "pride of place" in the "unsavoury netherworld," the bitterest invective is reserved for "Leda and the Swan," which

exhibits Senator Pollexfen Yeats in open rivalry with the "bestial genius" which Senator Yeats has so recently championed. For bestial is the precise and fitting word for this outburst of "poetry." The "swan-motive" has been prominent in the aesthete's circles for a year or more: it has now found characteristic utterance in the title and texture of these fourteen lines signed "W. B. Yeats." To such foul fruition have come the swan-sequence of Coole,[47] of the Liffey; the mutual prefaces, the mutual awards,[48] the posed photographs on the river-side, including Mr. Lennox Robinson, Senator Yeats, and the Senator who made the Offering of Swans to the river, and received from Senator Pollexfen Yeats therefor (*sic*) a wreath of laurel spray. Professor W. F. Trench is answered. We may even say that J. Joyce will be envious when he reads the effort of Yeats, and will call for a more effective rake. "Hell and the sewers" are not in it. It is when resort is had to the pagan world for inspiration in the "poetry" of the obscene, that the mere moderns can be outclassed in bestiality.

To Senator Yeats therefore must be accorded the distinction of bringing the Swan Stunt to its quite appropriate climax. The Swan Song which he has uttered will not be forgotten to him.[49]

This passage identifies correctly the concatenation of "motives" from the world of politics, culture, and real swans that helped to structure Yeats's sonnet. Yeats's friend Senator Oliver Gogarty, model for Buck Mulligan in *Ulysses*, was taken prisoner by the IRA. Swimming to safety across the Liffey he vowed to dedicate a pair of swans to the river should he survive. His much-photographed fulfillment of his promise was a melodramatic and self-promoting gesture. Corcoran's rage is directed at what he correctly identifies as a "stunt" on the part of Yeats and his friends: both the swan-launch and the swan-sonnet are cultural interventions by those seeking power and influence in the new State. "Ireland has been put into our hands that we may shape it" (*SS* 168), Yeats said in a speech on "The

Child and the State." From Corcoran's point of view, to grant Yeats that shaping power would be to continue the English occupation of Ireland by cultural rather than political means. Anglo-Ireland was construed as a sexual fifth column, an aristocratic serpent in the bourgeois Gaelic paradise. Sexuality and its representation in print, therefore, became a site of class as well as religious struggle. After the publication of *To-morrow*, "the filthy Swan Song of Senator W. B. Yeats," the "Stinking Sonnet" or the "putrid 'Swan Poem,'"[50] as it was variously termed, was used as a continual reminder of the danger to a Gaelic Catholic nation represented by the Cloacal Combine, denizens of the literary cesspool of Anglo-Ireland. The swan was indeed drifting upon a darkening flood.

The Catholic Bulletin constructed sexual purity as analogous to racial purity. Advocating an essentialist identity politics based on dubious biological foundations, the paper described the Anglo-Irish as "silly, sordid, and segregated."

The idea of a historic Irish nation, with its one Gaelic tradition, culture, and language, assimilating but dominating all adventitious elements – Norse, Norman, English – that idea is alone the true concept of Irish nationhood.[51]

Given the exclusivity and racism of Corcoran's formulation of Irish identity, it is surprising that the *Bulletin* exempted from comment Margaret Barrington's story "Colour," which deals with a white woman's desire for a negro. The Protestants acquired the dubious honor of condemning interracial attraction. Gregory reported that the Provost of Trinity thought Robinson's story "very offensive, also Yeats's Leda – 'so unlike his early poems'. Also another story in the same number 'one must speak plainly – it is about the intercourse of white women with black men.'"[52] (Barrington says that the "nigger" is sexy because "animal-like,"[53] but no one minded that.) The Provost's disgust, like Professor Trench's letter, complicates analysis of the dispute along purely sectarian lines and proves that Yeats and his co-conspirators were capable of promoting an unlikely union of hearts between the Gaelic propagandists and Trinity College. Jesuits and elderly male professors were equally horrified by the potential for species, class, and race miscegenation in the sexuality of swans, tramps, and black men.

Yeats, who frequently compared Joyce to Rabelais, was himself labelled as "rabelaisian" by *The Catholic Bulletin*.[54] Bakhtin's reading of Rabelais, which emphasizes the power of the low, the dirty, and the grotesque to unsettle the Law, may explain some of the impact of *To-morrow*. Stallybrass and White discard Bakhtin's occasionally simplistic opposition between the grotesque and the classical for his more complex appreciation of the way in which "the grotesque is formed through a process of hybridization or inmixing of binary opposites, particularly of high and low."[55] "Hybridization" is a paradigm for "Leda and the Swan," which posits no simple opposition between the carnal and the spiritual. The brutal rapist is Jove, omniscient as well as omnipotent. This confounding of categories is mirrored in the form: Leda's "loosening thighs" and the swan's orgasmic "shudder in the loins" insert a "low" or sexually explicit diction into the hegemonic "high" form of the sonnet. Yeats rarely used the classical sonnet:[56] he thought it a "lumbering" measure when it appeared in dramatic dialogue (*E&I* 240), and described Spenser's sonnets as "intolerably artificial" (*E&I* 362). "Leda" is itself a hybrid: an octave containing two Shakespearian quatrains and a Petrarchan sestet.

Yeats found the concept of the hybrid strategically useful against the unitary, totalizing vision of the "one Gaelic tradition." Although he intermittently presented himself as a eugenicist, parading his possession of "*blood / That has not passed through any huckster's loin*" (*VP* 269), and in late works like *Purgatory* and *On the Boiler* became preoccupied by class miscegenation, his position on purity and pollution was shifting and contradictory. Defending an Anglo-Ireland represented as "silly, sordid, and segregated"[57] he claimed that the real Irish tradition was mongrel rather than pure-bred. In 1925, introducing a translation of "The Midnight Court" by the eighteenth-century Gaelic poet Brian Merriman, he praised what to the Gaelic advocates of purity must have been an embarrassment: a bawdy comic masterpiece in the Irish language.[58] With an irony available only to those who had been following the "Leda" controversy, he wished

that a Gaelic scholar had been found, or failing that some man of known sobriety of manner and of mind – Professor Trench of Trinity College, let us say – to introduce to the Irish reading public this vital, extravagant, immoral, preposterous poem. (*Ex* 281)

"The Midnight Court" is a parodic inversion of legal practice, a Bakhtinian world-turned-upside-down in which the women are on top. The sheriff who calls the poet to the court is a gigantic woman;

the judge is the Queen of the Munster fairies, Eevell; judgment is given in favor of the women plaintiffs who protest the Irish practice of marrying for money rather than sex, attack clerical celibacy because the priests are a plump and tempting lot, and want to punish men for failing to satisfy their carnal appetites. Desire is sanctioned rather than restrained by the Law. Yeats notes that Merriman, writing in penal times, had seen Ireland's dismal political and economic state reflected in her loss of sexual energy: "your lads and lasses have left off breeding" (*Ex* 284). He disingenuously pretends to be scandalized by Merriman's crudity: "Certainly it is not possible to read his verses without being shocked and horrified as city onlookers were perhaps shocked and horrified at the free speech and buffoonery of some traditional country festival" (*Ex* 283–84). In identifying Merriman's poem with Bakhtinian carnival buffoonery, Yeats claims the grotesque for Gaelic literature. He also hybridizes "The Midnight Court" by crossing it with Anglo-Ireland and arguing that Merriman borrowed the structure of his poem from Swift's *Cadenus and Vanessa* (*Ex* 281–82). The great Gaelic language poem is not only "immoral," it is a literary half-breed. The vigor of bastardy is one of Merriman's themes, and Yeats quotes a passage that protests the social stigma of illegitimacy:

> For why call a Priest in to bind and to bless
> Before candid nature can give one caress?
>
> Since Mary the Mother of God did conceive
> Without calling the clergy or begging their leave,
>
> For love is a lustier sire than law.   (*Ex* 285)

Merriman's cheerful deployment of Mary's extra-marital impregnation, at issue both in the *To-morrow* and "Cherry Tree Carol" controversies, delighted Yeats, who enjoyed turning the Virgin against her clerical advocates.

"Leda and the Swan" can thus be read as an aristocratic liberal intervention in the cultural debate about post-Treaty Irish identity. Was Ireland to become, as Yeats wished, "a modern, tolerant, liberal nation" (*SS* 160), free to deploy the resources of pagan mythology and to admire naked Greek statuary? Sexuality, bodies, and their representations occupy center stage in this ideological struggle. The Swan symbolizes all those desires the censors found threatening: in the context of the poem's reception it embodies the forces of sexual liberation. Despite Foucault's warnings against construing erotic self-expression as politically emancipatory, the subsequent cultural and social history of Ireland makes it hard to dismiss this reading, especially as the clerical regulation of sexuality weighed most heavily upon women.[59]

The moral and political debate about "filth" and its exclusion from the national self-image, however, was conducted almost entirely between men. At issue was not the right of women to control and represent their own sexuality, but the male writer's freedom to use rape as a subject in a legitimate journal. Yeats's demand that the body be recognized as "the whole handiwork of God" is admirable, but no one at the time asked whether this liberalism justified his graphic depiction of a woman violently raped by an animal. Either the subject was condemned as pagan, or it was accepted as a classical myth that needed no defense. Yeats himself, however, was aware of the likely female response: when he was asked for the poem, he replied, "there is no typist here I would ask to copy it – one a few days ago wept because put to type a speech in favour of divorce I was to deliver in the Senate" (*L* 709).

Would Yeats's typist (her tears code her as female) have objected because of the poem's obscenity or because of its sexism? Might she have seen in the relation of famous poet to female stenographer a version of the power relation between the Swan and Leda? Women had had the vote for six years, but political representation did not guarantee economic or cultural power: Yeats's putative female reader is still a typist, a copier of other people's texts. The poem she would have read in 1924, however, is different from the one women readers encounter today: not simply because Yeats revised his words, but because feminism has created new conditions of reception for a poem about rape. Contemporary feminists challenge the credentials of a liberalism that privileges male subjectivity and freedom of speech at the price of female objectification. As Catherine MacKinnon argues, "Understanding free speech as an abstract system is a liberal position. Understanding how speech also exists within a substantive system of power relations is a feminist position."[60] The Irish historicist reading therefore needs to be articulated with a feminist approach that takes account of other histories: women's history, the history of pornography, the history of the sonnet form, and the textual history of the poem.

Contemporary feminist reactions to "Leda" must also negotiate the strategic problem of appearing to echo the original religious outrage. Objections to sexism are not the same as objections to sex, but they may sound alike. In a recent interview the Irish lesbian feminist writer Mary Dorcey sums up the problem posed by depictions of rape or violence against women in the Irish cultural context:

> When pornography is discussed by feminists...we run into trouble immediately with liberals and others who are determined to protect the small area of secular liberalism that has been won in Ireland. It is very difficult to make a case that is anti-pornographic but does not seem pro-censorship by the Catholic church and its various right-wing militias.[61]

Right-wing and religious moralists do not object to the degradation of women in pornography, but to "obscenity," a culturally relative term.[62] They are also likely to be the opponents of contraception, abortion, and divorce, the last two of which are still legally prohibited in Ireland. For this reason the feminist analysis of pornography has to be articulated with care.

"Pornography" may seem an extreme term to apply to "Leda and the Swan," which is protected from such judgments by its status as "high" art. Artistic merit is one of the grounds on which a work can be defined in law as *not* pornographic.[63] But what women dislike in pornography, they have been taught to accept in canonical literature.[64] Stripped of its artistic privilege and examined in terms of its content alone "Leda and the Swan" certainly qualifies as pornography, which according to MacKinnon is distinguished from erotica by

> the graphic sexually explicit subordination of women through pictures or words that also includes women dehumanized as sexual objects, things, or commodities; enjoying pain or humiliation or rape; being tied up, cut up, mutilated, bruised, or physically hurt; in postures of sexual submission or servility or display; reduced to body parts, penetrated by objects or animals, or presented in scenarios of degradation, injury, torture.[65]

Subordination, dehumanization, pain, rape, being reduced to body parts, and penetrated by an animal: Leda gets it all. Yeats's subject, moreover, is one that has been employed for centuries on the pornographic fringe of the fine arts. Representations of Jove's amours (accompanied by Aretine's licentious verses) were fashionable in Elizabethan bedchambers;[66] while Dijkstra catalogues the popularity of Leda in titillating late nineteenth-century painting.[67] Bestiality has always been an established sub-genre of pornography: offering a visual image of female degradation, it abrogates a woman's claim to be considered human.[68] When we encounter "Leda and the Swan" in its frame as modernist masterpiece, dirty postcards featuring women and donkeys do not suggest themselves as valid analogies, and we are likely to forget its extra-canonical pornographic pedigree.

Kappeler claims that what she calls "the pornography of representation" controls the focus of any poem written by a man depicting the body (let alone the bodily violation) of a woman. The male author/subject invites the male reader to enjoy a visual spectacle in which the woman becomes an object for his scrutiny and pleasure. Occasionally the representer may be female and the represented male, but "The history of representation is the history of the male gender representing itself to itself – the power of naming is men's... Culture, as we know it, is patriarchy's self-image."[69] Kappeler assumes that the structure of all male representation of women is pornographic: she sees no justification for female pleasure in viewing or reading the works of men except the (dubious) delights of masochism.[70] If we agree, it is pointless to analyze "Leda and the Swan" or, indeed, most Western art and literature. Berger, who draws a distinction between the objectification of most female nudes and the exceptional portrait of Hélène Fourment by Rubens, allows for the occasional rupture of the straitjacket of representation.[71] His less exclusivist theory allows us to read "Leda and the Swan" in search of Leda's almost obliterated subjectivity.

"Leda and the Swan" is a representation of a representation.[72] Gregory notes that "W. B. Y. finished his poem on Leda – showed me the reproduction of the carving on which it is founded,"[73] which confirms the hypothesis of Charles Madge that the most immediate visual source for "Leda" was a hellenistic bas-relief reproduced in Elie Faure's *History of Art* (1921), which Yeats owned (Fig. 6).[74] The carving corresponds to the configuration of bird and lady in Yeats's sonnet, and Faure's overheated commentary isolates precisely the features of the bas-relief that attracted Yeats's attention:

look at the "Leda" as she stands to receive the great swan with the beating wings, letting the beak seize her neck, the foot tighten on her thigh – the trembling woman subjected to the fatal force which reveals to her the whole of life, even while penetrating her with voluptuousness and pain.[75]

Figure 6 Hellenic bas-relief, *Leda and the Swan.*

The Sadean collocation of fatal force, voluptuousness and pain
identifies Faure as a Decadent, convinced not only that Leda did
"put on his knowledge with his power," but that she did so willingly:
she "receives" the god, "letting" his beak seize her neck. Faure
interprets Leda's rape as consensual intercourse.

The sestet of Yeats's poem remained the same in all printings, but
the octave as it appeared in *To-morrow* was closer than later versions
to its visual source: the first quatrain reads:

> A rush, a sudden wheel, and hovering still
> The bird descends, and her frail thighs are pressed
> By the webbed toes, and that all-powerful bill
> Has laid her helpless face upon his breast.[76]

As in the carving, the bird is "hovering" in the air and Leda's head
is pressed against his breast. The image is grotesque. The awkward

disposition of the swan's "webbed toes" is more apparent in the carving than in the sonnet, but the disparity in height between a standing woman and an attacking bird evokes an absurdly athletic image of an airborne rapist beating his wings furiously just to stay in place.

Yeats addresses these problems, which are simultaneously problems of poetics and of power, in the revised version of his first quatrain.[77] He decreases the clumsiness of the god, increases his violence, and frames that violence as seductive:

> A sudden blow: the great wings beating still
> Above the staggering girl, her thighs caressed
> By the dark webs, her nape caught in his bill,
> He holds her helpless breast upon his breast.   (*VP* 441)

The vagueness of "rush" and "wheel" and the discursiveness of "the bird descends" are condensed into the immediacy of "a sudden blow" from nowhere. The absurdity of the hovering rapist is transformed into the violent image of "great wings beating." The bird no longer hovers and descends at the same time: he is poised in the superior position, "above" his victim. In contrast with numerous versions of the myth that represent the encounter as pleasantly lubricious (HD's "Leda" or Correggio's painting, for example),[78] Yeats forces his readers to confront the brutality of rape. Leda, previously no more than a pair of "frail thighs" and a "helpless face," is finally characterized as "the staggering girl." "Staggering" conveys precisely her body's lurch under the weight from above: the violence has a specific target and physical effect.

The use of the patronizing word "girl" for a mythological heroine suggests Yeats's later poetic coaching of Swami Purohit, whom he persuaded to "call a goddess, 'this handsome girl' or even 'a pretty girl' instead of 'a maiden of surpassing loveliness'" (*LDW* 44). Even if we read "girl" primarily as an indication of Leda's youthfulness and physical frailty, it has a shockingly intimate effect, its colloquiality eliding the gap between the mythological past and the present. It may increase the erotic charge for certain male readers, who can repeat the action with "girls" of their own acquaintance.[79] An improvement in poetics intensifies the sexual and kinetic power of the verse. The notion that the "higher" the art the less pornographic it is surely requires reconsideration.

The poetically effective replacement of "her frail thighs are pressed / By the webbed toes" with "her thighs caressed / By the dark webs" strengthens the connection between male violence and male eroticism. The action is initially a straightforward exercise of force. MacKinnon suggests, however, that for many men violence and sexuality are indistinguishable.[80] In the final version the blow followed by the caress becomes a sinister form of seduction, as the swan's poetically ridiculous "webbed toes" are transformed into the metaphorically effective "dark webs." Leda is entangled in sexual webs constructed by the deceptive promise of gentleness. Her face is not merely "laid" on the swan's breast, her "nape" (another increase in physical and verbal precision at the expense of Leda's human individuality) is "caught" in his bill. The imbalance of face/breast is replaced by a constrained alliterative equivalence: "He holds her helpless breast upon his breast." Leda is held, but in a position that suggests lovemaking. The phrasing is taken from one of Yeats's first love poems in the female voice, "The Heart of the Woman":

> O, what to me the little room
> That was brimmed up with prayer and rest;
> He bade me out into the gloom,
> And my breast lies upon his breast.   (*VSR* 230)

For the female speaker this posture implies a mutuality for which she is ready to abandon religion and convention. In the story where it first appeared, however, "The Rose of Shadow," the girl's lover is revealed to be a demon, and his promise of love leads only to her death. The same irony recurs in "Leda," for the bird's expression of desire mimics the gestures of love until physical satiation reveals his indifference to his victim.

Yeats's insistence on the power differential between rapist and victim is more forcibly rendered in the final version. The descriptive, sequential, paratactic syntax – "and hovering still," "and her frail thighs are pressed," "and that all powerful bill" – is replaced by a series of clauses whose connectives have been suppressed in the interests of terseness. We are hurried on in search of the main verb, which appears dramatically late, at the beginning of the fourth line, emphasized by heavy alliteration: "He holds her helpless." Yeats thought "Leda" was a poem in which "it is not clear whether the speaker is man or woman" (*LMR* 30) but it is hard to imagine it as voiced from the subject position of the "helpless" victim.

The major obstacle to such a reading occurs in the second quatrain, where the relationship between male force and female consent is linguistically played out. Many previous versions of the myth show Leda as ready and willing: in a passage Yeats knew, Spenser writes:

> Whiles the proud Bird ruffing his fethers wyde,
> And brushing his faire brest, did her inuade;
> She slept, yet twixt her eyelids closely spyde,
> How towards her he rusht, and smiled at his pryde.[81]

This is not rape but pornographic pretense. Leda likes swans: she allows Jove to act out the violation scenario while secretly pursuing her own gratification. The scene embodies a number of classic male assumptions about female sexuality: women love a bit of force; or when a woman says no she means yes; or women like to degrade themselves with animals. In *The Player Queen* (1919) Yeats took a Spenserian view of his inherited material. Decima chooses deliberately between actors dressed as beasts:

> Shall I fancy beast or fowl?
> Queen Pasiphae chose a bull,
> While a passion for a swan
> Made Queen Leda stretch and yawn. (*VPL* 744)

In "The Adoration of the Magi," which originally contained no reference to Leda (*VRS* 166), and which Yeats revised at the time of the *To-morrow* controversy, the message given to the old men will "so transform the world that another Leda would open her knees to the swan, another Achilles beleaguer Troy" (*Myth* 310). The phrase "Open her knees to the swan" clearly implies Leda's consent.

Yeats's later lyric, "Lullaby" (1929), also implies that the woman enjoyed the experience. A mother elides violence as she wishes that her child may sleep like Jove,

> Such a sleep and sound as fell
> Upon Eurotas' grassy bank
> When the holy bird, that there
> Accomplished his predestined will,
> From the limbs of Leda sank
> But not from her protecting care. (*VP* 522)

The male rapist's "indifferent beak" contrasts with the "protecting care" offered by the woman to the sleeping bird at the end of "Lullaby." Yet as Shakespear perspicaciously observed: "Your lullaby, though very beautiful, is extremely unsuitable for the young! Leda seems to have a peculiar charm for you – personally I'm so terrified of swans, that the idea horrifies me – a feminine point of view."[82] Her half-humorous objection demonstrates how from "a feminine point of view" this mythological rape may cause terror unmitigated by pleasure.

As we have noted, however, in contrast with Spenser or with Yeats's other versions of the story, "Leda and the Swan" initially presents the rape as the forcible violation of an unsuspecting victim. The possibility of resistance is canvassed:

> How can those terrified vague fingers push
> The feathered glory from her loosening thighs?
> And how can body, laid in that white rush,
> But feel the strange heart beating where it lies?   (*VP* 441)

Seeking to adopt the victim's point of view, Yeats moves toward granting her a subject position of her own. Ignoring the divine rapist's state of mind, the narrating voice tries to gain access to Leda's consciousness via two rhetorical questions. The epithet "vague" suggests that she is too numb with shock to fight back: unlike Spenser's peeping Leda, she is "terrified." Disorientation renders effective struggle impossible: Yeats's first question implies that she could not have prevented the rape, and therefore was not responsible for it.

The questions, however, also contain certain assumptions in which male author and male reader are complicit. Leda's "loosening thighs" may be a straightforward representation of what happens when a rape victim is forced to give up the struggle, but they may also suggest that Leda's body responds to the rapist as physically erotic. Is it her consciousness or the narrator's that tropes her aggressor as "the feathered glory"? Kappeler argues that the idea that the woman's body will involuntarily desire the rapist panders to the male view of women as "naturally" lustful creatures.[83] The omission of the possessive pronoun before "body" suggests that both bodies "feel" the beating of the other's "strange" heart. The "heart" is culturally coded to suggest emotion: in "The Heart of the Woman" the line "My heart upon his warm heart lies" (*VP* 152) expresses the complete surrender of the female speaker. This rhetoric of feeling may suggest to a male reader that, if he behaves like the swan, women will find him emotionally as well as physically irresistible. Even when

Yeats abandons the beating heart to "turn" his sonnet on a contrasting image of sexuality as genital spasm, "a shudder in the loins," another suppressed possessive allows for the disturbing possibility of a simultaneous orgasm: a shudder in both sets of loins.

The question of Leda's sexual and emotional arousal engages with the legal attitude towards the plaintiff in a rape trial. If a woman appears as a sexual being in her dress, deportment, or actions; if it can be proved that she has had and enjoyed sex with other men, we have prima facie evidence of her consent, and no crime has been committed. Pursuing Merriman's idea that "love is a lustier sire than law," Yeats uses his description of rape to flout Irish taboos against the verbal expression of sexuality. In its repetition of male cultural assumptions about women's bodies, however, his poem paradoxically contributes to the disempowerment of the rape victim: if she brings a case against her abuser, the idea that women "naturally" desire their own violation will be used to discredit her testimony. Barthes suggests that in de Sade's system the victim can choose her relationship to what is being done to her: "The scream is the victim's mark; she makes herself a victim because she chooses to scream; if, under the same vexation she were to ejaculate, she would cease to be a victim, would be transformed into a libertine."[84] Do Leda's loosening thighs make her "a libertine"? I do not know if women ever find rape erotic, although I assume they do not; but I reject the Sadean notion of choice.[85] The rape happened to Leda; she was subjected to the swan's desire. If centuries of cultural conditioning have defined women as passive and masochistic, constructing female desire as the desire to be acted upon rather than to act, then the existence of female rape fantasies is not surprising. But the gap between fantasy (which a woman can control and which is painless) and the real thing (in which she is powerless and often suffers physical harm) makes male representations of rape as pleasurable for women extremely dangerous. Not only do they invite imitation on the grounds that a rapist is giving a woman what she really wants, but, as MacKinnon argues, "pornography institutionalizes the sexuality of male supremacy, which fuses the erotization of dominance and submission with the social construction of male and female."[86] Men represent submission as both erotic and feminine; women internalize male representations of their desire and their identity as women.

Paul Fussell's analysis of the structure of the sonnet form reveals how the language of criticism is permeated by the sexuality of male supremacy. "The [octave] builds up the pressure, the [sextet] releases it; and the turn is the dramatic and climactic center of the poem ... We may even suggest that one of the emotional archetypes of the Petrarchan sonnet structure is the pattern of sexual pressure and release."[87] Fussell's analogy is based on the mechanics of male sexual response, with its single moment of climax. His orgasmic poetics are certainly appropriate to "Leda and the Swan." "A shudder in the loins" is both linguistically graphic and physically climactic. Yeats's placement of this brutally naturalistic "low" diction at the "turn" between the octave and sestet, the place of maximum formal effect, demonstrates both his fidelity to the shape of the genre and, paradoxically, the way in which his attitude to the sublimated sexuality of the Petrarchan sonnet has changed.

Like all modifications of a generic form, the poem depends for its full effect on our knowing the convention that is being inverted. Originally the sonnet was the vehicle of idealized woman-worship,[88] in which the Lady disdained the helpless male lover, who was suspended in perennially unfulfilled desire; in Yeats's poem the woman is "helpless" before "the brute blood" of her male ravisher. Having overpaid his courtly dues in his youth, Yeats swung with corresponding intensity toward the opposite extreme: rape is the underside of Romance. In troubadour poetry the knight who restrains his desire for his idealized lady is encouraged to take advantage of peasant girls.[89] Yeats also alters the static poetics of the praise-sonnet, which represents the female beloved as a series of unlinked body parts suspended in the timeless present of her lover's vain desire.[90] Leda is characterized through the anatomical blazon (thighs, nape, breast, fingers); but so is the swan (wings, webs, bill, breast, loins). The achievement of orgasm, the "shudder in the loins," breaks the Petrarchan pattern of eternal frustration. The engendering of a new historical cycle is represented as a merely mechanical convulsion, but it releases the poet from the limbo of high diction and no action.

Yeats gets from the courtly sonnet ("The Folly of Being Comforted") to the rape sonnet, from stasis to action, via the unlikely mediation of the religious sonnet. Donne's "Batter My Heart, Three-Person'd God" is the only well-known sonnet before "Leda and the Swan" to focus on rape. Yeats thought Donne "could be as metaphysical as he pleased ... because he could be as physical as he pleased" (*Au* 326), and the abruptly violent openings of the two poems, "Batter my heart" and "A sudden blow," suggest an intertextual relation between them. Donne's image of himself as "an usurpt towne" under siege is echoed by Yeats's reference to the siege of Troy. Donne urges his besieging God "to breake, blowe, burn and make me new"; Yeats imagines "The broken wall, the burning roof and tower." Donne's sexual violence propels the metaphor of the love relation between the soul and God to a conclusion that mystics embrace but clerics regard with embarrassment:

> Take mee to you, imprison mee, for I
> Except you'enthrall mee, never shall be free,
> Nor ever chast, except you ravish mee.[91]

While Yeats approaches the female consciousness interrogatively, Donne adopts a "feminine" subject position and enthusiastically implores his own violation.

Shakespeare's sonnets habitually attempt to defeat time. "Leda and the Swan," however, incorporates time into the process of the poem. Although the traditional province of the sonnet is private experience,[92] in three lines typographically broken away from the sestet Yeats ruptures the shape of his poem and opens the present moment to its terrible future consequences. As in the Petrarchan model, the sestet alters the emotional trajectory of the poem. Instead of celebrating Leda's violation as necessary for the birth of a new civilization, a response his own historical philosophy might well have sanctioned, Yeats maintains that the rape of a woman will result in violence and destruction among men: historicizing the familiar trope, he shows a sexual act engendering death:

> A shudder in the loins engenders there
> The broken wall, the burning roof and tower
> And Agamemnon dead.   (*VP* 441)

Helen and Pollux issue from one of the eggs of Leda, Clytemnestra and Castor from the other (*AV*[*B*] 51). Representing the breach in the Trojan defenses in terms of sexual penetration, Yeats posits the war as equivalent to and deriving from Leda's violent defloration. "The broken wall" leads directly to murder, as though Clytemnestra's killing of Agamemnon were retribution for the rape. Clytemnestra, who killed her husband because he sacrificed their daughter Iphigenia, is not named in the sonnet, but she inhabits it as the subtextual threat of female retaliation against male brutality. The narrating voice wonders if Leda could foresee Clytemnestra's revenge:

> Being so caught up,
> So mastered by the brute blood of the air,
> Did she put on his knowledge with his power
> Before the indifferent beak could let her drop?   (*VP* 441)

The phrase "caught up" may suggest either the swan's physical victimization of Leda, or her intense participation in the event. In asking whether she "put on" his divine "knowledge" as he had carnal "knowledge" of her, Yeats provisionally evokes a moment of epiphany similar to that posited by Faure, in which the "fatal force" of the swan "reveals to her the whole of life." The verb "put on" is ambiguous, perhaps suggesting that she was not only "*over/* powered" but "*em/*powered" by the knowledge of her engendering role in future events. The contemporary poet Mona van Duyn, however, refuses to construe rape as epiphany: to Yeats's "did she?" she responds with an emphatic negative:

> Not even for a moment. He knew, for one thing, what he was.
> When he saw the swan in her eyes he could let her drop.
> In the first look of love men find their great disguise,
> and collecting these rare pictures of himself was his life.[93]

Van Duyn's Leda confirms the subjectivity of the male through her objectification. The "love" evoked in her by his violence turns her into a mirror for his vanity, a means by which he can represent himself to himself.

But Yeats also resists the temptation, implicit in the way he has constructed his question, to assume that being raped by a god is a glamorous experience worth any amount of inconvenience. Despite the ambiguity of the rhetorical question in the penultimate line, the final line, although it ends with a question mark, has the force of a declaration. Yeats places at the conclusion of his poem, and thus formally emphasizes, the fact that Leda has been victimized by an indifferent brute. Combining overwhelming force with seductive hints of tenderness, the god has betrayed Leda into a human response to a creature both less and more than human, who can never engage with her. When his "indifferent beak" lets her drop we understand, as Yeats does, that Leda has been both physically and emotionally used, objectified, and discarded.

When the Virgin Mary said, "Be it done unto me according to Thy Will," she too became a vessel of the Divine (Male) Purpose. As we have seen, the question of Mary's instrumental sexual relation to the Godhead was part of the controversy over the original publication of "Leda and the Swan," and in the first edition of *The Tower* Yeats affirmed the relation between Leda and Mary by juxtaposing his sonnet with the poem "Wisdom."[94] "Wisdom" contrasts the clerical, elaborately hieratical image of Mary and Jesus with the naturalistic reality of the child's conception and infancy. Giving a "chryselephantine" throne and "damask" robes to God's mother, the Byzantine Church erased the embarrassment of their deity's working-class origins. Through highly formalized artistic representations they

> Amended what was told awry
> By some peasant gospeller;
> Swept the sawdust from the floor
> Of that working-carpenter.   (*VP* 440)

But for Yeats, if Leda's rape was an Annunciation, Mary's Annunciation was a rape: a physical fact he wanted to rescue from bourgeois clerical obfuscation. In "The Mother of God" the Annunciation is a "terror" borne, like Leda's, by "Wings beating about the room"; the co-option of a "common woman" by indifferent forces that care nothing for her individuality (*VP* 499). "Wisdom" demonstrates how the rhetoric of religious representation deliberately erases Mary's bodily experience. Her rape is sanitized by abstract formulae, chosen by the priests because they sound good and obscure the horror of the events:

> King Abundance got Him on
> Innocence; and Wisdom He.
> That cognomen sounded best
> Considering what wild infancy
> Drove horror from His Mother's breast.   (*VP* 440)

The "horror" dispelled by the child's normal, wild infancy is the horror of his conception: "The threefold terror of love" (*VP* 499). The personifications Abundance, Innocence, and Wisdom disguise the trio of rapist, victim, and bastard child. "Wisdom," like "Leda and the Swan," demonstrates Yeats's identification with the human against the divine, with the peasant gospeller and the common woman against the priesthood. Defending the folk vision of the pregnant Virgin in "The Cherry Tree Carol," he declared, "the

Mother of God is no Catholic possession; she is a part of our imagination" (*UP2* 464).

Yeats's personal empathy with two female rape victims who were closely associated in his mythological imagination does not, however, entirely dispel the doubts of a feminist reader. "Leda and the Swan" demonstrates what happens when a writer cares more about using explicitly sexual situations as a strategy for challenging censorship than with the implications of that strategy for women, who are both the subjects of and subject to the power of his imagination. Yet it also exposes the brutality of the male or divine exercise of force. We cannot make a tidy separation between a positive liberal-historicist hermeneutic and a negative feminist one. Analyzing Swift's combination of misogyny with anti-imperialism, Laura Brown argues that we should bring "positive and negative hermeneutics together" to expose what she sees as "the necessary intimacy of structures of liberation and oppression in eighteenth-century culture."[95] To read "Leda and the Swan" along the contrasting axes of Irish history and women's history reveals a similar intimacy between liberation and oppression. In a Catholic culture the revision of Virgin into rape victim challenges the repressive ideology of female purity but risks reinscribing the woman into the equally repressive category "loose" (as in "loosening thighs"). To challenge the gathering impetus towards censorship Yeats flirts with pornography. A Foucauldian feminist might emphasize that the lifting of verbal sexual taboos does not necessarily liberate women; but a consideration of the effects of censorship in Ireland upon the dissemination of information about contraception suggests that the virtues of transgression should not be underestimated.

CHAPTER 9

The erotics of the ballad

Yeats's sequence of love poems, "A Man Young and Old," written during 1926 and 1927, was first published as "More Songs from an Old Countryman"[1] and "Four Songs from the Young Countryman."[2] In 1928 Yeats removed his attribution of the speaker's social origin, and placed the songs near the end of *The Tower*. These poems manifest a complex intersection between contemporary Irish social history and Yeats's modernization of the love lyric. As often in Yeats, this modernization consisted in a turning back: a reversion past the Renaissance iambic pentameter and the courtly sonnet to the popular ballad. Ballad metrics, folk simplicity, and peasant speakers combine to produce political as well as literary effects. "A Man Young and Old" begins the attempt to construct the erotic as a site of popular resistance that was to culminate in Crazy Jane's defiance of the Irish Episcopate.

Perloff has called these poems a "sequence of mythic ballads."[3] Their metrical pattern is consistent: alternating tetrameters and trimeters, rhyming on the even lines. Seven of the eleven poems use a six-line stanza rather than the Child quatrain: Yeats's formal models included literary ballads, translations from the Gaelic, and Anglo-Irish broadsides, which employ various stanzaic forms. By combining his rhyming units into longer stanzas, he also varies his structure without deviating from what he called "an old 'sing-song' that has yet a mathematical logic" (*UP2* 462). His *Oedipus* translation is in "fourteeners," or seven-stress lines: a form that Yeats found in the Irish street ballads collected by his brother Jack.[4]

Numerous twentieth-century English poets wrote "folk" poetry: Hardy, Houseman, De La Mare, and Auden, for example. Introducing his *Oxford Book of Modern Verse* Yeats noted that: "Folk-song, unknown to the Victorians as their attempts to imitate it show, must, because never declamatory or eloquent, fill the scene" (*OBMV* xiii).

In Yeats's devotion to the ballad form, however, aesthetics cannot be separated from national loyalties and social critique. The Irish ballad written in English has, since the late eighteenth century, frequently been the vehicle of anti-Imperialism,[5] and in his youth Yeats celebrated the propagandistic advantages of the genre. Adopting the form that was to dominate his later love poetry, "A Man Young and Old" signals a return to early enthusiasms. In "Popular Ballad Poetry of Ireland" (1889) he had praised the native Gaelic tradition that withered under colonial rule; but he also celebrated nineteenth-century translations and patriotic ballads written in English, "a pseudofolk tradition" that, according to Thuente, transformed the melancholy passivity of native folk poetry into stirring and "manly" nationalist verse.[6] He admired popular ballads that produced an image capable of arousing erotic desire and displacing it towards the nation: "Irish Jacobites... substituted some personification of Ireland, some Dark Rosaleen, for a mortal mistress" (*Ex* 283). Yeats's early project was the formation of the Irish subject into a nationalist subject through a poetics of desire for the free nation;[7] as a medium long associated in Ireland with both love and patriotism the ballad provided an appropriate vehicle.

Yeats included the Fenian Charles Kickham's "The Irish Peasant Girl" in his selections for *A Book of Irish Verse* (1895). Less obviously militaristic than Mangan's "Dark Rosaleen," Kickham's ballad nevertheless suggests the power of erotic sentimentality to form patriotic emotion. It is indebted to Wordsworth's "Lucy Grey":

> She lived beside the Anner,
> At the foot of Sliev-na-mon.[8]

It is therefore an imitation of an imitation, since, as Yeats observed, "Coleridge and Wordsworth were influenced by the publication of Percy's *Reliques* to the making of a simplicity altogether unlike that of old ballad-writers" (*Ex* 211). Yeats did not, however, dismiss literary ballads as inauthentic: in this he was in tune with anti-hierarchical thinking about the genre.[9] He bore personal witness to the emotive capacity of mediocre popular verse: "I began idly reading verses describing the shore of Ireland as seen by a returning, dying emigrant. My eyes filled with tears and yet I knew the verses were badly written" (*Au* 102). "The Irish Peasant Girl," which also deploys the well-used trope of the dying emigrant, plays skillfully with the pathos to be elicited when the victim is a pretty young girl. The fate of the dead girl is linked to the fate of her country: she becomes a surrogate for Ireland. Her death alone can move the hardened speaker to sympathy:

> Ah, cold, and well-nigh callous,
>   This weary heart has grown
> For thy helpless fate, dear Ireland,
>   And for sorrows of my own;
> Yet a tear my eye will moisten
>   When by Anner's side I stray,
> For the lily of the mountain foot
>   That withered far away.[10]

The tear that will moisten the speaker's otherwise dry eye represents the surplus emotion generated when the figure of Ireland's plight is also the focus of sexual desire. Yeats was determined to harness that surplus emotion while writing less hackneyed verse:

When the Fenian poet says that his heart has grown cold and callous – "For thy hapless fate, dear Ireland, and sorrows of my own" – he but follows tradition, and if he does not move us deeply, it is because he has no sensuous musical vocabulary. (*Au* 151)

Yeats's ambivalence about the literary quality of Anglo-Irish nineteenth-century ballads never led him to discount their popular appeal or their propagandistic value. At the end of his life he reiterated his appraisal of the ballad writers of *The Nation*: "they had one quality I admired and admire: they were not separated individual men; they spoke or tried to speak out of a people to a people; behind them stretched the generations" (*E&I* 510). He knew that "At the close of the eighteenth century Dublin street singers had some wealth and much influence; a political ballad had more effect than a speech." Arguing that in Ireland "The political ballads have never ceased to be written and sung,"[11] he returned to his earlier fusion of genre, class, and national pride:

It is centuries since England has written ballads. Many beautiful poems in ballad verse have been written; but the true ballad – the poem of the populace – she has let die; commercialism and other matters have driven it away: she has no longer the conditions. (*UP*1 147)

Yeats's early criticism is permeated by the materialist analysis of literature he learned from William Morris.[12] English "commercialism" accounts for the degeneracy of her artistic production, while Ireland's underdeveloped industries and rural economy allow access to the source of artistic health: the populace. Yeats views the Irish ballad as the oral expression of a communal folk culture, one he contrasts negatively with the bourgeois, capitalist, and individualist print culture of England. Unlike the purist devotees of Child, who established a rigid hierarchy of ballad genres, he does not scorn the hybrid form of the street or broadside ballad, which was particularly rich in Irish patriotic material. Since he does not distinguish between rural Gaelic, street, and political ballads,[13] his definition of "the populace" perforce includes the urban community. Many years after he had become "less of a Socialist" (*Mem* 21) he still saw the ballad as a crucial site of national and class antagonism. In 1906 he wrote:

Ireland, her imagination at its noon before the birth of Chaucer, has created the most beautiful literature of a whole people that has been anywhere since Greece and Rome, while English literature, the greatest of all literatures but that of Greece, is yet the literature of a few. Nothing of it but a handful of ballads about Robin Hood has come from the folk or belongs to them rightly, for the good English writers, with a few exceptions that seem accidental, have written for a small cultivated class; and is not this the reason? Irish poetry and Irish stories were made to be spoken or sung, while English literature, alone of great literatures, because the newest of them all, has all but completely shaped itself in the printing-press. In Ireland to-day the old world that sang and listened is, it may be for the last time in Europe, face to face with the world that reads and writes, and their antagonism is always present under some name or other in Irish imagination and intellect. (*Ex* 206)

Yeats's political partiality is evident in his canon construction: he excludes all but the Robin Hood ballads from "English Literature," he polemically (and incorrectly) assigns to the Celtic North all the ballads collected by Child in the 1890s,[14] and he persistently describes the traditional ballad as "Scots" (*Au* 150). He is, however, accurate in his identification of early twentieth-century Irish culture as more orally based than English culture. Even in 1982 Walter Ong could still call Ireland "a country which in every region preserves massive residual orality."[15]

The supposed orality of poetry became one of Yeats's central aesthetic principles. "I naturally dislike print and paper" (*E&I* 13), he claimed; and insisted hyperbolically: "I have remembered nothing that I read, but only those things that I heard or saw" (*Au* 47). His method of composition, which involved what Schuchard calls "eerie poetic murmuring," began with a sound scheme. From 1890 to 1912 he worked with Farr on chanting poems to the psaltery, an experiment that was crucially important for his "auditory poetics."[16] On revising the proofs of his collected edition in 1932 he observed that his lyric verse was "all speech rather than writing" (*L* 798). Whether or not this distinction is theoretically tenable, Yeats's aesthetic of speech imposed on his verse standards of comprehensibility and dramatic immediacy that distinguish it from that of elitist modernists like Eliot. In his 1935 collection of Broadsides Yeats noted that street singers "had to shout, clatter-bones in hand, to draw the attention of the passer-by."[17] For Yeats the poetics of orality is also a politics, which rejects bourgeois individualism and the solitude of the study in the interests of public, communal experience. His Utopian vision derives ultimately from the Tory medievalism of Carlyle and Ruskin, but Yeats acquired it from the communist William Morris, although Morris's own literary ballads failed to be "popular":[18]

I owe to him [Morris] many truths, but I would add to those truths the certainty that all the old writers, the masculine writers of the world, wrote to be spoken or to be sung, and in a later age to be read aloud for hearers who had to understand swiftly or not at all and who gave up nothing of life to listen, but sat, the day's work over, friend by friend, lover by lover. (*Ex* 221)

This passage was written in 1906, when Yeats was full of Nietzschean enthusiasm for virility. Masculinity is thus defined as the access to voice: it is manly to be oral. Elsewhere, however, Yeats associates orality with women: his storytelling mother and the women who transmit ballads through the family. Ong discusses what he calls the "psychodynamics of orality" in terms that resemble those of Yeats's ideal: "Oral communication unites people in groups. Writing and reading are solitary activities that throw the psyche back on itself."[19] Yeats, however, also celebrates the dialogue between literacy and orality. He was delighted by evidence that the popular voice could be anonymously augmented by the literate poet: "walking with Douglas Hyde I heard haymakers sing what he recognised as his own words and I begged him to give up all coarse oratory that he might sing such words" (*Ex* 337). For Yeats a necessary corollary of the communal ideal was the abdication of authorial privilege. He describes the anonymity conferred by absorption in the popular memory in terms that anticipate the currently accepted theory of communal recreation, which explains the ballads as individual compositions taken up, altered, and orally transmitted by illiterate people:[20]

In Ireland, where still lives almost undisturbed the last folk tradition of western Europe, the songs of Campbell and Colum draw from that tradition their themes, return to it, and are sung to Irish airs by boys and girls who have never heard the names of the authors. (*OBMV* xiii)

Yeats wanted to break away from the commodification of the word and the notion of literary proprietorship:[21] "I disliked the isolation of the work of art. I wished through the drama, through a commingling of verse and dance, through singing that was also speech, through what I called the applied arts of literature, to plunge it back into social life" (*Ex* 300).

Writing drama prompted a new appraisal of the Renaissance, which Yeats, following Ruskin and Morris, identified as the originary moment of capitalism: "The capture of a Spanish treasure ship in the time of Elizabeth made England a capitalist nation" (*Ex* 334). Capitalism spelt the end of orality, for in the time of Elizabeth "English ballad literature began to die" (*UP*1 147), while in subjugated but pre-capitalist Ireland the Gaelic ballad thrived. The poetic language of the English folk tradition was superseded by neo-classical models:

The metaphors and language of Euphuism, compounded of the natural history and mythology of the classics ... injured the simplicity and unity of the speech! Shakespeare wrote at the time when solitary great men were gathering to themselves the fire that had once flowed hither and thither among all men, when individualism in work and thought and emotion was breaking up the old rhythms of life, when the common people, sustained no longer by the myths of Christianity and of still older faiths, were sinking into the earth. (*E&I* 110)

Yeats's suspicion of English Renaissance individualism is inseparable from his suspicion of the blank verse line, which seems to him its prosodic expression: one wholly inappropriate to Irish culture:

When I wrote in blank verse I was dissatisfied ... our Heroic Age went better, or so I fancied, in the ballad metre of *The Green Helmet*. There was something in what I felt about Deirdre, about Cuchulain, that rejected the Renaissance and its characteristic metres ... When I speak blank verse and analyse my feelings, I stand at a moment of history when instinct, its traditional songs and dances, its general agreement, is of the past. (*E&I* 523–24)

Yeats's prosodic choices, therefore, are historically motivated and consciously oppositional. The lectures and pamphlets of Morris that turned him briefly into a socialist also enabled him to anticipate the speculations of critics like Easthope, who claims that the pentameter is a hegemonic form: "There is a solid institutional continuity of the pentameter in England from the Renaissance to at least 1900. Like linear perspective in graphic art and Western harmony in music, the pentameter may be an epochal form, one co-terminous with bourgeois culture from the Renaissance till now." Easthope sees the accentual-syllabic pentameter as relegating the older accentual or pure stress meter (four stresses to the line, with an indefinite number of unstressed syllables) to a subordinate or oppositional position as "the appropriate metre for nursery rhymes, the lore of school-children, ballad, industrial folk song."[22] Modernists like Ezra Pound, determined to break the tyranny of the "goddam iamb," move into free verse, but Yeats goes back to popular tradition for his metrics. Parkinson asserts that there is no reason to suppose that Yeats ever composed in accentual-syllabic feet, and identifies even those lines that appear to be pentameter as decasyllabics: "The main modes of his prosody are either the stress line or the syllabic line."[23] According to Easthope, one of the crucial distinctions between pure stress meter and pentameter is that

In accentual metre the stress of the intonation and the abstract pattern coincide and reinforce each other; in pentameter they are counterpointed. The coincidence in accentual metre calls for an emphatic, heavily stressed performance, one typically recited or chanted, often in association with rhythmic gestures, clapping, dancing. In chanting, rhythmic repetitions take complete priority over natural intonation, subsuming it, and this is the metrical "space" for a collective voice.[24]

Chanting to the psaltery involved reinforcing poetic rhythms by musical notes. In a late radio broadcast Yeats incorporated clapping into the recitation of his political ballad "Come Gather Round Me, Parnellites." Because he was tone deaf his command of pitch was non-existent, and appreciation of counterpoint impossible, but rhythm was paramount. He disliked "art" music, probably because he was unable to recognize its melodic and harmonic forms, and fought with composers who attempted to set his verse.[25] He never ceased, however, to search for the perfect marriage between words and music, one in which verse

must be set for the speaking voice, like the songs that sailors make up or remember, and a man at the far end of the room must be able to take it down on a first hearing ... I have but one art, that of speech, and my feeling for music dissociated from speech is very slight ... I hear with older ears than the musician, and the songs of countrypeople and of sailors delight me. (*Ex* 217–18)

Yeats's nautical poetics reinforced his folk aesthetics: sea shanties are work songs, organically connected to the labor of those who sing them. If as a child his absorption in traditional ballads stimulated a lonely longing "for some such end as True Thomas found" (*Au* 78), he also socialized with the sailors on his grandfather Pollexfen's vessels and with the fishermen and pilots of Rosses Point.

After 1926 the ballad came to compete with Yeats's more complex stanzaic forms, like the *ottava rima* and the *rime royale*, as the dominant prosodic structure of his verse. Always the vehicle of nationalist politics, it now became the vehicle of sexual politics as well. As we have seen, Yeats, opposing the clerical vision of the State, argued that censorship would exclude from Ireland "all great love poetry" (*SS* 177). In an erotophobic culture that tried to define indecency as "calculated to arouse sexual passion,"[26] he deployed love poetry as a strategy of poetic resistance. In a culture rapidly becoming bourgeois he marshalled the popular resonances of the ballad form. He adopted not only its metrical structure, but also the emotional atmosphere and attitude towards the body peculiar to the Child ballads, which are characterized by their casual acceptance of sexuality. Love is often passionate and enduring but seldom sentimentalized, and nearly always physically expressed: many ballad heroines become pregnant, and some are murdered by their relatives or lovers as a consequence.[27] This stark aesthetic is softened by neither chivalry nor religion.[28]

Just before he wrote "A Man Young and Old" Yeats was forcibly reminded of the power of ballad sexuality to disturb bourgeois clerical sensibilities when the Christian Brothers publicly burned "The Cherry Tree Carol," a folk ballad unusual in having a religious theme and treating it naturalistically: the pregnant Virgin feels a craving for cherries that the sexually jealous St. Joseph is disinclined to satisfy:

> Then up spake Joseph,
> With his words so unkind
> Let them gather cherries
> That brought thee with child.   (*UP2* 462)

The Christian Brothers reported their Nazi-style incendiarism to the Committee of Enquiry on Evil Literature with a mixture of self-advertisement and economic calculation that conveys the precise flavor of what Yeats was up against: "We telephoned to the *Evening Herald* for a photographer. On his arrival we set on fire all the collected specimens together with those we had in this office. The whole blaze cost us £4.10s.0d. plus a gallon of paraffin."[29] Yeats's brother Jack, a ballad enthusiast and collector, had published "The Cherry Tree Carol" in the Broadside series issued by Cuala Press from 1908 through 1915.[30] In "The Need for Audacity of Thought" (which was refused publication in *The Irish Statesman* by the prudent AE), Yeats defended both the orthodoxy of the carol and the class that made and sang it. It expresses the mystery of the Incarnation by showing "God, in the indignity of human birth ... I can see no reason for the anger of the Christian Brothers, except that they do not believe in the Incarnation." He concluded combatively that: "The intellect of Ireland is irreligious" (*UP2* 462–63, 464). Calling the carol a "masterpiece," he invoked the popular mind in its defense: "It has been sung to our own day by English and Irish countrymen, but it shocks the Christian Brothers" (*UP2* 462). In attacking a popular ballad, the priests attack the wisdom of the people, the countrymen.

Apart from Peter, "a pushing man" (*VP* 456), Yeats's "countrymen" are not the strong farmers, but the "peasantry" whom he instructed Irish poets to "Sing" in "Under Ben Bulben" (*VP* 639). The cultural values of the new state after 1922 were not only Catholic: they were rural petty-bourgeois. "Familism," which ensured the continuity of inheritance and prevented the splitting up of farms, encouraged sexual conservatism.[31] Against post-Famine sexual restrictiveness and consolidation of Church control, Yeats posited an image of the class below the farmers, the landless peasantry and the migrant laborers or "journeymen" (a class that rapidly declined in numbers after the Famine), as preoccupied with desire and sexuality. Studying the conservative small farmers of Clare in the 1930s, Arensburg and Kimball noted that landholders associated aberrant sexual behavior with "the debased conduct of the lower ranks of the landless and disreputable of the countryside."[32] Yeats's aristocratic "dream of the noble and the beggar-man" constructed the landless peasantry as desiring subjects in the new Free State, and the Free State itself as a political body open to desire. Hence the original attribution of "A Man Young and Old" to the young and old *Countryman*, and the claim, registered through the ballad meter and rhyme scheme, to participate in the popular consciousness.

It was not sufficient to posit the countryman as the locus of desire: at stake for a love poet was the question of what kind of desire, and for what kind of woman. In 1915 Yeats was still "The poet stubborn with his passion... / When age might well have chilled his blood" ("Broken Dreams," *VP* 356). Ten years later, the short lyrics of "A Man Young and Old" use the ballad form to reassess the assumptions and the diction of the Petrarchan lover. There is, however, a tension between the poems' autobiographical cast and the anonymity proper to the form: a tension that Yeats was not to resolve until he adopted the female voices of Crazy Jane and the Woman Young and Old.

The young countryman is a peasant afflicted by the courtly ethos. In "First Love" Yeats returns to the relation between the doomed lover and the murderous, moon-identified beauty that had provided the staple of his own early verse. His questioning of George Yeats's spirits had also returned obsessively to the theme:

> Though nurtured like the sailing moon
> In beauty's murderous brood,
> She walked awhile and blushed awhile
> And on my pathway stood
> Until I thought her body bore
> A heart of flesh and blood.

The aristocratic origins of the convention are undercut by the linguistic awkwardness of the peasant speaker, a parody of the "palely loitering" knight from the greatest of Romantic ballads, "La Belle Dame Sans Merci":

> She smiled and that transfigured me
> And left me but a lout,
> Maundering here, and maundering there.　　　　(*VP* 451)

The line "Maundering here, and maundering there" is deliberately anti-romantic. The lady is less a Keatsian "faery's child" than a version of the visionary *spéirbhean* of the *aisling* tradition. The quasi-oxymoronic expression "beauty's murderous brood" suggests both the famous oxymoron from "Easter 1916," the "terrible beauty" born of patriotic sacrifice, and the threatening "murderous innocence of the sea" from "A Prayer for my Daughter." The moon-woman has a "heart of stone," which reflects Yeats's previous fear that excess of nationalist desire "May make a stone of the heart"; and the image of the countryman "transfigured" into a lout bathetically undercuts the heroic transformation of the patriots of

"Easter 1916," who were "changed utterly." The flirtatious appeal of the lady who blocks the speaker's way, blushing and smiling, but who never delivers on her sexual promise, is related to the seductions of Cathleen ni Houlihan, who demands that her male devotees give her all but who has "never set out the bed for any" (*VPL* 226). "First Love" projects onto the female persona Yeats's negative feelings about the kind of state that had evolved after the revolution.

"Human Dignity" extends the imagery of moon and stone and continues the intertextual reference to "Easter 1916." The iconic moon, like the ideal of the patriot, repays no one on the personal level; in its universal "kindness" it is indifferent to particular sorrows or private desires. The lover invokes the verbal code of the Renaissance lyric in which the "kindness" of a mistress ought to signal her sexual willingness. The mistress refuses to recognize this code. Her "heart of stone" turns human sorrow into lapidary myth, "a scene / Upon a painted wall," and the dumbstruck lover himself into a "bit of stone" (*VP* 452).

In "The Mermaid" the lyric "I" yields to a condensed third person ballad narrative:

> A mermaid found a swimming lad,
> Picked him for her own,
> Pressed her body to his body,
> Laughed; and plunging down
> Forgot in cruel happiness
> That even lovers drown.   (*VP* 452–53)

Yeats here alludes to Burne Jones's *The Depths of the Sea* (Fig. 7),[33] in which an enigmatically smiling mermaid clasps a young man whose posture suggests that of a moribund captive. Yeats, however, is not merely reproducing the *fin de siècle* cliché of the vampire woman: the poem's context within this sequence suggests that he is criticizing male representations of the woman-nation, including his own, as insisting on the displacement of desire into death. Unlike the first two poems, "The Mermaid" figures a sexually confident woman who has "picked" the man and taken the physical initiative.[34] She appears absent-minded about his oxygen deficit, guilty not of murder but of negligence, yet her oxymoronic "cruel happiness" marks her as another "terrible beauty."

Reversing gender roles but retaining the tragic outcome, Yeats in "The Death of the Hare" reflects on woman as prey rather than

Figure 7 Sir Edward Burne Jones, *The Depths of the Sea*.

woman as predator. His juxtaposition of radically opposed definitions of the female role in love exhibits both representations as ideological. Acknowledging the coercive force of apparently dead metaphors, Yeats deliberately deconstructs the traditional trope of love as a hunt. If the male is a hunter, the only possible end for the prey is death. The game of compliment, the social equivalent of loosing the "yelling pack" on the hare, implies the curtailment of the woman's freedom, the loss of her "wildness."

> Then suddenly my heart is wrung
> By her distracted air
> And I remember wildness lost
> And after, swept from there,
> Am set down standing in the wood
> At the death of the hare. (*VP* 453)

Yeats, who valued wildness, understood that for women patriarchal marriage represents capture. On one of the rare occasions when his courtship of Gonne was going well, he wrote: "I had even as I watched her a sense of cruelty, as though I were a hunter taking captive some beautiful wild creature" (*Mem* 49). Of "The Death of the Hare" he said, "the poem means that the lover may, while loving, feel sympathy with his beloved's dread of captivity" (*L* 840–41). The young countryman poems thus provide meta-commentary on the traditional rhetoric of poetic love: its tropes point inexorably towards death for both male and female protagonists.

The poems attributed to the old countryman abandon this worn-out rhetoric to challenge the discourse of purity that controlled official Free State policy. In the process Yeats attempts a radical revision of romantic aesthetics, trying, despite the pessimistic concluding chorus from *Oedipus at Colonus*, to uncouple Eros from Thanatos, to celebrate sex without sacrifice. Anticipating his later declaration that lust and rage were just as appropriate for the pensioner as for the man in his prime, Yeats sets out to destroy the conventional image of the old as the peaceful repositories of wisdom and good counsel. The central trope in this poetics is that of desire out of season: the sexual desire of the old. Bakhtin considers old age to be a location of the oppositional grotesque:[35] in "A Man Young and Old" desire is rendered doubly anomalous and improper in being attributed to what Daniel O'Connell had called "the finest peasantry upon earth" (*Au* 204).

A satirical ballad that Yeats places immediately after "A Man Young and Old" provides the political context for the old country-man poems:

> They hold their public meetings where
> Our most renownèd patriots stand,
> One among the birds of the air,
> A stumpier on either hand;
> And all the popular statesmen say
> That purity built up the State
> And after kept it from decay;
> Admonish us to cling to that
> And let all base ambition be,
> For intellect would make us proud
> And pride bring in impurity:
> The three old rascals laugh aloud.   (*VP* 460)

"The Three Monuments" is usually glossed by Yeats's 1925 divorce speech in the Senate, in which he evidenced the sexual immorality of O'Connell, Nelson, and Parnell in order to oppose indissoluble marriage and affirm the sacredness of individual desire (*SS* 97–98). In a crude sexual pun the three "stand" in public to remind the Irish of the erotic energies they seek to suppress. Superior to contemporary "popular statesmen," they look down on their squeamish successors with Nietzschean gaiety: "The three old rascals laugh aloud." (Although Parnell died young Yeats makes him an honorary "old rascal," as if only in age can one cast prudery aside.) Ambition, intellect, and pride are boldly and approvingly associated with decay, baseness, impurity, and age. Yeats defends this paradoxical association with increasing energy in the last phase of his career.

Yeats's association of ribaldry with the countryman is not merely fanciful: writing of the late 1920s Arensburg and Kimball record that even the prudish small farmers indulge in "taunts about prowess and mild ridicule for the possession of a greater relish than is meet, or fanciful recitation of past magnificent misdeeds ... details of amorous desire and accomplishment are given with considerable gusto, and greeted and reiterated again and again amid hearty laughter." They caution, however, that the country tradition of verbal ribaldry is no indicator of sexual activity: it reinforces through the sanction of laughter the strict moral code of the farmers.[36] Yeats wishes to disrupt that code. The old countryman, instead of reflecting wisely at the fireside, is driven "crazy" by the thought of lost sexual opportunities.

"The Empty Cup" laments Yeats's inability to appreciate the sexual generosity of Shakespear,[37] to whom Yeats later wrote: "I shall be a sinful man to the end, and think upon my death-bed of all the nights I wasted in my youth" (*L* 790). "Moon-accursed" by the *femme fatale* of "First Love," the young man "Hardly dared to wet his mouth" with the sexual fluid contained in the symbolically feminine cup, for fear that he would be overwhelmed by the experience. Now the cup is "dry as bone" (*VP* 454). The lover exchanges the lyric form of Petrarchan sublimation for the ballad form of active and practical desire only to discover that although the spirit is willing the flesh is weak.

The decay of the body, however, increases the vehemence of desire. In "His Memories" the broken tree under which the young countryman lay in dumb endurance becomes a metaphor for the grotesque body of the old countryman, whose arms are "like the twisted thorn." The rural images that pervade the sequence become crudely colloquial as the old man, describing himself as a "holy show," asserts that women would "sooner leave their cossetting / To hear a jackass bray" (the jackass is a traditional image of sexual potency) (*VP* 454–55). Yeats's persona is autobiographical, but the "old sing-song" of the simple form permits him to take extravagant attitudes towards his experience. In a move that anticipates his later construction of female desire as obsessed with "desecration and the lover's night" (*VPL* 989), the old man reflects on his "magnificent misdeeds," bragging about his physical conquest of the *femme fatale* who once enjoyed his lovemaking with masochistic ecstasy:

> The first of all the tribe lay there
> And did such pleasure take –
> She who had brought great Hector down
> And put all Troy to wreck –
> That she cried into this ear,
> "Strike me if I shriek."   (*VP* 455)

The inaccessible woman, the Helen of "No Second Troy," is represented as eager for her own debasement, begging to be beaten. Even if this poem refers to Yeats's short-lived physical intimacy with Gonne, it remains problematic. In his eagerness to deconstruct the courtly form and to exalt the pleasures of the body, the speaker swings from deathly asexual adoration to sexual violence. The liberating power of female *jouissance* in a culture dominated by the

Virgin Mary is undercut by his presentation of that pleasure as another form of victimage. In this he may have been influenced by his formal model, the ballad, in which numerous heroines gladly endure physical abuse from the men they love.[38]

Ballad cruelty and the unsentimental tone of ballad narrative in the face of tragedy color Yeats's depiction of "The Friends of his Youth," Old Madge and Peter. In a new development of the "stone" image Madge carries "a stone upon her breast" and sings it a lullaby:

> She that has been wild
> And barren as a breaking wave
> Thinks that the stone's a child.   (*VP* 456)

The word "wild" carries stronger sexual connotations in Irish speech than in English, so we infer that Madge has had a promiscuous but infertile past; now in age her motherhood is a crazy masquerade. Through the image of the moon she is connected with the equally barren woman of "First Love," but in keeping with the coarseness of the old man's diction the moon is presented as "pot-bellied," pregnant, rather than as virginally romantic.

The image of the barren mother nursing a stone can be unpacked politically. Yeats thought Gonne's work to free the treason felony prisoners "brought to light the woman in her" and identified her with "Mother Ireland" (*Mem* 107). Later disillusionment with what he saw as her political inflexibility led him to formulate the idea that women "give themselves to an opinion as if [it] were some terrible stone doll" (*Mem* 192). "Easter 1916" took up the image of the stone as obsessive political commitment and contrasted it with the living mother who murmurs tenderly over her sleeping child. In the twenties Gonne was famous as one of the founders of the Women's Prisoners' Defense League, popularly known as "the Mothers." Every week, dressed in flowing black clothes, she led a march to O'Connell Street and made a speech demanding the release of Republican prisoners.[39] Yeats described with a mixture of awe and disapproval "those dwindling meetings assembled in O'Connell Street or at some prison gate by almost the sole surviving friend of my early manhood, protesting in sibylline old age, as once in youth and beauty, against what seems to her a tyranny" (*UP*2 487–88). One of "The Friends of his Youth," then, is certainly Gonne: not Gonne the mother of two but Gonne in her guise as Mother Ireland, the mother of prisoners, the woman who wrote to Yeats, "No power on earth can move the Mothers – the police know this" (*AYF* 435). After the experience of Civil War Yeats charges that Mother Ireland is barren: she has nursed not a living child but a nation with a heart of stone. Mrs. Tancred and Juno Boyle, mothers bereaved by the war in O'Casey's *Juno and the Paycock* (1924), use the same metaphor: "Mother o' God, Mother o' God, have pity on us all! Blessed Virgin, where were you when me darlin' son was riddled with bullets, when me darlin' son was riddled with bullets? Sacred Heart o' Jesus, take away our hearts o' stone, and give us hearts o' flesh!"[40] O'Casey responds intertextually to "Easter 1916," while Yeats in re-interrogating his own image must have had O'Casey's famous and twice-repeated prayer in his mind. Disillusionment with Mother Ireland was common in the 1920s: in *Ulysses* Joyce satirized her as the whining and bloodthirsty "old Gummy Granny,"[41] and after Republican women took the lead in objecting to *The Plough and the Stars*, O'Casey grumbled that "the one who had the walk of a queen could be a bitch at times." Hatred of a stereotype created by men slides easily into a hatred of women men see as conforming to that stereotype. O'Casey's vision of Cathleen is projected back onto Gonne, who supported Hannah Sheehy Skeffington at the debate on the play: "Sean saw, not her who was beautiful, and had the walk of a queen, but the Poor Old Woman, whose voice was querulous, from whom came many words that were bitter, and but few kind."[42] Yeats, on the other hand, refuses to dissociate himself from Old Madge. He had attacked the "shrieking" of political women in "Michael Robartes and the Dancer," but here the speaker admits with tears that "her shriek was love" (*VP* 456). Gonne wrote to Yeats that their shared belief in the "power of love & the sterility of hate" had led them in opposite directions: while he voted for harsh measures against Republican prisoners, she had founded the Women's Prisoners' Defense League: "I told them we were invincible because we relied on the greatest power in the Universe, love" (*AYF* 435). The politics of the oxymoron are the politics of admitted contradiction, opposites not reconciled but yoked by violence together. The paradox of the "terrible beauty" is that terror can still be beautiful, that excess of love is still love, and that the speaker's memories of Madge can be partly tender.

These memories are passionately evoked in "Summer and Spring," a parody of "Among School Children" (1926), in which Aristophanes' tale of lovers as separated halves of an original sphere symbolizes a moment of ecstatic union. In "Summer and Spring" the lecherous old countryman debunks the Aristophanic myth. He and Madge once sat under the old thorn-tree,

> And when we talked of growing up
> Knew that we'd halved a soul
> And fell the one in t'other's arms
> That we might make it whole.

Their symbolic mathematics, however, are confounded by the revelation that Madge has also halved a soul with Peter, and also healed the split "Under that very tree." The sphere was divided into three. Instead of developing the tragic potential of Peter's "murdering look" into a traditional ballad tale of violence occasioned by sexual jealousy, however, Yeats ends his poem with a jaunty and (in the Irish context) shocking affirmation of the wild woman with two lovers:

> O what a bursting out there was,
> And what a blossoming,
> When we had all the summer-time
> And she had all the spring!   (*VP* 456–57)

The word "blossoming" echoes the last stanza of "Among School Children," in which "The body is not bruised to pleasure soul" (*VP* 445). Here the reference is not ironic: the stately *ottava rima* and the brisk ballad meter carry the same impassioned protest against the mutilation of the whole person perpetrated by those who devalue physical experience.

It has been suggested that the traditional ballads were predominantly transmitted by women,[43] and "The Secrets of the Old" are female secrets, including the fact that older women fantasize more about sex than younger ones. The speaker's ignorance about what women really want is belatedly corrected by Madge, who "tells me what I dared not think / When my blood was strong." She and dumb-struck Marjorie are just as sex-obsessed as he is, sharing with him their memories of satisfied female desire: "How such a man pleased women most / Of all that are gone" and "Stories of the bed of straw / Or of the bed of down" (*VP* 457–58).

The "wildness" that in Yeats's poetic vocabulary is frequently attributed to women is transferred in "His Wildness" to the male speaker. He must "mount and sail up there," appropriate the woman's role as moon, because the female imaginative space is unoccupied:

> For Peg and Meg and Paris' love
> That had so straight a back,
> Are gone away.

Once up "there" with the sailing moon he will combine Peter's peacock cry of male pride with Madge's thwarted maternal impulse: "Being all alone I'd nurse a stone / And sing it lullaby (*VP* 458–59). Like the equally mysterious "What Magic Drum?" which also features a nursing male, "His Wildness" disturbs the categories of masculine and feminine by hybridization rather than inversion. Together with the "peacock cry" of male memory, the speaker takes on the lunar image of the traditional beloved, the maternal pose of Mother Ireland, and the barrenness of crazy Madge. His willingness to nurse a stone suggests an assumption of responsibility for the cultural and political conditions he intellectually deplores, and a desire to break down the intolerable separation imposed by gender between the male lover and the inaccessible woman with the "heart of stone."

Yeats has been linked with de Valera as responsible for imposing a constricting stereotype of Irish rural life upon the new State. "The pastoral Ireland of Yeats and de Valera has now become a downright oppression," writes Declan Kiberd. "The 'revival' which they led was in no sense a national revival, but a sentimentalisation of backwardness in Ireland, a surrender to what Marx once called 'the idiocy of rural life.'"[44] If we think only of the rural romanticism of Yeats's early writings, and of his attempt to replace the "stage Irishman" with the spiritual, organically rooted peasant,[45] we can agree. A comparison between his countryman ballads and de Valera's St. Patrick's day radio broadcast, however, invalidates the analogy. De Valera notoriously envisaged Ireland as

a land whose countryside would be bright with cosy homesteads, whose fields and villages would be joyous with the sounds of industry, with the romping of sturdy children, the contests of athletic youths and the laughter of comely maidens; whose firesides would be forums for the wisdom of serene old age.[46]

Yeats's ballad poetics of old age eschew wisdom for sexuality, exchange cosy homesteads for the open road and the broken thorn, replace athletic youths with twisted "holy shows" and comely maidens with demented old women whose memories are well stocked with illicit episodes. The romping of sturdy children (the only justification for desire in the Catholic sexual ethic) is notably absent as wild and barren Madge sings her lullaby to a stone. Neither Yeats's vision nor de Valera's has any claim to so-called objective truth; both are consciously ideological, and offer competing constructions of "the folk." No one knew better than Yeats that his countryman, like his legendary Fisherman, was "A man who does not exist, / A man who is but a dream" (*VP* 348). Although de Valera's speech was made in 1943, after Yeats's death, its contents epitomize the type of discourse against which the latter posed his defiant celebration of geriatric rural desire, itself a conscious fiction. As a popular form the ballad provided an appropriate vehicle for Yeats's construction of the countryman, and for his oppositional sexual poetics.

Desire and hunger in "Among School Children"

Paul de Man's deconstructive reading of "Among School Children" posits the concluding question as real rather than rhetorical: he thinks the speaker wants to distinguish the dancer from the dance. According to de Man, the poem enacts an "anguished" need to choose between "asceticism" (separation of dancer from dance) and the satisfactions of natural life (union of dancer and dance).[1] Syntactically one cannot determine whether a question is rhetorical: the context alone enables interpretation. In suggesting that "asceticism" was a valid option for Yeats's speaker de Man's ahistorical reading severs the poem's grammar from the material circumstances out of which it arose.

In resituating "Among School Children" in its historical context, however, I make no claim to objective truth. History too is created by perspective, made in answer to ideological pressures. For example, the "histories" studied by the children in Yeats's 1926 classroom are versions of the Irish past that are currently derided by revisionists as vulgar nationalism. As Ward has pointed out, women have been excluded from both the nationalist and the revisionist versions of the Irish story.[2] In reading the poem through the lens of Irish women's history I construct an alternative narrative, which resituates Gonne as social activist as well as hollow-cheeked Muse, writing subject as well as aesthetic object.

In Sonnet 71 of *Astrophil and Stella* Sidney voices the metaphorical connection between sexual appetite and physical hunger that is a commonplace of love poetry. Astrophil praises Stella's beauty in the approved platonic fashion because it leads the mind of her lover towards spiritual perfection: "So while thy beauty draws the heart to love, / As fast thy Virtue bends that love to good." Abruptly, however, Sidney interrupts the voice of platonic sublimation with the urgent cry of the body: "But ah, desire still cries: 'Give me some food.'"[3] Since we can live without sex but not without nourishment, the metaphor reinforces the sexual imperative by equating desire with necessity. It is a figure of speech that privileges the body over the spirit, consummated over platonic love. Arguing for the Irish right to divorce, Yeats used the familiar amatory trope, claiming that without sexual ties "the emotions and therefore the spiritual life may be perverted and starved" (*SS* 159). The juxtaposition of literary metaphor with political fact demonstrates the complex matrix of genre and history out of which both Yeats's poetry and his political interventions were generated. As a love poet Yeats could not have left the issue of divorce uncontested, since the proposed ban infringed the free expression of desire that was the basis of his art; and his position as a Senator involved in public debate about sexual mores informed his twenties love poetry.

The Free State inherited from the Imperial parliament the power to dissolve marriages, a power it immediately sought to renounce. In March 1925 Yeats published an "Undelivered Speech" in favor of divorce. Grounding his argument in the civil rights of the Southern Anglo-Irish minority, he warned against alienating the Northern Protestants, but his strongest claim was for sexual happiness. Gonne's traumatic marriage informed his conviction that:

Marriage is not to us a Sacrament, but, upon the other hand, the love of man and woman, and the inseparable physical desire, are sacred. This conviction has come to us through ancient philosophy and modern literature, and it seems to us a most sacrilegious thing to persuade two people who hate one another because of some unforgettable wrong, to live together. (*SS* 158–59)

The sacredness of physical desire, especially as sanctioned by "modern literature," was not a proposition calculated to appeal to Catholic sensibilities, especially in a culture that privileged celibacy. *The Catholic Bulletin* charged that Yeats's speech, a "pestilential effusion," was "on the same level, in regard to common decency and morality, as his notorious Swan Sonnet contributed to the filthy pages of the defunct Monthly called *To-morrow*."[4] "Leda and the Swan," with its graphic depiction of the sexual act, was the poetic correlative of Yeats's political defense of desire. Rape (unsanctioned union) and divorce (unsanctioned putting asunder) were cognate expressions of transgressive sexuality.

When he finally spoke in the Senate, Yeats supplemented his written arguments with an attack on the interference of the Church in the affairs of State. Admitting that "In the long warfare of this country with England the Catholic clergy took the side of the people, and owing to that they possess here an influence that they do not possess anywhere else in Europe" (*SS* 92–93), he nevertheless deplored the petrifying influence of churchmen of all denominations upon "the living, changing, advancing human mind." He argued that "Among modern communities there is a demand for happiness, which increases with education" (*SS* 96), insinuating those who would stifle happiness in the interests of morality were under-educated.

Yeats's defense of sexual happiness against clerical asceticism is fused poetically with the question of education in "Among School Children," a poem that is historically situated in the debate over the School Attendance Bill (1925), which closely followed the divorce controversy.[5] In May 1926, two months after his last Senate speech on the School Attendance Bill, Yeats told Shakespear, "I am writing poetry ... and as always happens, no matter how I begin, it becomes love poetry" (*L* 714–15). "Among School Children," which Ellmann dates June 1926, opens as the discursive memoirs of an elderly school inspector, but swiftly "becomes love poetry." Controlled by the traditional generic trope of desire as hunger, "Among School Children" implicitly poises Gonne's starvation of Yeats's sexual appetite against her feeding of poor school children, and ends with Yeats's most complete and satisfying celebration of the unbruised, undeprived body: the body whose desires have been fed.

As education spokesman, Yeats sought "to prepare for an Ireland that will be healthy, vigorous, orderly, and above all, happy" (*SS* 174), but the dilapidated and filthy condition of Irish schools was not conducive to happiness. Sectarian monopolies impeded government assistance, so in a speech on "The Child and the State" Yeats suggested that physical improvements should be financed by a county rate and supervised by county committees, without infringing the religious managers' right to control the intellectual life of the school (*SS* 170). In a long and hostile analysis of Yeats's speech, however, the *Bulletin* reaffirmed the principle of sectarian control. Claiming that, "It is obvious that Yeats and the Mutual Boosters mean to advance into the Educational Arena in 1926" and that "Pollexfen Yeats begirds himself for his new campaign of literary penetration" (surely not an innocent pun, considering "Leda"), the *Bulletin* explicitly warned Yeats off the educational grass.[6]

Yeats was not deterred. Accused by the Catholics of moral filth, he retaliated by charging that the schools controlled by religious managers were the sites of physical filth (*SS* 108). He became obsessed by cleanliness: George Yeats describes his interrogating the nuns at Waterford about how often the floors were washed.[7] School attendance, he argued, should not be compulsory unless the schools were likely to promote happiness as well as learning: "And if the children are going to be forced to school you must not only see that those schools are warm and clean and sanitary, but you must...see that children during school hours are neither half-naked nor starved" (*SS* 169). The children's food was as important as their cleanliness.

Yeats's work on the School Attendance Bill is a major political tribute to Gonne, though they had quarreled about his support for draconian Free State measures against Republicans.[8] Much of Gonne's earliest work in Ireland had taken place among the starving people of the West. During the 1898 famine in the Erris peninsula she and James Connolly drafted a pamphlet citing ecclesiastics on the right of the hungry to steal food. Yeats dedicated *The Countess Cathleen*, "the tale of a woman selling her soul to buy food for a starving people" (*Mem* 47), to Gonne. Like her model, Cathleen claims that:

> learned theologians have laid down
> That he who has no food, offending no way,
> May take his meat and bread from too-full larders.
>
> (*VPL* 67v, 69v)

Although the Countess refuses to gratify the erotic desires of her poet Aleel, she sacrifices herself to obtain food for her tenants.

Between 1910 and 1914 Gonne devoted herself to the private feeding of poor Irish school children while attempting to persuade municipal authorities to take up the burden. Her efforts to get the English School Meals Act (1906) extended to Ireland were opposed by some Catholic school managers, who feared that public control of the schools would endanger the sectarian monopoly. Gonne "tried to enlist the help of nuns to influence the Irish bishops on the matter, so that the 'secret opposition which we are meeting from some of the clergy in Ireland who seem to think it dangerous and subversive to feed starving school children' could be prevented."[9] The religious managers opposed humanitarian reform in the interests of spiritual control. Gonne hoped that nuns would be more responsive than bishops to the children's need for food, thus framing the dispute in gendered terms: female social compassion versus male religious intransigence, or love versus hate.

When during the Dublin Lock-Out of 1913 philanthropists proposed to send the starving children of the striking trade unionists to temporary fosterage in England, the Archbishop of Dublin condemned the scheme as likely to damage the children's religious faith; and Dublin priests encouraged hostile crowds to prevent their departure. Both the Lock-Out and the School Meals Act controversies poised Gonne's attempts to feed the hungry bodies of children against the Church's insistence on the preservation of pure souls. In a gesture reminiscent of the Countess Cathleen, she sold her jewels to provide food for the trade unionists.[10] Sharing Gonne's passionate concern about feeding the children,[11] Yeats wrote to Connolly's *Irish Worker* an indignant letter that accused the priests of turning "the religion of Him who thought it hard for a rich man to enter into the Kingdom of Heaven into an oppression of the poor" (*UP2* 407). In November 1913 Gonne thanked Yeats for a "generous subscription to the children's dinners" (*AYF* 329), while in his turn Yeats celebrated her social compassion and work for the poor in a remarkable group of love poems written in 1915.

"Broken Dreams" balances the poet's obsession with his mistress against the love she elicits from the old and the poor:

> Young men no longer suddenly catch their breath
> When you are passing;
> But maybe some old gaffer mutters a blessing
> Because it was your prayer
> Recovered him upon the bed of death. (*VP* 355)

The speaker recuperates her diminished beauty by remembering her work for the disadvantaged. In "Her Praise" he can find no one in his own intellectual or political circle willing to celebrate her, so he seeks out a beggar:

> If there be rags enough he will know her name
> And be well pleased remembering it, for in the old days,
> Though she had young men's praise and old men's blame,
> Among the poor both old and young gave her praise. (*VP* 351)

In "The People" she remembers how "Those I had served and some that I had fed" were turned against her by her enemies, but the speaker endorses her refusal to complain of "the people" (*VP* 352). All three love poems modify the individualism of the tradition through their celebration of her social labors, as opposed to her political ones. Writing to her in 1927, shortly after the composition of "Among School Children," Yeats connected her philanthropic work with an earlier occult vision in which

> the spirit showed you the circles of Heaven possible to you, of these the third & highest was "labour from devine [*sic*] love". Then in 1909 or 1910 when you were working on the feeding of school children I met you in Paris & you told me that you were convinced that all the misfortunes of your life had come upon you because you had taken up movements which had hate for their motive power.

In Yeats's mind the concepts of heavenly "labour" and Gonne's feeding of school children were closely associated, and opposed to what he identified as "labour from hatred" (*AYF* 443–44).

Although the School Meals Act was extended to Ireland in 1914, Gonne had to continue working to see that it did not "remain a dead letter" (*AYF* 388). In 1921 she told Yeats of a White Cross school meals campaign during which she had to arrange for the feeding of 2,500 children in Donegal (*AYF* 426–27, 524). In his Senate speech five years later, therefore, Yeats argued correctly that the operation of the Act was inadequate: while there were some arrangements for school meals in the towns,

> There are none in the country, and judging by my own countryside, where I live during the summer months, it is needed. Children will start early in the morning. They will be the greater portion of the day in school and they will have no adequate meals. They come away hungry, and it seems, if not very necessary, at least very desirable that they should have food. (*SS* 110)

Informed by his experiences as a school inspector, "Among School Children" shows Yeats attempting to adjust the imbalance between spiritual virtue and physical happiness through the "very desirable" feeding of the body. When he conjures Gonne's image into the pleasant Montessori classroom at Waterford, therefore, her presence is politically as well as emotionally appropriate.

St. Otteran's, the convent school at Waterford that is the site of the poem, was run by nuns who clearly did not subscribe to *The Catholic Bulletin* nor starve their children or their visitors. George Yeats recounts the lavish hospitality of the sisters, who in deference to the supposed worldliness of their distinguished guest swamped every dish on the long menu in alcohol.[12] Not all nuns were so liberal: Yeats wrote that, "Mrs. Kevin O'Higgins told me that a few years ago she was at a Retreat and on the day she left she and the others were addressed by the Mother Superior. They were told that there were two men 'they must never know, must not even bow to in the streets' – Lennox Robinson and W. B. Yeats" (*L* 747). His poetic compliment to a Catholic school is therefore strategic: he deliberately sites himself, a "filthy" and "Cromwellian" member of the New Protestant Ascendancy, next to a "kind old nun" who does *not* regard him as an enemy of her faith, the sort of nun to whom Gonne had appealed in her struggle against the male clergy. In the second stanza he follows the nun with a "Ledaean body": a deliberate allusion to his controversial "Swan Sonnet." Indeed, the subtext of "Among School Children" is "Leda and the Swan." Helen/Gonne, inheritor of the "Ledaean body," is one of the "daughters of the swan," while the speaker, though "never of Ledaean kind / Had pretty plumage once" (*VP* 443–44). Written two years after the *To-morrow* controversy, "Among School Children" redefines the place and nature of sexual love in the Catholic Free State through a meditation on desire, hunger, and the body.

Critics have contrasted the "masculine" volume *The Tower* with its "feminine" sequel *The Winding Stair*,[13] but "Among School Children," a poem dominated by representations of the feminine, fails to conform to this pattern. The children noticed by the speaker are all girls; the teacher is a nun; the poet remembers Gonne, evokes her mythical analogue Helen the daughter of Leda, and speculates about the feelings of a "youthful mother." The dancer, though grammatically ungendered (in the drafts there was once a "dancing couple"),[14] belongs to the tradition of the female performance artist represented by Jane Avril and Loie Fuller.[15] Only the philosophers and the poet are male, and the poet's masculinity is ambiguously figured. His alter ego is the nun, who has renounced sexuality. Her voluntary celibacy is linked with the comical impotence of her elderly questioner: Yeats enforces their relation by shared epithets: the nun is "kind" and "old"; while he is "A sixty-year old smiling public man" and "a comfortable kind of old scarecrow" (*VP* 443–44).

The male philosopher with whom Yeats struggles in "Among School Children" is Plato, source of the dualistic separation of soul from body that Yeats sees as constitutive of Irish Catholic teaching on sexuality: "Plato thought nature but a spume that plays / Upon a ghostly paradigm of things" (*VP* 445). Gonne's insistence on "an absolutely *platonic friendship* which is all I can or ever will be able to give" (*AYF* 85) laid the foundations of Yeats's later antipathy to the idea of "platonic" love, a love that denied nature. In *A Vision* Michael Robartes remembers "my past loves, neither numerous nor happy, back to the platonic love of boyhood, the most impassioned of all, and was plunged into hopeless misery" (*AV*[*B*] 40).

Ironically, Plato's Aristophanes perpetrates the romantic myth of perfect union between lovers. In *The Symposium* he describes an original splitting or self-alienation that can be overcome only in the arms of the missing other half. Zeus divided spherical mankind into two halves "like eggs which are cut with a hair," and the separated halves strove desperately to reunite. Love is "simply the name for the desire and pursuit of the whole."[16] In "Among School Children" Yeats remembers an occasion when

> it seemed that our two natures blent
> Into a sphere from youthful sympathy,
> Or else, to alter Plato's parable,
> Into the yolk and white of the one shell.   (*VP* 443)

Yeats "alters" Plato's parable by replacing the originary sphere with Leda's egg, suggesting that he and his beloved, like Helen and Pollux in some versions of the story, may have issued from "the one shell." The image conflates their "youthful sympathy" with Gonne's 1908 vision of astral union: "your lips touched mine. We melted into one another till we formed only *one being, a being greater than ourselves* who felt all & knew all with double intensity" (*AYF* 257). In the poem, however, the word "seemed" qualifies the image of two people blending into a perfect whole: spiritual union cannot satisfy the body's hungers.

Yeats therefore contrasts his vision of his beloved as an imaginary "living child" with her present image as a skeletally thin old woman. The crucial lines, "Hollow of cheek as though it drank the wind / And took a mess of shadows for its meat" (*VP* 444), suggest malnutrition as much as the ravages of time: wind and shadows are inadequate food and drink. Gonne had earlier described herself to Yeats as looking "thin & 'hungry'" (*AYF* 319). The "hollow" cheek, like the hollow moon of "Adam's Curse," evokes the emptiness of courtly frustration. The wind is Yeats's traditional image for unfulfilled desire; and he perhaps alludes to Hamlet's dissatisfactions:

"I eat the air, promise-crammed. You cannot feed capons so."[17] The phrase "took a mess of shadows for its meat" (originally "mass of shadows" [*VP* 444v]), also suggests Esau, who because he was hungry sold his birthright for a "mess of pottage." Yeats implies that Gonne has received nothing in exchange for her birthright: like the prisoners in Plato's Cave she has mistaken "shadows" for substantial food. She, who left her own children alone in Paris while she labored in Dublin to feed the school children of the poor, remains afflicted by unsatisfied hungers, while he is a bodiless "old scarecrow" who denies food to the birds. In "The Circus Animals' Desertion" he reiterates the metaphor of hunger: he was "starved for the bosom of his faery bride" (*VP* 629).

Gonne's letters to Yeats justifying her renunciation of the body after their brief affair in 1908[18] emphasize her deliberate suppression of physical desire:

I have prayed so hard to have all earthly desire taken from my love for you & dearest, loving you as I do, I have prayed & I am praying still that the bodily desire for me may be taken from you too. I know how hard and rare a thing it is for a man to hold spiritual love when the bodily desire is gone & I have not made these prayers without a terrible struggle. (*AYF* 258)

At this time Yeats noted the reawakening of the dread of physical love to which she had admitted in 1898 (*Mem* 134), but it is pointless to speculate about what Toomey calls Gonne's "essential sexual coldness."[19] When she promised to pray that "suffering & temptation may be taken from you as they have from me & that we may gain spiritual union stronger than earthly union could ever be" (*AYF* 271), was she saving Yeats's feelings? It is preferable to be renounced after a struggle with temptation than to suspect that you were never particularly tempting in the first place. Given the unreliability of contraception and the difficulties she had already endured in attempting to conceal the identity of her two illegitimate children, however, her physical withdrawal may have been warranted; and the theological register of her language also demonstrates a genuine, if relatively new, commitment to Catholic social teaching on sex. In May 1909 she wrote to Yeats in terms that anticipate the heroine of Graham Greene's *The End of The Affair*: "My loved one I belong to you more in this renunciation than if I came to you in sin." In November she added, "Willie I know we are doing the right thing. The love whose physical realization we deny here will unite us in another life – If we did the easy thing & yielded to it now, very likely it would *part us here* & after" (*AYF* 272, 283). Yeats's dislike of Catholic asceticism was strengthened by her theological justification of the deliberate starvation of desire. Her letters after 1908 sustain a running argument with him about the necessity of bodily fulfillment both to health and creativity. Yeats had obviously suggested that when "body is not bruised to pleasure soul" (*VP* 445) artistic productivity increases, but she insisted that, "Raphael bowed down to sex till it killed him when he was only 30, his painting is the essence of prettiness. Michael Angelo denied the power of sex, *for a year* while he was painting the marvel of the Sistine Chapel" (*AYF* 261). In her emphasis on the virtue of self-denial and the sinfulness of carnality she resembles the nun in "Among School Children," worshipping heartbreaking images that "keep a marble or a bronze repose" (*VP* 445).

Yeats occasionally uses the image of starvation to define left-wing activist women in negative terms: in "In Memory of Eva Gore-Booth and Con Markievicz" the "skeleton-gaunt" Eva Gore-Booth, trade-unionist, social worker, and suffragist, becomes "An image of such politics" (*VP* 475). The semiotics of hunger in the Irish context, however, are contradictory: connected both with the forced starvation of the Famine, image of England's genocidal colonial policies, and with the voluntary starvation of the hunger strike, an ancient Irish practice codified in the Brehon laws, and depicted approvingly by Yeats in his 1904 play *The King's Threshold*. The tactic was re-introduced by the suffragists and later adopted by the Republicans. Hannah Sheehy Skeffington wrote that in 1912 the hunger strike was "a new weapon – we were the first to try it out in Ireland – had we but known, we were the pioneers in a long line. At first Sinn Fein and its allies regarded the hunger strike as a womanish thing."[20] By 1926, however, many Republican prisoners, including Markievicz,[21] had followed the suffragist example. Gonne threatened to refuse food during her term of imprisonment in 1918 (*AYF* 395); she did not do so, but described herself to Yeats on her discharge as "*very thin*" (*AYF* 399). In 1920 Terence McSwiney, Republican Lord Mayor of Cork, died while on hunger strike against the British; and Yeats staged *The King's Threshold* in his honor, changing Seanchan's previous literal triumph over the King to a moral victory in death.[22] He labored to secure Gonne's release when, jailed for disseminating anti-government publications, she went on hunger strike in 1923:[23] after twenty

days in Kilmainham without food, her cheek was literally "hollow."
Yeats later claimed disapprovingly that the hunger strike had made
"deliberate suffering a chief instrument in our public life,"[24] yet in
his poem the ambiguity of an image that, despite its hollowness,
might have been fashioned by "Quattrocento finger," also suggests
admiration: Cleanth Brooks argues that Gonne's cadaverous physi-
ognomy is supposed to be "ideal."[25] Yeats compared Irishwomen
favorably with Englishwomen, who tend to run to fat; in London,

Certain old women's faces filled me with horror... the fat blotched faces,
rising above double chins, of women who have drunk too much beer and
eaten much meat. In Dublin I had often seen old women walking with erect
heads and gaunt bodies, talking to themselves with loud voices, mad with
drink and poverty, but they were different, they belonged to romance. Da
Vinci had drawn women who looked so, and so carried their bodies. (*Au*
155)

The image of the skeleton-gaunt woman, therefore, is a complex
amalgam of forced and voluntary starvation: she may be obsessed by
the wrong sort of activist politics, or she may be too poor to eat, but
she is visually preferable to the over-fed one: she belongs to Leonardo
and to romance.

The fifth stanza of the poem suggests that practical problems may
attend the "feeding" of desire; for consuming the "Honey of
generation" has material consequences in a culture without con-
traception. The child "betrayed" into the world (a strikingly
negative word) by the sexual activity of its parents may not want to
leave the pre-natal state of perfection; but the mother may feel
equally "betrayed" by her pregnancy (Yeats's syntax is ambiguous
at this point).[26] The stanza's representation of motherhood suggests
unwillingness followed by disappointment. The baby son is no more
than a somnolent or squalling "shape," the mother's "worship"
given to an image of possibility rather than to the actuality of beloved
flesh (*VP* 444–45). Yeats strongly advocated birth control as the
liberator of desire. Arguing against that section of the Censorship of
Publications Act that "forbids the sale or distribution of any
'appliances to be used for,' or any book or periodical which advocates
...'birth control,'" Yeats strategically produced St. Thomas
Aquinas as his authority:

Those who think it wrong to bring into the world children they cannot
clothe and educate, and yet refuse to renounce that "on which the soul

expands her wing," can say "no man knows whether the child is for love's sake, the fruit for the flower, or love for the child's sake, the flower for the fruit"; or quote the words of St. Thomas: "Anima est in toto corpore." (*SS* 177–78)

Yeats had used a similar organic metaphor in "Among School Children": "Are you the leaf, the blossom or the bole?" (*VP* 446). If generation is not to be a "betrayal" of sexual love then the "labour" of childbirth must be a welcome "blossoming" rather than Eve's curse: "I will greatly multiply thy sorrow and thy conception; in sorrow thou shalt bring forth children."[27]

Yeats was pleased to marshall so respectable a Catholic authority as Aquinas in his defense of birth control. Gonne commented shrewdly on his strategy: "You hate the Catholic Church with the hate of the Daemon condemned by the old monk of the Mariotic Sea & when you take your stand on certain papal Encyclicals you always remind me of Satan rebuking Sin" (*AYF* 442). In "The Censorship and St. Thomas Aquinas" Yeats attacked the Censorship Bill's proposed definition of indecency as "calculated to excite sexual passion." Claiming that this definition "must be sacrilegious to a Thomist," he ironically expressed surprise that Catholic lawyers and ecclesiastics could make such a blunder as to call natural bodily desires indecent. He tendentiously referred to his opponent in the "Leda" controversy: "Had Professor Trench made it [the blunder] I would understand, for his sort of evangelical belief, whatever it owes to the ascetic Platonism of the seventeenth century, owes nothing to Aquinas." "Anima est in toto corpore" lines up Aquinas in defense of sexual passion, against Plato and Descartes, "who both consider the soul as a substance completely distinct from the body." The contentious definition of "indecency" became the focus of Yeats's opposition to the Censorship Bill, which he represented as the repression of "sexual passion" by "ascetic Platonism." Yeats's politically motivated debate with Plato and "the Platonizing theology of Byzantium" (*UP2* 477–78) informs both "Among School Children" and almost all his love poetry between 1926 and 1932.

St. Thomas's maxim "Anima est in toto corpore" also helped Yeats to avoid a simplistic binarism in his poetic representations of the body. The Church bruised the flesh to pleasure the soul, but Yeats resisted the temptation to banish soul in the interests of corporeal reality. The soul was too important to be left to priests or philosophers. In "Among School Children" Yeats remembers Plato's parable of the soul as a winged charioteer with two horses, one docile, the other (symbolizing physical appetite) wild and unruly. In the drafts he refers to "the souls horses";[28] in the finished work he echoes Plato's phrase "the soul's plumage" in his own former "pretty plumage" (*VP* 444). Through appetite, Plato's charioteer loses the feathers from his wings, and sinks down into the incarnate state, "the pollution of the walking sepulchre which we call a body."[29] Memory alone can rescue man: under the form of time it becomes Eros or love of beauty, which will enable the soul of the philosopher to "regain its wings" through recollection of the heavenly vision.[30] Platonic Eros is thus not what we (or Yeats) would call erotic.

In *The Symposium* Plato distances Eros still further from sexual love: Diotima tells Socrates that the object of love is not beauty but "to procreate and bring forth in beauty" because "love is love of immortality as well as of the good."[31] The highest kind of procreation is not that of the youthful mother, but that of the celibate philosopher, whose issue is wisdom. Yeats, however, denies that the spiritual procreators, the philosophical lovers of wisdom, will succeed in growing wings again. Plato has despised the living beauty of the body in favor of abstraction, "a ghostly paradigm of things," while "Solider Aristotle played the taws / Upon the bottom of a king of kings" (*VP* 445). Like a dour Scottish schoolmaster, Aristotle has "bruised" the body of the young Alexander with the "taws." During debates on the School Attendance Bill Yeats argued that children should not be unjustly disciplined, and urged the scrupulous keeping of "punishment books" as a check on bad-tempered masters (*SS* 109). He sought to avoid the "harsh reproof" that turns "some childish day to tragedy." Plato and Aristotle, the philosophical founders of Western patriarchy, are scarecrows designed to keep Nature away from Culture: "Old clothes upon old sticks to scare a bird." They not only fail to regain their plumage; they drive away those who still have feathers from the food they desire. They are the agents of punishment and starvation.

Yeats sees Plato's teaching as having had a destructive influence both on Christian assumptions about sex and on the ideology of romantic love, since Platonic dualism informs our privileging of male over female, soul over body, heaven over earth. Platonic binary oppositions are always hierarchical. Decades before Derrida, Yeats attempted to hybridize them without discarding difference. *A Vision* is founded on the alternation and interpenetration of oppositions:

Yeats had "never thought with Hegel that the two ends of the see-saw are one another's negation, nor that the spring vegetables were refuted when over" (*AV[B]* 72–73). Plato's lover is committed to the metaphysical absolute, not the dialogical: "treating his beloved as if he were himself a god, he fashions and adorns an image, metaphorically speaking, and makes it the object of his honour and worship."[32] Or as Yeats puts it: "Both nuns and mothers worship images" (*VP* 445). The Platonic Presences represent absolute truth, "Yet even the truth into which Plato dies is a form of death, for when he separates the Eternal Ideas from Nature and shows them self-sustained he prepares the Christian desert and the stoic suicide" (*AV[A]* 183). Those self-born images of unreachable perfection that inspire the "passion" of the lover, the "piety" of the nun, and the "affection" of the mother may symbolize heavenly glory, but in despising Nature they lead to frustration, celibacy, and despair: the body is not fed, but "bruised to pleasure soul."

In describing how ascetic art inspired by "the Platonizing theology of Byzantium" was replaced in the Renaissance by "an art of the body" Yeats contrasted "a pinched, flat-breasted" Byzantine Virgin with the "voluptuous" women of Titian's *Sacred and Profane Love*. Still pursuing his debate with Gonne about the beneficial effects of sexual fulfillment on the artist, and remembering her denigration of Raphael as one who bowed down to sex until it killed him, he wrote, "The next three centuries changed the likeness of the Virgin from that of a sour ascetic to that of a woman so natural nobody complained when Andrea del Sarto chose for his model his wife, or Raphael his mistress, and represented her with all the patience of his 'sexual passion'" (*UP2* 478–79). In "Among School Children" Yeats moved from Plato's sour asceticism towards his own "art of the body."

Yet he could not originally summon the energy to challenge Plato's "Presences." In earlier drafts the poem ended after stanza seven in a mood of despondency appropriate to Yeats's gloomy initial notes, which emphasize that children can never fulfill their teachers' hopes, and that all life is a preparation for something that never happens.[33] Yeats transformed the ending of his poem by deciding to apostrophize the "self-born mockers of man's enterprise." He rhetorically defies the heartbreak enforced by Platonic idealism in love and religion by employing a trope that foregrounds his own poetic and bodily presence in the poem. Culler calls apostrophe a device which the poetic voice uses to establish with an object a relationship which helps to constitute him. The object is treated as a subject, an *I* which implies a certain type of *you* in its turn. One who successfully invokes nature is one to whom nature might, in turn, speak. He makes himself poet, visionary. Thus, invocation is a figure of vocation ... The poet makes himself a poetic presence through an image of voice, and nothing figures voice better than the pure *O* of undifferentiated voicing.[34]

In concluding his poem with five apostrophes Yeats constitutes himself as someone to whom an answer must be returned. Since voice implies a body to speak from, Yeats's apostrophes are the formal equivalent of materiality: the signifier as pure sound. The Presences from whom he demands an answer are not, as in most Romantic apostrophes, material beings. They are supernatural Platonic forms: the religious icons of Catholic Ireland, the secular icons of lovers and mothers.

Yeats's apostrophes locate him not only as the speaking subject of the poem, but also as a spokesman for others: the school children of Ireland, Gonne's special care, whose bodies need food, warmth, and cleanliness before they can begin to acquire wisdom. Arguing in the Senate that "we ought to be able to give the child of the poor as good an education as we give to the child of the rich" (*SS* 111), Yeats upheld the rights of the voiceless and underprivileged. It is often assumed that by the last stanza of the poem Yeats has "transcended" the local and particular historical incident out of which it arose. On the contrary, we are never closer to the prosaic material details of the School Attendance Bill, and to Yeats's experiences (both good and bad) as a school inspector, than in the lines

> Labour is blossoming or dancing where
> The body is not bruised to pleasure soul,
> Nor beauty born out of its own despair,
> Nor blear-eyed wisdom out of midnight oil. (*VP* 445–46)

This evocation of unalienated labor and joyful learning can be read both as an impossible Utopia and as a plea for a humane and decent system of primary education. Yeats was certain that "for a child to spend all day in school with a stupid, ill-trained man under an ill-planned system, is less good for that child than that the child should be running through the fields and learning nothing" (*SS* 110). Amid the general "bitterness" (Yeats's word) of *The Tower* (*L* 742), "Among School Children" offers a romantic image of happiness and liberation comparable to the image of the child (a Wordsworthian

child escaped momentarily from the prison house of learning)
"running through the fields."

Yeats saw himself primarily as a tragic artist, but at moments he
longed to be otherwise. Calling William Morris "The Happiest of the
Poets," he once claimed that, despite the fact that he could not value
Morris's verse very highly, "I would choose to live his life, poetry and
all, rather than my own or any other man's" (*Au* 141). In 1927 he
reflected to Gonne about the change in his political beliefs:

> In some ways you & I have changed places. When I knew you first you were
> anti-Drefusard all for authoritative government ... and I was Drefusard &
> more or less vaguely communist under the influence of William Morris.
> Today if I lived in France I would probably join your old party – though
> with some reservations – & call myself a French nationalist. You I imagine
> would join the communists. (*AYF* 437)

When he worked for the good of others, however, Yeats instinctively
readopted Morris's Utopian frame of mind. In one of the pamphlets
that turned the young Yeats "vaguely communist," Morris had
asserted the human right to bodily integrity:

> To feel mere life a pleasure; to enjoy the moving one's limbs and exercising
> one's bodily powers; to play, as it were, with sun and wind and rain; to
> rejoice in satisfying the due bodily appetites of a human animal without fear
> of degradation or sense of wrong-doing: yes, and therewithal to be well-
> formed, straight-limbed, strongly knit, expressive of countenance – to be, in
> a word, beautiful – that also I claim. If we cannot have this claim satisfied,
> we are but poor creatures after all; and I claim it in the teeth of those terrible
> doctrines of asceticism, which, born of the despair of the oppressed and
> degraded, have been for so many years used as instruments for the
> continuation of that oppression and degradation.[35]

Only in the fallen world of capitalism must one labor to be beautiful:
for Morris beauty is a right which socialism will restore. In play,
pleasure, and the satisfaction of bodily appetite it will blossom
naturally. Remembering Morris as he wrote "The Trembling of the
Veil" in 1922, Yeats praised his revolutionary vision: "He imagined
... new conditions of making and doing" (*Au* 143). Following Morris,
Yeats bases his new conditions of making and doing, blossoming and
dancing, on physical perfection, rather than on the images of bodily
torture offered by the Catholic iconography. His Christ was not the
Crucified One, but that "Unity of Being Dante compared to a
perfectly proportioned human body" (*E&I* 518). Returning to
"Adam's Curse," Yeats redefines in "Among School Children" the

"labour" that constituted for poets and beautiful women the consequences of the Fall. In *A Vision* he wrote that at Phase Fifteen, the phase of greatest perfection, "The ascetic, who had a thousand years before attained his transfiguration upon the golden ground of Byzantine mosaic, had turned not into an athlete but into that unlabouring form the athlete dreamed of: the second Adam had become the first" (*AV*[*B*] 291–92). The second Adam, the crucified Christ whose image inspires the asceticism of nuns, is replaced by the bodily beauty of Michaelangelo's "half-awakened Adam" (*VP* 638), an "unlabouring," unfallen Adam as yet uncursed by the need to earn his bread by the sweat of his brow. Asserting that "labour" is blossoming or dancing, Yeats replicates the Utopian ethos of Morris's *News from Nowhere*, in which work brings joy to the laborers. Eve, cursed by God with labor pains and subordination to her husband, is metaphorically liberated from "the pang of...birth" (*VP* 444) (perhaps Yeats has contraception in mind) and from the labor of being beautiful.

The last stanza affirms the unalienated bodies of tree and dancer. Two apostrophes combine with two rhetorical questions to produce a heightened coda in which the individualist "I" is replaced by the collective "we":

> O chestnut-tree, great-rooted blossomer,
> Are you the leaf, the blossom or the bole?
> O body swayed to music, O brightening glance,
> How can we know the dancer from the dance?   (*VP* 446)

Yeats's choice of the dancer as a non-ascetic image of bodily sanity, grace, and wholeness is partly a product of his oppositional dialogue with the voices of Catholic Ireland. While Kermode reads her as an icon of the decadent tradition, a faintly sinister female symbol left over from the nineties,[36] Yeats's dancer also manifests a contemporary social combativeness. The Irish bishops were obsessed by "foreign corrupting dances," which were not "the clean, healthy, National Irish dances ... [but] importations from the vilest dens of London, Paris and New York – direct and unmistakable incitements to evil thoughts, evil desires, and grossest acts of impurity."[37] Yeats's dancer, body sensuously "swayed to music," is certainly not performing a "healthy" Irish reel.

Sending Gonne a copy of *The Tower*, Yeats told her that she would find "a reference to your self in 'Among School Children,'" adding,

"I do not think it will offend you." It did not: she thought it "kind" (*ATF* 445). "Among School Children" is Yeats's most Utopian poem. For him Utopia and femininity were related terms, although not always complimentary ones: he accused the social worker Eva Gore-Booth of dreaming "Some vague Utopia" (*VP* 475). In the historical speculations of *A Vision* he gendered the democratic politics of social concern: a primary civilization is "levelling, unifying, feminine, humane, peace its means and end" (*AV[B]* 263). Yeats's equation of femininity with humanity, democracy, unity, and peace is essentialist: women are stereotyped as caregivers and mediators. Essentialism, however, led to a progressive social praxis, and to a poem whose almost universal appeal lies precisely in what Yeats would call its "femininity": its celebration of the material body, informed but not dominated by the spirit.[38] "Among School Children" also provides the context for Yeats's experiment in female speech, "A Woman Young and Old," begun in the same month.[39]

CHAPTER II

Writing the female body: women young and old

A man who writes in the voice of a woman risks accusations of appropriation or insincerity; of indulging in "a narcissistic exercise," or "literary masquerade." Anne Taylor claims that "certain fictional women are primarily their male authors in disguise."[1] Naturally a man does not become a woman when he writes as one, yet cross-gendered composition can be practiced with successful poetic and political effects. Taylor discusses novelists, but because of the generic presupposition of intimacy (lyric as "overheard" rather than dramatized voice) the poet who speaks as a woman is attempting a more transgressive and more perilous task. Since the romantic lyric poet conventionally speaks from the depths of his being, to figure those depths as female invites psychoanalytic investigation.

Psychoanalytic critics, however, celebrate literary cross-dressing: according to Freud everyone is bisexual anyway, and Jung exhorts men to discover and liberate the *anima*. Kristeva sees no reason why biological men should not produce womanly (semiotic) writing; while Cixous argues that poets, because their work derives more directly from the unconscious than that of novelists, can break through the structures of patriarchal ideology and voice the repressed, figured as woman.[2]   Heath notes that "semiotics, psychoanalysis, deconstruction" have taught readers "not to confuse the sex of the author with the sexuality and sexual positioning inscribed in a text." Since the dominant discursive structures are male, however, Heath recognizes that writing (or reading) as a man is normative. For male modernists, therefore, "writing differently has seemed to be naturally definable as writing feminine, as moving across into a woman's place."[3] Like Kristeva and Cixous, Heath adduces Joyce as his example of avant-garde "feminine" writing. Various male critics have approached Yeats in a similarly hopeful spirit, although with different methodologies. Keane admires Yeats's "'feminist' sensibility" and "the deeper wisdom he seems to have attained by submitting himself to the female perspective of Crazy Jane and a Woman Young and Old." He praises Yeats for understanding "the mystery of the feminine, the fecund darkness of woman and of Nature."[4] If Yeats figures woman as fecund darkness, however, there is nothing necessarily feminist about such a well-worn representational move.

Yet it cannot be argued that no man has the right to speak for or in the voice of a woman: such essentialism appeals to the overriding authority of biology. Said has rightly protested against the idea that "only women can understand feminine experience."[5] Yeats's most intense friendships and professional collaborations were with women, and by 1926 he had labored long and intimately with his wife over the intellectual and sexual materials of *A Vision*. Joseph Boone posits "alternatives beyond 'appropriation' – instances, however rare, when [the male writer] has let femaleness transform, redefine, his textual erotics, allowed himself *to be read through* femininity and femaleness."[6] Does Yeats provide such an alternative? He sought poetic impersonality by speaking in female voices, but since the poems are signed such impersonality is shadowed by Yeats's sexual identity. The poems are double-voiced: the poet as male is textually absent but contextually present.

Yeats's lyric gender-changes, however, are enabled as much by drama as by psychology. Writing to Margot Ruddock he assumes the theatrical nature of all lyric voice, denaturalizing even the process of speaking as a man: "In the list of poems ... I notice two in which I dramatise myself as a man, 'Broken Dreams', 'May God be thanked for Woman'. You should as far as possible select poems where a woman speaks or where it is not clear whether the speaker is man or woman" (*LMR* 30). Poetic voice, then, male or female, is constructed rather than given. A corollary of Yeats's theatrical lyric mode is his refusal to speak as Woman, his voicing of many different aspects of female erotic experience: lust, coquetry, spiritual love, maternal affection, unsatisfied desire, and sexual mockery. Yeats's use of the ballad form reinforces his attempt to displace the romantic male self: as anonymous compositions constantly modified by the women and blind men who primarily transmitted them,[7] the ballads provide an appropriately non-canonical form for a man trying to speak as a woman. Woolf speculates that "It was a woman ... who made the ballads and the folk-songs, crooning them to her children, beguiling her spinning with them, or the length of the winter's night,"[8] and Yeats describes how "Barbara Allen" has "come down…from mother to daughter."[9] In "A Woman Young and Old" he imagines an older woman passing on her love-secrets to "some new-married bride" (*VP* 535).

The ballad helps Yeats to reinflect the canon of Western male love poetry by presenting it from the woman's point of view: inverting the master tropes of the genre he allows the object of the gaze to interrogate the gazer. She speaks in answer to many a lover's complaint: "Why should he think me cruel / Or that he is betrayed?" (*VP* 532). She also speaks in defiance of Irish Catholic puritanism. As Marjorie Howes has shown, State regulation of sexuality through the refusal of divorce and contraception and the promotion of motherhood as a full-time occupation particularly affected Irish women.[10] In their 1927 Pastoral Letter the bishops reiterated that, "in woman, especially, purity is the crowning glory."[11] Yeats, however, supported divorce, defended women's right to work outside the home after marriage, and opposed censorship because it would ban not only contraceptive advertisements, but most great love poetry. The love poems of "A Woman Young and Old" respond to the Irish social context of the late 1920s: contraception and love poetry, material and ideological products, are mutually imbricated.

In "Father and Child" Yeats mocks those who were alarmed by the "loosening of the bonds of parental authority…and a general impatience under restraint that drives youth to neglect the sacred claims of authority and follow its own capricious ways."[12] Fresh from his Senatorial defense of school children against cruel masters, Yeats chooses a young woman (historically his pre-teenage daughter, but poetically a desiring female) through whom to challenge the Irish patriarchy. Critics have noted his reversal of Herbert's "The Collar,"[13] in which the soul declares its independence of paternal authority only to return humbled to its allegiance to the Divine Father:

> She hears me strike the board and say
> That she is under ban
> Of all good men and women,
> Being mentioned with a man
> That has the worst of all bad names.   (*VP* 531)

"Father" is the commonest Irish Catholic term of address for a priest. The Father of "Father and Child" is first "Yeats," father of Anne Yeats, and secondarily the generic "Father" of "Bless me Father, for I have sinned," the formula for a Catholic confession. The sequence contains two poems, "A First Confession" and "A Last Confession," which bear out Foucault's analysis of confession as the putting of sex into discourse; but although one is encouraged to voice sexuality in the confessional one is not supposed to publish the results. Lyn Innes argues that in the larger context of *The Winding Stair* the woman's "critique of male power becomes concerned with a sterile Christian morality which Yeats contrives to divorce from political or economic structures."[14] In Ireland, however, a critique of Christian morality is inevitably political. Since the Christian ethic embodies contempt for women, associating their bodies with sin, this critique also has feminist implications.

Yeats quoted his daughter directly. When George Yeats told Anne that her friend was a nasty little boy, she replied, "Yes but he has such lovely hair and his eyes are cold as a March wind."[15] Like "The People," "Father and Child" foregrounds the words of a woman. After the moralism of the father, whose choice of adjectives ("good," "bad," "worst") is judgmental and poetically uninteresting, her figurative language, illogical in terms of reason, triumphs rhetorically: "his hair is beautiful, / Cold as the March wind his eyes" (*VP* 531). In "A Prayer for my Daughter" Yeats had endorsed a safe, aristocratic marriage, but now he recognizes that desire cannot be contained by custom and ceremony. The March wind of the daughter's metaphor, like the screaming sea wind of the earlier poem, overturns conventional social wisdom.

Yeats's late love poems frequently rework his early ones. "Father and Child" responds to "The Heart of the Woman," which appeared in "The Rose of Shadow" (1894), a story that resembles the ballad "The Demon Lover." Yeats's heroine Oona defies parental disapproval of her dead lover:

> O, what to me my mother's care,
> The home where I was safe and warm?
> The shadowy blossom of my hair
> Will hide us from the bitter storm.   (*VSR* 230–31)

The girl's attraction to her brutal lover is masochistic: he subdued women "through that love of strength which is deep in the heart of even the subtlest among them" (*VSR* 228). Oona's rebellion against home, prayer, and parental authority, therefore, replaces domestic and religious confinement by sexual slavery. When Creed's ghost appears, Oona is helpless: "out of her eyes looked all the submission which had been in the heart of woman from the first day." The story ends with her vision of "the shape of a man crouching on the storm" (*VSR* 231), and the death of the whole family.

Yeats suppressed the story after the 1897 printing, but in "Father and Child" he took up the association of the sexually compelling male with the storm. Both poems use hair to represent desire and rebellion: the hair of the girl will replace the domestic roof; and the boy's "beautiful" hair prompts the daughter's rejection of "all good men and women." In "Father and Child," however, the daughter's submission to her lover disappears, and her defiance of the father becomes central. Gendered power relations are thus refigured: "The Rose of Shadow" exhibits female helplessness, but "Father and Child" affirms female desire. Moreover, Yeats pursues his debate with Plato, deconstructing the binary opposition between all "good" men and women and the boy's "bad" name with the question: what does virtue have to do with beauty? Love in *The Symposium* posits the beautiful and the good as synonymous: but Yeats denies that premise, setting at odds his daughter's desire and the Platonic apparatus of erotic sublimation. Like Derrida, he sees Woman as the Other who will destabilize the Platonic hierarchies and challenge the hegemony of male reason.[16]

Plato's ghost also haunts "Before the World was made," which Howes reads as satirizing the idea of Eternal Beauty.[17] Yeats ironically rewrites "The Rose of the World," in which Woman precedes the archangels:

> Before you were, or any hearts to beat...
> He made the world to be a grassy road
> Before her wandering feet.   (*VP* 112)

The ostensibly frivolous "Before the World was made," however, is not entirely satirical.[18] The Ideal Forms may be self-born mockers of woman's enterprise, but the speaker manipulates them to justify neither ascetic self-denial nor the Platonic view of worldly beauty as "a mass of perishable rubbish,"[19] but her own preoccupation with her painted face. As Aquinas was turned against the bishops, so Plato is turned against Plato in a complex maneuver that places philosophy at the service of a woman's desire. The make-up artist claims that "artificial" feminine beauty has a legitimate relationship to the "artifice of eternity":

> If I make the lashes dark
> And the eyes more bright
> And the lips more scarlet,
> Or ask if all be right
> From mirror after mirror,
> No vanity's displayed:
> I'm looking for the face I had
> Before the world was made. (*VP* 531–32)

Mascara, eyeshadow, and lipstick, conventionally denigrated as weapons in the "low" armory of feminine deceit, are revealed as the agents of a "high" and heroic self-creation. Yeats, however, does not invert the Platonic hierarchies: he hybridizes them. If female flesh is an imperfect copy of the Ideal Form, the woman is justified in improving it. She wittily deconstructs the Platonic binary opposition between Essence and Appearance, liberating herself from the essentializing identification with Nature so pervasive in male love poetry.

The make-up debate begins with Ovid, who in the *Ars Amatoria* offers conspiratorial advice to his female readers: advice that Yeats copied when telling women that, like poets, they must labor to appear effortlessly beautiful:

> You know how to brighten your complexion
> With powder, add rouge to a bloodless face,
> Skillfully block in the crude outline of an eyebrow ...
> But don't let your lover find all those jars and bottles
> On your dressing-table: the best
> Make-up remains unobtrusive ...
> The result may be attractive, but the *process* is sickening –
> Much that is vile in the doing gives pleasure when done.[20]

Ovid's misogynistic emphasis on the repulsive process of the cosmetic arts undermines his sophisticated acceptance of the finished product. Propertius, however, demonstrates that the opposite attitude also creates problems. In "Truth is Beauty" he condemns "artifice":

> Why drench your hair with Syrian scent, and try
> To sell yourself in foreign finery,

While shop-bought fashion, spoiling nature's line,
Allows your own fair form no chance to shine?
Such doctoring, take my word, is all in vain:
Love wears no clothes, and likes his beauty plain.

Propertius' attitude initially appears more complimentary than Ovid's: his beloved's body needs no adornment. His aesthetic, however, is organic and biologistic. If women are supposed to stay as nature made them in matters of dress and make-up, by implication they should stay as nature made them in everything else as well. Propertius' essentialism has a potentially reactionary vegetable foundation: "Look, earth brings forth her colours and is fair, / And ivies flourish best, without our care."[21] The appeal to nature easily becomes a coercive strategy, and denigration of women's "painting" as an indicator of their duplicitous natures and frivolous extravagance is a familiar misogynist trope: Pope's Belinda and Swift's Celia are notable poetic examples.

Hamlet has always been especially useful to anti-feminist moralists. At a meeting of the Catholic Truth Society in 1925 an Irish would-be Hamlet, Mr. Daniel O'Brien, K.C., complained that:

The women of Ireland – heretofore renowned for their virtue and honour – now borrowing the vicious customs of other countries, go about furnished with the paint-pot, the lip-stick and the rest of a meretricious armoury, justifying in their very persons the reproach, "God hath given you one face and you make yourselves another."[22]

In this context, the defense of a woman's right to use make-up is also a defense of her freedom from the constricting definitions of womanhood that supported the idea of an essential Irish identity. Ovid's "Art" of love asserts that desire and beauty are constructed rather than natural. Yeats the masker agrees. When his daughter began to use make-up, he praised the "admirable results" (*L* 887). Unlike Michael Robartes's dancer, the woman in "Before the World was made" consults the mirror to adjust her mask, not to admire her lover's wage. She vehemently denies the moralizing male interpretation of the looking-glass trope: "No vanity's displayed" (*VP* 532).

She is also a figure for the artist: a metaphor that has contradictory implications. No longer merely her lover's spoil, she is nevertheless confined to the physical sphere. In "To A Young Beauty" Iseult Gonne was advised to "keep in trim" (*VP* 336). Placed immediately after "A Song," in which Yeats disciplines his own body with "dumb-bell and foil" (VP 334), the poem suggests that she sculpt her flesh into perfection. In A Vision Yeats denigrates a hypothetical "natural" woman, a "woman of New York or Paris who has renounced her rouge pot to lose her figure and grow coarse of skin and dull of brain, feeding her calves and babies somewhere upon the edge of the wilderness" (AV[A] 213). "To a Young Beauty," like "Adam's Curse," equates the discipline of the rouge pot with the labor of the poet: Iseult Gonne is addressed as a "fellow-artist," and Yeats commiserates with her upon a footing of equality: "I know what wages beauty gives, / How hard a life her servant lives" (VP 336). The relation between beautiful girl and beauty-creating poet is intended to be flattering but can also justify a limiting obsession with good looks, and reify male standards of perfection into physical ideals as destructive as Plato's Presences. There is nothing natural about the politics of the female body. Social power circulates invisibly through women's internalization of a model of "femininity" that serves the interests of patriarchy. In the labor of diet, exercise, fashion, and make-up, body may indeed be bruised to pleasure men. During a debate on "Men and Women in Politics" in late 1925, the Auditor of the Solicitors' Apprentices Debating Society attacked female suffrage and disparaged the literary achievements of women. In reply, Yeats adopted the chauvinist tone of the all-male occasion:

The Auditor had told them that a woman never wrote a masterpiece. They never did, never would, and would never want to. The reason was that women between the ages of 15 and 35, decently good-looking, got greater honour than was ever conferred on anybody, be he the greatest statesman or a man victorious in war. Why, then, should she toil for many years to produce a masterpiece? Looking into her glass, she saw a greater masterpiece than had ever been created in art or in sculpture.[23]

Rehearsing the cliché that a woman is a poem and therefore need never write one, Yeats ignores women older than thirty-five or not "decently good-looking." What if they see in the glass a form that does not comply with the male standard of the beautiful? Yeats's argument (a commonplace in poems advocating that women think through the body) was worthy of an evening in which the only female work acknowledged as a "masterpiece" was Isabella Beeton's cookery book.

The make-up artist, then, is an equivocal figure. She is her own masterpiece, but she may be nothing else. Yet the made-up woman is a woman in disguise, and although love is a game played by male rules, disguise is one form of sexual freedom, power, and control. "Before the World was made" draws on "The Mask," in which the male lover's desire to know "if hearts be wild and wise, / And yet not cold" is rebuffed by the female speaker, who favors the superior eroticism of anonymity.[24] Passion has no need of sincerity:

> "It was the mask engaged your mind,
> And after set your heart to beat,
> Not what's behind." *(VP 263)*

The speaker of "Before the World was made" similarly dismisses male complaints against the cold-hearted *femme fatale* whose apparent compliance masks "a heart of stone":

> What if I look upon a man
> As though on my beloved,
> And my blood be cold the while
> And my heart unmoved?
> Why should he think me cruel
> Or that he is betrayed? *(VP 532)*

Rephrasing the arguments of the woman in "The Mask," she claims that since what attracts the man is a façade constructed according to the rules of a male-defined game, he cannot complain if her heart is not engaged. Like the women of "Never Give all the Heart," she plays his game better than he does:

> For they, for all smooth lips can say,
> Have given their hearts up to the play.
> And who could play it well enough
> If deaf and dumb and blind with love? *(VP 202)*

"Before the World was made" posits the male gaze as its own punishment: if "love comes in at the eye" ("A Drinking Song," *VP* 261) it is limited to appearances. When Yeats says of Gonne, "My devotion might as well have been offered to an image in a milliner's window" (*Au* 399), he criticizes a system of representation that privileges the visual. The lover has condemned himself to worship a Platonic form that cannot return his love in the created world. The woman proffers a heartless consolation: through her, the lover may learn that ideal beauty is no guarantee of emotional reciprocity: "I'd have him love the thing that was / Before the world was made" (*VP* 532).

The metaphor of vision dominates "A First Confession." In 1899 Yeats quoted Coleridge's definition of sexual attraction as a state of disequilibrium: the man desires the woman, but the woman desires "the desire of the man" (*VP* 807). Here the coquette "admits" to the priest that to awaken male desire she has resorted to "dissembling." Miming conventional gendered relations of power, she plays helpless in the briars:

> My blenching and trembling
> Nothing but dissembling,
> Nothing but coquetry.

Like the woman of "Before the World was made" she exposes the strategies of the game: she knows what men require in love. She does not challenge the priest's moral judgment:

> I long for truth, and yet
> I cannot stay from that
> My better self disowns,
> For a man's attention
> Brings such satisfaction
> To the craving in my bones.

Her "better self" prompts the submission to spiritual authority implied in the act of confession. Yet she uses the occasion for self-justification rather than penitence:

> Brightness that I pull back
> From the Zodiac,
> Why those questioning eyes
> That are fixed upon me?
> What can they do but shun me
> If empty night replies?   (*VP* 532–33)

The male cliché "Your eyes are like stars" is appropriated by the woman, who actively pulls back instead of merely reflecting brightness. Her strategy is a response to male interrogation: "Why those questioning eyes / That are fixed upon me?" Anticipating Berger, Yeats's speaker argues that the male gaze constructs femininity as something to be surveyed. Women have become icy idols or dissembling flirts because they have learned that certain visual cues will attract the gaze to its object: "What can they do but shun me / If empty night replies?"

"Her Triumph," however, reconsiders game-playing, challenging the casual attitude to love professed in the 1920s as sexual liberation. Free love may be just another form of enslavement:

> I did the dragon's will until you came
> Because I had fancied love a casual
> Improvisation, or a settled game
> That followed if I let the kerchief fall:
> Those deeds were best that gave the minute wings
> And heavenly music if they gave it wit.   (*VP* 533)

Yeats's speaker was initially immersed in "shame" and kept bad company: "A friend of mine takes drugs, another friend / Has drunk to drown a melancholy fit."[25] The finished poem, though it lightens the moral tone and diminishes the implications of promiscuity, retains its skepticism about casual sex. Her "triumph" is the miracle of reciprocal affection: a moment without masks or games in which love is real and mutual:

> And then you stood among the dragon-rings.
> I mocked, being crazy, but you mastered it
> And broke the chain and set my ankles free,
> Saint George or else a pagan Perseus;
> And now we stare astonished at the sea,
> And a miraculous strange bird shrieks at us.   (*VP* 533–34)

As in "A Memory of Youth," the bird's cry indicates love's triumph: "marvellous" in the earlier poem (*VP* 314), "miraculous" here. Do we celebrate this mutuality[26] or deplore Yeats's reinscription of the myth of a woman's need for a hero to "master" the dragon? The sexually liberated woman can manipulate the love game. What does she gain when she is "freed" from the position of relative power occupied by the speakers of "Before the World was made" and "A First Confession," inveterate game-players both?

David Clark identifies the poem's principal visual source as Burne-Jones's *The Doom Fulfilled*.[27] Ingres's *Ruggiero Freeing Angelica*, which Yeats mistakenly referred to as "the *Perseus*" (*Au* 550), is another (Fig. 8). Both Ingres and Burne-Jones focus on the nude body of Andromeda, foregrounding the implicit erotic clash between the woman's vulnerable nakedness and the knight's armored body. The eroticism is most blatant in Ingres, where a full-frontal Angelica hangs from her chains like a bondage pornography model while Ruggiero thrusts a phallic spear down the throat of the sea monster

Figure 8 Jean-Auguste-Dominique Ingres, *Ruggiero Freeing Angelica.*

in a displaced act of rape. In this picture, according to Yeats, Ingres staked his claim to be considered one of "the great myth-makers and mask-makers" (*Au* 550), but the nature of the myth may give us pause. Invoking it at the climactic moment of "Her Triumph," Yeats strips his modern woman of her clothing and her power in the love-game and restores her, naked and grateful, to her rock by the sea. There is something disturbingly Lawrentian about the abandonment of superficial liberation for a mutual sexual commitment, the rejection of twentieth-century social *mores* for the world of nature.

In "Consolation," which is funnier and less ambiguous than "Her Triumph," Yeats's female speaker answers the sages, the canonical "ancient writers" of the *Oedipus at Colonus* chorus from "A Man Young and Old." For them, love is a curse, and life a cruel disappointment: "Never to have lived is best" is their pessimistic conclusion (*VP* 459). In jaunty ballad sixains the woman grants their premise: "O but there is wisdom / In what the sages said." Agreeing that life is a crime for which we are all under sentence of death, however, she uses this existential insight as an aphrodisiac:

> How could passion run so deep
> Had I never thought
> That the crime of being born
> Blackens all our lot?

Even the "black" knowledge of pain and death can be held at bay by the "comfort" of sexual intercourse:

> But stretch that body for a while
> And lay down that head
> Till I have told the sages
> Where man is comforted. (*VP* 534)

Bodily pleasures are still pleasures despite their ultimate end. The first stanza appears to resituate the woman in her usual position as man's comforter, but the second reveals that she is pursuing her own desire for passion and oblivion. Like the Wild Old Wicked Man the speaker is content to "choose the second-best" and "forget it all awhile" (*VP* 590) in the ephemeral but intense joys of copulation: "But where the crime's committed / The crime can be forgot" (*VP* 534). Canonical seriousness is displaced by flippancy from the female margins. Poetic humor, almost entirely absent from "A Man Young and Old," pervades "A Woman Young and Old." Tragedy is punctured by the laughter of the woman who acknowledges life's bitterness but refuses to take it solemnly. After the heavy auto-biographical freight of "A Man Young and Old," the woman's voice distances Yeats's own desires and failures.

Speaking as a woman also enabled Yeats's revisionary dialogue with the canon of male love poetry. The stanza form of "Chosen" derives from Donne's elegy for the Countess of Bedford: a gloomy meditation upon "absence, darknesse, death; things which are not."[28] In 1926 Yeats re-read "that intoxicating 'St. Lucies Day' which I consider always an expression of passion and proof that he was the Countess of Bedford's lover" (*L* 710). Wilson argues that while Yeats owes his form and much of his imagery to Donne, "Chosen" is actually "a refutation of ... one of the most pessimistic of his lyrics."[29] Like most classical elegies, "St. Lucies Day" is primarily preoccupied not with the elegized object but with the grieving poet, who immerses himself in the darkness of a night figured as feminine:

> Since shee enjoyes her long nights festivall,
> Let mee prepare towards her, and let mee call
> This hour her Vigill, and her Eve, since this
> Both the yeares, and the dayes deep midnight is.[30]

"Chosen" rewrites a famous poem (which Yeats took to be a love poem) from the woman's point of view, and offers a bracing reply to Donne's lament. Yeats had earlier crossed the love lyric with the elegy;[31] here he transforms Donne's elegy into love poem.

Since death and parting are inevitable, the woman opens herself to pain by choosing to love. Hers is a destiny accepted before birth, in the pre-natal state where Plato's souls choose their "lots" or future lives:

> The lot of love is chosen. I learnt that much
> Struggling for an image on the track
> Of the whirling Zodiac.

In the "whirling" of the sexual gyres love is transitory: Yeats here symbolizes it as a single brief night.

> Scarce did he my body touch,
> Scarce sank he from the west
> Or found a subterranean rest
> On the maternal midnight of my breast
> Before I had marked him on his northern way,
> And seemed to stand although in bed I lay.   (*VP* 534–35)

The woman of "Chosen" is both lover and mother: Yeats changes Donne's "deep midnight" into "maternal midnight." In a typescript note on the poem he wrote:

In "A First Confession", "The Choice" and "The Parting" I have made use of that symbolic marriage of the Sun and Light with the Earth and Darkness, current in literature since the Renaissance. The sun's northern (not northward) way is his passage under the earth, his sojourn in the bed of love. Earth would bar his way and so prevent the dawn.[32]

Yeats's use of these mythical archetypes is problematic. The woman is celebrated for her unsentimental acceptance of the cost of passion, presented as less self-pitying than the famous love poet to whom she responds, and accorded all the rhetorical power accruing to a voice perceived by the reader as "realist." In terms of subject position, however, she is where she always was: subterranean, maternal, dark, and prone, an obstruction to the progress of the male Light. Yeats endows his female speaker with qualities that he sees as natural and life-affirming: feminists see them as socially constructed characteristics that maintain gender inequality. Yet Yeats's praise of women is genuine. To appreciate it we need to take "the risk of essence," and to acknowledge that, as Diana Fuss has argued, anti-essentialist positions are always deeply implicated in the essentialism they purport to reject.[33] Yeats's mythical archetypes are not always negative stereotypes.[34] We might affirm as politically and socially enabling qualities that are the products of oppression, like the stoicism, humor, and maternality of this speaker.

The maternal metaphor is common in Yeats's love poetry. In the autobiographical novella *John Sherman* he revealed his need, never satisfied by Susan Yeats, for mothering in love: "She looked upon him whom she loved as full of a helplessness that needed protection, a reverberation of the feeling of the mother for the child at the breast" (*JS* 111). In "Three Things," which he considered one of his best poems, "all praise of joyous life" (*L* 758), a dry bone sings of "Three dear things that women know": the joy of suckling a child, the joy of satisfying a lover, and finally the joy of desiring her own "rightful man." Yeats gives uncensored voice to female sensual pleasures, including the pleasure of giving. He parallels the lover's satisfaction with that of the child at the mother's breast:

> "A child found all a child can lack,
> Whether of pleasure or of rest,
> Upon the abundance of my breast."

> "A man if I but held him so
> When my body was alive
> Found all the pleasure that life gave."

The woman is not fecund, earthy darkness, but clean and pure, "*A bone wave-whitened and dried in the wind.*" She nevertheless longs for the return of her bodily "abundance," figured in synecdoche by her breast (*VP* 521). Although Bonnie Kime Scott asserts that "the erotics of nursing are a female experience,"[35] Yeats represents breast-feeding as sexually gratifying for the mother.

The "Lullaby" that Shakespear considered so unsuitable for the young opens with the woman's prayer for the child at her breast: "Beloved, may your sleep be sound / That have found it where you fed." The model for the poem is Grania's song over her sleeping lover Diarmuid (*Au* 457–58), and Yeats's choice of the appellation "Beloved," more appropriate to an erotic poem than to a lullaby, leaves us initially uncertain whether the addressee is a man or an infant. Perhaps the man finds satisfaction in love where he once found it as a nursing child, a Freudian reading that recalls Yeats's metaphorical conflation of desire and hunger, and is reinforced by his examples, in which slumber is post-coital rather than post-prandial:

> What were all the world's alarms
> To mighty Paris when he found
> Sleep upon a golden bed
> That first dawn in Helen's arms?   (*VP* 522)

The sexuality of Helen and Paris, Tristram and Isolde, and Leda and the Swan, eroticizes the lullaby. Yeats's attribution of the poem to a mother (*L* 760) rather than to Grania suggests that the satiation of the sleeping baby evokes in her the sensations of fulfilled erotic love: in giving the breast she satisfies her own desire as well as the infant's.

For the stillness of post-coital satisfaction the maternal woman of "Chosen" is willing to pay the price of the "horror of daybreak":

> If questioned on
> My utmost pleasure with a man
> By some new-married bride, I take
> That stillness for a theme
> Where his heart my heart did seem
> And both adrift on the miraculous stream
> Where – wrote a learned astrologer –
> The Zodiac is turned into a sphere.   (*VP* 535)

Female sexual knowledge is passed from the old woman to the new-married bride. Women speak of sex among themselves, in community. The old woman celebrates the pleasure of the brief instant when transience is forgotten, the Zodiac "changed into a sphere." Like the "miraculous" bird at the end of "Her Triumph," the sphere represents the mutuality of married love. In *A Vision* the marriage bed, "the symbol of the solved antinomy" (*AV*[*B*] 52), recalls Aristophanes' myth of the spherical union of two in one. But the marriage bed is only a symbol, the hearts only "seem" to be one. Reality breaks in with "Parting," originally conceived as the conclusion to "Chosen."[36]

Yet "Parting" is also the most literary poem in the sequence, the most conscious of its generic origins in the troubadour aubade.

Yeats's sources have been identified as adaptations or translations of the convention: Swinburne's "In the Orchard"; Pound's "Alba Inominata" and "Vergier"; Shakespeare's lark or nightingale debate from *Romeo and Juliet*.[37] "Parting" combines Swinburne's eroticism, Pound's verbal economy, and Shakespeare's dialogue form. Yeats gestures at the sonnet in the fourteen short lines, the abba rhyme in the first quatrain, and the tantalizing dbeecd pattern of the sestet. The allusion to *Romeo and Juliet* sustains the theme of the defiant young woman broached in "Father and Child" and concluded in the last poem of the sequence, "From the Antigone." Love in the aubade is forbidden and perilous, subject to discovery by the "household spies." Birdsong, miraculous to the mutual lovers at the end of "Her Triumph," here signifies limit and defeat: "That song announces dawn." As in "Chosen," the woman is identified with the darkness, with the nightingale whose "loud song reproves / The murderous stealth of day" (*VP* 536). The word "murderous" emphasizes the threat to the male lover if he should stay: Romeo finally wins Juliet's consent to his departure by exclaiming: "Come, death, and welcome! Juliet wills it so."[38]

The pleasures of love are more luridly shadowed by death in Swinburne's "In the Orchard," where the woman is bent on becoming an erotic victim before the dawn can quench desire: "Nay, slay me now; nay, for I will be slain; / Pluck thy red pleasure from the teeth of pain."[39] Juliet, less pathological than Swinburne's speaker, finally admits that "It is the lark that sings so out of tune"[40] and sends Romeo to Mantua. Yeats defies literary convention when his female speaker ignores the lark:

> Let him sing on,
> I offer to love's play
> My dark declivities. (*VP* 536)

As in Donne's "The Sunne Rising" the lover's desire bends nature to her will: the darkness of her "declivities" will eclipse the sun. Although the title "Parting" implies the normal termination of the aubade, the poem ends surprisingly, on the brink of a renewed sexual encounter. The interplay between linguistic formality and frank reference to female genitalia in the word "declivities" creates a powerful erotic effect. The woman in "A First Confession" constructed herself as an object of sight, but the speaker of "Parting" offers what cannot be seen, even by the lover. Like "Crazy Jane on the Day of Judgment" she is both "Naked and hidden away" (*VP* 510), offered and occulted. Although gynephobia is common in poems about sexual women, Yeats's fascination with "dark declivities" seems purely sensual. It is congruent with his frequent use of the word "labyrinth" to suggest the sexual and emotional depths and complexities of women: "The labyrinth of her days" from "Against Unworthy Praise" (*VP* 260), and the "labyrinth of another's being" from "The Tower" (*VP* 413); and cognate images like the "wildering whirls" of the shell in "The Sad Shepherd" (*VP* 69) and "that shell's elaborate whorl" from "Crazy Jane Reproved" (*VP* 509).[41]

"Parting" affirms love as "play" and darkness as benign: a genial vision contradicted by the succeeding poem, "Her Vision in the Wood." Before claiming lust and rage as an old man's only "spurs," Yeats gave them to an old woman:

> Dry timber under that rich foliage,
> At wine-dark midnight in the sacred wood,
> Too old for a man's love I stood in rage
> Imagining men.

The "dark declivities" of the previous poem are desiccated, the old woman's breasts flat and fallen. In the "wine-dark midnight" she is but "dry timber": only "wine-dark" blood can lubricate the sexual aridity of age. Since sex is denied her, the old woman resorts to the pleasures of pain: she masochistically tears her own body "that its wine might cover / Whatever could recall the lip of lover." Holding up her bloodstained fingers she magically evokes a group of women bearing a bleeding man. Although we recognize him as the dying god of Frazer's fertility myths, the woman knows him as her lover:

> That thing all blood and mire, that beast-torn wreck,
> Half turned and fixed a glazing eye on mine,
> And, though love's bitter-sweet had all come back,
> Those bodies from a picture or a coin
> Nor saw my body fall nor heard it shriek,
> Nor knew, drunken with singing as with wine,
> That they had brought no fabulous symbol there
> But my heart's victim and its torturer.   (*VP* 536–37)

Like "Crazy Jane grown old looks at the Dancers," with which it has many affinities, "Her Vision in the Wood" may suggest the erotic violence of de Sade or Baudelaire.[42] Gould argues that despite its Frazerian resonances, the poem also derives from a pagan procession in Flaubert's decadent *Temptation of Saint Anthony*.[43] Sexual passion is neither "comfort" as in "Consolation"; miracle as in "Her Triumph"; "play" as in "Parting"; nor a symbol of eternity as in "Chosen." It is torture: "*Love is like the lion's tooth*" (*VP* 514). What distances Yeats from Sade's pornographic sexism is that he never seeks images of male violence to women to stimulate erotic appetite. If he envisages love as torture, even as "murder" in "Solomon and the Witch" (*VP* 388), he differs from de Sade about who is doing the murdering. De Sade shows women beaten, tortured, raped, and killed by men. In "Her Vision in the Wood" Yeats is closer to Blake than to de Sade. Both the idea of love as reciprocal and equal agony for the partners and the discrepancy between the ages of the dying young man and the aging woman suggest Blake's poem "The Mental Traveller," which Yeats cites in *A Vision* as a source for his theory of the opposing gyres:

> Her fingers number every nerve
> Just as a miser counts his gold;
> She lives upon his shrieks and cries
> And she grows young as he grows old.
> Till he becomes a bleeding youth
> And she becomes a virgin bright;
> Then he rends up his manacles
> And binds her down to his delight.

According to Yeats, Blake's "woman and the man are two competing gyres growing at one another's expense" and their conflict is "that in all love ... which compels each to be slave and tyrant by turn." Were male or female to achieve victory, they would die, for "The existence of one depends on the existence of the other" (*AV*[*A*] 133–34). "Her Vision in the Wood" replicates the sexual foundations of *A Vision*. The poem also addresses the interplay between the immutable forms of art, the "bodies from a picture or a coin," and the personal experience of abjection that creates and sustains them: "That thing all blood and mire, that beast-torn wreck" (*VP* 537). The formal *ottava rima* that "Her Vision in the Wood" shares with "Among School Children," a poem written in the same year, connects the "Quattrocento painter's throng" with the "Presences" that break human hearts.

Scott doubts "whether men are sufficiently informed to write convincingly" about female eroticism, and notes "The limits of Yeats's writing of the female body."[44] Yeats indeed has limits, but a comparison between "A Last Confession" and a contemporaneous sonnet by Edna St. Vincent Millay may historicize them. In "I, being born a woman," Millay's speaker takes an unromantically direct view of female bodily pleasure:

> I, being born a woman and distressed
> By all the needs and notions of my kind,
> Am urged by your propinquity to find
> Your person fair, and feel a certain zest
> To bear your body's weight upon my breast:
> So subtly is the fume of life designed,
> To clarify the pulse and cloud the mind,
> And leave me once again undone, possessed.
> Think not for this, however, the poor treason
> Of my stout blood against my staggering brain,
> I shall remember you with love, or season
> My scorn with pity, – let me make it plain:
> I find this frenzy insufficient reason
> For conversation when we meet again.[45]

Montefiore claims that many of Millay's poems succeed "as a statement of female desire" and that their "bold references to lovemaking break consciously with Victorian conventions of purity and high-mindedness."[46] If Montefiore can describe sonnets such as "I, being born a woman" as both accurate and "bold," there is no reason to deplore the "limits" of these lines:

> What lively lad most pleasured me
> Of all that with me lay?
> I answer that I gave my soul
> And loved in misery,
> But had great pleasure with a lad
> That I loved bodily.
>
> Flinging from his arms I laughed
> To think his passion such
> He fancied that I gave a soul
> Did but our bodies touch,
> And laughed upon his breast to think
> Beast gave beast as much.   (*VP* 538)

The tonal similarities between Yeats and Millay suggest that a man writing as a woman encounters the same generic problems and opportunities as a woman composing within the male-dominated tradition of poetic love. The impulse to debunk is strong, and the most tempting target is the obdurately chaste and beautiful Beloved, object but not subject of desire. The woman who has had many carnal lovers and neglected to take them with the seriousness demanded by the tradition provides a powerful oppositional and parodic voice. Millay and Yeats agree that a woman has imperative physical "needs" that can be satisfied by sex without the framework of romantic love. Neither is willing to soften or cloud the facts of sexual desire with poetic diction. They transfer the traditional objectification of the female beloved onto the "lively lad" and the "fair" lover who attracts simply because of his "propinquity." The cool, rational women speakers regard their male sex objects with "scorn" and "laughter": unlike their deluded partners they know that the lusts of the body are not to be equated with the desires of the "soul" (Yeats) or the judgment of the "mind" (Millay). In adopting the male subject position for the female speaker, they usurp its power to define the experience and appropriate the freedom to be witty at the man's expense. Neither Millay nor Yeats, however, thought that women love this way all the time: Millay in the rest of her sequence and Yeats in the last two stanzas of his poem explore quite different attitudes to female passion.

"A Last Confession," a rudimentary dramatic monologue, begins as an old woman's deathbed confession. She mocks her confessor by unrepentantly verbalizing her sexual exploits: "I gave what other women gave / That stepped out of their clothes." She commits heresy in affirming sex beyond the grave:

> But when this soul, its body off,
> Naked to naked goes,
> He it has found shall find therein
> What none other knows,
>
> And give his own and take his own
> And rule in his own right;
> And though it loved in misery
> Close and cling so tight,
> There's not a bird of day that dare
> Extinguish that delight.   (*VP* 538)

This ecstatic affirmation shatters the propriety of confessional discourse. The speaker's flouting of the priest, however, entails spiritual submission to her lover. This is a post-mortem version of "Her Triumph," the masterful Perseus replaced by a male soul who will "rule in his own right." The limits of this poem lie not in Yeats's writing of the female body, but in his inability to imagine a love without tyrants and slaves, even if those tyrants and slaves frequently exchange positions.

"A Last Confession" mimics the trajectory of Yeats's struggle with the Catholic Church in the 1920s. Within the framework of religious discourse, the confession, Yeats introduces the oppositional voice of defiant female sexuality; then in a characteristic rhetorical turn he re-appropriates the religious discourse for his own ends. The liberationary aspects of his poetic and political efforts, however, are shadowed by the reinscription of female submission within the ostensibly oppositional discourse of frank sexuality. A suspicious reader of "A Woman Young and Old" might argue that Yeats gives a voice to formerly silenced female desire only so that it may say the things a man wants to hear. Women are freed from the oppressions of Victorian chastity to become not the partners but the slaves of liberated men. Stephen Heath demonstrates how supposedly free "sexuality" is produced and commodified within the capitalist system as a new mode of conformity. Nevertheless, he admits that the sexual revolution (the dissemination of contraception, widely available information about sexuality, increased social toleration) represents a massive advance over Victorianism.[47] Heath writes from an English perspective: the sexual revolution in Ireland is even today still unfinished. Yeats, with few effective allies, contributed his poetic talent and his prestige to the struggle. Readers must balance the genuinely progressive against the reactionary implications of his work.

The last poem of "A Woman Young and Old," however, presents a woman for whom sex is less important than principle: Yeats concludes with his version of the Eros chorus from Sophocles' *Antigone*. Sophocles acknowledges the power of love with dread rather than exhilaration,[48] but Yeats takes a romantic view of Eros in its relation to Thanatos: love is a violent "calamity," but also a "great glory" that drives men "wild" (*VP* 540): Yeats, according to Clark, is "cheering Love on."[49] The value we give to Antigone as the closing image of "A Woman Young and Old" depends on her relation to Love. The Chorus speaks just after the quarrel between Creon and Haemon, and it refers to the power of Eros over the rebellious young man. Antigone loves Haemon, but her transgression is political, and is motivated not by Eros but by family loyalty. She argues coldly that husbands are replaceable while brothers are not.[50] Her "soft cheek" may be the dwelling place of Eros, but she herself resists his power. As she goes to her death she laments that she goes unwed and without children, but she says nothing about Haemon; it is he who makes the "wild" romantic gesture of killing himself upon her body. Keane is infected by the same romanticism: "Sophocles has already established Antigone as a paragon to admire; now he gives us a woman for whom we, like Haemon, would be prepared to die."[51] Being a "woman" as opposed to a "paragon" means being married and having children, and letting male critics do the dying for you. It is precisely in her refusal of such definitions of femininity that Antigone commands attention. If the young woman of "Father and Child" rebels in the name of Eros, Antigone rebels in her rejection of Eros: she obeys an older law than Creon's.

Antigone, in fact, is a political figure; a champion of family duty, religious obligation, and freedom of conscience against the tyranny of the secular patriarchal State. To align her closely to the girl at the opening of Yeats's sequence, as Keane does, is to trivialize her. Keane uses her to claim Yeats for feminism: "We expect to find Antigone championed by a writer like Virginia Woolf – for whom Sophocles' heroine was a symbolic presence from the outset of her career, with Creon rightly emblematic of weak yet oppressive male society. It is a pleasant surprise to encounter a similar response in W. B. Yeats."[52] But did Antigone mean the same thing for Yeats as for Woolf? Woolf said that *Antigone* could be used as anti-fascist propaganda, with Creon as Hitler or Mussolini and the heroine as Mrs. Pankhurst or the anti-Nazi Frau Pommer.[53] For her, fascism was the political expression of patriarchy. But Yeats's poem was originally entitled "Oedipus' Child";[54] Antigone is referred to by that title; and at the time of its composition Yeats had just finished his adaptation of *Oedipus at Colonus*, in which Antigone plays not a rebellious but a devotedly filial role:

> Antigone here, ever since she grew up
> To womanhood, has been an old man's nurse.[55]

Antigone's love for her father is as absolute as her respect for her dead brother. She lives a martyr to his needs and dies a martyr to his lusts, "Doomed to this death by the ill-starred marriage."[56] When Freud nicknamed his devoted daughter Anna "Antigone" he was surely thinking of her filial rather than her political dimension.

Neither as daughter subject to a father nor as citizen rebelling against the State, however, does Antigone act as the mouthpiece of

Eros: Eros is set aside for moral and political reasons. Antigone's descent into "the loveless dust" (*VP* 540) provides a sombre conclusion to a cycle in which Yeats's female speakers attempt to define their widely differing sexual identities within the patriarchal frame voiced by the father and the male chorus. But if fathers are dismayed by daughters who demand their sexual freedom, tyrants like Creon are even more alarmed by women who put political rights and religious duties above sex: who are willing to descend into the "loveless dust" rather than yield to a male despot.

CHAPTER 12

Crazy Jane and the Irish episcopate

Yeats's last year in the Senate, 1928, saw the introduction of the Censorship of Publications Bill, which generated in the aging poet an extraordinary combativeness:

I am in the throes of a violent conflict here. Holy Church – no, the commercial tourist agency that conducts the annual Lourdes pilgrimage, and the Catholic Truth Society, and The Society of Angelic Welfare have pressed on the Government a bill which will enable Holy Church to put us all down at any moment. I know from the anonymous letters that the Catholic press is calling me all the names it can think of. I am in the highest spirits. (L 746–47)

The high spirits characteristic of Yeats in a fight were dampened shortly afterwards by an illness that almost claimed his life, but strengthened his determination to speak boldly before it was too late. "In the spring of 1929 life returned to me as an impression of the uncontrollable energy and daring of the great creators ... I wrote ... almost all that group of poems, called in memory of those exultant weeks *Words for Music Perhaps*" (*VP* 831). He associates song with energy, the return from death to life, defiance, resistance. Against the power of what he called the "ecclesiastical mind, Protestant and Catholic" (*SS* 117) he pitted an erotic and licentious female figure, the old madwoman Crazy Jane, who disputes through her ballad poetics and carnivalesque insistence on the grotesque body the monologic identity constructed by a celibate clergy, and enshrined in law by the State. Although Hynes claims that Crazy Jane is "the changeless female principle ... living ... out of history,"[1] she is rooted in the repressive social and religious circumstances symbolized by her antagonist the Bishop.

Foucault warns us not to define sexuality as resistance to the law. Seeking to discredit the "repressive hypothesis," he argues that sex has been incessantly produced and put into discourse by the medical, legal, and social bureaucracies through which power circulates in the modern state.[2] Mary Lydon suggests that "if the repressive hypothesis were to hold good anywhere, it ought to be in Ireland, that Galapagos of sexual life where the Jansenist species reportedly still survives."[3] She asserts, however, that even in Ireland the conversation about sex has been incessant: in advocating the rhythm method, the Irish bishops publicly discuss vaginal secretions. There is a difference, however, between the circulation of sex in discourse and the regulation of sex by law, which Foucault's analysis blurs. His rejection of the supposed opposition between sexuality and the law is questionable in a country where sexual legislation still oppresses women. The bishops had to talk about ovulation in public because all contraceptive practices other than the rhythm method were illegal. As a result of refusing women control over their reproductive functions, the law produced an official discourse about sex. Foucault's argument is a luxury that a country with limited access to contraception, no abortion, no divorce, and socially stigmatized illegitimacy, cannot politically afford. Without claiming sexuality as the lynchpin of identity, we can nevertheless argue that sexual self-determination is imperative. Endless talk about sex in the confessional there may have been, as Molly Bloom bears witness: "he touched me father and what harm if he did where and I said on the canal bank like a fool."[4] Yet the sexologists, doctors, and psychoanalysts who produced the late nineteenth-century discourse of sex hardly broke the public silence in Ireland during Yeats's lifetime. He wrote in the first draft of his *Autobiography* a brave account of his experiences with masturbation, "that some young man of talent might not think as I did that my shame was mine alone" (*Mem* 71). When it came to publication, however, even Yeats lost his nerve, and the passage was deleted.

Although Bakhtin paid even less attention than Foucault to the nuances of gender in the discourse of sexuality, his theories are nevertheless productive for a political reading of the sexuality of Yeats's Crazy Jane. Clair Wills suggests that women and carnival may be related, since "they are both placed together in the zone of the anomalous." She fears, however, that if "'public' women become associated in male fantasy with the witch and the prostitute," their outspokenness will reinforce negative stereotypes.[5] Yeats approves of Crazy Jane, but can he avoid reinscribing her as spectacle within the visual economy of the male gaze? Eagleton celebrates Bakhtin's "explosive politics of the body, the erotic, the licentious and semiotic"[6] as a subversion of Stalinism: if we substitute for Stalinism the Society of Angelic Welfare, then Jane's occult and sexual energies signal resistance rather than co-option.

In 1930 Yeats suggested a paradoxical similarity between the Bolshevik cultivation of mass emotion and his own imaginative return to the oral popular culture of the Irish peasantry:

> Is not the Bolshevist's passion for the machine, his creation in the theatre and the schools of mass emotion, a parody of what we feel? We are casting off crown and mitre that we may lay our heads on Mother Earth. (*Ex* 336)

Yeats's metaphor of "discrowning" also permeates *Rabelais and His World*, on which Bakhtin worked from 1934 to 1940, during the expropriation of the Russian peasant farmers and the Stalinist terror.[7] While the historical analogies between Bakhtin's Marxist espousal of the folk and Yeats's aristocratic "dream of the noble and the beggarman" cannot be pressed too far, their juxtaposition is suggestive. Yeats, who had a lifelong interest in Frazer's *Golden Bough* and in popular folklore, was thoroughly familiar with the concept of carnival.[8] The "discrowning" populism he shares with Bakhtin defines itself in opposition to the social and political repression that followed the Irish and Bolshevik revolutions. At a time when the Russian peasants were resisting forced collectivization, Bakhtin celebrated the spontaneous collectivity of folk festival and humor. In the supposedly Free State Yeats, who had supported the Irish rejection of the Imperial crown, now opposed the Roman mitre. Reading Yeats through the lens of carnivalesque dialogism reveals Crazy Jane not as the eccentric spokeswoman for Yeats's private desires, but as the figure for an eroticized politics of female transgression. Yeats's contention that the removal of crown and mitre allows us to "lay our heads on Mother Earth" provides a metaphorical starting point for an investigation of the relation of Bakhtinian carnivalesque and Yeatsian female masquerade both to each other and to the discourse of feminism.

The rhetorical invocation of "Mother Earth" is problematic. Is it the familiar containment of women within the stereotype of maternality and materiality or a challenge to male transcendence through the generative power of female immanence? Bakhtin's work is permeated by a positive equation of woman with womb, grave, and excrement. In celebrating the regenerative capabilities of the grotesque carnival body, he continually tropes that body as female, without interrogating the gender implications of his metaphors. Admitting that Rabelais did not take a progressive position in the sixteenth-century *Querelle des femmes*, Bakhtin nevertheless distances Rabelais from clerics hostile to the female body as the incarnation of sin and presents him as adhering to the comic, folk view of woman:

> The popular tradition is in no way hostile to woman and does not approach her negatively. In this tradition woman is essentially related to the material bodily lower stratum; she is the incarnation of this stratum that degrades and regenerates simultaneously. She is ambivalent. She debases, brings down to earth, lends a bodily substance to things, and destroys; but, first of all, she is the principle that gives birth. She is the womb. Such is woman's image in the popular comic tradition.[9]

Bakhtin is so firmly wedded to the virtues of degradation that he cannot imagine a woman objecting to his characterizing her as the mindless representative of the lower body: the endlessly reproducing womb.

Stallybrass and White qualify Bakhtin's joyfully positive celebration of carnival by reminding us that "the politics of carnival cannot be resolved outside of a close historical examination of particular conjunctures: there is no a priori revolutionary vector to carnival and transgression." The same is true of the sexual politics of festivity. The female role in Renaissance carnival was ambivalent: in the process described by Stallybrass and White as "*displaced abjection*," carnival's violent energies might be turned not against the official hierarchy but against powerless marginal groups like Jews, or against women,[10] for whom the danger was rape.[11] The woman's symbolic role in carnival practices, however, was central. Men dressed as dominant, unruly viragos, and "in hierarchical and conflictful societies that loved to reflect on the world-turned-upside-down, the *topos* of the woman on top was one of the most enjoyed."[12] Woolf suggests that such symbolic use of the female serves only to sustain her social marginality: "Imaginatively she is of the highest importance; practically she is completely insignificant."[13] Her objection speaks to Bakhtin's idealization of carnival: as a licensed transgression and inversion it may be no more than "a permissible rupture of hegemony, a contained popular blow-off."[14] Simple inversion of categories reinforces hierarchy: as Shakespeare acknowledges, "There is no slander in an allowed fool,"[15] and, Woolf would add, no threat in the representation of a woman ruling a man. Bakhtin, however, emphasized that only to the extent that it enters into antagonistic dialogue with "official" discourse can the energies of carnival become politically transformative. This "hybridization" or mixing of messages corresponds to the dialogism of Yeats's Blakean occult philosophy, in which "a negation is not a contrary" (*AV*[*B*] 72).

Davis provides an optimistic reading of the trope of the unruly woman that may be applied to Yeats's Crazy Jane. She argues that the representation of a disobedient, transgressive, verbally abusive female offers women a politically useful model for domestic and public behavior. The model can operate positively only in specific historical contexts, where "sexual symbolism had a close connection with questions of order and subordination ... [and] the stimulus to inversion play was a double one – traditional hierarchical structures *and* disputed changes in the distribution of power in family and political life."[16] Both of these conditions applied to post-Treaty Ireland: woman had traditionally been represented as virgin or mother, an image deployed politically to generate sacrificial idealism in patriotic males; and pressures to modernize in social and sexual life were resisted by government and clergy as emanating from the political enemy, England. This idealization of the female persisted in Irish cultural consciousness long after the establishment of the Free State: it was maintained by a religious devotion to the Virgin Mary with which it had always been intertwined. Throughout the Crazy Jane poems the symbiosis between the pure woman and the nation, a product of male fantasy, is ironized and ruptured.

In a poem contemporary with the Crazy Jane sequence, "The Mother of God," Yeats emphasizes Mary's common humanity rather than her purity. He is indebted to Mary Coleridge (1861–1907), whose poem "Our Lady" he reprinted in his *Oxford Book of Modern Verse*. Coleridge is concerned to establish Our Lady as a proto-socialist "daughter of the people," whose Magnificat is defiantly addressed to men "in woman's tongue" and whose message is revolutionary: "*He hath filled the hungry with good things ... And the rich He hath sent empty away.*" The word "common" is repeated with approving emphasis:

> Mother of God! no lady thou:
> Common woman of common earth
> *Our Lady* ladies call thee now;
> But Christ was never of gentle birth;
> A common man of the common earth.   (*OBMV* 62)

Coleridge's humble rather than hieratic version of the gospel appealed to the same instinct in Yeats that had affirmed "The Cherry Tree Carol": Christ in the mystery of *human* birth. Yeats's "Mother of God," like Coleridge's, is a "common woman":

> Had I not found content among the shows
> Every common woman knows,
> Chimney corner, garden walk,
> Or rocky cistern where we tread the clothes
> And gather all the talk? (*VP* 499)

In "Wisdom" (1927) Yeats mocks the Byzantine transformation of the wife of a "working-carpenter" into a majestic figure "damask clothed and on a seat / Chryselephantine." Reversing the late troubadour iconography of the Virgin as the lofty and inaccessible Beloved, he reconstitutes Christianity as the religion of the common woman and her "peasant gospeller" (*VP* 440).

Yeats saw the Irish hierarchy and the Catholic politicians conspiring to impose censorship in order to occlude what Bakhtin called "the life of the belly and the reproductive organs."[17] The establishment was bent on eradicating filth and silencing hetero-glossic voices. Crazy Jane speaks as a sexual woman, but also as one of the disenfranchised rural poor: the Catholic state, neglecting the radical message of Mary's "Magnificat," had little interest in the dispossessed. Although Yeats romanticizes Jane and Jack the Journeyman instead of analyzing the economic basis of their predicament, class and gender issues meet in the personae of the defiant old peasant woman and her lover outfacing the bourgeois and puritanical Bishop. The "journeyman," a craftsman who hires himself out for a day's wages, is a man of no property, and free of the sexual conservatism that accompanies land ownership. Yeats intuits that, since the landless had nothing to inherit or bequeath, sexual caution was not mandatory.

Introducing "The Midnight Court," Yeats related its frank expression of desire to the license of peasant carnival, to "the free speech and buffoonery of some traditional country festival" (*Ex* 284). His construction of the peasantry as desiring subjects parallels Bakhtin's vision of the early Renaissance folk: both serve political ends. Jameson endorses "the reconstruction of so-called popular cultures... from the fragments of essentially peasant cultures: folk songs, fairy tales, popular festivals, occult or oppositional systems of belief such as magic and witchcraft."[18] As opposed to Nazi propaganda about the *Volk* or the "Stalinization of Russian folklore,"[19] both of which subsume a sanitized idea of the people within the totality of the State, Yeats and Bakhtin emphasized the messy, libidinous, and subversive powers of folk culture.

In her deployment of the transgressive power of anomaly, Crazy Jane embodies the carnival folk grotesque. Her obsession with copulation, defecation, and degradation contaminates the purity of monologic Catholic doctrine. As Rabelais mocks the clergy, Jane, with her "flat and fallen" breasts, her public, open body "like a road / That men pass over," her preoccupation with "The place of excrement," and her continual obscene punning on "whole/hole," taunts the Bishop. She is the unruly woman, "proud and stiff," a shrew and a termagent (*VP* 512–13). "I can scoff and lour / And scold for an hour" she warns her lover, who responds resignedly: "*That's certainly the case*" (*VP* 510). According to Bakhtin, craziness like Jane's "makes men look at the world with different eyes, not dimmed by 'normal,' that is by commonplace ideas and judgments. In folk grotesque, madness is a gay parody of official reason, of the narrow seriousness of official 'truth.'"[20] Jane appears more "gay" in Yeats's letters than she does in the poems. Her parody of "official reason" targets a petty-bourgeois shopkeeper's wife:

Crazy Jane is more or less founded upon an old woman who lives in a little cottage near Gort. She ... [has] an amazing power of audacious speech. One of her great performances is a description of how the meanness of a Gort shopkeeper's wife over the price of a glass of porter made her so despair of the human race that she got drunk. The incidents of that drunkenness are of an epic magnificence. She is the local satirist and a really terrible one. (*L* 785–86)

Like an ancient Irish bard endowed with the power of cursing, Jane is committed to the culture of orality. She uses her "amazing power of audacious speech" to tell satirical stories "of an epic magnificence" that Yeats calls "performances." Yeats conducts his resistance to censorship through a poetics of desire in which sexuality is celebrated in the metrics, stanzas, and refrains of the popular ballad form.

English broadside ballads, which had a long tradition of anti-Puritanism, were often used to disseminate verses too bawdy for genteel publication. Mixing the rural and the urban, the Irish and the English traditions, Yeats crosses the meter of the ballad with the brevity of a folk lyric to create a hybrid: the poem of emotion framed in a form associated with anonymity and collectivity. Although Bakhtin contrasted the unity of poetic style and form with the novel's heteroglossic carnival of voices,[21] the ballad Yeats inherits and uses is dialogic in both history and form. Ballads depend on a process of communal re-creation that disperses the monologic voice of the poet among singers who modify and transmit his creation. The ballad also foregrounds direct speech, often in the form of questions and answers, as in, for example, "Edward." In "Crazy Jane on the Day of Judgment" Jane's voice alternates with the laconic responses of her lover; in "Crazy Jane talks with the Bishop" she satirically quotes the words of her clerical opponent. Most significant for a dialogic reading of the poems, however, is Yeats's use of the ballad refrain, a voice without a subjectivity that complicates the univocality of the poetic text. In "Crazy Jane Reproved" the refrain, "*Fol de rol, fol de rol*," flippantly derides the injunction, spoken by an anonymous "reprover" (the Bishop, perhaps), "never hang your heart upon / A roaring, ranting journeyman" (*VP* 509). In "Crazy Jane on God" the words one might expect from the Bishop are in fact contained in the refrain, which is strikingly juxtaposed with Jane's account of her sexual openness:

> I had wild Jack for a lover;
> Though like a road
> That men pass over
> My body makes no moan
> But sings on;
> *All things remain in God.*
>
> (*VP* 512)

Challenging Bakhtin's over-simple equation of woman with flesh, Yeats turns the religious refrain into the voice of Jane's body.

A female speaker created by a man, Crazy Jane is inescapably hybrid. She undermines Yeats's representation of himself as a "sixty-year-old smiling public man" (*VP* 443). "Senator Yeats" with his Nobel Prize, his silk hat, and his armed guards, was an establishment persona with whom Yeats was never completely at ease. Crazy Jane is both his opposite and his grotesque alter ego: unlike him she is mad; like him she is old but still a desiring subject. Bakhtin has identified old age as a component of the oppositional grotesque,[22] and in what David Lloyd has aptly termed a "poetics of old age"[23] Yeats marshals all the power that anomaly, ambiguity, and hybridization can provide. An old woman's sexual desire is out of place in the cycles of generation. Unmarried and past childbearing, Jane lacks a Catholic justification for her sexuality. Economic considerations might sanction the marriage of an older farmer with a young woman, but in the Irish countryside, according to Arensburg and Kimball, "the old person who has already had his or her day of childgetting and childbearing, and yet still persists in manifesting sexual aspirations, is a stock figure of fun."[24] Post-menopausal desire is rare in the love lyric: Crazy Jane's lust violates generic expectations.

The form of her speech, its economical urgency and strongly marked ballad rhythms, and its approximation to the language of oral poetry, expresses both Yeats's stylistic ideal and his realization of himself as a man in permanent opposition:

I tried to make the language of poetry coincide with that of passionate, normal speech. I wanted to write in whatever language comes most naturally when we soliloquise, as I do all day long, upon the events of our own lives or of any life where we can see ourselves for the moment. I sometimes compare myself with the mad old slum women I hear denouncing and remembering; "How dare you," I heard one say of some imaginary suitor, "and you without health or a home!" If I spoke my thoughts aloud they might be as angry and as wild. (*E&I* 521)

"Wildness" was often for Yeats a feminine attribute. In the articulation of his own wildness he found a woman's voice indispensably liberating: not until he had written the Crazy Jane poems could he claim to be the "Wild Old Wicked Man" *in propria persona*. Crazy Jane was both Yeats's attempt to speak the Other and a strategy for evading his own internal censor. His wife's mediumship gave him an occult model for the writing of poetry: Crazy Jane became one of his "controls." The control was a way for female mediums to express forbidden materials:[25] Crazy Jane offered Yeats a similar license. As a result he, to whom composition had been a torture, "never wrote with greater ease" (*L* 759). When he grew tired of Crazy Jane he was unable simply to discard her: he had to "exorcise"[26] or "shake [her] off" (*L* 788).

Crazy Jane is, therefore, occult, *unheimlich*, and anomalous. Her ambiguous position in society is a source of both power and danger. Her opening poem, "Crazy Jane and the Bishop," is a female curse against patriarchal ecclesiastical authority:

> Bring me to the blasted oak
> That I, midnight upon the stroke,

> (*All find safety in the tomb.*)
> May call down curses on his head
> Because of my dear Jack that's dead.   (*VP* 507–08)

An aged female who calls down midnight curses at a blasted oak is figuratively a witch. The clergy were the traditional persecutors of witches; unsurprisingly, Jane's primary antagonist is the Bishop, who represents the forces of organized society and culture arrayed against the marginal female figure.

Jane as witch is also in dialogue with the male canon. Bakhtin, who understands language as rooted in social context and words as having meaning in relation to the words of others, sees texts as the site of multiple historical voices. When Crazy Jane situates herself under the "blasted oak" in order to curse the Bishop, her occult power and prophetic capabilities anticipate her later allusion to Macbeth's witches: "Fair and foul are near of kin" (*VP* 513). The "coxcomb" in the refrain "*The solid man and the coxcomb*" (*VP* 508) suggests Lear's fool, exposed on the heath to a storm like the one that rages in "Crazy Jane Reproved." Shakespeare's prophetic witches and wise fools represent the uncanny in dialogue with official reason.

The oak tree under which Jane takes up her station is similarly intertextual: it was Burke's image of the healthy state, one Yeats frequently borrowed for poetic and polemical purposes. "Burke [proved] that the State was a tree, no mechanism to be pulled in pieces and put up again, but an oak tree that had grown through centuries" (*SS* 172). Here it is blasted by the repressive Catholicism that Yeats had spent his Senate term opposing. Yeats's post-Treaty poetics challenge the organic ethos common to romanticism and nationalism alike with a deliberately anti-organic use of allegory and emblem, which reminds his readers that the poetic identity between symbol and concept is constructed rather than natural.[27] Burke's oak is no longer the living tree, but a dead trunk: no more blossoming or dancing will occur, by order of the hierarchy.

Crazy Jane's farmyard curses are Bakhtinian "billingsgate":[28] a low discourse that mimics the official Catholic discourse of ex-communication once pronounced by the Bishop "when his ban / Banished Jack the Journeyman." Her spontaneous orality contrasts with his dependence on print: his "ban," which comes from an officially sanctioned text, reminds Yeats's audience that their bishops were eager to "ban" books and behavior that challenged canonical standards of moral decency: "Yet he, an old book in his fist, / Cried that we lived like beast and beast" (*VP* 508). Linking potency and orality, "Crazy Jane on the Mountain" associates the Bishop with clothing, textuality, and male impotence:

> I am tired of cursing the Bishop
> (Said Crazy Jane)
> Nine books or nine hats
> Would not make him a man.   (*VP* 628)

There's more enterprise in walking naked. The Bishop had charged that her physical relationship with Jack was the mating of "beast and beast." Using the abusive catalogue or popular blazon described by Bakhtin, which is "related to animal traits, bodily defects,"[29] Jane inverts the religious condemnation of the animal body by associating the Bishop with various birds: goose, heron, and (once the Bishop is identified with the "coxcomb" of the slippery refrain) cock. The Bishop's cock, however, is flaccid, while Jack's is "solid," tree-like:

> The Bishop has a skin, God knows,
> Wrinkled like the foot of a goose,
> (*All find safety in the tomb.*)
> Nor can he hide in holy black
> The heron's hunch upon his back,
> But a birch-tree stood my Jack:
> *The solid man and the coxcomb.*   (*VP* 508)

The Bishop's ban ended Jack and Jane's love before it could exhaust itself through fulfillment: they are still bound to one another by unsatisfied longing. The "Crazy Jane" of English folklore was traditionally represented as deserted by her lover,[30] but Jack's name, repeated in every stanza, may suggest the banished Jacobite prince of the popular Gaelic *aisling* tradition, in which Ireland waits for an exiled Stuart to return.

In Jack's absence, however, Jane has entertained numerous lovers, some of whom have exploited her:

> That lover of a night
> Came when he would,
> Went in the dawning light
> Whether I would or no;
> Men come, men go.

Bakhtin's celebration of woman as the open body leaves her vulnerable to male predators. If Jane resembles an unpaid prostitute, however, she validates her chosen way of life: "My body makes no moan" (*VP* 512). Yeats's celebration of female sexual transgression opens an imaginative space for women's desire and pleasure in a culture that occludes them, and recuperates the desires and pleasures of women from Ireland's mythological past. Jane's multiplicity of lovers and unquenchable sexual appetites associate her with the promiscuous Queen Maeve and the Cailleac Beare, whom Joyce had evoked in the opening chapter of *Ulysses*:

Old shrunken paps ... Old and secret she had entered from a morning world, maybe a messenger ... a witch on her toadstool ... Silk of the kine and poor old woman, names given her in old times. A wandering crone, lowly form of an immortal serving her conqueror and her gay betrayer, their common cuckquean, a messenger from the secret morning.[31]

Yeats would have recognized his own Cathleen, who has turned back into the poor old woman: as O'Casey put it, "the proud step gone that was once the walk of a queen; bent now like the old Hag of Beara."[32] Joyce's old woman is witch, crone, sexually promiscuous, but "maybe a messenger." Completing an intertextual transmission from Yeats to Joyce and back again, her "old shrunken paps" cue the Bishop's taunt "Those breasts are flat and fallen now" (*VP* 513). On the hint provided by Joyce's "common cuckquean" the virgin Cathleen ni Houlihan reverts to the randy Crazy Jane, whose decrepitude implies that, because of Ireland's mangled political independence, the goddess of sovereignty is still unsatisfied. Blood sacrifice has failed to renew her youth, and in post-Treaty, partitioned Ireland no one is offering her any sex. Free of English rule, Southern Ireland has been reimprisoned by the Church.

Yeats was unwilling to concede the sacred to the bishops, however. Jane argues in "Crazy Jane and Jack the Journeyman" that sexuality must express itself here and now to free the soul for its encounter with divinity. The famous lines "The more I leave the door unlatched / The sooner love is gone" are not lament but celebration, for

> I – love's skein upon the ground,
> My body in the tomb –
> Shall leap into the light lost
> In my mother's womb.   (*VP* 511)

These poems deny not divinity but the bishops' right to legislate how it may be attained. Jane does not invert the Church's demand for purity with a monologic demand for carnality: anti-Manichaean, she claims that soul and body must be joined. Women must challenge the priestly definition of their sexuality as the site and origin of sin. In a carnival inversion Yeats equates sinfulness with premature renunciation of the flesh: "To seek God too soon is not less sinful than to seek God too late; we must love, man, woman, or child, we must exhaust ambition, intellect, desire, dedicating all things as they pass, or we come to God with empty hands" (*E&I* 483). The Bishop does not represent the male "high" against the female "low," for Jane claims both "bodily lowliness" and "the heart's pride" for the desiring phallic woman, "proud and stiff" in her pursuit of love. As she says in "Crazy Jane on the Day of Judgment,"

> "Love is all
> Unsatisfied
> That cannot take the whole
> Body and soul." (*VP* 510)

The Bishop tells Jane to observe the Platonic binary opposition between heaven and earth that informs clerical contempt for female sexuality: "Live in a heavenly mansion, / Not in some foul sty." But she refuses to separate mansion from sty, grave from bed, lowliness from pride, or the whole from the ruptured: "Fair and foul are near of kin, / And fair needs foul" (*VP* 513).

As we have seen in discussing "Leda and the Swan," the public debate over Irish sexual identity was couched in excremental terms: the Sewage School, the Cloacal Combine, and the literary cesspool. The Dublin Catholic weekly *The Standard* recommended the censorship bill as "a sound measure of moral sanitation."[33] Crazy Jane complicates the repeated insults of the Catholic press by connecting excrement with pride and love:

> "A woman can be proud and stiff
> When on love intent;
> But Love has pitched his mansion in
> The place of excrement;
> For nothing can be sole or whole
> That has not been rent." (*VP* 513)

Yeats's strategy is a perilous one. The use of the drains as a displaced metaphor for sex, traditional in the negative discourse of the body from St. Augustine to Bataille, springs from fear and contempt of female sexuality rather than from a joyful acceptance of the mingling of base and sacred during sexual intercourse. Male depiction of female defecation in poetry is uniformly misogynistic. In "The Lady's Dressing Room" Swift's Strephon nauseatedly explores his nymph's chamberpot, which sends up "an excremental smell." He is overwhelmed with revulsion at the unsurprising truth that "Celia, Celia, Celia shits."[34] Rochester's jaunty rhyme cannot mask his loathing of female bodily oozings:

> It is a thing unfit
> That men should fuck in time of flowers,
> Or when the smock's beshit.[35]

In the first draft of *The Waste Land* Eliot, sharing the disgust of Swift and Pope, depicts Fresca at "needful stool."[36]

Crazy Jane's assertion that "Love has pitched his mansion in / The place of excrement" therefore risks siting itself in a misogynist Waste Land of bodily issues. Bataille argues that there are "unmistakable links between excreta, decay and sexuality" and that "The sexual channels are also the body's sewers; we think of them as shameful and connect the anal orifice with them. St. Augustine was at pains to insist on the obscenity of the organs and function of reproduction. 'Inter faeces et urinam nascimur.'"[37] The discourse of shame and "obscenity" voiced by Irish supporters of censorship and intellectual pornographers like Bataille betrays their common revulsion from the female body as reproductive site.

Through symbolic substitution and contiguity, the connection between excreta and sexuality also models that between sexuality and death. In her essay on abjection, Kristeva argues that "These body fluids, this defilement, this shit are what life withstands, hardly and with difficulty, on the part of death."[38] Crazy Jane presents the inextricability of fair and foul as "a truth / Nor grave nor bed denied" (*VP* 513). Her juxtaposition of grave and bed evokes the association of love and death in "Crazy Jane grown old looks at the Dancers." Yeats had dreamed of a dancing couple in which the male had the weapon and was the sexual and physical aggressor: "I knew that he did not know whether he would strike her dead or not, and both had their eyes fixed on each other, and both sang their love for one another. I suppose it was Blake's old thought 'sexual love is founded upon spiritual hate'" (*L* 758). While Bataille insists on women's erotic passivity and victimage, Yeats alters his dream to affirm sexually egalitarian violence: he puts a knife into the woman's hand and leaves the outcome ambiguous:

> Did he die or did she die?
> Seemed to die or died they both?
> God be with the times when I
> Cared not a thraneen for what chanced
> So that I had the limbs to try
> Such a dance as there was danced –
> *Love is like the lion's tooth.*   (*VP* 514–15)

Whether the connection between sex and death is viewed as socially constructed or essential, Yeats's deployment of it must be distinguished from de Sade's and Bataille's sexist philosophizing and pornographic practice. Bakhtin helps us to separate Yeats from the gynephobes and pornographers. He interprets the interconnection of Eros and Thanatos as a positive oppositional strategy, a method of resistance and regeneration:

Degradation ... means coming down to earth, the contact with earth as an element that swallows up and gives birth at the same time. To degrade is to bury, to sow, and to kill simultaneously, in order to bring forth something more and better. To degrade also means to concern oneself with the lower stratum of the body, the life of the belly and the reproductive organs; it therefore relates to acts of defecation and copulation, conception, pregnancy, and birth. Degradation digs a bodily grave for a new birth; it has not only a destructive, negative aspect, but also a regenerating one.[39]

Bakhtin genders the birthing Earth as feminine, but Yeats's validation of female sexuality goes beyond Bakhtin's when Crazy Jane opposes the sterility of the celibate Bishop without offering herself as an Earth Mother. Jane's erotic life is determined not by her reproductive function, but by her desire to keep repeating the intense moment when "looks meet" and she "tremble[s] to the bone" (*VP* 511). She affirms the pleasures both of deep passion and casual sex without the justification of maternity.

Bakhtin claims that the carnival use of excrement to mock all that is "high, spiritual, ideal, abstract" is positive: "in the images of urine and excrement is preserved the essential link with birth, fertility, renewal, welfare."[40] Yeats, who in his younger days had read Bourke's *Scatalogic Rites ... A Dissertation upon the Employment of Excrementitious Remedial Agents in Religion, Therapeutics, Divination, Witchcraft, Love-Philters, etc., in all Parts of the Globe*, was familiar with the uses of excrement in folk rituals and remedies. He described a wife taken by the fairies who instructed her husband to rescue her by throwing "fowl droppings and urine" at her as she passed (*UP*2 99). Bourke's discussion of the folk practice of sewing dung into the clothes of a bride to protect her, and of the use of urine in love-philters,[41] is congruent with Crazy Jane's association of love and excrement. Praising Cuchulain's wife Emer because she is "Great-bladdered" (*VP* 628), Crazy Jane suggests that the interplay of disgust and desire generates energy. "Byzantium," a poem about power and purgation written at the same time as the Crazy Jane series, also defines power as produced by "The fury and the mire of human veins." "Complexities of mire or blood" are opposed to the spiritual flames that may purify but that "cannot singe a sleeve." The "unpurged" prostitutes and soldiers dismissed in the opening lines covertly return in the "mire and blood" of the dolphins at the end of the poem (*VP* 497–98). Sexuality and violence structure human life and ensure its continuation. The "mire" liberally spread through the lines of "Byzantium" comes straight from Crazy Jane's "foul sty."

Yeats associated the word "mire" with pigs, as does the OED: "The sowe that was waszhed is turned again unto hir walowynge in the mire." It may also mean "dung." In "Her Vision in the Wood" the dying body, "That thing all blood and mire" (*VP* 537), has been savaged by a boar. The Swineherd from *A Full Moon in March* confirms the association: "There in the dust and mire / Beasts scratched my flesh" (*VPL* 981). An animal that devours its own excrement and wallows in filth, the pig symbolizes uncleanness for both Jews and Christians. Colonial discourse had long bestialized the Irish as pigs: they were characterized as living in a "foul dunghill" in their "swinesteads."[42] While the Bishop mimics colonialist denigration of the Irish peasantry, however, Crazy Jane affirms the vital energies of the "foul sty."

Yeats had always been fascinated by symbolic pigs. His note on "The Valley of the Black Pig" (1896) is an essay in Frazerian folklore that identifies the Black Pig with "the boar that killed Adonis; the boar that killed Attis" (*VP* 809).[43] Like Bakhtin, however, Yeats sees the pig as ambivalent: merely material, as in "this pragmatical, preposterous pig of a world, its farrow that so solid seem" (*VP* 481), or materially powerful.[44] As Chairman of the Coinage Committee he lamented changes imposed by the Ministry of Agriculture on the original design of the sow and her litter because "With the round cheeks of the pig went the lifted head, the look of insolence and of wisdom, and the comfortable round bodies of the little pigs" (*SS* 166). Attacking these "grotesque designs from the farm and poultry yards of Yeats" as "un-Christian," the *Catholic Bulletin* ridiculed "the pig-litter coinage,"[45] thus giving Yeats further reason to set the pig against the Bishop. The pig's "insolence and wisdom" befit that independent-minded inhabitant of the "foul sty," Crazy Jane. Symons had depicted suffragists as descending into the "mire" with man, fighting "for leave to ply / A friendly muckrake with him in his sty."[46] Yeats revalues Symons' metaphor.

For Yeats, excrement is a route to the divine. Recalling Bloom defecating in the outhouse, he speaks of "James Joyce in his Ulysses lying 'upon his right and left side' like Ezekiel and eating 'dung' that he might raise 'other men to a perception of the infinite'" (*UP*2 464). Coprophilia grants prophetic status: the low provides access to the high. Yeats had earlier observed that Donne's "pedantry and his obscenity" were "the rock and the loam of his Eden" (*L* 570), obscenity and "loam" being paired. As Bloom makes his way to the outhouse, he too meditates on the Edenic properties of loam:

Want to manure the whole place over, scabby soil... All soil like that without dung. Household slops. Loam, what is this that is? The hens in the next garden: their droppings are very good top dressing. Best of all though are the cattle, especially when they are fed on those oilcakes. Mulch of dung. Best thing to clean ladies' kid gloves. Dirty cleans. Ashes too. Reclaim the whole place.[47]

"Dirty cleans" expresses Bakhtin's notion that degradation digs a grave for a new birth, that destruction and regeneration are linked. Only those obsessed with the Manichaean claim that the body is inherently sinful fail to apprehend that waste and death are not the binary opposites of purity and life, but their necessary complement. Since the 1934 Congress of Soviet Writers had declared *Ulysses* "a heap of dung teeming with worms,"[48] Bakhtin could not mention Joyce in *Rabelais and His World*. Yeats, however, argued in the Senate in 1928 that Rabelais "is looked upon as one of the greatest masters of the past, and what is to be said of James Joyce may be said of Rabelais" (*SS* 147). He praised Rabelais for escaping from the Catholic sense of sin by virtue of his "vast energy" (*L* 807).

Douglas argues that rituals of exclusion depend on the belief that "to be holy is to be whole, to be one; holiness is unity, integrity." Blood, urine, faeces, and spittle are taboo because they traverse the body's boundary. Cultures that "most explicitly credit corrupt matter with power are making the greatest effort to affirm the physical fullness of reality ... cultures which frankly develop bodily symbolism may be seen to use it to confront experience with its inevitable pains and losses. "[49] Through Crazy Jane, Yeats challenged the cultural exclusions by which the Free State was attempting to assert its body/boundary/identity against the encroachments of modernism. If "nothing can be sole or whole / That has not been rent" (*VP* 513), Ireland must symbolically accept the orifices and excreta of the body as part of the body politic. Writing on divorce Yeats asserted that union with the North could be achieved only through dialogue and the acceptance of difference: the Ulster Protestants "cannot be won if you insist that the Catholic conscience alone must dominate the public life of Ireland" (*SS* 157). Yeats prophetically argued that the nation could not be made "whole" until it tolerated the "rending" of its ideological purity by minority views and practices: contraception, divorce, foreign dances, and books like *Ulysses*. His argument was largely strategic, since Ulster Protestantism, though it permits divorce and contraception, was and is otherwise illiberal in sexual matters. Yet Yeats's claim that a whole nation must comprise heteroglossic voices (women, the rural poor, the Anglo-Irish, the Ulster Protestants) challenges the totalizing monoglot discourse of Irish Catholicism.

CHAPTER 13

Supernatural sex

Yeats had always believed that sexuality and creativity were indissolubly connected: in youth he had asserted that "All the arts sprang from sexual love" (*SB* 106). He associated the creative potency of Synge with the aggressively displayed sexuality of Don Juan in Hell, where the eunuchs "rail and sweat / Maddened by that sinewy thigh" (*VP* 294v). According to Yeats, opponents of the *Playboy* had suffered "a deprivation which is the intellectual equivalent to the removal of the genitals" (*Mem* 176). He celebrated Synge as one who had "brought back masculinity to Irish verse with his harsh disillusionment" (*OBMV* xiv). Yeats's admiration for literary virility and scorn for eunuchs reveals his masculine sexual bravado, but in his mid-sixties his confidence was shattered by the return of what he called "my inhibition" (*LMR* 32): his early impotence with Shakespear. Once a nervous problem, the "inhibition" was now organic. When in early 1934 Yeats consulted the London surgeon Norman Haire he said: "for about three years...he had lost all inspiration and been unable to write anything new."[1] He tried to jump-start the creative process through drama, hoping to "write lyrics out of dramatic experience, all my personal experience having in some strange way come to an end" (*L* 819). As Ellmann puts it: "Versemaking and lovemaking were always connected in his mind. Not to be able to do the one meant not to be able to do the other."[2]

Gilbert and Gubar discuss the patriarchal trope of the pen as penis without noting that the latter is frequently subject to embarrassing dysfunctions.[3] Rochester's "The Imperfect Enjoyment" belongs to a well-established genre in which the poet laments the humiliations to which his organ exposes him:

> But when great Love the onset does command,
> Base recreant to thy prince, thou dar'st not stand.[4]

Great anxiety attaches to a theory of creativity dependent on a part of the body not subordinate to the will. Yeats's worries about potency, however, did not generate the literary sex warfare Gilbert and Gubar see as epidemic among male modernists. They cite Yeats's "globe-trotting Madam," aroused by Michaelangelo's Adam "Till her bowels are in heat" (*VP* 638), as analogous to Prufrock's pseudo-cultivated vampiric women who talk of Michaelangelo: Yeats's speaker, they claim, is alarmed by Madam's "bowels" and her libidinous energy.[5] Yeats, however, validated her erotic reception of high art: he thought artists should depict desirable people, and viewers should desire them. Michaelangelo's representation of male sexuality turns a vacuous tourist into an orgasmic art-lover. In "Long-legged Fly" the speaker wants Michaelangelo left undisturbed so "That girls at puberty may find / The first Adam in their thought" (*VP* 617). Yeats neither imagines the "maimed, unmanned, victimized characters ... obsessively created by early twentieth-century literary men"[6] nor portrays women as monstrous castrating figures. Perhaps because his impotence was caused by arteriosclerosis rather than by a panic reaction to the shift in power between the sexes, he did not blame his insecurities on women.

Yeats's sexual problems were reflected in other spheres, however. In July 1933, at the height of his brief enthusiasm for the Blueshirts, he wrote: "There is so little in our stocking that we are ready at any moment to turn it inside out, and how can we not feel emulous when we see Hitler juggling with his sausage of stocking" (*L* 812). The semi-comic "sausage of stocking" is also so blatantly phallic that Yeats, who knew a little about Freud (*YVP*2 444), must have used it advisedly. The analogous idea that having nothing in your stocking produces compensatory violence was explored by Yeats in a letter to Margot Ruddock in November 1934: "I got up in utter black gloom, 'perhaps after all' I thought 'this nervous inhibition has not left me' – I pictured Margot unsatisfied and lost. How could I finish the poem? How could I finish anything?" The plaintive question refers to his own inability to reach sexual climax, but he was also concerned about his lover's satisfaction. To cheer himself up Yeats invited a Blueshirt comrade to dinner:

His wounds had given him my inhibition and several others. He had cured himself by Oriental meditations. Every morning he stands before his mirror and commands himself to become more positive, more masculine, more independent of the feelings of others. Six months ago he was ordered off the hunting field by a political enemy. He turned his horse and rode the man down. If he goes on with these meditations he will be murdered. (*LMR* 31–32)

Yeats's account of how MacManus cured his impotence by meditations on masculinity, defined as independence of other people's feelings, and flaunted his cure by riding a man down, illustrates the displacement of sexual inhibition into fascist violence. Although Yeats swiftly dropped the Blueshirts, some of his late love poetry offers a violent compensation for lost potency. The metaphor of Hitler as circus clown, however, reveals Yeats's admiration for aggressive masculinity as partially ironic. During the Blueshirt excitement Yeats was writing an account of Bhagwan Shri Hamsa's pilgrimage to Tibet: his vacillation between Western politics and Eastern meditation informs his poetry.

The Steinach operation performed by Haire in April 1934 was intended to rejuvenate Yeats and restore his ability to write. A partial vasectomy (no glands, whether of goats or monkeys, were involved) was supposed to increase the production of testosterone and back it up into the body: this would supposedly slow or reverse the effects of aging. Yeats's experiment with his own anatomy, which he did not attempt to conceal, evinces his willingness to "seem / For the song's sake a fool" (*VP* 553). Yet Steinach, although mistaken, was not a quack, and Yeats was one of many notable men, including Freud, to submit to the operation in the twenties and thirties.[7] In connecting creativity with testosterone, however, Yeats assents to a biologistic model in which great men write out of their essential maleness.[8] Renoir said he painted with his prick.

Yeats probably hoped that the operation would restore his potency as well as his youth. His letter to Ruddock, written eight months after the operation ("perhaps after all... this nervous inhibition has not left me"), suggests as much (*LMR* 31). Ellmann, however, testifies that "Norman Haire, whom Yeats authorized to discuss his case, said to me what a woman friend[9] of Yeats's confirmed... that the operation had no effect upon his sexual competence. He could not have erections, Haire told me."[10] Discussing male sexual ideology Brittan focuses on the centrality of erection to the construction of masculinity: "A man is only a man in so far as he is capable of using his penis as an instrument of power."[11] Yeats, however, uncoupled male sexuality from its dependence on erection, and had several affairs before his death. The renewal of sexual desire to which he testified reopened his access to language and to women's bodies; but the loss of phallic potency forced him to find alternative expressions of that desire and different ways of pleasing his lovers. It is no accident that many of his women friends were lesbians. The Pruitts argue that in his emphasis on the body as the place of writing Yeats reveals himself as a materialist, who sought the magical elixir of youth in the guise of science.[12] Yeats's "materialism," however, can be defended as an extension of his debate with Plato, as a continuation of his dispute with the Manichaean ethic of Irish Catholicism, and as a defense of the marginalized desires of the old.

The "Supernatural Songs," written just after the Steinach operation, celebrate the return of Yeats's sexual desire, but undermine traditional conceptions of masculinity. They also articulate Yeats's opposition to established social and religious power in Ireland. Once again he sought to wrest the high ground from the supporters of orthodoxy by invading, appropriating, and hybridizing rather than simply opposing their theological discourse. The hero of his nineties novel *The Speckled Bird* had articulated a lifetime project: to "reconcile religion with the natural emotions" (*SB* 106). In 1932, when Dublin was in a ferment of religiosity before the Eucharistic Congress, AE wrote to Yeats: "Ireland today forces us to a heretical revolt ... I cannot imagine so much musty piety to exist without some ribald iconoclast being constrained to cry out its opposite."[13] Yeats, who had just written "Crazy Jane talks with the Bishop," was already in heretical revolt. He understood that "The educated Catholics, clerics or laymen, know we are fighting ignorance" (*L* 840), but uneducated Catholics were in the political majority. The "Supernatural Songs" are the verses of a ribald iconoclast who is out to disturb musty piety, but is nevertheless serious about reconciling divine love with the natural emotion of human passion.

The seed of the "Supernatural Songs" lies in the anti-clerical "The Wanderings of Oisin," which Yeats re-read with approval in 1924.[14] Returning to Ireland, the aged Oisin rejects the rosary offered by St. Patrick: "I will pray no more with the smooth stones!" Pagan to the last, he resolves to "go to the house of the Fenians, be they in flames or at feast" (*VP* 63v). In revision the rosary became a "chain": a chain that had tightened its stranglehold by 1934, when Yeats charged that "the Church and the State / Are the mob that howls at the door!" (*VP* 554). In "Supernatural Songs" Ribh, an ancient hermit whose Christianity comes not from Rome but from

Egypt (*VP* 837), takes up Oisin's role in the "old dialogues where Oisin railed at Patrick" (*Ex* 285). Yeats remembered among the Irish peasantry "visionaries of whom it was impossible to say whether they were Christian or Pagan" (*E&I* 429): his hermit Ribh, one of these hybrids, crosses theological, geographical, and gender boundaries. Attempting to circumvent both a Protestantism "that suggested by its blank abstraction chloride of lime" (*E&I* 428) and a Catholicism whose distrust of nature was symbolized by St. Bernard passing the Swiss Lakes "with averted eyes" (*E&I* 431), Yeats shows Patrick's Romanized Christianity as a parvenu in Ireland by evoking anterior religious traditions.

In his Commentary on the "Supernatural Songs" Yeats observed that he "associated early Christian Ireland with India" (*VP* 837), an association strengthened by his friendship with Shri Purohit Swami, which began in 1931. Yeats's long-standing interest in Indian philosophy was reinforced by politics. Ireland and India were fellow-victims of the political and linguistic imperialism that Yeats denounced during a Pen Club dinner in 1934:

I looked round, saw several Indian authors & a lot of refugees from Germany, got the impression every woman there was a Britannia and was suckling a little Polish Jew. Result I devoted my speech to denouncing the Indians for writing in English & England for compelling Indians to conduct government business and all higher education in English "Go back to India," I said, "boycot the English language. Compell (*sic*) your masters to talk Pigeon Bengali, Pigeon Hindi, Pigeon Marratti. Thrust upon them the indignity they thrust upon you." (*AYF* 449)

Maternal Britannia poses as the protectress of Jews and guardian of freedom in Europe, but Yeats reminds her of colonial misdeeds: she has done to Indians what Germany is doing to the Jews. Yeats's "orientalism" was neither frivolous decoration nor the quest for knowledge as a mode of domination described by Said,[15] but the establishment of a circuit between two points on the periphery: an acceptance of ways of knowing deemed marginal by rationalist Western culture. In constructing a mock case against Yeats, Auden appeals to Western ethnocentrism: "in 1930 we are confronted with the pitiful, the deplorable spectacle of a grown man occupied with the mumbo-jumbo of magic and the nonsense of India."[16] Yeats, however, did not regard the philosophy of an ancient civilization as "nonsense." He wrote an introduction for the Swami's spiritual

autobiography, and collaborated with him on a translation of the
Upanishads. Their intimacy between 1932 and 1936 was reflected
both in "Supernatural Songs" and in his important essays, "The
Holy Mountain" and "The Mandukya Upanishad."

"Ribh at the Tomb of Baile and Aillinn" draws on the Swami's
tales of saintly Indian hermits, and crosses them with the Irish myth
retold in Yeats's early poem "Baile and Aillinn" (1901). In the
mythic source Baile and Aillinn both expired upon being given false
reports of the other's death. Identifying the lying messenger as
Aengus, Yeats implies that the god of love prefers supernatural to
natural consummation. The poem's speaker celebrates the death of
lovers as preventing the death of love:

> *Their love was never drowned in care*
> *Of this or that thing, nor grew cold*
> *Because their bodies had grown old.*   (*VP* 189)

The narrative of "Baile and Aillinn" employs the familiar early-
Yeatsian *Liebestod* in which permanent love occurs only in the grave.
When in 1934 Yeats returned to their story, however, his interest in
sex after death was no longer a deferral of experience but an old
man's search for something to anticipate. In proclaiming that "only
two topics can be of the least interest to a serious and studious mind
– sex and the dead" (*L* 730), he was not joking. Baile and Aillinn
meet to make love each year on the "anniversary" of their death (*VP*
555). Harold Bloom has noted the logical discrepancy between their
supposedly eternal and timeless love and the temporality of their
encounters.[17] Ghosts who return annually, however, are a crucial
part of the Irish folk conception of the supernatural. Sheeran notes
the overwhelming importance in Irish culture of the death anni-
versary: "In Irish idiom the word anniversary...is used almost
exclusively with reference to death."[18]

In 1909 Yeats's longing for physical satisfaction had caused him to
doubt Gonne's promise of union "in the blinding light beyond the
grave" (*VP* 258); but his spiritualist experiments after 1911
convinced him that there was indeed a world elsewhere. He wrote to
her: "It changes life to believe all the new intimate knowledge, not
theoretical merely, that love & friendship last beyond the grave"
(*AYF* 323). Despite their later sharp exchanges about his Senate
votes for "flogging bills & Treason Acts & Public Safety Acts" (*AYF*
435), Yeats defused his desire to criticize Gonne by remembering that

"Somewhere beyond the curtain / Of distorting days" her beauty still lived on ("Quarrel in Old Age," *VP* 504). The parts of *A Vision* that deal with the soul's "dreaming back" after death through the events of its life and the cycles of reincarnation through which it must proceed are constructed to give philosophical support to the *Liebestod*: a generic cliché is reanimated through spiritualist testimony and Indian belief.

Describing "Ribh at the Tomb of Baile and Aillinn," Yeats reflected to Shakespear in July 1934: "Strange that I should write these things in my old age, when if I were to offer myself for new love I could only expect to be accepted by the very young wearied by the passive embraces of the bolster" (*L* 824–25). Yeats implies that he would be an improvement on the bolster, since his embraces would be active rather than passive. Like Yeats, Ribh is too old for phallic sex, but he sympathizes with the lovers whose non-phallic intercourse he observes and whom, in a move reminiscent of Donne, he has "*Canoniz'd* for Love."[19]

> The miracle that gave them such a death
> Transfigured to pure substance what had once
> Been bone and sinew; when such bodies join
> There is no touching here, nor touching there,
> Nor straining joy, but whole is joined to whole;
> For the intercourse of angels is a light
> Where for its moment both seem lost, consumed. (*VP* 555)

Drawing on "that saying of Swedenborg's that the sexual intercourse of the angels is a conflagration of the whole being" (*L* 805), Yeats imagines how in heaven "an improvement in sense" can far surpass the unsatisfactory mechanics of earthly copulation. He cited Dryden's translation of Lucretius on the failure of penetration to achieve perfect union between lovers:

> They grip, they squeeze, their humid tongues they dart,
> As each would force their way to t'other's heart:
> In vain; they only cruise about the coast;
> For bodies cannot pierce, nor be in bodies lost,
> As sure they strive to be, when both engage
> In that tumultuous momentary rage.[20]

Yeats's dictum, "the tragedy of sexual intercourse is the perpetual virginity of the soul,"[21] echoes Lucretius. But Baile and Aillinn, no longer dependent on uncertain male potency or on the "straining joy" of hard-working Lucretian sexual partners, truly merge. Penetration is irrelevant when every part of the body is in erotic conflagration: to abandon masculinity's exclusive concentration on the penis is to liberate hitherto unsuspected erogenous zones. "The intercourse of angels" may have been a model for Yeats's own late sexual practice. Donne's "The Extasie," more optimistic than Lucretius in its characterization of sexual intercourse, had claimed that "soule into the soule may flow, / Though it to body first repaire." Yeats stresses the "pure substance" (does his emphasis fall on "pure" or on "substance"?) of what he still insists are the "bodies" of the angels. For Yeats as for Donne, "Loves mysteries in soules doe grow, / But yet the body is his booke."[22]

The Swami reawakened Yeats's interest in esoteric Tantric philosophy, popularized by Blavatsky in *The Secret Doctrine*. In 1962 Mrs. Yeats showed the scholar Naresh Guha a complete set of Woodroffe's *Tantrik Texts*, which Yeats had bought on their publication in 1913.[23] Victorian scholars viewed Tantra as a revolting mixture of sex and black magic posing as religion: a combination guaranteed to appeal to Yeats. He even speculated that Tantric philosophy might have created European romance:

Did this worship, this meditation, establish among us romantic love, was it prevalent in Northern Europe during the twelfth century? In the German epic *Parsifal* Gawain drives a dagger through his hand without knowing it during his love-trance, Parsifal falls into such a trance when a drop of blood upon snow recalls to his mind a tear upon his wife's cheek. (*E&I* 484)

Although Vedantic and Buddhist disdain for the manifest world and quest of the Nirvana of non-being devalues fleshly pleasures, Indian temple sculptures depict mythological figures enjoying enthusiastic and complicated congress. Guha argues that without a knowledge of the esoteric sexual lore of Tantra, "it would be impossible to explain the affirmative character of the major portion of the ancient sculpture in India."[24] Devotees of Tantra had the same goal as their ascetic counterparts: the nothingness of ultimate reality. They believed, however, in reaching Nirvana by exhausting rather than denying the passions. In his 1935 essay "The Mandukya Upanishad," Yeats described

the Tantric philosophy, where a man and woman, when in sexual union, transfigure each other's images into the masculine and feminine characters of God, but the man must not finish, vitality must not pass beyond his body, beyond his being. There are married people who, though they do not forbid the passage of the seed, practise, not necessarily at the moment of union, a meditation, wherein the man seeks the divine Self as present in his wife, the wife the divine Self as present in the man. There may be trance, and the presence of one with another though a great distance separates. (*E&I* 484)

Although Tantra does permit penetration, Yeats emphasizes the non-orgasmic nature of the caress: "the man must not finish." For a man able neither to penetrate nor to finish, the idea must have been attractive. The acceptance of sex as a road to divinity in Tantra satisfied Yeats's desire for a philosophy that would affirm "an alliance between body and soul our theology rejects" (*E&I* 451).

In Tantric sex the goal of losing self in union with the Godhead is not abandoned but postponed. Yeats knew that "the last kiss is given to the void" (*LTSM* 154). Nevertheless, he wanted to put off the last kiss as long as possible, especially since he had wasted his youth in sexual self-denial. It was religious to make up for lost time; a spiritual requirement to approach God with all passion spent: "Sexual desire dies because every touch consumes the Myth, and yet a Myth that cannot be so consumed becomes a spectre" (*LTSM* 154). His Young Girl agrees:

> Such body lovers have,
> Such exacting breath,
> That they touch or sigh.
> Every touch they give,
> Love is nearer death.
> *Prove that I lie.* (*VP* 517)

Through a hermeneutics partly derived from Indian thought, Yeats challenges the tendency of Western poets to disparage the available woman because the female body is "Enjoyed no sooner but despised straight." For Yeats the extinction of male sexual desire in satisfaction is not an "expense of spirit in a waste of shame,"[25] but the necessary death of the romantic Myth, a Myth that if not consumed becomes a spectre or vampire.

Yeats refuses to write of the demythologized beloved or the sexual act with the savage abhorrence expressed in Shakespeare's Sonnet 129. Although he lamented that "my loves drank their oil and died – there has been no ever-burning lamp" (*AV*[*B*] 40), he did not blame his lovers. The alternation between lust and disgust in Sonnet 129 produces a binary opposition between the Heaven of desire and the Hell of repentance. Yeats, however, argues that even brief love is good: it should be enjoyed and relinquished. In Blake's words, "he who kisses the joy as it flies / lives in eternity's sun rise."[26] The love that cannot be realized, and therefore can never die, becomes a spectre. In *A Vision* Yeats posed the problem philosophically:

Love contains all Kant's antinomies, but it is the first that poisons our lives. Thesis, there is no beginning; antithesis, there is a beginning; or, as I prefer: thesis, there is an end; antithesis, there is no end. Exhausted by the cry that it can never end, my love ends; without that cry it were not love but desire, desire does not end. (*AV*[*B*] 40)

Yeats's perception – love dies, desire does not – anticipates his pragmatic deconstruction of the poisonous antinomy: the exhaustion of one love-Myth entails its immediate replacement by another. The youth who had thought one woman enough for a lifetime becomes an aged philanderer: "When life puts away her conjuring tricks one by one, those that deceive us longest may well be the wine-cup and the sensual kiss" (*Myth* 332). In his poetry after 1928 Yeats affirms the brevity of love: if every touch consumes the Myth, then every touch brings us closer to the emptiness of union with the Divine. Theory became practice in his affairs, sanctioned by the logic of a desire that "does not end" and by the speculations of Indian philosophy.

"Crazy Jane and Jack the Journeyman," in which Jane claims that "A lonely ghost the ghost is / That to God shall come" (*VP* 511), was written in 1931, just after Yeats met the Swami.[27] Shri Purohit's ideas strengthened Jane's determination to exhaust her passion by leaving the door unlatched for passing lovers. Despite his admiration for the ascetic Bhagwan Shri Hamsa, Yeats was not attracted by Vedantic ideals of renunciation: according to Naresh Guha, he preferred Blavatsky's Puranic or popular mythological Hinduism:

Whereas Matter is "Illusion" in Vedanta, in Puranic Hinduism it has become *Devi* (the Goddess), or *Sakti* (Power), the Eternal Feminine Principle of creation. The whole external universe is the product of the union of the two – the Spirit and the Goddess, and is, therefore, sacred. The world should not therefore be devalued or discarded as illusion. Even liberation becomes meaningless to a worshipper of the Goddess.[28]

When Yeats claims that "Matter is the source of all energy, all creative power, all that separates one thing from another" (*E&I* 461), he deconstructs the Platonic hierarchical opposition between male Spirit and female Nature. The *Yoga-Sutras* of Patanjali, to which Yeats wrote an introduction, represented the Goddess as neither passive primal slime awaiting the breath of God, nor as a degraded but necessary vehicle for male semen, but as Herself a source of primary power. In "Supernatural Songs" the Swami's Eastern metaphysics challenge Plato's Western philosophy. The dualistic privileging of spirit over matter, argues Brittan, "is central to the masculinist ethos."[29] In "Ribh denounces Patrick" Yeats shows Western Christianity as enslaved by the masculine bias of Platonism. The Trinity is absurd because it excludes the female, both as engenderer and offspring:

An abstract Greek absurdity has crazed the man,
Recall that masculine Trinity. Man, woman, child (a daughter or a son),
That's how all natural or supernatural stories run.   (*VP* 556)

Yeats knew from Burkitt's *Early Eastern Christianity* that the Holy Spirit was figured as feminine,[30] but his potential female Christ ("a daughter or a son") is revolutionary.

Ribh, the first of Yeats's dramatic speakers since Crazy Jane, shares more with her than his advanced age. Her denunciation of the Bishop's prudery parallels his blasphemous insistence to Patrick that there must be copulation in Heaven, since there is plenty on earth:

Natural and supernatural with the self-same ring are wed.
As man, as beast, as an ephemeral fly begets, Godhead begets Godhead,
For things below are copies, the Great Smaragdine Tablet said. (*VP* 556)

Substituting the sexually active divine Mother for the Virgin Mary, Yeats imagines frenetic heterosexual begetting in the beyond. "Ribh in Ecstasy" eavesdrops as "Godhead on Godhead in sexual spasm begot / Godhead." Auditor of divine intercourse, Ribh is brought to onanistic "ecstasy" by hearing the gods' "amorous cries" (*VP* 557). In 1931 Yeats wrote: "Heaven is an improvement of sense – one listens to music, one does not read Hegel's logic" (*L* 781). Although old and impotent, Ribh hears the music of eternal sexuality, and his perpetually copulating gods derive from Indian sculptures and Tantric sexual practices.

Human orgasms differ from divine ones, however. Lacking contraception earthly lovers must reproduce themselves ad infinitum, "increase their kind" and surrender to the "mirror- scalèd serpent" of multiplicity, whereas God can eternally reproduce itself as an unchanging, never increasing trio of "Man, woman, child." Human passion is only a symbol of eternity:

When the conflagration of their passion sinks, damped by the body or the
  mind,
That juggling nature mounts, her coil in their embraces twined.

Ribh suggests that if perfect love were possible on earth it would result in perfect contraception: juggling nature would gain no purchase on lovers who "could beget or bear themselves could they but love as He" (*VP* 556). The Catholic injunction to go forth and multiply is challenged by Yeats's Trinitarian ideal family: a heterosexual couple and one child. As Sheeran has suggested, this obscure metaphysical poem encodes a subtle comment on Catholic reproductive theology.[31]

Yeats's heterodox religious temper conditions his presentation of gender in "What Magic Drum?" which combines the Swami's miraculous tales of his master Bhagwan Shri Hamsa with Swedenborgian androgyny:

He holds him from desire, all but stops his breathing lest
Primordial Motherhood forsake his limbs, the child no longer rest,
Drinking joy as it were milk upon his breast.   (*VP* 559)

Critics disagree about the number of figures in this tableau: does it comprise man, woman, and child,[32] or father and baby?[33] The latter reading, which I prefer, suggests that the male protagonist has achieved "Primordial Motherhood" himself through the suspension of masculine desire, and the line "Drinking joy as it were milk upon his breast" grants the nurturing function to the father. Peter Middleton relates this image to "A Dialogue of Self and Soul," where the line "So great a sweetness flows into the breast" (*VP* 479) also establishes man as "nurturing maternal creator."[34] Yeats wrote that "in Swedenborg alone the conscious and the subconscious became one – as in that marriage of the angels, which he has described as a contact of the whole being – so completely one indeed that Coleridge thought Swedenborg both man and woman" (*Au* 244). If "Ribh at the Tomb of Baile and Aillinn" abolishes the prominence of the phallus in the androgynous intercourse of angels, "What Magic Drum?" imagines an androgynous maternal male. Yeats found his metaphor in the Swami's account of Bhagwan Shri

Hamsa's pilgrimage to Mount Kailas, when Lord Dattatreya "lifted me up like the Divine Mother and hugged me to His breast and caressed me all over the body" (*E&I* 479). Conflating mystical, parental, and sexual love, Yeats blurs gender identity and sexual orientation:

> Through light-obliterating garden foliage what magic drum?
> Down limb and breast or down that glimmering belly move his mouth
>   and sinewy tongue.
> What from the forest came? What beast has licked its young? (*VP* 560)

The licking of the child is highly erotic, and Yeats's use of the word "sinewy" to describe the tongue of the beast is a significant displacement of the "sinewy thigh" that signalled the potency of Synge to the eunuchs in Hell. This polymorphous, dispersed sexuality was a characteristic of the Swami's poetry:

all his poems are love-songs, lullabies, or songs of loyalty to friend or master, for ... he can but offer to God the service learnt in service of man or woman; nor can any single service symbolise mans's relation to God. He must be sung as the soul's husband, bride, child, and friend. (*E&I* 434)

As if in emulation of the Swami's creative fusion of love and religious worship, Yeats adapted Lord Dattatreya's words to Bhagwan Shri Hamsa, "O my child, O my dear" (*E&I* 460), as the refrain for his ballad about sexuality, "The Three Bushes."

The "Supernatural Songs" are unconventional love poems that extend the possibilities of the genre through hybridization with the cognate genre of divine poetry. Like the Swami, divine poets in the West, from the Song of Songs through Donne, Herbert, and Hopkins, have often borrowed the metaphors of secular love, while the mystics of the Church have also used the vocabulary of erotic desire to convey the essence of union with the divine. In the "Supernatural Songs" Yeats takes advantage of the historical cross-fertilization between the genres. In "Ribh considers Christian Love insufficient," the speaker reinforces his dismissal of love through the ancient gendered trope of the soul of man as the Bride of Christ. Choosing hatred as a "besom" or broom to clear the soul of "impurities," he evokes the biblical image of the soul swept and garnished to await the bridegroom's coming. In 1909 Yeats had defined hatred as antithetical to desire, as producing eunuchs: "Hatred as a basis of imagination ... helps to dry up the nature and makes the sexual abstinence, so common among

young men and women in Ireland, possible. This abstinence reacts in
its turn on the imagination, so that we get at last that strange eunuch-
like tone and temper" (*Mem* 177). In this poem, however, hatred
replaces desire as a creative force: hate is more powerful than love
because love as defined by Irish Catholicism is "trash and tinsel":

> Then my delivered soul herself shall learn
> A darker knowledge and in hatred turn
> From every thought of God mankind has had.
> Thought is a garment and the soul's a bride
> That cannot in that trash and tinsel hide:
> Hatred of God may bring the soul to God.   (*VP* 558)

Ribh employs a negative theology that rejects not the love of God but
all human conceptions of that love, and all institutions that claim to
control access to it.[35] Yeats was familiar with the *via negativa* espoused
by St. John of the Cross and by exponents of the Christian mystical
tradition like Meister Eckhardt: "The soul honours God most in
being quit of God."[36]

Ribh's use of traditional religious metaphors, however, carries a
crude sexual charge. Coarsening his reference to the Song of Songs,
Ribh ends with a series of rhetorical questions that imply the soul's
complete subservience to her Master:

> What can she take until her Master give!
> Where can she look until He make the show!
> What can she know until He bid her know!
> How can she live till in her blood He live!   (*VP* 558)

The soul is blind, ignorant, and unliving. The Master is the agent of
sight, knowledge, and power. At midnight, the moment of death, the
soul must strip naked and the Master must "give" her the gift of his
semen, parade his erection for her benefit ("make the show"),
"know" her carnally, and "live" in the blood of her defloration,
possibly even her murder. Hopkins's address to Jesus in *The Wreck of
the Deutschland*, "What was the feast followed the night / Thou hadst
glory of this nun,"[37] deploys a similarly violent though less explicit
spiritual erotics. Like Donne's speaker in "Batter My Heart, Three-
Person'd God," Ribh represents the submission of a man's soul to its
Creator in terms of a sexual dominance fantasy. To represent the
imbalance of power between God and man, many male religious
poets use, and thus naturalize, the unbalanced relation between man
and woman.

Yeats, however, follows "Ribh considers Christian Love insuf-
ficient" with an antidote. Although it deploys the well-worn
metaphor of woman as reflected rather than original light, "He and
She" represents the soul as refusing sexual obliteration. As the moon
flirtatiously approaches and avoids the stronger light of the sun, the
soul escapes the pornographic "show" of the Master by declining to
look at it: "His light had struck me blind / Dared I stop." Her
strategy is not to challenge his power but to acknowledge that her
own increases when she is farthest away from him. The poem
celebrates an independent identity:

> She sings as the moon sings:
> "I am I, am I;
> The greater grows my light
> The further that I fly".
> All creation shivers
> With that sweet cry.   (*VP* 559)

Bloom, antagonistic to female independence, calls this "a slight but
bitterly charming lyric, on woman's fickleness and power of self-
assertion."[38] While the shiver that runs through "all creation" may
be apprehension or delight, however, Yeats presents the cry "I am I,
am I" as unambiguously "sweet." The soul has reclothed herself in
the garment of selfhood that was stripped from her in the previous
poem, and Yeats rejoices in her freedom.

Freedom, however, is obliterated in "Whence had they Come?"
which, like "Leda and the Swan," represents history as fuelled by
libido, political and sexual apocalypse as cognate. Lovers think
themselves unique, but their play is already scripted:

> girl or boy
> Cry at the onset of their sexual joy
> "For ever and for ever"; then awake
> Ignorant what Dramatis Personae spake.

In the grip of passion we are "ignorant," driven by the unconscious.
Ascetics who imagine they can subdue the flesh are impelled by Eros
to acts of religious mortification. Yeats had read Flaubert's *Temptation
of St. Anthony* and understood the Swinburnian algolagnia of the
monks in the desert:

> The Flagellant lashes those submissive loins
> Ignorant what that dramatist enjoins,
> What master made the lash.

Like Ribh, the dramatist of world history has a sado-masochistic imagination. The sacred drama, the orgasm, and the omnipresent lash are metonymically connected:

> Whence had they come,
> The hand and lash that beat down frigid Rome?
> What sacred drama through her body heaved
> When world-transforming Charlemagne was conceived? (*VP* 560)

The hand and lash belong to Jesus Christ, deity of the Flagellants, whose masochistic sacrifice unleashed a "Galilean turbulence" upon the cold rationality of the Age of Augustus: at his birth "The Roman Empire stood appalled" (*VP* 437–38). In the eighth century Charlemagne revived Rome by uniting secular with Christian power; in the "sacred drama" of his mother's orgasm the Holy Roman Empire was conceived. Yeats challenges the frigidity of contemporary Holy Rome by exposing the erotic foundations of religious power. Having described the sexual prohibitions of the Catholic Church as "icebergs in warm water" (*SS* 97), he tries to heat up the water with a sacred "coming." As the futility of Yeats's challenge to musty piety became evident during the thirties, his language became more violent and extreme. The stridency of "Whence had they Come?" like that of "Ribh considers Christian Love insufficient," is the stridency of combative defeat. When Yeats closes his sequence with an image of Indian ascetics exposed to the "drifted snow" on Mount Meru, he adopts a less aggressive attitude to his enemies, for Eastern wisdom reminds us that all things pass away: "Egypt and Greece, good-bye, and good-bye Rome!" (*VP* 563).

CHAPTER 14

A foolish passionate man

Yeats knew that his readers, male and female alike, would "think it horrible that lust and rage / Should dance attendance upon my old age" (*VP* 591). To continue to write of desire, passion, and power, he risked both giving offense and seeming foolish. "A Prayer for Old Age," written in August 1934, articulates a defiant ballad poetics in which the claims of the body's "marrow-bone" must be sustained beyond the boundaries of propriety in order to guarantee a "lasting song." Yeats did not write the body in order to shock: he could not write without it. He therefore prayed "That I may seem, though I die old, / A foolish, passionate man" (*VP* 553).

After retiring from the Senate in 1928 Yeats continued to combat censorship with unceasing vigor and little success: post-revolutionary conservatism increased. De Valera's Constitution of 1937, affirming the "special position" of the Catholic Church and enshrining its view of women as the home-bound agents of reproduction, is unashamedly theocratic: the sexual division of labor is given the double force of state approval and religious blessing. The Constitution is also masculinist in its assumption of hegemonic heterosexuality and its validation of the patriarchal family. Yeats reasserted that he was a nationalist of the school of John O'Leary because nationalism of an unenlightened Catholic type now dominated Irish public life: "The beggars have changed places, but the lash goes on" (*VP* 590). He poetically reopened the cases of Protestant patriots like Parnell and Casement who were marginalized because of their aberrant sexuality. For Mother Ireland he substituted his "old bawd" Mrs. Mary Moore, whose scandalous tales would horrify the clergy: "And O! but she had stories, / Though not for the priest's ear" (*VP* 620).

Yeats also scandalized the younger English poets. MacNeice felt that "the septuagenarian virility is sometimes too exhibitionist,"[1] while Auden wrote prissily of Yeats's "embarrassing insistence upon an old man's virility, which some one who was more self-critical, not as a poet, but as a man, would have avoided."[2] Today Yeats's pose as Wild Old Wicked Man appears either provocatively carnivalesque, a comic assault on censorship and ageism, or a pathetic over-compensation for impotence. Yet his connection of passion with age challenged the thirties cult of youth and the misogyny of the English Old Boy literary network. Citing the chauvinist opinions of Auden, Day Lewis, Tolkein, Waugh, and Williams, Cunningham suggests that being "mad about women" (*VP* 587) was unfashionable among thirties writers.[3] Yeats's late work needs to be assessed not only against the climate of censorship in Ireland, but against the cultural norms of the English literary establishment. In 1937 he told Wellesley that while Mallarmé escapes from history, "you and I are in history, the history of the mind. Your 'Fire' has a date or dates, so has my 'Wild Old Wicked Man'" (*L* 887). The date of his poem suggests that it is an attempt to neutralize the loss of authority and prestige inevitably incurred by an old man among "the boys" of the thirties.[4]

This most notorious of Yeats's late ballads originated in his wish to visit India with the Swami's disciple Lady Elizabeth Pelham,[5] who refused to be drawn into intimacy with him. Sex spurs the ascent of the holy mountain: "Because I am mad about women / I am mad about the hills." In old age Yeats thought the supreme experience available to men and women was to share profound thought and then to touch, and his speaker links language with body: "Kind are all your words, my dear, / Do not the rest withhold." Assuming that his rivals are youths, he uses his verbal superiority as a seduction strategy:

> I have what no young man can have
> Because he loves too much.
> Words I have that can pierce the heart,
> But what can he do but touch?

A man unable to have an erection has a vested interest in the idea that words go deeper than penises. His rival, however, is no young stud, but an even "older man." With rosary-wielding Catholic piety the woman asserts her prior commitment to

> That old man in the skies.
> Hands that are busy with His beads
> Can never close those eyes.   (*VP* 588)

Beaten in sexual competition with God, the old man, his phallic "stout stick under his hand," turns from the reluctant virgin to the sailors' whores, the "Girls down on the sea shore / Who understand the dark." But the refrain, "*Day-break and a candle end,*" undercuts his sexual bravado with its suggestion of drooping, melting wax. Perhaps his stick is not so stout after all. Even with the whores the Wild Old Wicked Man must insist on verbal instead of physical virility: he can "touch" these women more profoundly than their other clients, the sexually vigorous "warty lads." He takes pride in pleasing the women about whom he is mad. Age has tempered the impetuousness of youthful masculinity with a subtler, androgynous intuition: he "Can touch by mother wit / Things hid in their marrow bones" (*VP* 589). Women know what women like; men feminized by age and impotence understand, as lesbians do, those female pleasures not dependent upon an erect penis. Yeats's image covertly suggests the replacement of phallic thrust by clitoral stimulation. Far from being a sexist hymn to copulation, "The Wild Old Wicked Man" tells of rejection, compensation for lost potency, and desire to give as well as to receive sexual pleasure. The "old man in the skies" may ultimately cauterize the body with a stream of lightning, but the "coarse old man" (like the old woman of "Consolation") will immerse himself in the darkness of a physical pleasure imaged, as often in Yeats, as the child's return to the lost mother:

> I choose the second-best,
> I forget it all awhile
> Upon a woman's breast. (*VP* 589–90)

Yeats's late affairs, all with Englishwomen, were conducted in England, where sexual tolerance was greater than in Ireland. What Margot Ruddock, Dorothy Wellesley, Edith Shackleton Heald, and Ethel Mannin also had in common was their pursuit of a career: Mannin was a novelist, Ruddock an actress, Heald a journalist, and Wellesley a poet.[6] Yeats maintained to the last his habit of choosing women who had their own creative or professional bent, and encouraging them to pursue it. But what of his wife, the medium, collaborator, secretary, and nurse, upon whom he depended so completely? George Yeats, like the wives of many literary men, was exploited. She accepted her subordinate position and tolerated his infidelities:

Mrs. Yeats knew how important they were to him and, conscious of her role as a poet's wife, she countenanced more than she discountenanced them.

"After your death," she once said to him, "people will write of your love affairs, but I shall say nothing, because I will remember how proud you were."[7]

Her comment implies that Yeats's liaisons might make him appear ridiculous, and some of them certainly had their tragi-comic aspects. There was nothing ridiculous, however, about his enduring need for female friendship. In 1936 he wrote to Mannin, "We poets would die of loneliness but for women, and we choose our men friends that we may have somebody to talk about women with... I don't think women choose their women friends to talk of men" (*L* 867). Yeats acknowledged and envied the self-containment of female friendship because he found friendship with other men competitive and difficult. He had told Gregory, "I have always believed that the chief happiness & favour of my life has been the nobility of three or four women friends."[8] After her death he acquired three or four more. By then the distinction between friendship and passion that had seemed absolute in his youth had broken down. He wrote to Margot Ruddock:

I understand what you feel about the word "love". I too hate that word and have I think avoided it. It is a name for the ephemeral charm of desire – desire for its own sake. I do not think that it is because I have grown old, that I value something more like friendship because founded on common interest, and think sexual pleasure an accessory, a needful one where it is possible. Paris and Helen were Romantic Love, and both were probably fools; Odysseus returning to Penelope through ten years' heroic toil (though frequently unfaithful on the way), Penelope's patient waiting, was the classical ideal of man's and woman's wisdom. Both had Ithaca to think of. (*LMR* 42)

Yeats's mature redefinition of Romantic Love as folly and valorization of friendship founded on common interest, however, is compromised by his acceptance of the stereotypes of the wandering man and the patiently waiting wife. In his search for multiple female friendships Yeats cast George Yeats as Penelope to his frequently unfaithful Odysseus.

Margot Ruddock was the first woman to engage Yeats's affections after the Steinach operation. Their relationship, which culminated with her despair about her poetry, her arrival on Yeats's doorstep, and her mental breakdown, followed the father-daughter model: the older, world-famous male dominating the unstable, unknown female pupil. His poems about her, however, disturb this power relation.

The draft material for "Margot" and the unpublished fragment "Portrayed before his Eyes"[9] approaches inequality in love with a directness that Ellmann finds "near-sentimental":

> All day you flitted before me
> Moving like Artemis
> I longed to clasp your knees in worship
> When I sat down to rest you stood beside me as a child.
> My eyes dimmed with tears
> O beloved come to me when the night thickens
> That I may hope [to end] in the bed's friendship
> This heart-breaking inequality.[10]

The straightforward address of lover to beloved, the traditional comparison of the woman to a goddess, and the simple seduction motive mark this "theme for a poem" as a generic classic. The sentimentality Ellmann discerns is a function of diction. Yeats's goddess "flitted" before him; he longed "to clasp your knees in worship"; his eyes predictably "dimmed with tears." Under the stress of an immediate and painful inspiration, Yeats's first resort is the language of convention, which suggests the power of that convention and the formal effort it took him to remake it. Yet his wish to end love's "heart-breaking inequality" in the charmingly prosaic "bed's friendship" reworks convention. Love unfulfilled creates the disequilibrium Yeats experienced with Gonne: the woman is either chaste goddess or child, the man abject worshipper or anxious protector. In the last draft Yeats evokes a temporary balance of power contingent upon fulfillment: "In Love's levelling bed / All gyres lie still."[11] Sexual hierarchies are abolished in the democracy of the sheets.

"Margot," a love poem included in a letter but unpublished until recently, is the nearest Yeats comes to unmediated intimacy in the genre. Although he had praised the love songs of Connacht because they were made not by conscious artists but by "people very desperately in love" (*UP*I 292), his usual practice in his later verse was to create poetic voices distinct from his own. He addressed no other poem to a woman by her first name. To match the unguardedness of the title Yeats employs the "I/you" form of address in "Margot." This poem, constructed to thank, praise, and cajole the recipient, successfully braves sentimentality in the interests of communication. There is a difference between a poem meant to move a particular person, which constructs a relationship between sender and receiver, and a poem that uses love as an occasion for public performance. "Margot," Yeats's closest approach to a confessional love poem, presents the speaker in the sentimental pose of an old man dependent on the sexual generosity of a young woman: "All famine struck sat I, and then / Those generous eyes on mine were cast." Love is a two-way process rather than a bravura posture: relinquishing the power of the gaze to his beloved, Yeats tries to see himself through her eyes. With wry irony he acknowledges that only by squinting can she perceive him in a romantic light:

> O how can I that interest hold?
> What offer to attentive eyes?
> Mind grows young and body old;
> When half closed her eye-lid lies
> A sort of hidden glory shall
> About these stooping shoulders fall.

Her "generous" and "attentive" eyes must be veiled during their affair, but,

> When my brief final years are gone
> You shall have time to turn away
> And cram those open eyes with day.   (*LMR* 33–34)

The generosity he celebrates in her is reciprocated. He will not detain her long in the geriatric twilight, and when he is dead she can return to the sunlit world where no illusions are necessary to sustain desire. No love poem can be free of pose, which is implicit in the act of writing rather than embracing; poems like "Margot," however, create that illusion of eavesdropping implied in Mill's definition of lyric as "overheard."

Yeats's hope that his affair with Margot Ruddock would cost her little was not fulfilled, although her crisis was caused less by sexuality than by his criticism of her verse: "Did words of mine put too great strain / On that woman's reeling brain?" (*VP* 632). Initially acknowledging her as a "fellow artist" (*LMR* 19), he suggested that they "collaborate in half a dozen poems" (*LMR* 32), and much of their correspondence concerns the improvement of her poetry, which he included in his Oxford anthology. Sensing that their professional relation broke down gender barriers she sought his opinion of her poems "as man to man" (*LMR* 78). Yeats also encouraged her career, writing: "I am glad you are to go back to the stage...Act constantly, act anywhere, so that you act" (*LMR* 64). When she lamented the difficulty of combining career and childcare his solution was economic: act more, and earn enough money "to hire a proper nurse" (*LMR* 67). As he had said in the Senate, defending women's right to work after marriage, "I have not noticed that when an actress gets married she retires from the stage" (*SS* 104). While Ruddock's bout of insanity in May 1936 cooled their personal relationship, Yeats still gave his prestigious imprimatur to her book of verse, *The Lemon Tree*, and they continued to work together on broadcasts of his poetry. The ending of their sexual friendship did not entail the abandonment of their professional relation.

Unlike "Margot," Yeats's canonical poems about Ruddock's madness conceal their personal roots. In "Sweet Dancer" the patronizing designation "girl" and the adjective "crazy" distance speaker and reader from the object of their gaze, who is isolated by her insanity. As if to counter this traditional rendition of female madness as aesthetic spectacle, however, Yeats explicitly rejects conventional consolation: "do not say / That she is happy being crazy." Her madness is tragic rather than pathetic; her dance demands its appropriate conclusion: "Let her finish her dance." The poet sides with the dancer rather than with the threatening "strange men" who come to incarcerate her. "Sweet Dancer" is recognizable as a love poem by its refrain, "*Ah, dancer, ah, sweet dancer!*" (*VP* 568), in which the repeated interjection conjures an emotional and regretful speaker. As in the refrain of "The Three Bushes," "Ah" and "O" are codewords for sexual feeling: Yeats rescues the apostrophe from Victorian "poeticism" and reclaims it for modern love poetry.

"A Crazed Girl" also affirms the female creator as she improvises "her music, / Her poetry, dancing upon the shore." In *New Poems* "A Crazed Girl" follows "Beautiful Lofty Things," where Yeats had celebrated Gregory and at last named "Maud Gonne at Howth station waiting a train, / Pallas Athene in that straight back and arrogant head." As an artist and a brave woman Ruddock too merits the epithet "beautiful lofty thing":

> No matter what disaster occurred
> She stood in desperate music wound,
> Wound, wound, and she made in her triumph
> Where the bales and the baskets lay
> No common intelligible sound
> But sang, "O sea-starved, hungry sea." (*VP* 578)

Her "desperate music" is canonized a "triumph," its unintelligibility coded as aristocratic avoidance of the "common." Roger McHugh finds it ironic that in *New Poems* "A Crazed Girl" precedes "To Dorothy Wellesley," since Yeats's relationship with Wellesley was ripening just as he was ending his intimacy with Ruddock (*LMR* 116). Both poems, however, celebrate the solitary heroism of female artists. While Ruddock is separated from the "common" by her madness, Wellesley is a wealthy aristocrat, but both are driven by their different Furies.

Yeats's meeting with Wellesley in 1935 brought him into a circle of cultured English lesbians who had artistic and social ties with the remnants of Bloomsbury. Vita Sackville-West had been Wellesley's lover, but left her for Woolf. Sackville-West later fell in love with Hilda Matheson, a formidable professional woman[12] whom Yeats much admired (*LDW* 147). When Sackville-West's passion cooled, Matheson and Wellesley became lovers, remaining together until Matheson's death in 1940.

Wellesley encouraged Yeats to read Sackville-West's novels and poems. Although he disliked *The Edwardians* he nevertheless found it compelling. He commented that "Miss Sackville West sees only the futility of her own class – & all that is admirable," but argued that she was mistaken to suppose that "it is easier to live a profound life in an arctic hut than at Knowle" (*LDW* 55–56). Yeats, who did not view money as an impediment to creativity, liked the wealthy upperclass life Wellesley lived at Penns-in-the-Rocks, which became for him a substitute for the lost Coole Park, as the aristocratic Wellesley was a substitute for Gregory. Wellesley urged Yeats to "study Virginia Woolf's books, *all of them*" (*LDW* 57). Woolf and Yeats had already met twice, as Woolf records in her letters and diaries. In 1930, she wrote that he was "vital, supple, high charged & altogether seasoned & generous,"[13] and she thought him "our only living poet – perhaps a great poet: anyhow a good poet."[14] In 1934 Yeats praised Woolf's *The Waves*, an approbation that sustained her in the face of a spiteful review by Wyndham Lewis. She "felt Yeats' extreme directness, simplicity, & equality: liked his praise; liked him."[15] Woolf intuited correctly that Yeats recognized women artists on a footing of equality.

Wellesley's revelation to Yeats that she was a lesbian only deepened the intensity of their friendship, though it precluded a physical affair. Yeats had always sympathized with homosexual men like Wilde, for in his own social milieu, "historical knowledge had lessened or taken away the horror or disgust at his form of vice prevalent elsewhere in England" (*Mem* 79). Outraged by the supposed forgery of Casement's diaries he demanded: "If Casement were a homo-sexual what matter!" (*LDW* 128). Edward Martyn had once commented maliciously that Yeats's "weird appearance" was "triumphant with middle-aged masculine women,"[16] meaning Gregory and Horniman, whose supposed "masculinity" lay as much in their money and commanding personalities as in their persons. A woman-identified man, impotent but still sexually active, Yeats in his later years was happy surrounded by lesbian or bisexual women. His last passionate affair was with the wealthy feminist journalist Edith Shackleton Heald, who after his death lived for many years with the lesbian painter Hannah Gluckstein.[17] The lesbians Heald, Wellesley, and Matheson were at his deathbed with George Yeats. Women who loved women also loved Yeats. At a time when de Valera was consolidating the regressive sexual policies of the post-Treaty era in his 1937 Constitution, Yeats had to go to England to find unconventional sexualities.

Both Yeats and the women in this circle theorized lesbianism in terms of androgyny: the woman in man and the more socially transgressive man in woman. Yeats wrote to Wellesley after their conversation about lesbianism: "O my dear I thank you for that spectacle of personified sunlight. I can never while I live forget your movement across the room ... made to draw attention to the boy in yourself ... at last an intimate understanding is possible" (*LDW* 99). Yeats had already created his most striking female voices in Crazy Jane and the Woman Young and Old, but now he wrote: "My dear, my dear – when you crossed the room with that boyish movement, it was no man who looked at you, it was the woman in me. It seems that I can make a woman express herself as never before. I have looked out of her eyes. I have shared her desire" (*LDW* 108). None of his female personae had gone so far. The desire Yeats wishes to share is lesbian desire: "your lines have the magnificent swing of your boyish body. I wish I could be a girl of nineteen for certain hours that I might feel it even more acutely" (*LDW* 113). Yeats's identification of poetry with femininity, pervasive in his earlier work, suppressed with Nietzschean firmness in his middle years as he attempted to create a masculine poetics, re-emerged at the end of his life.

Yeats appropriated only an imaginative femininity: in 1935 he told Mannin, "You are doubly a woman, first because of yourself and secondly because of the muses, whereas I am but once a woman" (*L* 831).[18] Although his interest in androgyny dates from the nineties, his thinking in the thirties shows the influence, mediated through Wellesley, of Woolf. Although no record exists of his having read *A Room of One's Own*, Wellesley had certainly done so. In showing Yeats "the boy in herself," she was acceding to Woolf's definition of androgyny:

in each of us two powers preside, one male, one female, and in the man's brain the man predominates over the woman, and in the woman's brain the woman predominates over the man. The normal and comfortable state of being is that when the two live in harmony together, spiritually cooperating. If one is a man, still the woman part of the brain must have effect; and a woman also must have intercourse with the man in her. Coleridge perhaps meant this when he said that a great mind is androgynous. It is when this fusion takes place that the mind is fully fertilised and uses all its faculties. Perhaps a mind that is purely masculine cannot create, any more than a mind that is purely feminine, I thought.[19]

The phrasing of Yeats's letters to Wellesley suggests that they had discussed Woolf's analysis: "Have you noticed that the Greek androginous [*sic*] statue is always the woman in man, never the man in woman? It was made for men who loved men first" (*LDW* 114). In *Orlando* and *Three Guineas* Woolf addressed the social construction of femininity, but Yeats follows her earlier, essentialist theory when he discusses androgyny in terms reminiscent of the Jungian animus and anima. Dollimore warns that androgyny may create "a genderless transcendent which leaves sexual difference in place."[20] For example, Yeats wrote to Wellesley: "What makes your work so good is the masculine element allied to much feminine charm" (*LDW* 113); he applauded her "powerful onrushing masculine rhythm" (*LDW* 24) in combination with womanly grace and elegance. The conventional assignation of gender characteristics persists, although they exist side by side in one woman's boyish body and masculine verse.

Showalter, however, attacks Woolf's "flight into androgyny" as an inhuman retreat into the sphere of the eunuch: according to her, androgyny does not reify sexual difference but elides it altogether.[21] Yet Woolf's famous metaphor for the androgynous state involves no sexless fusion, but a man and a woman together in a taxi. Heilbrun celebrates Woolf's search for a new synthesis of human qualities without conceding that such a synthesis would be either inhuman or sexless,[22] while Moi argues that in theorizing androgyny Woolf deconstructs "the death-dealing binary oppositions of masculinity and femininity," and that "a theory that demands the deconstruction of sexual identity is indeed authentically feminist."[23] Whether we see Woolf's androgyny as essentialist or deconstructive, however, it is crucial to situate it historically. As Dollimore argues, we may want to reject essentialism as the basis of a current politics, but we must "do justice to its histories, avoiding at all costs a 'theoreticist' writing off of them."[24] In embracing androgyny in 1935 Yeats responded positively to the most advanced feminist thought available to him.

Wellesley's lesbianism shifted their relationship towards intimate friendship and collaboration, which suited them both despite Yeats's frustrated yearning to be a girl of nineteen. His poem "To Dorothy Wellesley," originally entitled "To a Friend," offers her the respect due to an artistic equal, and attempts to render poetically the androgynous personality, the man in woman. The poem evokes a woman of great economic power. Wellesley is enjoined to stretch out and grasp the trees: "tighten that hand / As though to draw them closer yet." Her firm control of the natural world transforms trees into "old upholsteries," furnishings for a stately home. Her isolation is guaranteed by money, "For since the horizon's bought strange dogs are still." Her own dog, Brutus, sleeps by her side: a woman's ownership of a Great Dane metonymically indicates her power. Remembering that, in Woolf's words, "a woman must have money and a room of her own if she is to write fiction,"[25] Yeats situates Wellesley in a "chamber full of books": alone, and therefore symbolically free of family responsibilities, she awaits a supernatural visitation:

> What climbs the stair?
> Nothing that common women ponder on
> If you are worth my hope! Neither Content
> Nor satisfied Conscience, but that great family
> Some ancient famous authors misrepresent,
> The Proud Furies each with her torch on high.   (*VP* 579)

Finneran suggests that Yeats drew on Jane Ellen Harrison's *Prolegomena to the Study of Greek Religion* for his descriptions of the Furies.[26] Harrison was one of the first to argue that the plot of the

Oresteia describes symbolically the social transition "between kinship through the mother and through the father," a version of Engels' world historical defeat of the female sex. She claims that Aeschylus misrepresents the Erinyes by turning them from justifiably angry male or female avenging ghosts into "a lower and more loathsome, because wholly human, horror,"[27] the female monsters who hound Orestes for his murder of his mother Clytemnestra. Harrison regrets that Aeschylus

seems to have seen only the evil of the Earth-Spirits, only the perennial damnation of the blood-feud. It is impossible to avoid regret that he did not see that these Earth-Spirits were for blessing as for cursing, and that he stooped to the cheap expedient of maligning his spiritual foes.[28]

After their defeat by the male-identified goddess Athena, Aeschylus further misrepresents the Furies by domesticating them: they become the Semnae, peaceable Athenian deities. In *A Room of One's Own* Woolf reinstates the Furies in the person of Jane Harrison herself: on the terrace at Fernham walks

a bent figure, formidable yet humble, with her great forehead and her shabby dress – could it be the famous scholar, could it be J--- H--- herself? All was dim, yet intense too, as if the scarf which the dusk had flung over the garden were torn asunder by star or sword – the flash of some terrible reality leaping, as its way is, out of the heart of the spring.[29]

Like "The Proud Furies each with her torch on high" who illuminate the moonless midnight of Wellesley's estate, Harrison brings "the flash of some terrible reality" to the dim garden of Fernham College. In his poem Yeats accepts Harrison's defense of the Furies as spirits who bring joy and blessing as well as terror, energy and pride as well as vengeance.

　　Yeats suggests that a woman has the right to reject heterosexual domesticity for "that great family" of three female Furies, as Harrison, herself a lesbian, did. He invokes the Furies as the mentors of women who have the courage to reject the feminine virtues and their rewards, urging Wellesley to dispense with the "Content" offered by traditional marriage and the satisfied "Conscience" obedient to conventional morality. Wellesley records that, "Within two minutes of our first meeting at my house he said: 'You must sacrifice everything and everyone to your poetry.' I replied: 'I have children and cannot'" (*LDW* 46). Her worries, however (the estate, the servants, and bringing out her daughter) were ones that many women would envy. Yeats's progressive deconstruction of gender stereotypes is accompanied by a conservative reinscription of class hierarchies. The modest legacy that Woolf considered necessary to the woman writer was in Wellesley's case extremely large, and she is celebrated for qualities that "common women" cannot share because their social and economic position forbids it. Yeats is willing to leave Content and satisfied Conscience to conventional females, provided the world supplies him with enough of the other sort.

Money and class are not the only difficult issues in Yeats's last love poems. Blood, both the good blood of eugenically sound breeders and the spilt blood of massacre, is omnipresent. "To Dorothy Wellesley" is linked with "Hound Voice" through their portrayal of unconventional women who derive strength from the knowledge of terror and violence. To Wellesley Yeats formulated the governing aesthetic of his later verse:

the passion of the verse comes from the fact that the speakers are holding down violence or madness – "down Hysterica passio". All depends on the completeness of the holding down, on the stirring of the beast underneath. Even my poem "To D. W." should give this impression. The moon, the moonless night, the dark velvet, the sensual silence, the silent room and the violent bright Furies. (*LDW* 86)

The "hysterical women" of "Lapis Lazuli" cannot hold down the beast, but the aristocratic Wellesley has her environment firmly in control: the "violent bright Furies," therefore, bless her with creative energy rather than hysteria. In "Hound Voice" Yeats's female friends and lovers form an elite tested by terror:

> The women that I picked spoke sweet and low
> And yet gave tongue. "Hound voices" were they all.
> We picked each other from afar and knew
> What hour of terror comes to test the soul,
> And in that terror's name obeyed the call,
> And understood, what none have understood,
> Those images that waken in the blood. (*VP* 622)

Yeats had compared Gonne to Diana of the Crossways, who uses her huge dog Leander to ensure her independence.[30] Wellesley, like Gonne the owner of a Great Dane, was also for "many years companioned by a hound" (*VP* 621). Yeats salutes Ascendancy huntswomen and female warriors from Irish myth, but his praise is problematic. Appropriating Lear's patriarchal commendation of

Cordelia, "Her voice was ever soft, / Gentle, and low, an excellent thing in woman,"[31] Yeats celebrates women who accede to voice and power without becoming hysterical. The baying female, however, is no improvement on the screaming harridan; while the "blood-dark track," "the kill," and the "chants of victory amid the encircling hounds" (*VP* 622), sound sinister in a poem written just before the Second World War.

One cannot label all of Yeats's late love poetry as incipiently fascistic, however. Like "To Dorothy Wellesley," individual poems are complex and indeterminate, and there are differences in tone and attitude between poems. "Hound Voice" shares with "A Bronze Head" its aristocratic Chaucerian *rime royale*. When Yeats deploys the simplicity of ballad meters his attitudes are less hierarchical. In 1936 he and Wellesley engaged in a verse-writing competition on the topic of "the lady, the poet, & the maid" (*LDW* 64). Although Armstrong describes "The Three Bushes" as an act of "(amicable) usurpation,"[32] Yeats's poem was written before he saw Wellesley's: after finishing it he wrote to her "I am longing to read your ballad. I will not send you mine until yours is finished" (*LDW* 69). Yeats was, however, eager to revise Wellesley's poem for their series of Broadsides, because collective authorship was appropriate for a ballad; moreover, literary collaboration was a version of the sexual act: "Ah my dear how it added to my excitement when I re-made that poem of yours to know it was your poem. I re-made you and myself into a single being" (*LDW* 82). Wellesley, however, objected to literary intercourse: she thought it was cheating.

Yeats was the more poetically progressive of the two. As Woolf wrote: "masterpieces are not single and solitary births; they are the outcome of many years of thinking in common, of thinking by the body of the people, so that the experience of the mass is behind the single voice."[33] In *A Room of One's Own* she uses "Mary Hamilton"[34] (the ballad of Mary Stuart's maid, who, having killed the illegitimate child she has conceived by the king, is hanged for her transgression) to highlight the sexual exploitation of women by the patriarchy. Yeats employs the example of "Mary Hamilton" for different ends:

Neither scholars nor the populace have sung or read anything generation after generation because of its pain. The maid of honour whose tragedy they sing must be lifted out of history with timeless pattern, she is one of the four Maries, the rhythm is old and familiar, imagination must dance, must be carried beyond feeling into the aboriginal ice. (*E&I* 523)

Woolf insists that women be reinserted into history, not lifted out of it. Nevertheless, in "The Three Bushes" Yeats takes up the ballad triangle of the servant exploited by the king and forsaken by the queen, and rewrites it to honor the chambermaid, who, like Mary Hamilton, is the plaything of her aristocratic employers. The ballad vindicates the servants who were supposed to do our living for us.

Just before Yeats began the poem, Margot Ruddock wrote to him about male fetishization of the inaccessible woman:

Really men are most extraordinary. You can go and practically offer to sleep with them, in fact one might almost say implore them to take one ... and they won't so much as blink an eyelid with passion. Yet if you walk off and leave them they nearly die wanting you. I don't understand it at all. (*LMR* 77–78)

In "The Three Bushes" Yeats explores Ruddock's bewilderment as he again demystifies the courtly ethic. His Lady recognizes that theories of sexuality have changed since the medieval revival of the nineteenth century. Gonne had told Yeats that her sexual refusal and his subsequent unhappiness had enabled him to produce beautiful poetry. This lady, however, has read some Freud and some popular sexology – perhaps Havelock Ellis – and worries about the effect of sublimation on her poet's creative output.

> "None can rely upon
> A love that lacks its proper food;
> And if your love were gone
> How could you sing those songs of love?
> I should be blamed, young man." (*VP* 569)

Yeats had made poetic capital out of the idea that to satisfy love is to end it. Here he suggests the contrary: that love dies when it is not satisfied, and poetry dies with it. In his early poem "Words," it was precisely the lack of "proper food" that kept the poet's "songs of love" in circulation: his speaker agreed with Gonne that if he had been physically requited he "might have thrown poor words away / And been content to live" (*VP* 256). The Lady, however, believes sex rather than sublimation keeps creation going, that hunger must be fed; and thus attacks a love tradition that depends upon frustration for its continuance. Her justification lies in the poet's love song, which unites sacred and profane: "A laughing, crying, sacred song, / A leching song" (*VP* 570). Sex with the chambermaid enables the lover to transcend the sterility of courtliness while remaining in touch with the sacred. The Lady's stratagem, however, is undermined by the fact that the song makes him late and thus leads to his death, while she too succumbs in an abrupt ballad *Liebestod*. She had thought that she would "drop down dead" if she indulged in sex; ironically she "dropped and died" of romantic love instead.

The song also undermines her defense of her chastity: if sex is healthy for her lover and the chambermaid, why not for her? Class is the answer. Only the aristocratic woman's chastity has positive value: the chambermaid's virginity is worthless because non-dynastic. The lady also regards her lover as a sexual beast, albeit a noble one. She is a Victorian prude with a clear-headed modern analysis of the division of labor between the angel in the house and the prostitute on the streets, a division made necessary by a man's uncontrollable sexual urges and a lady's natural distaste for passion. Yeats subtly conveys the extent of her self-deception, for she is sexually jealous if not actively sexual: she "heaved a sigh if the chambermaid / Looked half asleep all day." Despite her hypocrisy and prudery, however, she suspects that the sexual act may be democratic:

> maybe we are all the same
> Where no candles are,
> And maybe we are all the same
> That strip the body bare. (*VP* 570)

Like the Woman Old who "gave what other women gave / That stepped out of their clothes" (*VP* 538), or the speaker of "Portrayed before his Eyes" who longs for "Love's levelling bed,"[35] the Lady suggests that nakedness knows no class distinctions.

The chambermaid's opinions are never explored: she appears as passive as the lover in the toils of her conniving mistress, and unromantically lives on long after the drama is over. Yet at the end of the ballad Yeats's Priest validates her actions:

> She made a full confession.
> Long looked he in her face,
> And O he was a good man
> And understood her case.

The confession motif is significant. The Abbé Michel de Bourdeille praises the anonymous priest who absolves the chambermaid. This mediation of the story through two clerics connects the ballad with Yeats's Ireland. The tolerance of the priest, who recognizes the claim of the body as equal to the claim of the soul and orders that this claim be recognized in death as it was not in life, stands in satirical contrast to the erotophobia of the Dublin clergy.

Parodying the ubiquitous ballad trope of the rose bush uniting the graves of two lovers, a symbol of perfect union after death, the priest provides a non-canonical extra rose bush that unites three graves and raises all sorts of awkward questions about sex in the afterlife:

> He bade them take and bury her
> Beside her lady's man,
> And set a rose-tree on her grave,
> And now none living can,
> When they have plucked a rose there,
> Know where its roots began. (*VP* 571)

Wellesley's ballad keeps the serving maid in proper class position even after death: "And she was put between their graves / That each might on her call" (*LDW* 96). When autumn leaves fall she rises from the dead to sweep her employers' graves. Yeats's chambermaid, however, is placed "Beside her lady's man" and incorporated into the aristocratic emblem of the Rose.

Yeats's use of the word "rose-tree" instead of "rose bush" recalls his nationalist ballad "The Rose Tree," which he had just reprinted on a Broadside with the Protestant ballad about the defeat of James II, "Boyne Water." The collocation of Catholic and Protestant songs suggests a political agenda for "The Three Bushes." If Ireland was a Rose Tree watered by nationalist blood, it also contained a powerful Protestant tradition. Yeats wanted to establish the impossibility of disentangling the "roots" of Irish cultural, sexual, and class identities. To juxtapose "The Rose Tree" with "Boyne Water" suggests that both belong to past history, 1916 no less than 1690. In "The Three Bushes," the rose tree that rises from the graves no longer signifies sacrifice, but the triumph of love.

The apotheosis of the chambermaid also challenges the Madonna/Whore polarity, a creation of men who are unable to sleep with the woman they respect or to respect the woman they have enjoyed. Crazy Jane and the chambermaid demonstrate that the body is not necessarily an occasion of sin, while the Lady's purity is dubious. Wellesley called her Lady "a minx, a demi-vierge, an 'allumeuse' … A mental baggage, a jade, hussy, slut, demirep" (*LDW* 80). Yeats's Lady, flirting with a voyeuristic knowledge of transgression, hopes to hear but not touch the phallic "contrapuntal serpent" through her stand-in the chambermaid (*VP* 573). Yeats wrote that "The man who ignores the poetry of sex ... finds the bare facts written up on the walls of a privy, or himself is compelled to write them there" (*L* 818–19). The Indian tradition helped him to break down the opposition between chastity and pollution deeply embedded in the Lady's Pauline conception of sex as bestial:

> Our moral indignation, our uniform law, perhaps even our public spirit, may come from the Christian conviction that the soul has but one life to find or lose salvation in: the Asiatic courtesy from the conviction that there are many lives. There are Indian courtesans that meditate many hours a day awaiting without sense of sin their moment, perhaps many lives hence, to leave man for God. For the present they are efficient courtesans. Ascetics ... have lived in their houses and received pilgrims there. (*E&I* 436)

The chambermaid plays "efficient courtesan," and although some sense of sin must have prompted her confession, the Priest relieves her of moral responsibility. She is a victim of the self-deceptions of the upper classes, not a whore. Yeats's poignant refrain, "*O my dear, O my dear*," its lamenting cadence suggesting both desire and regret, is initially addressed to the Lady, but by the end of the poem it belongs to the chambermaid.

In "A Model for the Laureate" and "Come Gather Round Me, Parnellites" Yeats uses the ballad to foreground the choice of love over political power made by public men implicated in divorce scandals. In August 1936 Henry Harrison told Yeats that O'Shea had accepted money to leave Mrs. O'Shea free, and would have let himself be divorced if Parnell could have raised a bribe of £20,000: "The Irish Catholic press ... preferred to think that the Protestant had deceived the Catholic husband. He begged me to write something in verse or prose to convince all Parnellites that Parnell had nothing to be ashamed of in her love" (*L* 863). Yeats had argued in the Senate that divorce enabled Parnell to behave honorably by marrying Kitty O'Shea. Now he used the ballad to condemn the Church, expose O'Shea's economic motive, attack the hypocrites who objected to divorce but not to adultery, and affirm both Parnell's patriotism and his love:

> The Bishops and the Party
> That tragic story made,
> A husband that had sold his wife
> And after that betrayed;
> But stories that live longest

Are sung above the glass,
And Parnell loved his country
And Parnell loved his lass.   (*VP* 587)

The paratactic sentence structure suggests that patriotism and romance are parallel but not synonymous. The Englishwoman Mrs. O'Shea is no virginal Cathleen ni Houlihan but a ballad "lass," and Parnell died of illness, not of love.

Divorce was controversial in December 1936 when Edward VIII abdicated to marry the divorcée Wallis Simpson. Yeats noted "an outbreak among the young in favor of the king, which has astonished everybody. For the first time in the history of Ireland they are loyal" (*LDW* 111). Consistently pro-divorce, Yeats "thought the ex-king's broadcast moving, restrained & dignified, & of what I hear the Archbishop's was the reverse" (*LDW* 113). When a few months later Edward married Simpson Yeats wrote "A Marriage Ode," which was "the kind of thing I would have written had I been made Laureate, which is perhaps why I was not made Laureate" (*LDW* 141). Deriding the English monarchy, he congratulates the Windsors on escaping it. Kingship once merited the sacrifice of romance, but now Edward is right to put sex before duty because "The Muse is mute when public men / Applaud a modern throne." No "decent man" would "keep his lover waiting" in order to be King of degenerate England (*VP* 597–98).

Bradshaw has shown that the idea of degeneracy became an obsession with Yeats in his last years.[36] The decline in the European birthrate between 1880 and the Second World War caused observers from all shades of the political spectrum to embrace eugenic ideas.[37] Foucault calls eugenics one of "the two great innovations in the technology of sex of the second half of the nineteenth century."[38] The regulation of sex in the interests of racial health preoccupied birth-control crusaders like Marie Stopes and Margaret Sanger; Fabians like Shaw and Webb; sexologists like Ellis; and gynecologists like Yeats's homosexual Jewish doctor Haire.[39] A few suffragists were able to reconcile the demand for the vote with the exaltation of race-motherhood,[40] but eugenicists commonly opposed feminism because educated and politically active women were likely to sacrifice breeding to careers. Woolf, suggesting that the state should pay a wage to mothers, wrote, "Consider ... what effect this would have upon the birth-rate, in the very class where the birth-rate is falling, in the very class where births are desirable – the educated class."[41]

When Wellesley argued that no woman of genius should be expected to rear children, Yeats, "raising his hand and speaking like the prophets of old, replied: 'No, we urgently need the children of women of genius!'" (*LDW* 178).

Stanfield observes that in the late thirties Yeats gave a scientific name to his long-standing interest in breeding, inheritance, and racial or familial degeneration.[42] Expounding standard eugenical wisdom, he warned that since 1900 "the better stocks have not been replacing their numbers, while the stupider and less healthy have been more than replacing theirs" (*Ex* 423). Yeats liked eugenics because he thought that it was a revolutionary movement "with that element of novelty and sensation which sooner or later stir men to action" (*Ex* 437). Yet eugenics challenges the sacredness of personal choice upon which romantic love depends. It exposes the connection between private erotic fulfillment and the public arena of state power. It therefore has serious implications for love poetry.

Yeats's eugenic poetics are contradictory. Against the romantic individualists, Parnell, Edward VIII, and the speaker of "Politics," stands the tinker Mannion, who promises to "Throw likely couples into bed / And knock the others down" (*VP* 606). Exemplifying by exaggeration the anti-individualist, anti-democratic, class-biased, and racist nature of eugenics, Mannion demonstrates more clearly than its responsible advocates the nature of genetic planning. Beating up "the common sort" and throwing likely couples into bed is a more accurate representation of the violence behind policies designed to preserve racial purity than was the idea that sterilization programs for the unfit could be operated voluntarily. A serious eugenicist reading these lines in 1938 would have deplored Yeats's extremism,[43] but Mannion exemplifies the historical connection between eugenics and fascism. By making him a degenerate descendant of the sea-god Manannan, however, Yeats ironically undermines his authority: we cannot read him simply as the poet's mouthpiece.

In the twenties Yeats saw birth control as saving romantic love from "juggling nature"; in the thirties it was a way of controlling the Irish poor. Flouting both liberals and Bishops he asserts: "Sooner or later we must limit the families of the unintelligent classes, and if our Government cannot send them doctor and clinic it must, till it gets tired of it, send monk and confession-box" (*Ex* 426). The "likely couples" whom Mannion will encourage to breed are either upper class or physically exceptional: an enterprising "man-picker" barmaid (*Ex* 433) may be a eugenically sound breeder despite her class disadvantage: "We should count men and women who pick, as it were, the dam or sire of a Derby winner from between the shafts of a cab, among persons of genius, for this genius makes all other kinds possible" (*Ex* 430). Havelock Ellis denied the accusations of a critic who wrote that he wanted to breed human beings "like race horses!"[44] but Yeats was franker. The barmaid and the cab-horse can "double their mettle" and revitalize exhausted aristocratic stock if they "pick" luckily. Yeats's use of the word "pick" implicates "Hound Voice," in which the speaker and his lovers "picked each other from afar" (*VP* 622), in the eugenic program.

Yeats had always entertained the idea of marriage as the choice of a type rather than an individual. If all the arts are the expression of desire, they control the sexual ideology of future breeders. Yeats therefore preferred the representation of archetypal beauty (Greek statues, Rossetti women, Botticelli nymphs) to individuality or "character." Realism is anti-eugenic because it represents the degenerate present rather than the glorious past on which we should model a racially healthy future. The coercion of women implied by the representation of a male ideal of female perfection is less obvious in love poetry than on the pages of *Vogue*, but when Yeats evokes as his eugenic model "a Swedish actress standing upon some boat's edge between Portofino and Rapallo, or riding the foam upon a plank towed behind a speed-boat," he could be writing for a women's magazine, covering some fashionable Riviera playground where "the lucky or the well-born uncover their sunburnt bodies" (*Ex* 451). Eugenics implicates love poetry with money, class, and the bodies of starlets on the Riviera. Yeats appreciates the role of art in the hegemony of the dominant caste:

If... the family is the unit of social life, and the origin of civilisation which but exists to preserve it... it seems more natural than it did before that its ecstatic moment, the sexual choice of man and woman, should be the greater part of all poetry. A single wrong choice may destroy a family, dissipating its tradition or its biological force, and the great sculptors, painters, and poets are there that instinct may find its lamp. When a young man imagines the woman of his hope, shaped for all the uses of life, mother and mistress and yet fitted to carry a bow in the wilderness, how little of it all is mere instinct, how much has come from chisel and brush. (*Ex* 274–75)

This is a functionalist and instrumental view of love poetry as the educator and selector of the genes. No longer the expression of one man's desire for a particular woman, it is a template by which to create and verify the proper kind of love: that which will produce intelligent and well-grown offspring. The body of the woman is not merely the receptacle for male seed; it contributes equally to the genetic pattern of the offspring. So the woman must be maternal, sexual, and amazonic at the same time. Her strength must complement that of her mate: Aoife chose Cuchulain to father her son because he was the only man who had ever beaten her in battle.

"The Statues" is a eugenic love poem, or rather a poem about the determination of love by eugenics. The Greek boys and girls who press "Live lips upon a plummet-measured face" are interested not in the unique individual – the statues lack "character" – but in the racial type. For the purposes of reproductive health "passion could bring character enough." Sexual choice is the foundation of civilization, and art, which ideologically enforces the correct choices, is the agent, not the result, of historical and cultural change; for Europe defeated the Eastern world when Phidias "Gave women dreams and dreams their looking-glass" (*VP* 610). In Darwinian theory, the male must compete, either in strength or looks, for the attention of the female. Women's dreams are not the manifestations of individual preference, but biological guidelines for the improvement of the stock. Elsewhere Yeats also cites approvingly the ancient Irish custom of allowing females to compete physically for males: great-bladdered Emer is chosen by Cuchulain for a power that has little to do with visual attraction, while Finn watches from a hilltop as two thousand women strive to reach him first and claim his seed (*Ex* 433). In Gonne Yeats had "picked" an amazonic woman whose classic "lineaments," in his view, resembled a Greek statue. He thought she made a disastrous eugenic choice in mating with the base blood of John MacBride. Echoes of that choice reverberate through "The Statues" as through *Purgatory*, which is a lament for the destruction of a dynasty through a lady's mating with a drunken vainglorious lout. Yeats exhorts the Irish, thrown on the "spawning" tide of modern racial degeneration, to choose their mates according to the Greek standard of physical perfection and the heroism represented by Emer and Cuchulain; to trace "The lineaments of a plummet-measured face" (*VP* 611). Romantic love serves only to disguise the violence of the sex drive.

In a lyric originally intended for *The King of the Great Clock Tower*, however, Yeats theorizes the difference between romantic and eugenic love without validating either. His musician recalls the intercourse of Baile and Aillinn, who,

> Cast out by death and tethered there by love,
> Touch nerve to nerve throughout the sacred grove
> And seem a single creature when they please.

These are romantic lovers whose love defies mortality but produces no offspring. A second musician evokes a "harsher" vision of sexuality as applied eugenics:

> I call to mind the iron of the bell
> And get from that my harsher imagery,
> All love is shackled to mortality,
> Love's image is a man-at-arms in steel;
> Love's image is a woman made of stone;
> It dreams of the unborn; all else is naught;
> To-morrow and to-morrow fills its thought;
> All tenderness reserves for that alone.

Yeats glosses these lines: "One might say that the love of the beloved seeks eternity, that of the child seeks time" (*L* 817). "A Bronze Head," one of Yeats's last love poems about Gonne, can be read in the light of these opposing definitions.

The love of the beloved seeks eternity, so Yeats, coming full circle from "He wishes his Beloved were Dead," begins this love-elegy for a still-living woman by wondering what will remain of her in the "distant sky" after her death: "Something may linger there though all else die." The "head" into which she has been transformed suggests a death mask, and Yeats evokes her as a "dark tomb-haunter," the woman who kept the plight of Republicans buried alive in prison before the consciousness of the Dublin public. The epithet "tomb-haunter" also suggests Republican devotion to the graves of nationalist martyrs, which Yeats shared in the days when Gonne thrilled crowds by her challenge: "Must the graves of our dead go undecorated because Victoria has her Jubilee?" (*Au* 367). He is faithful to her complexities when he contradicts his first negative image of darkness and death:

> her form all full
> As though with magnanimity of light,
> Yet a most gentle woman; who can tell
> Which of her forms has shown her substance right.

Looking for the essence of Gonne's character, Yeats is baffled. He admits that the quest for essence is philosophically futile:

> Or maybe substance can be composite,
> Profound McTaggart thought so, and in a breath
> A mouthful held the extreme of life and death.

So to ask whether Gonne is human or superhuman, light or dark, gentle or terrible, is to force her into the familiar dichotomous stereotypes of angel or devil, life-giving or death-dealing goddess, child or destroying harpy. A composite substance contains extremes that do not negate each other.

After this insight, generated by a love that has paid minute attention to the individual character of the beloved, the poem degenerates. Eugenic racehorse rhetoric reinforces the vulgar stereotype of the woman as nervous thoroughbred filly: "But even at the starting-post, all sleek and new, / I saw the wildness in her." The deliberate "harshness" of the last stanza exemplifies the conjunction of class, gender, and violence sanctioned by Yeats's eugenic theories:

> Or else I thought her supernatural;
> As though a sterner eye looked through her eye
> On this foul world in its decline and fall;
> On gangling stocks grown great, great stocks run dry,
> Ancestral pearls all pitched into a sty,
> Heroic reverie mocked by clown and knave,
> And wondered what was left for massacre to save.   (*VP* 618–19)

These lines, which develop his earlier idea that heroic beauty is "not natural in an age like this" (*VP* 257), represent a poetic betrayal of Gonne. Although she had advocated violence in her youth, and remained a supporter of the IRA, the "massacre" she saw when nursing the wounded in a French hospital during World War I diminished her taste for indiscriminate bloodshed. She was interested in Hitler's Germany, as were numerous Irish people, not for eugenic but for nationalist reasons.[45] As a champion of the disadvantaged she would have been dismayed by Yeats's remedy for social degeneration, a war between the masses and the eugenic aristocrats, "with the victory of the skilful, riding their machines as did the feudal knights their armoured horses" (*Ex* 425). That the saving massacre is envisaged by a "sterner" eye that looks through hers cannot excuse Yeats's poetic implication of Gonne in his eugenic program. Although eugenics may enable poems about human sexual instinct like "The Statues," the last stanza of "A Bronze Head" demonstrates that eugenic ideas are at odds with both love and love poetry.

As if to qualify the extremism of "A Bronze Head," Yeats ordered his *Last Poems* so that his poetic *œuvre* would close with "The Circus Animals' Desertion" and "Politics." Written in *ottava rima* and ballad quatrains respectively, the two poems epitomize opposite formal tendencies in Yeats's work; but both enact similar rhetorical gestures. "The Circus Animals' Desertion" makes poetry out of Yeats's inability to write poetry, as "Politics" evokes history in rejecting history. Both poems attempt to cast off superfluities in order to reach the bedrock of emotional experience. Both poems, finally, are about love: Yeats's earliest poetic subject also closes his last volume. "The Circus Animals' Desertion" returns again to "Maud Gonne," whom the speaker wrongly identifies as the inspiration for "The Wanderings of Oisin," and correctly names as the original of *The Countess Cathleen.* Yeats examines for the last time the relationship between personal experience and genre, between love and the epic or dramatic "shows" that he equates with circuses. "The Wanderings of Oisin" belongs to the tradition of "old songs or courtly shows," but the genre of romance epic is less important than the urgency of personal deprivation: "But what cared I that set him on to ride, / I, starved for the bosom of his faery bride?" (*VP* 629). Yeats remembers his rationale for the creation of a National Theater as private rather than public:

> I though my dear must her own soul destroy,
> So did fanaticism and hate enslave it,
> And this brought forth a dream ...

This ruthless over-simplification of his complex and undoubtedly patriotic motives in founding the theater, and of Gonne's character, resembles the speaker's attempt to delegitimize history in favor of the heart in "Politics." He acknowledges, however, that the "dream" acquired its own momentum, leaving "Heart-mysteries" behind: "Players and painted stage took all my love, / And not those things that they were emblems of" (*VP* 630).

Now, however, the ringmaster can no longer put his circus animals "on show," no longer deploy his "masterful images" of completion, because he is "but a broken man." The "manly" genres of epic and

drama, the exploits of Oisin or Cuchulain, are beyond the reach of an
old and impotent poet whose phallic ladder is gone. All he can
manage is another lyric: "I must be satisfied with my heart." The
circus show was in any case "stilted," and the off-hand casualness of
"Lion and woman and the Lord knows what" reveals the speaker's
impatience with "burnished" things. Although Malachi Stilt-Jack
claims that "Processions that lack high stilts have nothing that
catches the eye" and affirms the popular demand for "Daddy-long-
legs upon his timber toes" (*VP* 622–23), the Antaeus-like speaker of
"The Circus Animals' Desertion" must discard his stilts to seek
regeneration through contact with the earth, with the fecundity of
Crazy Jane's foul sty:

> Those masterful images because complete
> Grew in pure mind, but out of what began?
> A mound of refuse or the sweepings of a street,
> Old kettles, old bottles, and a broken can,
> Old iron, old bones, old rags, that raving slut
> Who keeps the till. Now that my ladder's gone,
> I must lie down where all the ladders start,
> In the foul rag-and-bone shop of the heart.   (*VP* 630)

"The Circus Animals' Desertion" is Yeats's last statement of the idea
that "Love has pitched his mansion in / The place of excrement"
(*VP* 513), although Crazy Jane gets a new, urban persona as she
keeps the greasy till in the foul rag-and-bone shop. Her charac-
terization as a "slut" may sound offensive, but for Yeats the term
connotes the fusion of filth, sexual promiscuity, and poetic energy. As
Jane rejected the "heavenly mansion" offered by the Bishop, so
Yeats, to achieve "perfection of the work," must also "refuse / A
heavenly mansion, raging in the dark" ("The Choice," *VP* 495).
The choice, then, is gendered: between the ringmaster, reason, "pure
mind"; and the raving slut, old rags, "the heart." The terms of the
opposition – Jane and the Bishop, pollution and purity, the rent and
the whole, emotion and reason – are familiar. Yeats's endorsement
of the "foul rag-and-bone shop" and its female inhabitant con-
trasts with his condemnation of "this foul world in its decline and
fall…Ancestral pearls all pitched into a sty" (*VP* 619), and
demonstrates that the eugenic violence of "A Bronze Head" is only
one facet of his late love poetry. As Prospero abjures his "rough
magic," abandons his "so potent art" and vows "to break my

staff, / Bury it certain fathoms in the earth,"[46] so the "broken man" who affirms the primacy of pollution over purity symbolically relinquishes the ringmaster's control over his stilted and burnished circus animals, "Lion and woman and the Lord knows what" (*VP* 629).

Notes

INTRODUCTION

1 Jameson, *Political Unconscious* 17.
2 Friel, *Translations* 43.
3 Finneran, *Editing Yeats's Poems* 26.
4 Harwood, "Secret Communion" 8.
5 Adorno, "Lyric Poetry" 56–71.
6 Jameson, *Political Unconscious* 141.
7 La Rochefoucauld, *Maxims* 58.
8 Millett, *Sexual Politics* 36–37.
9 Berger, *Ways of Seeing* 47.
10 Stewart, *Jane Ellen Harrison* 140.
11 Rich, *On Lies* 39.
12 Woolf, "Mr. Bennett and Mrs. Brown" 96.
13 Eliot, *Collected Poems* 5.
14 Received critical wisdom as characterized by Rosmarin, *Power of Genre* 7.
15 Cixous, "Sorties" 98.
16 Woolf, *Room* 97–98.
17 See Praz, *Romantic Agony*; Auerbach, *Woman and the Demon*; Dijkstra, *Idols*; Marcus, *Art and Anger* 3–4.
18 See Gilbert and Gubar, *No Man's Land* 1: 35–36.
19 See Cullingford, *Yeats, Ireland and Fascism* 16–28.
20 See Laity, "Yeats and Farr" passim.
21 MacBride, *Servant* 291.
22 Lyons, *Ireland* 231.
23 Foster, "Protestant Magic" 244–46.

1 THE ANXIETY OF MASCULINITY

1 For an account of the relation between nationality and manliness, see Mosse, *Nationalism* 77–80.
2 Gilbert and Gubar, *Madwoman* 3–7.
3 Mary Ellmann, *Thinking* 15.
4 Castle, "Lab'ring Bards" 197–205.
5 Friedman, "Creativity" 56.
6 See Webster, *Yeats* 7.

7 Lynch, *Yeats* 47–51.
8 Kiberd, *Men and Feminism* 127–30.
9 Praz, *Romantic Agony* 366.
10 Marcus, *Art and Anger* 251.
11 Fuss, *Essentially Speaking* xi.
12 Heilbrun, *Androgyny* ix.
13 Nandy, *Intimate Enemy* 8.
14 Moore, *Unicorn* 216.
15 I owe this observation to Warwick Gould.
16 For "manliness" in the folklore of Irish nationalism in the nineteenth century see Thuente, "Folklore" 45, 47, 56.
17 Parker, *Literary Fat Ladies* 66.
18 Reproduced in *Yeats Annual* 4, Plate 16.
19 Grossman, *Poetic Knowledge* 55–56.
20 Cixous, "Sorties" 98.
21 Marvell, *Andrew Marvell* 25.
22 Shakespeare, *Complete Works* 341.
23 See Ortner, "Is Female to Male" for a feminist discussion of the Woman/Nature, Man/Culture opposition first analyzed by Levi-Strauss.
24 Waller, *Poems* 128.
25 Herrick, *Poetical Works* 84.
26 The similarities between these poems have been more frequently noted than their differences (see, for example, Mackey, "Yeats's Debt to Ronsard").
27 Ronsard, *Oeuvres* 2: 286–87.
28 Broadbent, *Poetic Love* 153.
29 Stallworthy, *Love Poetry* 25.
30 Shakespeare, *Complete Works* 1620.
31 Shakespeare, *Complete Works* 1629.

2 AT THE FEET OF THE GODDESS: YEATS AND THE FEMINIST OCCULT

1 For chivalry in this poem see Grossman, *Poetic Knowledge* 195.
2 Lewis, *Allegory* 2.
3 Benton, "Clio and Venus" 37.
4 Dronke, *Medieval Latin* xi.
5 See Kendrick, *Game of Love* 6.
6 Goldin, *Lyrics of the Troubadours* 217.
7 Goldin, *Lyrics of the Troubadours* 129.
8 Gould, "A Lesson for the Circumspect" 259–60.
9 Here he serves his patron rather than his lover, but on the rhetorical identity of political and amatory codes in Renaissance lyric see Parker, *Literary Fat Ladies* 61.
10 Goldin, *Lyrics of the Troubadours* 125.

11 Shahar, *Fourth Estate* 131–38.
12 Bogin, *Women Troubadours* 53–54.
13 See Bogin, *Women Troubadours,* for an anthology of their poems. See also Kelly, *Women, History and Theory* 29.
14 Shahar, *Fourth Estate* 161.
15 Bogin, *Women Troubadours* 89.
16 Benton, "Clio and Venus" 34–35; Shahar, *Fourth Estate* 163–64.
17 Kendrick, *Game of Love* 7–10.
18 Goldin, *Lyrics of the Troubadours* 125, argues that "the language of their piety comes from the songs of the courtly circle," that the Virgin owes more to the Lady than the Lady does to the Virgin.
19 Kelly, *Women, History and Theory* 36.
20 Joyce, *Portrait* 252.
21 I am assuming the existence of a real woman, whether or not she was actually Beatrice Portinari. See Potter, "Beatrice, Dead or Alive" 60, 70.
22 Rossetti, *Poems* 348. I quote Dante in Rossetti's translation, because Yeats used it (*Myth* 329).
23 Rossetti, *Poems* 328.
24 Spivak, *Other Worlds* 20.
25 Rossetti, *Poems* 345–46.
26 For the impact of medievalism on Victorian culture see Girouard, *Return to Camelot.*
27 Hough, *Last Romantics* 72.
28 Loizeaux, *Visual Arts* 7.
29 See Dijkstra, *Idols* 3–24.
30 Yeats mistakenly called this picture *Pomegranate.*
31 Loizeaux, *Visual Arts* 27.
32 Auerbach, *Woman and the Demon* 48.
33 Rossetti, *Poems* 166.
34 Hunt, *Pre-Raphaelite Imagination* 144.
35 Auerbach, *Woman and the Demon* 39.
36 Dobbs, *Rossetti* 86; Gaunt, *PreRaphaelite Tragedy* 45.
37 Dobbs, *Rossetti* 96, 106.
38 Millet, *Sexual Politics* 37.
39 Rossetti, quoted in Gaunt, *PreRaphaelite Tragedy* 128.
40 Burne-Jones, *Memorials* 1: 169.
41 Harwood, *Olivia Shakespear* 71–73.
42 Grossman, *Poetic Knowledge* 163, 159.
43 Daly, *Beyond God the Father* 96.
44 See Stanton, "Difference on Trial" 170.
45 Moi, *Sexual/Textual Politics* 13.
46 Felski, *Beyond Feminist Aesthetics* 119.
47 Stanton, "Difference on Trial" 174.
48 Moi, "Feminism, Postmodernism, and Style" 7.
49 Murphet, *When Daylight Comes* 8; Symonds, *Madame Blavatsky* 226.

50 Murphet, *When Daylight Comes* 99.
51 Quoted in Symonds, *Madame Blavatsky* 89.
52 F. A. C. Wilson, Kathleen Raine, James Olney, George Mills Harper, Allen Grossman.
53 Deane, "Blueshirt" 24.
54 Tuchman, "Hidden Meanings" 18; Mosse, "Origins" 81–96.
55 It never existed in Germany. Howe, *Magicians* 284.
56 Murphet, *When Daylight Comes* 128–29.
57 Quoted in Symonds, *Madame Blavatsky* 205.
58 Gandhi, *Autobiography* 91.
59 Murphy, *Women's Suffrage Movement* 4.
60 Harper, *Golden Dawn* 3.
61 Howe, *Magicians* 55.
62 Blavatsky, *Key to Theosophy* 34.
63 See also Blunt, *My Diaries* 2: 310.
64 Brandon, *Spiritualists* 8.
65 Campbell, *Ancient Wisdom* 20.
66 Brandon, *Spiritualists* 12.
67 Henderson, "Fourth Dimension" 223.
68 Besant, *Autobiography* 64–68, 159.
69 Dinnage, *Besant* 106–14.
70 Besant, *Autobiography* 3, 57–63, 153, 235, 249.
71 Cousins, *We Two Together* 75.
72 Lewis, *Eva Gore Booth* 150–54.
73 Mulvihull, *Charlotte Despard* 99–100.
74 Cousins, *We Two Together* 121–22, 131.
75 Howe, *Magicians* 54, 49.
76 Frazier, *Behind the Scenes* 155–57.
77 Harper, *Golden Dawn* 193.
78 Tickner, *Spectacle of Women* 247–48.
79 Quoted in Dinnage, *Besant* 78.
80 Grossman, *Poetic Knowledge* 211–12; Jonas, *Gnostic Religion* 104–11.
81 Pagels, *Gnostic Gospels* 60, 66.
82 Quoted in Grossman, *Poetic Knowledge* 87.
83 Scholem, *Origins of the Kabbala* 163. For this reference I am indebted to Deirdre Toomey.
84 Quoted in Rich, *On Lies* 75.
85 See Coward, *Patriarchal Precedents* 28–29.
86 Engels, *Origin of the Family* 87, 93.
87 Pomeroy, *Goddesses* 15.

3 THE *LIEBESTOD*

1 Quoted in Bataille, *Erotism* 11.
2 Freud, *Standard Edition* 11: 188–89.
3 Plato, *Symposium* 76–77.

4 Freud, *Standard Edition* 18: 38.
5 Bataille, *Erotism* 61–62.
6 Information from Warwick Gould.
7 Freud, *Standard Edition* 19: 161.
8 Bataille, *Erotism* 18.
9 Freud, *Standard Edition* 14: 88–89. For a discussion of Freud on narcissistic women, see Kofman, *Enigma of Woman* 50–65.
10 Ellmann, *Thinking* 67.
11 Rose, *Sexuality* 10.
12 Groult, "Night Porters" 69.
13 Cixous, "Laugh of the Medusa" 255.
14 Rose, *Sexuality* 16.
15 Rose, *Sexuality* 23.
16 De Rougemont, *Love* 284–85.
17 Bataille, *Erotism* 20.
18 Ramazani, *Yeats* 21.
19 MacBride, *Servant* 147.
20 Adam, *Axel* 285.
21 Adam, *Axel* 293.
22 Swinburne, *Selected Poems* 73.
23 Rossetti, *Poems* 4.
24 Freud, *Standard Edition* 18: 62.
25 See Praz, *Romantic Agony* 215–321.
26 Rossetti, *Poems* 146.
27 Kermode, *Romantic Image* 73–77.
28 Pater, *Renaissance* 83.
29 See Frazier, *Behind the Scenes* 158–59.
30 Moore, *Unicorn* 148–49.
31 Bataille, *Erotism* 92.
32 Ramazani, *Yeats* 19–22, comes to a similar conclusion.
33 See Bloom, *Yeats* 128–29; Kline, *Last Courtly Lover* 83–87.
34 Hone, *Yeats* 321.
35 See Harwood, *Olivia Shakespear* 63.
36 Yeats, *Fairy and Folk Tales* 383.
37 Thuente, "Folklore" 56.

4 THINKING OF HER AS IRELAND

1 For this debate see, in chronological order, O'Brien, "Unhealthy Intersection"; Kearney, "Myth and Motherland"; *Mother Ireland*, dir. Crilly; Boland, "Woman Poet"; Cullingford, "Thinking of Her... as Ireland"; Longley, *From Cathleen to Anorexia*; Loftus, *Mirrors*; Wills, "Mothers and Strangers."
2 Loftus, *Mirrors* 44.
3 Said, *Yeats and Decolonization* 10; Lloyd, "Nationalism and the Feminine."
4 See O Corráin, "Women in Early Irish Society."

5 Clark, *Great Queens* 186–96.
6 Warner, *Alone of All Her Sex* 77.
7 Heaney, "Mother Ireland" 790.
8 Heaney, *North* 40–45.
9 Kermode is similarly suspicious of the political implications of mythical thinking. See *Romantic Image* 107–08.
10 O'Brien, "Unhealthy Intersection" 5–6.
11 Longley, "Poetry and Politics" 26.
12 Clair Wills clarified my ideas on this point.
13 Dalton, "Tradition of Blood Sacrifice" 343–45.
14 MacCana, "Women in Irish Mythology" 7–10.
15 Kennelly, *Book of Irish Verse* 64.
16 For Yeats's impressionistic handling of the Irish mythical materials, see Kelleher, "Irish Materials" 115–25. For a justification of his treatment of Clooth-na-Bare as deriving from oral tradition see Thuente, *Yeats and Folklore* 144–47.
17 Ní Dhomhnaill, "Myth of Sovereignty"; Clark, *Great Queens* 4–8.
18 O Tuama, *An Duanaire* 189.
19 See Kearney, "Myth and Motherland" 76–78.
20 Toomey, "*Bards of the Gael and Gall*" 207–08.
21 Quoted in Toomey, "*Bards of the Gael and Gall*" 207.
22 Bessai points out, however, that Mangan's version has close affinities with the *aisling*: "Dark Rosaleen" 74–78.
23 O'Sullivan, *Songs* 133.
24 Hardiman, *Irish Minstrelsy* 1: 351; Lloyd, *Nationalism* 85–88.
25 O'Sullivan, *Songs* 130.
26 Bessai, "Dark Rosaleen" 62.
27 Renan, *Poetry of the Celtic Races* 81.
28 Arnold, *Lectures and Essays* 82.
29 Nandy, *Intimate Enemy* 7–10.
30 Kearney, "Myth and Motherland" 76.
31 Toomey, "Labyrinths" 95–112.
32 MacCana, "Women in Irish Mythology" 8.
33 Toomey, "Labyrinths" 100.
34 Toomey, "Labyrinths" 101.
35 Toomey discusses the image in "Labyrinths" 112–14.
36 MacCana, "Women in Irish Mythology" 9.
37 O'Sullivan, *Songs* 141–42.
38 See Nash, "Yeats and Heffernan" 201–02.
39 Preminger, *Princeton Encyclopedia* 64.
40 Pethica, "Our Kathleen."
41 Lloyd, "Nationalism and the Feminine."
42 Marcus, "Asylums of Antaeus" 64.
43 Kearney, "Myth and Motherland" 65–71; Deane, "Heroic Styles" 52–55. Kiberd disputes the revisionist connection between the myths of 1916 and the contemporary IRA ("Elephant" 13) while Laffan reasserts it ("Insular Attitudes" 113).

44 See Dhonnchadha and Dorgan, *Revising the Rising* passim.
45 See especially his short story "The Roads."
46 Pearse, *Works: Plays, Stories, Poems* 323.
47 Pearse, *Works: Political Writings* 300–1.
48 Pearse, *Works: Plays, Stories, Poems* 15, 31, 10.
49 Pearse, *Works: Plays, Stories, Poems* 333.
50 See Kiberd, "Inventing Irelands" 17.
51 Typescript of *A Vision* [A], transcribed by Ellmann.
52 Yeats, "Modern Ireland" 266.
53 MacNeice, *Poems* 132.
54 Directed by Anne Crilly, Derry Film and Video, 1988.
55 MacBride, *Servant* 7, 134, 136, 241.
56 Cardozo, *Lucky Eyes* 404.
57 Markievicz, *Prison Letters* 155, 189.
58 MacBride, "Yeats and Ireland" 20.

5 VENUS OR MRS. PANKHURST: FROM LOVE TO FRIENDSHIP

1 Adorno, "Lyric Poetry" 61.
2 Symons, *Knave of Hearts* 50.
3 Beckson, *Arthur Symons* 253.
4 Beckson, *Arthur Symons* 281–82.
5 Owens, "How We Won the Vote" 4.
6 See *AYF* 504.
7 Johnson, *Florence Farr* 48; Laity, "Yeats and Farr" 626, 632–33.
8 Tickner, *Spectacle of Women* 24.
9 Tickner, *Spectacle of Women* 247–48.
10 MacBride, *Servant* 85.
11 For the most recent discussion of suffrage agitation in Ireland see Murphy, *Women's Suffrage Movement*.
12 Ward, *Maud Gonne* 65–68.
13 Ward, *Unmanageable Revolutionaries* 69.
14 Quoted in Balliett, "Maud Gonne" 31.
15 See also Balliett, "Maud Gonne" 36; Ward, *Maud Gonne* 86–87.
16 Quoted in Laity, "Yeats and Farr" 628–29.
17 Laity, "Yeats and Farr" 628.
18 Gordon and DuBois, "Seeking Ecstasy" 16–18.
19 See Tickner, *Spectacle of Women* 223.
20 Ward, *Maud Gonne* 101–02.
21 *Votes for Women* 14 October 1910: 21.
22 Mackenzie, *Shoulder to Shoulder* 28.
23 Tickner, *Spectacle of Women* 59.
24 Tickner, *Spectacle of Women* 10, 89–90.
25 Sheehy Skeffington, "Reminiscences" 13.
26 Oppel, *Mask and Tragedy* 72, 84.

27 Quoted in Tickner, *Spectacle of Women* 80.
28 Marcus, *Art and Anger* 22.
29 Meredith, *Diana of the Crossways* 18.
30 Marcus, *Art and Anger* 20.
31 Meredith, *Diana of the Crossways* 18–19.
32 Marcus, *Suffrage and the Pankhursts* 9.
33 Kelly, *Women, History and Theory* 33–36.
34 See also *AYF* 166, 224–25, 231.
35 See his "Perseus."
36 Quoted in Tickner, *Spectacle of Women* 199–200.
37 See Toomey, "Labyrinths" 112–13.
38 The ambivalence towards independent women revealed in this poem was pointed out to me by Lyn Innes.
39 Berger, *Ways of Seeing* 47, 51.
40 Meredith, *Essay on Comedy* 92–93.
41 For Yeats's fluctuating attitude towards Manet, see Schuchard, "Yeats, Titian and the New French Painting."
42 Mackenzie, *Shoulder to Shoulder* 258–59.
43 Mackenzie, *Shoulder to Shoulder* 261.
44 Harwood, "Secret Communion" 9.
45 Yeats, National Library of Ireland, Ms. 5919.
46 Kline, *Last Courtly Lover* 46.
47 Donne, *Poetical Works* 106.
48 Shelley, *Poetical Works* 621; Bloom, *Yeats* 167.
49 Yeats, *Tower of Polished Black Stones* 22, 44.
50 Shelley, *Poetical Works* 18.
51 Yeats, *Tower of Polished Black Stones* 23.
52 Woolf, *Room* 37.
53 See Gould, "An Empty Theatre?" pp. 86–89.
54 Cross and Slover, *Ancient Irish Tales* 87.
55 Jeffares, *New Commentary* 123.
56 Toomey, "Worst Part of Life" 224–25; Harwood, *Olivia Shakespear* 136–37.
57 Pethica, "Patronage" 68–69.
58 For the second affair see Toomey, "Worst Part of Life" 224, and Harwood, *Olivia Shakespear* 135–37.
59 Parkinson, *Later Poetry* 90–91; Toomey, "Worst Part of Life" 226; Harwood, *Olivia Shakespear* 184–86.

6 THE OCCULT EPITHALAMIUM

1 Frye, "Approaching the Lyric" 32.
2 MacBride, *Servant* 329–30.
3 Gilbert and Gubar, *No Man's Land* 1: 3–62.
4 Woolf, "Mr. Bennett and Mrs. Brown" 96.
5 Schenk, "Corinna Sings" 41–45.

6 Donne, *Poetical Works* 128.
7 Carew, *Poems* 80.
8 For the forms of epithalamium see Greene, "Spenser" 40–44.
9 Adorno, "Lyric Poetry" 58–59.
10 Harwood, *Olivia Shakespear* 153–60; Ellmann, *Man and Masks* xii.
11 Letter to Shakespear of 9 July 1926, quoted in Moore, *Unicorn* 253. See also Ellmann, *Man and Masks* xii-xiii.
12 Harper, "The Medium as Creator" 49.
13 Harper, "The Message is the Medium" 36–37.
14 Owen, *Darkened Room* 236.
15 Goldman, "Yeats, Spiritualism" 108–29. See Yeats's "Introduction" to *The Words Upon the Window-pane* (*Ex* 363–69).
16 Vendler, private communication.
17 See Harper, *Making of a Vision* 2: 17, 75.
18 Ellmann, "At the Yeatses'" 244.
19 For the relationship between the *Arabian Nights* and "The Gift of Harun Al-Rashid," see Gould, "A Lesson for the Circumspect" 246–50.
20 Yeats had two editions of Sappho: O'Shea, *Catalog* 236.
21 Sappho, *Poems*, Nos. 29, 32, 34, 36.
22 Lynch, *Yeats* passim; Harwood, *Olivia Shakespear* 50–51.
23 Schenk, "Corinna Sings" 43.
24 Quoted in Harwood, *Olivia Shakespear* 157.
25 Harwood, *Olivia Shakespear* 160.
26 Quoted in Harwood, *Olivia Shakespear* 157.
27 Harper, "The Medium as Creator" 63.
28 Toomey, "Unwilling Persephone."
29 Harper, "The Message is the Medium" 51.
30 The automatic writing continued from October 1917 to March 1920; the "sleeps" began March 1920 and ended July 1922.
31 Harper, "The Medium as Creator" 52.
32 Owen, *Darkened Room* [iv], 31, 10, 212.
33 Brennan, "Yeats, Clodd, *Scatalogic Rites*" 210–14.
34 Hynes, "All the Wild Witches" 569–71.

7 SHRILL VOICES, ACCURSED OPINIONS

1 Mayhew, "Yeats's 'Easter 1916'" 69–71.
2 Ward, *Maud Gonne* 111.
3 Haverty, *Markievicz* 105–06, 110–11; Innes, "Yeats's Female Voices" 57.
4 Quoted in Haverty, *Markievicz* 41.
5 Innes, "Yeats's Female Voices" 56–58.
6 Stallworthy, *Between the Lines* 172.
7 Stallworthy, *Between the Lines* 172, 169, 171.
8 Stallworthy, *Between the Lines* 168.
9 See Bornstein, *Yeats and Shelley* 29–66.

10 Shelley, *Poetical Works* 19, 15.
11 Dalton, "Tradition of Blood Sacrifice" 350–51. Yeats had a copy of Le Fanu's poems: O'Shea, *Catalog* 150.
12 Shelley, *Poetical Works* 582–83.
13 Toomey, "Labyrinths" 103.
14 MacBride, "Yeats and Ireland" 32.
15 Dalton, "Tradition of Blood Sacrifice" 343–45.
16 See Harwood, *Olivia Shakespear* 52, for a more negative reading of her motives.
17 Kiberd, "War against the Past" 39.
18 Ellmann dates the poem January 1919, but since Gonne was released in October 1918 it must have been begun earlier.
19 Jeffares, *New Commentary* 195.
20 For Clarke's account see *Revolutionary Woman* 150–66.
21 Markievicz, *Prison Letters* 149.
22 Broadcast, "Poems about Women," 10 April 1932. National Library of Ireland, MS. 30117.
23 O'Casey, *Drums under the Windows* 212.
24 Stallworthy, *Between the Lines* 29, 31.
25 Haverty, *Markievicz* 201.
26 Stallworthy, *Between the Lines* 17.
27 Stallworthy, *Between the Lines* 29, 38–42.
28 Chesler, *Women and Madness* 43.
29 Perloff, "Between Hatred and Desire" 39–40. Harwood, "Secret Communion" 4–8, correctly challenges Perloff's biographical theory about Yeats's reawakened love for Gonne, but her point about his poetic emphasis still stands.
30 Harwood, "Secret Communion" 6–7.
31 Stallworthy, *Between the Lines* 29, 31.
32 Quoted in Markievicz, *Prison Letters* xxxi.
33 Hassett, *Yeats* passim.
34 For another view see Perloff, "Between Hatred and Desire" 43.
35 Lloyd, *Man of Reason* 104.
36 Wordsworth, *Poetical Works* 32.
37 Oates, "At Least I Have Made a Woman of Her" 17.
38 Harris, *Yeats* 146; Archibald, *Yeats* 8.
39 Stallworthy, *Between the Lines* 43.
40 Boose, "The Father and the Bride" passim.

8 SWANS ON THE CESSPOOL: LEDA AND RAPE

1 See Kearney, "Faith and Fatherland" 60.
2 Herr offers an essentialist account of Irish sexual paralysis, "The Erotics of Irishness" 6–7, 13.
3 Scheper-Hughes, *Saints, Scholars, and Schizophrenics* 119.
4 Cairns and Richards, *Writing Ireland* 60–63.

5 "The Tipperary Man's Courtship," from "Irish Street Ballads," a scrapbook of original nineteenth-century broadsheets in the Humanities Research Center, U of Texas.
6 Unpublished letters transcribed by Ellmann.
7 Foster, *Modern Ireland* 534–35; Cairns and Richards, *Writing Ireland* 114–20.
8 Douglas, *Purity and Danger* 124.
9 See Kearney, "Faith and Fatherland" 62–64.
10 Lee, *Ireland* 159.
11 *Irish Catholic Register* (1925): 559.
12 *Catholic Bulletin* 14.10 (1924): 877.
13 Lee, *Ireland* 157–58.
14 Whyte, *Church and State* 59.
15 MacKinnon, *Feminism Unmodified* 184–86.
16 Douglas, *Purity and Danger* 53.
17 Gregory, *Journals* 1: 477.
18 Melchiori, *Whole Mystery of Art* 77.
19 Gregory, *Journals* 1: 563.
20 Molloy, "*To-morrow*" 215.
21 See Gregory *Journals* 1: 584, 592. For what happened to Robinson, see Molloy, "*To-morrow*" 219–22.
22 Miles, "The Virgin's One Bare Breast," passim.
23 Torchiana, *Yeats and Georgian Ireland* 142–44; Costello, *Heart Grown Brutal* 249–53.
24 Gregory, *Journals* 1: 609, 614, 624.
25 Keogh, *Vatican* 168.
26 Kearney, "Between Politics and Literature" 165.
27 O'Callaghan, "Language" 235.
28 Adams, *Censorship* 67, asserts that they were written by Corcoran. Torchiana, *Yeats and Georgian Ireland* 143, says they were "allegedly" his. Brown, *Ireland* 63, says Corcoran was "a frequent anonymous contributor" to the *Bulletin*.
29 See Keogh, *Vatican* 30.
30 Lee, *Ireland* 134.
31 For Corcoran's response to Yeats on this issue see *Catholic Bulletin* 14.8 (1924): 659–60.
32 Brown, *Ireland* 62–63.
33 See *Catholic Bulletin* 14.8 (1924): 660.
34 In "What is the Text of a Poem by Yeats?" Bornstein emphasizes the possible multiplicity of textual "versions."
35 Gregory, *Journals* 1: 563.
36 Gregory, *Journals* 1: 563.
37 *Irish Statesman* 23 August 1924: 753.
38 *Irish Statesman* 30 August 1924: 790.
39 *Catholic Bulletin* 15.1 (1925): 1.
40 *Catholic Bulletin* 14.12 (1924): 1020.

41 Maddox, *Nora* 139–47.

42 In his copy there are "some pp. uncut after p. 433, mostly in Circe." O'Shea, *Catalog* 143.

43 Joyce, *Critical Writings* 151.

44 *Catholic Bulletin*, 14.10 (1924): 837.

45 See Gregory, *Journals* 1: 527.

46 *Irish Statesman* 16 August 1924: 736.

47 *The Wild Swans at Coole.*

48 Yeats wrote the preface to Gogarty's *An Offering of Swans*, which was awarded one of the Tailteann literary prizes by Yeats and his committee.

49 *Catholic Bulletin* 14.11 (1924): 930.

50 *Catholic Bulletin* 15.1 (1925): 4, 5; 14.11 (1924): 934.

51 *Catholic Bulletin* 15.2 (1925): 103.

52 Gregory, *Journals* 1: 592.

53 *To-morrow* 8.

54 *Catholic Bulletin* 14.12 (1924): 1027.

55 Stallybrass and White, *Politics and Poetics* 44.

56 Cruttwell, *English Sonnet* 51. Jochum, however, argues that Yeats's use of the sonnet has been unjustly neglected. See "Yeats's Sonnets" 43, for his list of sonnets.

57 *Catholic Bulletin* 15.2 (1925): 103.

58 Deane ranks it as one of "the language's greatest masterpieces": *Short History* 24–25.

59 Howes, "*The Winding Stair.*"

60 MacKinnon, *Feminism Unmodified* 140–41.

61 Dorcey, "Spaces Between the Words" 23.

62 Kappeler, *Pornography* 102.

63 See Kappeler, *Pornography* 53–57, for a discussion of the privileging of the aesthetic category.

64 Kappeler, *Pornography* 103.

65 MacKinnon, *Feminism Unmodified* 176.

66 Melchiori, *Whole Mystery of Art* 280–81.

67 Dijkstra, *Idols* 314–18.

68 Griffin, *Pornography and Silence* 24–29.

69 Kappeler, *Pornography* 52–53.

70 See Boose, "The Family in Shakespeare Studies" 725, for a discussion of the opposition between feminism and pleasure.

71 Berger, *Ways of Seeing* 60–61.

72 See Melchiori, *Whole Mystery of Art* 151–63, and Fletcher, "Leda" 92–100, for a summary of the possible visual sources.

73 Gregory, *Journals* 1: 476.

74 Madge, "Leda" 532. The detail about Faure was added by Fletcher, "Leda" 99.

75 Faure, *History of Art* 1: 197. The carving is reproduced at the beginning of the book, facing 3.

76 *To-morrow* 2.

77 For a study of the poem's evolution that comments on the *To-morrow* version see Parkinson, *Later Poetry* 136–42.

78 On HD see Sword, "Leda" 313–15. Sword also lists non-violent literary (306) and visual (315) versions.

79 See Roth, *Portnoy's Complaint* 191–94.

80 MacKinnon, *Feminism Unmodified* 85–92.

81 See Melchiori, *Whole Mystery of Art* 112.

82 Harwood, "Olivia Shakespear: Letters" 71.

83 Kappeler, *Pornography* 158.

84 Quoted in Kappeler, *Pornography* 90.

85 In this I am in agreement with Kappeler, *Pornography* 91.

86 MacKinnon, *Feminism Unmodified* 148.

87 Fussell, *Poetic Meter* 116.

88 Fuller, *Sonnet* 6–7.

89 Ferrante, "Male Fantasy" 69–76.

90 Vickers, "Diana Described" 96–97.

91 Donne, *Poetical Works* 299.

92 Even Milton uses the sonnet more for autobiography than for purely political or public verses. See Fuller, *Sonnet* 7.

93 Van Duyn, *To See, To Take* 98. Kline, *Last Courtly Lover* 38, also notes Van Duyn's poem.

94 In the 1933 *Collected Poems* he moved "Wisdom" to a different position. Adams has noted the relation between the two poems: *Book of Yeats's Poems* 173–74.

95 Brown, "Reading Race and Gender" 426.

9 THE EROTICS OF THE BALLAD

1 Numbers 6,7,8,10.

2 Numbers 1–4.

3 Perloff, "Heart Mysteries" 270.

4 Pyle, *Jack Yeats* 67–68.

5 See Thuente, "Folklore" passim.

6 Thuente, "Folklore" 42, 46–47.

7 Lloyd, "*The Tower.*"

8 Yeats, *Book of Irish Verse* 180.

9 See Bratton, *Victorian Popular Ballad* 4–7.

10 Yeats, *Book of Irish Verse* 180–81.

11 Yeats, "Foreword" to *Broadsides* n.p.

12 See Cullingford, *Yeats, Ireland and Fascism* Chapter 2.

13 Meir, *Ballads and Songs* 8–9.

14 See Hodgart, *Ballads* 19.

15 Ong, *Orality and Literacy* 69.

16 Schuchard, "Yeats and the Imagists" 223, 215.

17 Yeats, "Foreword" to *Broadsides* n.p.

18 Bratton, *Victorian Popular Ballad* 152–53.

19 Ong, *Orality and Literacy* 69.
20 *Princeton Encyclopedia* 63.
21 See Ong, *Orality and Literacy* 131.
22 Easthope, *Poetry as Discourse* 53, 65.
23 Parkinson, *Later Poetry* ix, 187.
24 Easthope, *Poetry as Discourse* 73.
25 See Mann, "Yeats and Music."
26 For Yeats's objection to this definition see "The Censorship and St. Thomas Aquinas," *UP*2 477–80.
27 See, for example, "Jellon Grame," "Child Waters," "Fair Annie," "Leesome Brand."
28 Hodgart, *Ballads* 129–30, 135.
29 Quoted in Adams, *Censorship* 204.
30 Broadside No.7, Dublin: Cuala Press, 1909.
31 Arensburg and Kimball, *Family and Community* 195–223.
32 Arensburg and Kimball, *Family and Community* 204.
33 Yeats probably saw this picture when it was displayed at the New Gallery during the Burne-Jones exhibition of 1898 (information from Deirdre Toomey).
34 Perloff sees the mermaid as Gonne ("Heart Mysteries" 270); Harwood as Shakespear (*Olivia Shakespear* 183).
35 Bakhtin, *Rabelais* 25.
36 Arensburg and Kimball, *Family and Community* 199–200.
37 See Harwood, *Olivia Shakespear* Chapter 3, for the 1896 affair.
38 For example, Burd Ellen in "Child Waters." See also "Fair Annie," "Jellon Grame," "Lord Thomas and Fair Annet."
39 Ward, *Maud Gonne* 134–36, 153–55.
40 O'Casey, *Three Plays* 71–72.
41 Joyce, *Ulysses* 485–86, 490.
42 O'Casey, *Inishfallen* 176, 178–79.
43 Bold, *The Ballad* 33; Woolf, *Room* 50–51.
44 Kiberd, "Inventing Irelands" 13.
45 Hirsch, "Imaginary Irish Peasant" 1126.
46 de Valera, *Speeches and Statements* 466.

10 DESIRE AND HUNGER IN "AMONG SCHOOL CHILDREN"

1 de Man, *Rhetoric of Romanticism* 200–05.
2 Ward, *Missing Sex* 5–12.
3 Sidney, *Sir Philip Sidney* 182.
4 *Catholic Bulletin* 15.6 (1925): 530.
5 See Torchiana, "Among School Children" passim.
6 *Catholic Bulletin* 16.1 (1926): 7, 8.
7 Saddlemyer, "George Yeats."
8 MacBride, "Yeats and Ireland" 25.

9 Ward, *Maud Gonne* 98–99.
10 Information from Deirdre Toomey.
11 "Meals for School Children," *Irish Times* 29 October 1913: 8; Torchiana, "Among School Children" 138.
12 Saddlemyer, "George Yeats."
13 See, for example, Innes, "Yeats's Female Voices" 56; Keane, *Yeats's Interactions with Tradition* 286.
14 For the poem's genesis see Parkinson, *Later Poetry* 92–103.
15 Kermode, *Romantic Image* 70–72.
16 Plato, *Symposium* 60–64.
17 Shakespeare, *Complete Works* 1089.
18 Ellmann, *Man and Masks* xxii–xxiii, and Bradford, "Yeats and Maud Gonne" 464–66, have discussed this affair. See *AYF* 255–83, for her letters between June 1908 and July 1909.
19 Toomey, "Labyrinths" 96.
20 Sheehy Skeffington, "Reminiscences" 23.
21 Haverty, *Markievicz* 218–19.
22 Cullingford, *Yeats, Ireland and Fascism* 105–06.
23 Ward, *Maud Gonne* 139–40.
24 Yeats, "Modern Ireland" 266.
25 Brooks, *Well Wrought Urn* 167.
26 See Parkinson, *Later Poetry* 99.
27 Genesis 3: 16.
28 Parkinson, *Later Poetry* 102.
29 Plato, *Phaedrus* 57.
30 Plato, *Phaedrus* 55–66.
31 Plato, *Symposium* 87.
32 Plato, *Phaedrus* 60.
33 Parkinson, *Later Poetry* 93–4, 104–05.
34 Culler, *Pursuit of Signs* 142.
35 Morris, *Works* 23: 17.
36 Kermode, *Romantic Image* 60–65.
37 *Irish Catholic Register*, 1925: 562–63.
38 Innes, "Yeats's Female Voices" 56.
39 Ellmann dates "A Last Confession" as June 1926.

11 WRITING THE FEMALE BODY: WOMEN YOUNG AND OLD

1 Taylor, *Male Novelists* 2–3.
2 Cixous, "Sorties" 98.
3 Heath, "Male Feminism" 25, 27.
4 Keane, *Yeats's Interactions with Tradition* 17, 40, 41.
5 Said, "Intellectuals" 55.
6 Boone, "Of Me(n) and Feminism" 18.
7 Bold, *The Ballad* 33.

8 Woolf, *Room* 51.

9 Yeats, "Foreword" to *Broadsides* n.p.

10 Howes, " *The Winding Stair.*"

11 *Catholic Bulletin* 17.11 (1927): 1200.

12 "Pastoral Address," *Catholic Bulletin* 17.11 (1927): 1200.

13 Keane, *Yeats's Interactions with Tradition* 125–26; Innes "Yeats's Female Voices" 65; Howes, " *The Winding Stair.*"

14 Innes, "Yeats's Female Voices" 69.

15 Yeats, diary entry, quoted in Parkinson, *Later Poetry* 64.

16 For Derrida on woman as "the very figure of undecidability" see Fuss, *Essentially Speaking* 12–18.

17 Howes, " *The Winding Stair.*"

18 See Ellmann, "At the Yeatses'" 25–26.

19 Plato, *Symposium* 95.

20 Ovid, *Erotic Poems* 220.

21 Propertius, *Poems* 40.

22 *Catholic Bulletin* 15.11 (1925): 1110–11.

23 *Catholic Bulletin* 15.12 (1925): 1249.

24 See *VPL* 738–39 for the gender of the speakers.

25 Clark, *Yeats* 98.

26 Cavanaugh, *Love and Forgiveness* 116–17; Kline, *Last Courtly Lover* 143–44.

27 Clark, *Yeats* 98.

28 Donne, *Poetical Works* 40.

29 Wilson, *Yeats and Tradition* 206. Wilson 205–11, and Melchiori, *Whole Mystery of Art* 179–85, have explicated Yeats's occult symbolism and much of his debt to Donne.

30 Donne, *Poetical Works* 41.

31 Ramazani, *Yeats* 17–26.

32 Quoted in Stallworthy, *Between the Lines* 139.

33 Fuss, *Essentially Speaking* 1–21.

34 For this distinction see Scott, "Feminist Theory" 58.

35 Scott, "Feminist Theory" 60.

36 Stallworthy, *Between the Lines* 137–63.

37 Stallworthy, *Between the Lines* 142–43.

38 Shakespeare, *Complete Works* 1007.

39 Swinburne, *Selected Poems* 66.

40 Shakespeare, *Complete Works* 1007.

41 For a discussion of the labyrinth as both a negative and positive image see Toomey, "Labyrinths" 112–15.

42 Ellmann, *Second Puberty* 42.

43 Gould, "Frazer, Yeats" 140–41.

44 Scott, "Feminist Theory" 56–57.

45 Millay, *Collected Sonnets* 41.

46 Montefiore, *Feminism and Poetry* 117.

47 Heath, *Sexual Fix* 3.

48 Keane, *Yeats's Interactions with Tradition* 289.

49 Clark, *Yeats* 224.
50 Sophocles, *Theban Plays* 150.
51 Keane, *Yeats's Interactions with Tradition* 288.
52 Keane, *Yeats's Interactions with Tradition* 304.
53 Woolf, *Three Guineas* 169–70.
54 Clark, *Yeats* 215.
55 Sophocles, *Theban Plays* 81.
56 Sophocles, *Theban Plays* 149.

12 CRAZY JANE AND THE IRISH EPISCOPATE

1 Hynes, "All the Wild Witches" 580.
2 Foucault, *History of Sexuality* 1: 17–35.
3 Lydon, "Foucault and Feminism" 136.
4 Joyce, *Ulysses* 610.
5 Wills, "Upsetting the Public" 138, 140.
6 Eagleton, *Walter Benjamin* 144.
7 Bakhtin, *Rabelais* xvii-xix.
8 Gould, "Frazer, Yeats" 144–46.
9 Bakhtin, *Rabelais* 240.
10 Stallybrass and White, *Politics and Poetics* 16, 19.
11 Russo, "Female Grotesques" 217.
12 Davis, *Society and Culture* 136–38, 129.
13 Woolf, *Room* 45.
14 Eagleton, *Walter Benjamin* 148.
15 Shakespeare, *Complete Works* 334.
16 Davis, *Society and Culture* 131, 150.
17 Bakhtin, *Rabelais* 21.
18 Jameson, *Political Unconscious* 85–86.
19 Holquist, "Prologue," *Rabelais* xix.
20 Bakhtin, *Rabelais* 39.
21 Bakhtin, *Dialogic Imagination* 264.
22 Bakhtin, *Rabelais* 25.
23 Lloyd, "*The Tower.*"
24 Arensburg and Kimball, *Family and Community* 212.
25 Owen, *Darkened Room* 11.
26 Unpublished letter to George Yeats, quoted in Jeffares, *New Commentary* 307.
27 See de Man, *Rhetoric of Romanticism* passim, and Lloyd, "The Poetics of Politics" 83.
28 Bakhtin, *Rabelais* 16–17.
29 Bakhtin, *Rabelais* 430.
30 For this tradition see Munch-Pederson, "Crazy Jane."
31 Joyce, *Ulysses* 12.
32 O'Casey, *Inishfallen* 148.
33 Quoted in Adams, *Censorship* 42.

34 Swift, *Poems* 451. See also "Cassinus and Peter" 466.
35 Rochester, *Poems* 139.
36 Eliot, *Waste Land* 23.
37 Bataille, *Erotism* 58, 57.
38 Kristeva, *Powers of Horror* 3.
39 Bakhtin, *Rabelais* 21.
40 Bakhtin, *Rabelais* 19, 148.
41 Brennan, "Yeats, Clodd, *Scatalogic Rites*" 210.
42 Stallybrass and White, *Politics and Poetics* 132.
43 Gould, "Yeats, Frazer" 128–29.
44 See Chapter 4, "Thinking with Pigs," Stallybrass and White, *Politics and Poetics*.
45 *Catholic Bulletin* 18.1 (1928): 19–21.
46 Symons, *Knave of Hearts* 50.
47 Joyce, *Ulysses* 55–56.
48 Eagleton, *Marxism* 38.
49 Douglas, *Purity and Danger* 54, 120.

13 SUPERNATURAL SEX

1 Ellmann, *Second Puberty* 28.
2 Ellmann, *Second Puberty* 28.
3 Gilbert and Gubar, *Madwoman* 3–7.
4 Rochester, *Poems* 39.
5 Gilbert and Gubar, *No Man's Land* 1: 32–35.
6 Gilbert and Gubar, *No Man's Land* 1: 36.
7 See Pruitt, "Yeats and the Steinach Operation" 112–13.
8 See Armstrong, "Giving Birth" 50.
9 Possibly Mannin.
10 Ellmann, *Second Puberty* 28.
11 Brittan, *Masculinity* 47.
12 Pruitt, "Yeats and the Steinach Operation" 123.
13 Finneran, Harper, and Murphy, *Letters to Yeats* 531.
14 Gregory, *Journals* 1: 589.
15 See Said, *Orientalism*.
16 Auden, "Prosecution and Defence" 59.
17 Bloom, *Yeats* 408–09.
18 Sheeran, "Supernatural Songs."
19 Donne, *Poetical Works* 15.
20 Dryden, *John Dryden* 284–85. Yeats alludes to this passage in *AV[B]* 214. See also Hassett, *Yeats* 92–95.
21 Conversation with John Sparrow quoted in Jeffares, *Yeats* 267.
22 Donne, *Poetical Works* 47–48.
23 Guha, *Yeats* 144. O'Shea, *Catalog* 134, records only Avalon's translation of *Hymns to the Goddess* (London: Luzac, 1913).
24 Guha, *Yeats* 121.

25 Shakespeare, *Complete Works* 1642.
26 Blake, *Complete Writings* 179; see Whitaker, *Swan and Shadow* 113.
27 Harwood, "Olivia Shakespear: Letters" 102.
28 Guha, *Yeats* 37, 60.
29 Brittan, *Masculinity* 201.
30 Burkitt, *Early Eastern Christianity* 88–90.
31 Sheeran, "Supernatural Songs."
32 Bloom, *Yeats* 415.
33 Adams, *Book of Yeats's Poems* 218; Whitaker, *Swan and Shadow* 119.
34 Middleton, *Inward Gaze*, forthcoming.
35 For a Gnostic reading of this poem see Hassett, *Yeats* 108–18.
36 Sheeran, "Supernatural Songs."
37 Hopkins, *Poetical Works* 127.
38 Bloom, *Yeats* 414.

14 A FOOLISH PASSIONATE MAN

1 MacNeice, "Yeats's Epitaph" 45.
2 Auden, "Yeats: Master of Diction" 48–49.
3 Cunningham, *British Writers* 152.
4 See Cunningham, *British Writers* 110–11 for a collection of references to "the boys."
5 Jeffares, *New Commentary* 390.
6 Hassett, "The Chief Consolation" 55–67.
7 Ellmann, "At the Yeatses'" 253.
8 Quoted in Kelly, "Friendship" 234.
9 Gould, "Portrayed before his Eyes" 219.
10 Ellmann, *Identity* 209–10.
11 Gould, "Portrayed before his Eyes" 214.
12 Glendinning, *Vita* 208–12.
13 Woolf, *Diary* 3: 329.
14 Woolf, *Letters* 4: 250.
15 Woolf, *Diary* 4: 260, 257.
16 Gwynn, *Edward Martyn* 154.
17 Souhami, *Gluck* 211–18.
18 Armstrong, "Giving Birth" 40, also makes this point.
19 Woolf, *Room* 97.
20 Dollimore, *Sexual Dissidence* 262.
21 Showalter, *Literature* 285–89.
22 Heilbrun, *Androgyny* 151–67.
23 Moi, *Textual/Sexual Politics* 13–14.
24 Dollimore, *Sexual Dissidence* 45.
25 Woolf, *Room* 6.
26 Finneran, editorial note in Yeats, *The Poems Revised* 673–74.
27 Harrison, *Prolegomena* 246, 224.
28 Harrison, *Themis* 414–15.

29 Woolf, *Room* 18–19.
30 Meredith, *Diana* 131.
31 Shakespeare, *Complete Works* 1217.
32 Armstrong, "Giving Birth" 53.
33 Woolf, *Room* 66.
34 See Marcus, *Virginia Woolf* 163–64.
35 Gould, "Portrayed before his Eyes" 214.
36 Bradshaw, "Eugenics Movement" passim.
37 Soloway, *Demography* xvii-xviii.
38 Foucault, *History of Sexuality* 1: 118.
39 Grosskurth, *Havelock Ellis* 410–13.
40 Soloway, *Demography* 130–31.
41 Woolf, *Three Guineas* 111.
42 Stanfield, *Yeats* 145–58.
43 Bradshaw, "Eugenics Movement" 210–11.
44 Grosskurth, *Havelock Ellis* 413.
45 Ward, *Maud Gonne* 180–82.
46 Shakespeare, *Complete Works* 1554.

Works cited

Adam, Villiers de L'Isle. *Axel.* Trans. H. P. R. Finberg. London: Jarrolds, 1925.

Adams, Hazard. *The Book of Yeats's Poems.* Tallahassee: Florida State UP, 1990.

Adams, Michael. *Censorship: The Irish Experience.* University, Alabama: U of Alabama P, 1968.

Adorno, Theodor W. "Lyric Poetry and Society." *Telos* 20 (1974): 56–71.

Archibald, Douglas. *Yeats.* Syracuse: Syracuse UP, 1983.

Arensburg, Conrad M., and Solon T. Kimball. *Family and Community in Ireland.* 2nd ed. Cambridge, Mass.: Harvard UP, 1968.

Armstrong, Tim. "Giving Birth to Oneself: Yeats's Late Sexuality." *Yeats Annual* 8 (1991): 39–58.

Arnold, Matthew. *Lectures and Essays in Criticism.* Ed. R. H. Super. Ann Arbor: U of Michigan P, 1973.

Auden, W. H. "Prosecution and Defence." *Yeats: Poems, 1919–1935: A Casebook.* Ed. Elizabeth Cullingford. London: Macmillan, 1984. 57–62.

"Yeats: Master of Diction." *Yeats: Last Poems: A Casebook.* Ed. Jon Stallworthy. London: Macmillan, 1968. 47–49.

Auerbach, Nina. *Woman and the Demon: The Life of a Victorian Myth.* Cambridge, Mass.: Harvard UP, 1982.

Bakhtin, Mikhail. *The Dialogic Imagination.* Ed. Michael Holquist. Trans. Caryl Emerson and Michael Holquist. Austin: U of Texas P, 1981.

Rabelais and His World. Trans. Helen Iswolsky. Bloomington: Indiana UP, 1984.

Balliett, Conrad A. "The Lives – and Lies – of Maud Gonne." *Eire-Ireland* 14.3 (1979): 17–44.

Bataille, Georges. *Erotism: Death and Sensuality.* Trans. Mary Dalwood. San Francisco: City Lights, 1986.

Beckson, Karl. *Arthur Symons: A Life.* Oxford: Clarendon P, 1987.

Benton, John F. "Clio and Venus: An Historical View of Courtly Love." *The Meaning of Courtly Love.* Ed. F. X. Newman. Albany: State U of New York P, 1967. 19–42.

Berger, John. *Ways of Seeing.* Harmondsworth: Penguin, 1972.

Besant, Annie. *An Autobiography.* 3rd ed. Adyar: Theosophical Publishing House, 1939.

Bessai, Diane E. "'Dark Rosaleen' as Image of Ireland." *Eire-Ireland* 10.4 (1975): 62–84.

Blake, William. *Complete Writings*. Ed. Geoffrey Keynes. Rev. ed. London: Oxford UP, 1972.

Blavatsky, Helena Petrovna. *The Key to Theosophy*. Simplified ed. Adyar: Theosophical Publishing House, 1953.

Bloom, Harold. *Yeats*. London: Oxford UP, 1970.

Blunt, W. S. *My Diaries*. 2 vols. New York: Knopf, 1923.

Bogin, Meg. *The Women Troubadours*. New York: Norton, 1980.

Boland, Eavan. "The Woman Poet in a National Tradition." *Studies* 76.302 (1987): 148–58.

Bold, Alan. *The Ballad*. London: Methuen, 1979.

Boone, Joseph A. "Of Me(n) and Feminism." *Engendering Men: The Question of Male Feminist Criticism*. Ed. Joseph A. Boone and Michael Cadden. New York: Routledge, 1990. 11–25.

Boose, Lynda E. "The Family in Shakespeare Studies." *Renaissance Quarterly* 40.4 (Winter 1987): 707–42.

"The Father and the Bride in Shakespeare." *Publications of the Modern Language Association* 97 (1982): 325–47.

Bordo, Susan. "Anorexia Nervosa: Psychopathology as the Crystallization of Culture." *Feminism and Foucault: Reflections on Resistance*. Ed. Irene Diamond and Lee Quinby. Boston: Northeastern UP, 1988. 87–117.

Bornstein, George. "What is the Text of a Poem by Yeats?" Unpublished paper, ACIS conference, Galway 1992.

Yeats and Shelley. Chicago: U of Chicago P, 1970.

Bradford, Curtis B. "Yeats and Maud Gonne." *Texas Studies in Language and Literature* 3 (1962): 452–74.

Bradshaw, David. "The Eugenics Movement in the Thirties and the Emergence of *On the Boiler*." *Yeats and Women*. Ed. Deirdre Toomey. *Yeats Annual* (A Special Number) 9 (1991): 189–215.

Brandon, Ruth. *The Spiritualists: The Passion for the Occult in the Nineteenth and Twentieth Centuries*. Buffalo: Prometheus, 1984.

Bratton, J. S. *The Victorian Popular Ballad*. London: Macmillan, 1975.

Brennan, Genevieve. "Yeats, Clodd, *Scatalogic Rites* and the Clonmel Witch Burning." *Yeats Annual* 4 (1986): 207–15.

Brittan, Arthur. *Masculinity and Power*. Oxford: Blackwell, 1989.

Broadbent, J. B. *Poetic Love*. London: Chatto, 1964.

Brooks, Cleanth. *The Well Wrought Urn: Studies in the Structure of Poetry*. New York: Reynal, 1947.

Brown, Laura. "Reading Race and Gender: Jonathan Swift." *Eighteenth Century Studies* 23.4 (1990): 425–43.

Brown, Terence. *Ireland: A Social and Cultural History* 1922–1985. 2nd ed. London: Fontana Press, 1985.

Browning, Robert. *Poetical Works*. Ed. Ian Jack, Margaret Smith, and Rowena Fowler. 3 vols. Oxford: Clarendon P, 1983–88.

Burkitt, F. Crawford. *Early Eastern Christianity*: *St. Margaret's Lectures* 1904 *on the Syriac-Speaking Church*. London: Murray, 1904.

Burne-Jones, Georgiana. *Memorials of Edward Burne-Jones*. 2 vols. London: Macmillan, 1904.

Cairns, David, and Shaun Richards. *Writing Ireland*: *Colonialism, Nationalism and Culture*. Manchester: Manchester UP, 1988.

Campbell, Bruce F. *Ancient Wisdom Revived*: *A History of the Theosophical Movement*. Berkeley: U of California P, 1980.

Cardozo, Nancy. *Lucky Eyes and a High Heart*. Indianapolis: Bobbs Merrill, 1978.

Carew, Thomas. *Poems*. Ed. Rhodes Dunlap. Oxford: Clarendon P, 1949.

Castle, Terry. "Lab'ring Bards: Birth *Topoi* and English Poetics 1660–1820." *Journal of English and Germanic Philology* 78 (1979): 193–208.

The Catholic Bulletin, Dublin, 1924–28.

Cavanaugh, Catherine. *Love and Forgiveness in Yeats's Poetry*. Ann Arbor: UMI, 1986.

Chesler, Phyllis. *Women and Madness*. New York: Avon, 1973.

Cixous, Hélène. "The Laugh of the Medusa." *New French Feminisms*: *An Anthology*. Ed. Elaine Marks and Isabelle de Courtivron. New York: Schocken, 1981. 245–64.

——— "Sorties." *The Newly Born Woman*. Trans. Betsey Wing. Minneapolis: U of Minnesota P, 1986. 63–132.

Clark, David R. *Yeats at Songs and Choruses*. Amherst: U of Massachussetts P, 1983.

Clark, Rosalind. *The Great Queens*: *Irish Goddesses from the Morrígan to Cathleen ní Houlihan*. Gerrards Cross: Colin Smythe, 1991.

Clarke, Kathleen. *Revolutionary Woman*, 1878–1972: *An Autobiography*. Ed. Helen Litton. Dublin: O'Brien P, 1991.

Condren, Mary. *The Serpent and the Goddess*: *Women, Religion, and Power in Celtic Ireland*. San Franciso: Harper, 1989.

Costello, Peter. *The Heart Grown Brutal*. Dublin: Gill, 1977.

Cousins, James H., and Margaret E. *We Two Together*. Madras: Ganesh, 1950.

Coward, Rosalind. *Patriarchal Precedents*: *Sexuality and Social Relations*. London: Routledge, 1983.

Cross, Tom Peete, and Clark Harris Slover. *Ancient Irish Tales*. 1936. New Jersey: Barnes and Noble, 1969.

Cruttwell, Patrick. *The English Sonnet*. London: Longmans, 1966.

Culler, Jonathan. *The Pursuit of Signs*: *Semiotics, Literature, Deconstruction*. Ithaca: Cornell UP, 1981.

Cullingford, Elizabeth Butler. "How Jacques Molay Got Up the Tower." *English Literary History* 50 (1983): 763–89.

——— "Thinking of Her... as Ireland." *Textual Practice* 4.1 (1990): 1–21.

——— *Yeats, Ireland and Fascism*. London: Macmillan, 1981.

Cunningham, Valentine. *British Writers of the Thirties*. Oxford: Oxford UP, 1988.

Dalton, G. F. "The Tradition of Blood Sacrifice to the Goddess Eire." *Studies* 63.252 (1974): 343–54.

Daly, Mary. *Beyond God the Father*. 2nd ed. Boston: Beacon P, 1985.

Davis, Natalie Zemon. *Society and Culture in Early Modern France*. Stanford: Stanford UP, 1965.

Deane, Seamus. "Blueshirt." *London Review of Books*, 4 June 1981. 23–24.

    Celtic Revivals: Essays in Modern Irish Literature, 1880–1980. London: Faber, 1985.

    "Heroic Styles: The Tradition of an Idea." *Ireland's Field Day*. Notre Dame, Indiana: U of Notre Dame P, 1986. 45–58.

    A Short History of Irish Literature. London: Hutchinson, 1986.

de Man, Paul. *The Rhetoric of Romanticism*. New York: Columbia UP, 1984.

de Rougemont, Denis. *Love in the Western World*. Trans. Montgomery Belgion. 2nd ed. Princeton: Princeton UP, 1983.

de Valera, Eamon. *Speeches and Statements*: 1917–73. Ed. Maurice Moynihan. Dublin: Gill, 1980.

Dijkstra, Bram. *Idols of Perversity: Fantasies of Feminine Evil in Fin de Siècle Culture*. New York: Oxford UP, 1988.

Dinnage, Rosemary. *Annie Besant*. Harmondsworth: Penguin, 1986.

Dobbs, Brian, and Judy Dobbs. *Dante Gabriel Rossetti*. London: Macdonald, 1977.

Dollimore, Jonathan. *Sexual Dissidence: Augustine to Wilde, Freud to Foucault*. Oxford: Clarendon P, 1991.

Donne, John. *Poetical Works*. Ed. Sir Herbert Grierson. London: Oxford UP, 1933.

Dorcey, Mary. "The Spaces Between the Words: Mary Dorcey Talks to Nuala Archer." *Women's Review of Books* 8.3 (1990): 21–24.

Douglas, Mary. *Purity and Danger: An Analysis of the Concepts of Pollution and Taboo*. New York: Praeger, 1966.

Dronke, Peter. *Medieval Latin and the Rise of the European Love Lyric*. 2 vols. Oxford: Clarendon P, 1965.

Dryden, John. *John Dryden*. Ed. Keith Walker. Oxford: Oxford UP, 1987.

Eagleton, Terry. *Marxism and Literary Criticism*. London: Methuen, 1976.

    Walter Benjamin or Towards a Revolutionary Criticism. London: Verso, 1981.

Easthope, Antony. *Poetry as Discourse*. London: Methuen, 1983.

Eliot, T. S. *Collected Poems* 1909–1962. New York: Harcourt, 1963.

    The Waste Land. Ed. Valerie Eliot. London: Faber, 1971.

Ellmann, Mary. *Thinking About Women*. New York: Harcourt, 1968.

Ellmann, Richard. "At the Yeatses'." *a long the riverrun: Selected Essays*. New York: Knopf, 1989. 239–55.

    The Identity of Yeats. London: Faber, 1964.

    W. B. Yeats's Second Puberty. Washington: Library of Congress, 1986.

    Yeats: The Man and the Masks. 2nd ed. New York: Norton, 1978.

Engels, Friedrich. *The Origin of the Family, Private Property, and the State*. Harmondsworth: Penguin, 1985.

Faure, Elie. *History of Art.* Trans. Walter Pach. 4 vols. New York: Harper, 1921–24.

Felski, Rita. *Beyond Feminist Aesthetics: Feminist Literature and Social Change.* Cambridge, Mass.: Harvard UP, 1989.

Ferrante, Joan M. "Male Fantasy and Female Reality in Courtly Literature." *Women's Studies* 11/12.1 (1984): 67–98.

Finneran, Richard J. *Editing Yeats's Poems: A Reconsideration.* New York: St. Martin's Press, 1990.

     with George Mills Harper and William M. Murphy, eds. *Letters to W. B. Yeats.* 2 vols. New York: Columbia UP, 1977.

Flaubert, Gustave. *The Temptation of Saint Antony.* Trans. D. F. Hannigan. 2 vols. London: Nichols, 1895.

Fletcher, Ian. "'Leda and the Swan' as Iconic Poem." *Yeats Annual* 1 (1982): 82–113.

Foster, R. F. *Modern Ireland, 1600–1972.* Harmondsworth: Allen Lane, 1988.

     "Protestant Magic: W. B. Yeats and the Spell of Irish History." *Proceedings of the British Academy* 75 (1989): 243–66.

Foucault, Michel. *The History of Sexuality: Volume 1: An Introduction.* Trans. Robert Hurley. New York: Vintage, 1980.

Frazier, Adrian. *Behind the Scenes: Yeats, Horniman, and the Struggle for the Abbey Theatre.* Berkeley: U of California P, 1990.

Freud, Sigmund. *The Standard Edition.* Trans. James Strachey. 24 vols. London: Hogarth Press, 1974.

Friedman, Susan Stamford. "Creativity and the Childbirth Metaphor: Gender Difference in Literary Discourse." *Feminist Studies* 13.1 (1987): 49–82.

Friel, Brian. *Translations.* London: Faber, 1981.

Frye, Northrop. "Approaching the Lyric." *Lyric Poetry: Beyond New Criticism.* Ed. Chaviva Hosek and Patricia Parker. Ithaca: Cornell UP, 1985. 31–37.

Fuller, John. *The Sonnet.* London: Methuen, 1972.

Fuss, Diana. *Essentially Speaking: Feminism, Nature and Difference.* New York: Routledge, 1989.

Fussell, Paul. *Poetic Meter and Poetic Form.* Rev. ed. New York: Random House, 1979.

Gandhi, M. K. *Autobiography.* Trans. Mahadev Desai. Washington: Public Affairs P, 1948.

Gaunt, William. *The PreRaphaelite Tragedy.* London: Cape, 1942.

Gilbert, Sandra, and Susan Gubar. *The Madwoman in the Attic: The Woman Writer and the Nineteenth-Century Literary Imagination.* New Haven: Yale UP, 1979.

     No Man's Land: The Place of the Woman Writer in the Twentieth Century. 2 vols. New Haven: Yale UP, 1988–89.

Girouard, Mark. *The Return to Camelot: Chivalry and the English Gentleman.* New Haven: Yale UP, 1981.

Glendinning, Victoria. *Vita: The Life of V. Sackville-West.* New York: Knopf, 1983.

Goldin, Frederick. *Lyrics of the Troubadours and Trouveres: An Anthology and a History.* Gloucester, Mass.: Smith, 1973.

Goldman, Arnold. "Yeats, Spiritualism, and Psychical Research." *Yeats and the Occult.* Ed. George Mills Harper. Macmillan of Canada: Maclean-Hunter P, 1975.

Gordon, Linda, and Ellen DuBois. "Seeking Ecstasy on the Battlefield: Danger and Pleasure in Nineteenth-Century Feminist Sexual Thought." *Feminist Studies* 9.1 (1983): 7–25.

Gould, Warwick. "An Empty Theatre? Yeats as Minstrel in *Responsibilities.*" *Studies on W. B. Yeats.* Ed. Jacqueline Genet. Paris: CNRS, 1989. 79–118.

"Frazer, Yeats and the Reconsecration of Folklore." *Sir James Frazer and the Literary Imagination.* Ed. Robert Fraser. London: Macmillan, 1990. 121–53.

"'A Lesson for the Circumspect': W. B. Yeats's Two Versions of *A Vision* and the *Arabian Nights.*" *The Arabian Nights in English Literature: Studies in the Reception of the Thousand and One Nights into British Culture.* Ed. Peter L. Caracciolo. London: Macmillan, 1988. 244–80.

"'Portrayed before his Eyes': an Abandoned Late Poem." *Yeats Annual* 6 (1988): 214–21.

Greene, Thomas M. "Spenser and the Epithalamic Convention." *Edmund Spenser: Epithalamion.* Ed. Robert Beum. Columbus: Merrill, 1968. 37–52.

Gregory, Isabella Augusta. *Lady Gregory's Journals.* Ed. Daniel Murphy. 2 vols. New York: Oxford UP, 1978.

Griffin, Susan. *Pornography and Silence: Culture's Revenge against Nature.* London: Women's P, 1981.

Grosskurth, Phyllis. *Havelock Ellis: A Biography.* New York: Knopf, 1980.

Grossman, Allen. *Poetic Knowledge in the Early Yeats: A Study of The Wind among the Reeds.* Charlottesville: UP of Virginia, 1969.

Groult, Benoîte. "Night Porters." *New French Feminisms: An Anthology.* Ed. Elaine Marks and Isabelle de Courtivron. New York: Schocken, 1981. 68–75.

Guha, Naresh. *W. B. Yeats: An Indian Approach.* Calcutta: Jadavpur, 1968.

Gwynn, Denis. *Edward Martyn and the Irish Literary Theatre.* New York: Lemma P, 1974.

Hardiman, James, ed. *Irish Minstrelsy: The Bardic Remains of Ireland.* 1831. 2 vols. Shannon: Irish UP, 1971.

Harper, George Mills. *The Making of Yeats's A Vision: A Study of the Automatic Script.* 2 vols. Carbondale: Southern Illinois UP, 1987.

Yeats's Golden Dawn: The Influence of the Hermetic Order of the Golden Dawn on the Life and Art of W. B. Yeats. Wellingborough: Aquarian P, 1987.

Harper, Margaret Mills. "The Medium as Creator: George Yeats's Role in the Automatic Script." *Yeats: An Annual of Critical and Textual Studies* 6 (1988): 49–71.

"The Message is the Medium: Identity in the Automatic Script." *Yeats: An Annual of Critical and Textual Studies* 9 (1991): 35–54.

Harris, Daniel. *Yeats: Coole Park and Ballylee.* Baltimore: Johns Hopkins UP, 1974.

Harrison, Jane Ellen. *Epilegomena to the Study of Greek Religion and Themis.* New York: University Books, 1962.

   Prolegomena to the Study of Greek Religion. 2nd ed. Cambridge: Cambridge UP, 1908.

Harwood, John, ed. "Olivia Shakespear: Letters to W. B. Yeats." *Yeats Annual* 6 (1988): 59–107.

   Olivia Shakespear and W. B. Yeats: After Long Silence. London: Macmillan, 1989.

   "'Secret Communion': Yeats's Sexual Destiny." *Yeats and Women.* Ed. Deirdre Toomey. *Yeats Annual* (A Special Number) 9 (1991): 3–30.

Hassett, Joseph M. "Yeats and the Chief Consolation of Genius." *Yeats: An Annual of Critical and Textual Studies* 4 (1986): 55–67.

   Yeats and the Poetics of Hate. Dublin: Gill, 1986.

Haverty, Anne. *Constance Markievicz: An Independent Life.* London: Pandora, 1988.

Heaney, Seamus. "Mother Ireland." *Listener* [London] 27 Nov. 1972. 790.

   North. London: Faber, 1975.

   Preoccupations: Selected Prose 1968–1978. London: Faber, 1980.

Heath, Stephen. "Male Feminism." *Men in Feminism.* Ed. Alice Jardine and Paul Smith. New York: Methuen, 1987. 1–32.

   The Sexual Fix. London: Macmillan, 1982.

Heilbrun, Carolyn G. *Toward a Recognition of Androgyny.* 1964. New York: Norton, 1982.

Henderson, Linda. "Mysticism, Romanticism, and the Fourth Dimension." *The Spiritual in Art.* Los Angeles: Abbeville P, 1986. 219–37.

Herr, Cheryl. "The Erotics of Irishness." *Critical Inquiry* 17.1 (1990): 1–34.

Herrick, Robert. *Poetical Works.* Ed. L. C. Martin. Oxford: Clarendon P, 1956.

Hirsch, Edward. "The Imaginary Irish Peasant." *PMLA* 106.5 (1991): 1116–33.

Hodgart, M. J. C. *The Ballads.* London: Hutchinson, 1950.

Hone, Joseph. *W. B. Yeats, 1865–1939.* 2nd ed. London: Macmillan, 1962.

Hopkins, Gerard Manley. *The Poetical Works.* Ed. Norman H. Mackenzie. Oxford: Clarendon P, 1990.

Hough, Graham. *The Last Romantics.* London: Duckworth, 1949.

Howe, Ellic. *The Magicians of the Golden Dawn.* London: Routledge, 1972.

Howes, Marjorie. "*The Winding Stair.*" Unpublished lecture, Yeats International Summer School, Sligo, 1990.

Hunt, John Dixon. *The Pre-Raphaelite Imagination.* London: Routledge, 1968.

Hynes, Samuel. "All the Wild Witches: The Women in Yeats's Poems." *Sewanee Review* 85.4 (1977): 565–82.

Innes, C. L. "Yeats's Female Voices: Crazy Jane and Other Women in *The Winding Stair and Other Poems.*" *Text and Context* 3 (Autumn 1988): 55–70.

The Irish Catholic Register. Dublin, 1925.

The Irish Statesman. Dublin, 1924–25.

Jameson, Frederic. *The Political Unconscious.* Ithaca: Cornell UP, 1981.

Jeffares, A. Norman. *A New Commentary on the Poems of W. B. Yeats.* Stanford: Stanford UP, 1984.

W. B. Yeats: Man and Poet. 2nd ed. London: Routledge, 1962.

Jochum, K. P. S. "Yeats's Sonnets." *Modern British Literature* 4.1 (1979): 33–42.

Johnson, Josephine. *Florence Farr: Bernard Shaw's "New Woman".* Gerrards Cross: Smythe, 1975.

Johnson, Toni O'Brien, and David Cairns, eds. *Gender in Irish Writing.* Milton Keynes: Open UP, 1991.

Jonas, Hans. *The Gnostic Religion: The Message of the Alien God and the Beginnings of Christianity.* 2nd ed. Boston: Beacon P, 1963.

Joyce, James. *The Critical Writings.* Ed. Ellsworth Mason and Richard Ellmann. New York: Viking P, 1964.

A Portrait of the Artist as a Young Man. Harmondsworth: Penguin, 1960.

Ulysses. Ed. Hans Walter Gabler. New York: Vintage, 1986.

Kappeler, Susanne. *The Pornography of Representation.* Minneapolis: U of Minnesota P, 1986.

Keane, Patrick J. *Terrible Beauty: Yeats, Joyce, Ireland and the Myth of the Devouring Female.* Columbia: U of Missouri P, 1988.

Yeats's Interactions with Tradition. Columbia: U of Missouri P, 1987.

Kearney, Richard. "Between Politics and Literature: The Irish Cultural Journal." *The Crane Bag* 7.2 (1983): 160–71.

"Faith and Fatherland." *The Crane Bag* 8.1 (1984): 55–66.

"Myth and Motherland." *Ireland's Field Day.* Notre Dame: U of Notre Dame P, 1986. 59–80.

Kelleher, John V. "Yeats's Use of Irish Materials." *Tri-Quarterly* 4 (1965): 115–25.

Kelly, Joan. *Women, History and Theory.* Chicago: U of Chicago P, 1984.

Kelly, John. "Friendship is the Only House I Have: Lady Gregory and W. B. Yeats." *Lady Gregory, Fifty Years After.* Ed. Ann Saddlemyer and Colin Smythe. Gerrards Cross: Smythe, 1987. 179–257.

Kendrick, Laura. *The Game of Love.* Berkeley: U of California P, 1988.

Kennelly, Brendan, ed. *The Penguin Book of Irish Verse.* Harmondsworth: Penguin, 1970.

Keogh, Dermot. *The Vatican, the Bishops and Irish Politics, 1919–39.* Cambridge: Cambridge UP, 1986.

Kermode, Frank. *Romantic Image.* London: Routledge, 1986.

Kiberd, Declan. "The Elephant of Revolutionary Forgetfulness." *Revising the Rising.* Ed. Máirín Ní Dhonnchadha and Theo Dorgan. Derry: Field Day, 1991. 1–28.

"Inventing Irelands." *The Crane Bag* 8.1 (1984): 11–23.

Men and Feminism in Modern Literature. London: Macmillan, 1985.

"The War against the Past." *The Uses of the Past: Essays on Irish Culture.* Ed. Audrey S. Eyler and Robert F. Garratt. Newark: U of Delaware P, 1988. 24–54.

Kline, Gloria C. *The Last Courtly Lover: Yeats and the Idea of Woman.* Ann Arbor: UMI P, 1983.

Kofman, Sarah. *The Enigma of Woman: Woman in Freud's Writings.* Trans. Catharine Porter. Ithaca: Cornell UP, 1985.

Kristeva, Julia. *Powers of Horror: An Essay on Abjection.* Trans. Leon S. Roudiez. New York: Columbia UP, 1982.

Laffan, Michael. "Insular Attitudes: The Revisionists and their Critics." *Revising the Rising.* Ed. Máirín Ní Dhonnchadha and Theo Dorgan. Derry: Field Day, 1991. 106–21.

Laity, Cassandra. "W. B. Yeats and Florence Farr: The Influence of the 'New Woman' Actress on Yeats's Changing Images of Women." *Modern Drama* 28 (1985): 621–37.

La Rochefoucauld, François, Duc de. *The Maxims.* Trans. Constantine FitzGibbon. London: Wingate, 1957.

Lee, J. J. *Ireland 1912–1985: Politics and Society.* Cambridge: Cambridge UP, 1989.

Lewis, C. S. *The Allegory of Love: A Study in Medieval Tradition.* 2nd ed. New York: Oxford UP, 1958.

Lewis, Gifford. *Eva Gore Booth and Esther Roper: A Biography.* London: Pandora, 1988.

Lloyd, David. "Nationalism and the Figuration of the Feminine." Unpublished lecture, Gender and Colonialism Conference, Galway, 1992.

Nationalism and Minor Literature: James Clarence Mangan and the Emergence of Irish Cultural Nationalism. Berkeley: U of California P, 1987.

"The Poetics of Politics: Yeats and the Founding of the State." *Qui Parle* 3.2 (1989): 76–114.

"*The Tower.*" Unpublished lecture, Yeats International Summer School, Sligo, 1990.

Lloyd, Genevieve. *The Man of Reason: "Male" and "Female" in Western Philosophy.* London: Methuen, 1984.

Loftus, Belinda. *Mirrors: William III & Mother Ireland.* Dundrum, Co. Down: Picture P, 1990.

Loizeaux, Elizabeth Bergmann. *Yeats and the Visual Arts.* New Brunswick: Rutgers UP, 1986.

Longley, Edna. *From Cathleen to Anorexia: The Breakdown of Irelands.* Dublin: Attic Press, 1990.

"Poetry and Politics in Northern Ireland." *The Crane Bag* 9.1 (1985): 26–40.

Lydon, Mary. "Foucault and Feminism: A Romance of Many Dimensions." *Feminism and Foucault: Reflections on Resistance.* Ed. Irene Diamond and Lee Quinby. Boston: Northeastern UP, 1988. 135–47.

Lynch, David. *Yeats: The Poetics of the Self.* Chicago: U of Chicago P, 1979.

Lyons, F. S. L. *Ireland Since the Famine.* London: Wiedenfeld, 1971.

MacBride, Maud Gonne. *Always Your Friend: Letters between Maud Gonne and W. B. Yeats, 1893–1938.* Ed. Anna MacBride White and A. Norman Jeffares. London: Hutchinson, 1992.

A Servant of the Queen. London: Gollancz, 1938.

"Yeats and Ireland." *Scattering Branches.* Ed. Stephen Gwynn. New York: Macmillan, 1940. 16–33.

MacCana, Proinsias. "Women in Irish Mythology." *The Crane Bag* 4.1 (1980): 7–11.

Mackenzie, Midge. *Shoulder to Shoulder: A Documentary.* 2nd ed. New York: Vintage, 1988.

Mackey, William F. "Yeats's Debt to Ronsard on a *Carpe Diem* Theme." *Comparative Literature Studies* 5.19 (1946): 4–7.

MacKinnon, Catherine A. *Feminism Unmodified: Discourses on Life and Law.* Cambridge, Mass.: Harvard UP, 1987.

MacNeice, Louis. *Collected Poems.* Ed. E. R. Dodds. New York: Oxford UP, 1967.

"Yeats's Epitaph." *Yeats: Last Poems: A Casebook.* Ed. Jon Stallworthy. London: Macmillan, 1968. 44–46.

Maddox, Brenda. *Nora: A Biography of Nora Joyce.* 2nd ed. London: Minerva, 1989.

Madge, Charles. "Leda and the Swan." *Times Literary Supplement* 20 July 1962: 532.

Mann, Ann. "Yeats and Music." Unpublished lecture, Yeats International Summer School, Sligo, Ireland, 1989.

Marcus, Jane. *Art and Anger: Reading Like a Woman.* Columbus: Ohio State UP, 1988.

"The Asylums of Antaeus." *Feminism and Critical Theory: The Differences Within.* Ed. Elizabeth Meese and Alice Parker. Amsterdam: Benjamins, 1988.

Virginia Woolf and the Languages of Patriarchy, Bloomington: Indiana UP, 1987.

Marcus, Jane, ed. *Suffrage and the Pankhursts.* London: Routledge, 1987.

Markievicz, Constance. *Prison Letters of Countess Markievicz.* Intro. Amanda Sebestyen. London: Virago, 1987.

Marvell, Andrew. *Andrew Marvell.* Ed. Frank Kermode and Keith Walker. Oxford: Oxford UP, 1990.

Mayhew, George. "A Corrected Typescript of Yeats's 'Easter 1916.'" *Huntington Library Quarterly* 7.1 (1963): 53–71.

Meir, Colin. *The Ballads and Songs of W. B. Yeats: The Anglo-Irish Heritage in Subject and Style.* London: Macmillan, 1974.

Melchiori, Giorgio. *The Whole Mystery of Art: Pattern into Poetry in the Work of W. B. Yeats.* Westport: Greenwood P, 1979.

Meredith, George. *Diana of the Crossways.* Intro. Arthur Symons. New York: Modern Library, n.d.

An Essay on Comedy and the Uses of the Comic Spirit. Ed. Lane Cooper. Rev. ed. Ithaca: Cornell UP, 1956.

Middleton, Peter. *The Inward Gaze*. London: Routledge, forthcoming.

Miles, Margaret R. "The Virgin's One Bare Breast: Female Nudity and Religious Meaning in Tuscan Early Renaissance Culture." *The Female Body in Western Culture: Contemporary Perspectives*. Ed. Susan Rubin Suleiman. Cambridge, Mass.: Harvard UP, 1986. 193–208.

Millay, Edna St. Vincent. *Collected Sonnets*. New York: Harper, 1941.

Millett, Kate. *Sexual Politics*. 2nd ed. London: Virago, 1977.

Moi, Toril. "Feminism, Postmodernism, and Style." *Cultural Critique* (1988): 3–22.

Sexual/Textual Politics: Feminist Literary Theory. London: Methuen, 1985.

Molloy, F. C. "Francis Stuart, W. B. Yeats, and *To-morrow*." *Yeats Annual* 8 (1991): 214–24.

Montefiore, Jan. *Feminism and Poetry: Language, Experience, Identity in Women's Writing*. London: Pandora, 1987.

Moore, Virginia. *The Unicorn: W. B. Yeats' Search for Reality*. New York: Macmillan, 1954.

Morris, William. *Collected Works*. Ed. May Morris. 24 vols. London: Longmans, 1910–15.

Mosse, George L. "The Mystical Origins of National Socialism." *Journal of the History of Ideas* 22.1 (1961): 81–96.

Nationalism and Sexuality. New York: Fertig, 1985.

Mother Ireland. Researched and directed by Anne Crilly, produced by Derry Film and Video, 1988.

Mulvihull, Margaret. *Charlotte Despard: A Biography*. London: Pandora, 1989.

Munch-Pederson, Ole. "Crazy Jane: A Cycle of Popular Literature." *Eire-Ireland* 14 (1979): 56–73.

Murphet, Howard. *When Daylight Comes: A Biography of Helena Petrovna Blavatsky*. Wheaton, Ill.: Theosophical Publishing House, 1975.

Murphy, Cliona. *The Women's Suffrage Movement and Irish Society in the Early Twentieth Century*. New York: Harvester, 1989.

Murphy, William Martin. *Prodigal Father*. Ithaca: Cornell UP, 1978.

Nandy, Ashis. *The Intimate Enemy: Loss and Recovery of Self Under Colonialism*. Oxford: Oxford UP, 1983.

Nash, Nancy Rutowski. "Yeats and Heffernan the Blind." *Yeats Annual* 4 (1986): 201–06.

Ní Dhomhnaill, Nuala. "Yeats and the Myth of Sovereignty." Unpublished lecture, Yeats International Summer School, Sligo, 1987.

Ní Dhonnchadha, Máirín, and Theo Dorgan, eds. *Revising the Rising*. Derry: Field Day, 1991.

Oates, Joyce Carol. "'At Least I Have Made a Woman of Her': Images of Women in Twentieth-Century Literature." *Georgia Review* 37.1 (1983): 7–30.

O'Brien, Conor Cruise. "An Unhealthy Intersection." *New Review* 2.16 (1975): 3–8.

O'Callaghan, Margaret. "Language, Nationality and Cultural Identity in the Irish Free State, 1922–7: The *Irish Statesman* and the *Catholic Bulletin* Reappraised." *Irish Historical Studies* 24.94 (1984): 226–45.

O'Casey, Sean. *Autobiography Book 3: Drums under the Windows*. London: Pan, 1972.

Autobiography Book 4: Inishfallen Fare Thee Well. London: Pan, 1972.

Three Plays. London: Macmillan, 1966.

O Corráin, Donncha. "Women in Early Irish Society." *Women in Irish Society*. Ed. M. MacCurtain and D. O Corráin. Westport, Conn.: Greenwood P, 1979. 1–13.

Olney, James. *The Rhizome and the Flower*. Berkeley: U of California P, 1980.

Ong, Walter J. *Orality and Literacy: The Technologizing of the Word*. London: Methuen, 1982.

Oppel, Frances Nesbitt. *Mask and Tragedy: Yeats and Nietzsche, 1902–1910*. Charlottesville: UP of Virginia, 1987.

Oppenheim, Janet. *The Other World: Spiritualism and Psychical Research in England, 1850–1914*. Cambridge: Cambridge UP, 1985.

Ortner, Sherry. "Is Female to Male as Nature is to Culture?" *Woman, Culture and Society*. Ed. Michelle Rosaldo and Louise Lamphere. Stanford: Stanford UP, 1974. 67–88.

O'Shea, Edward. *A Descriptive Catalog of W. B. Yeats's Library*. New York: Garland, 1985.

O'Sullivan, Donal, ed. *Songs of the Irish: An Anthology of Irish Folk Music and Poetry with English Verse Translations*. New York: Crown, 1960.

O Tuama, Séan, and Thomas Kinsella, eds. *An Duanaire 1600–1900: Poems of the Dispossessed*. Trans. Thomas Kinsella. Portlaoise: Dolmen P, 1981.

Ovid. *The Erotic Poems*. Trans. Peter Green. Harmondsworth: Penguin, 1982.

Owen, Alex. *The Darkened Room: Women, Power and Spiritualism in Late Victorian England*. London: Virago, 1989.

Owens, Rosemary Cullen, "How We Won the Vote." *Votes for Women: Irish Women's Struggle for the Vote*. Ed. A. D. Sheehy Skeffington and Rosemary Owens. Dublin: n.p., 1975. 4–11.

Smashing Times: A History of the Irish Women's Suffrage Movement. Dublin: Attic P, 1984.

Pagels, Elaine. *The Gnostic Gospels*. New York: Random House, 1979.

Parker, Patricia. *Literary Fat Ladies: Rhetoric, Gender, Property*. London: Methuen, 1987.

Parkinson, Thomas. *W. B. Yeats Self-Critic and The Later Poetry: Two Volumes in One*. Berkeley: U of California P, 1971.

Pater, Walter. *The Renaissance*. Ed. Donald Hill. Berkeley: U of California P, 1980.

Pearse, Padraic H. *Collected Works*. 3 vols. Dublin: Maunsel, 1918–22.

Perloff, Marjorie. "Between Hatred and Desire: Sexuality and Subterfuge in 'A Prayer for my Daughter.'" *Yeats Annual* 7 (1990): 29–50.

"'Heart Mysteries': The Later Love Lyrics of W. B. Yeats." *Contemporary Literature* 10.2 (1969): 266–83.

Pethica, James. "'Our Kathleen': Yeats's Collaboration with Lady Gregory in the Writing of *Cathleen ni Houlihan.*" *Yeats Annual* 6 (1988): 3–31.

"Patronage and Creative Exchange: Yeats, Lady Gregory and the Economy of Indebtedness." *Yeats and Women.* Ed. Deirdre Toomey. *Yeats Annual* (A Special Number) 9 (1991): 60–94.

Plato. *The Phaedrus and the Seventh and Eighth Letters.* Trans. Walter Hamilton. Harmondsworth: Penguin, 1973.

The Symposium. Trans. Walter Hamilton. Harmondsworth: Penguin, 1951.

Pomeroy, Sarah. *Goddesses, Whores, Wives, and Slaves.* New York: Schocken, 1975.

Potter, Joy Hambuechen. "Beatrice, Dead or Alive: Love in the *Vita Nuova.*" *Beatrice Dolce Memoria, 1290–1990.* Special issue of *Texas Studies in Literature and Language* 32.1 (1990): 60–84.

Praz, Mario. *The Romantic Agony.* Trans. Angus Davidson. 2nd ed. London: Collins, 1960.

Preminger, Alex., ed. *Princeton Encyclopedia of Poetry and Poetics.* Enlarged Edition. Princeton: Princeton UP, 1974.

Propertius. *The Poems.* Trans. A. E. Watts. Harmondsworth: Penguin, 1966.

Pruitt, Virginia D., and Raymond D. Pruitt. "Yeats and the Steinach Operation: A Further Analysis." *Yeats: An Annual of Critical and Textual Studies* 1 (1983): 104–24.

Pyle, Hilary. *Jack B. Yeats: A Biography.* Rev. ed. London: Deutsch, 1989.

Ramazani, Jahan. *Yeats and the Poetry of Death: Elegy, Self-Elegy, and the Sublime.* New Haven: Yale UP, 1990.

Renan, Ernest. *The Poetry of the Celtic Races.* London: Scott, n.d.

Rich, Adrienne. *On Lies, Secrets, and Silence: Selected Prose 1966–1978.* New York: Norton, 1979.

Rochester, John Wilmot, Earl of. *The Complete Poems.* Ed. David M. Vieth. New Haven: Yale UP, 1968.

Ronsard, Pierre de. *Oeuvres.* Ed. Isidore Silver. 7 vols. Chicago, U of Chicago P, 1966.

Rose, Jacqueline. *Sexuality in the Field of Vision.* London: Verso, 1986.

Rosmarin, Adena. *The Power of Genre.* Minneapolis: U of Minnesota P, 1985.

Rossetti, Dante Gabriel. *Poems and Translations: 1850–1870.* London: Oxford UP, 1926.

Roth, Philip. *Portnoy's Complaint.* New York: Random House, 1967.

Russo, Mary. "Female Grotesques: Carnival and Theory." *Feminist Studies/Critical Studies.* Ed. Teresa de Lauretis. Bloomington: Indiana UP, 1986. 213–29.

Saddlemyer, Ann. "George Yeats." Unpublished lecture, Modern Language Association Convention, Chicago 1990.

Said, Edward. "Intellectuals in the Post-Colonial World." *Salmagundi* 70–71 (1986): 44–81.

Orientalism. New York: Vintage, 1979.

Yeats and Decolonization. Derry: Field Day, 1988.

Sappho. *Poems.* Trans. Mary Barnard. Berkeley: U of California P, n.d.

Schenk, Celeste. "'Corinna Sings': Women Poets and the Politics of Genre." *Decolonizing Tradition: New Views of Twentieth-Century "British" Literary Canons.* Ed. Karen R. Lawrence. Urbana: U of Illinois P, 1992. 37–69.

Scheper-Hughes, Nancy. *Saints, Scholars, and Schizophrenics: Mental Illness in Rural Ireland.* Berkeley: U of California P, 1979.

Scholem, Gershom. *Origins of the Kabbalah.* Princeton: Princeton UP, 1987.

Schuchard, Ronald. "'As Regarding Rhythm': Yeats and the Imagists." *Yeats: An Annual of Critical and Textual Studies* 2 (1984): 209–26.

"An Attendant Lord: H. W. Nevinson's Friendship with W. B. Yeats." *Yeats Annual* 7 (1990): 90–130.

"Yeats, Titian and the New French Painting." *Yeats the European.* Ed. A. Norman Jeffares. Gerrards Cross: Colin Smythe, 1989. 142–59.

Scott, Bonnie Kime. "Feminist Theory and Women in Irish Writing." *The Uses of the Past: Essays on Irish Culture.* Ed. Audrey S. Eyler and Robert F. Garratt. Newark: U of Delaware P, 1988. 55–63.

Shahar, Shulamith. *The Fourth Estate: A History of Women in the Middle Ages.* London: Methuen, 1983.

Shakespeare, William. *The Complete Works.* Ed. David Bevington. 4th ed. New York: HarperCollins, 1992.

Sheehy Skeffington, Hanna. "Reminiscences of an Irish Suffragette." *Votes for Women: Irish Women's Struggle for the Vote.* Ed. A. D. Sheehy Skeffington and Rosemary Owens. Dublin: n.p., 1975. 12–26.

Sheeran, Patrick. "Supernatural Songs." Unpublished lecture, Yeats International Summer School, Sligo, 1990.

Shelley, Percy Bysshe. *The Complete Poetical Works.* Ed. Thomas Hutchinson. 2nd ed. London: Oxford UP, 1969.

Showalter, Elaine. *A Literature of Their Own: British Women Writers from Brontë to Lessing.* Princeton: Princeton UP, 1977.

Sidney, Sir Philip. *Sir Philip Sidney.* Ed. Katharine Duncan-Jones. Oxford: Oxford UP, 1989.

Soloway, Richard A. *Demography and Degeneration: Eugenics and the Declining Birthrate in Twentieth-Century Britain.* Chapel Hill: U of North Carolina P, 1990.

Sophocles. *The Theban Plays.* Trans. E. F. Watling. Harmondsworth: Penguin, 1947.

Souhami, Diana. *Gluck 1895–1978: Her Biography.* London: Pandora, 1988.

Spivak, Gayatri Chakravorty. *In Other Worlds: Essays in Cultural Politics.* New York: Routledge, 1988.

Stallworthy, Jon. *Between the Lines: Yeats's Poetry in the Making.* Oxford: Clarendon P, 1963.

Vision and Revision in Yeats's Last Poems. Oxford: Clarendon P, 1969.

Stallworthy, Jon, ed. *The Penguin Book of Love Poetry.* Harmondsworth: Penguin, 1976.

Yeats: *Last Poems*: *A Casebook*. London: Macmillan, 1968.

Stallybrass, Peter, and Allon White. *The Politics and Poetics of Transgression*. London: Methuen, 1986.

Stanfield, Paul Scott. *Yeats and Politics in the* 1930*s*. London: Macmillan, 1988.

Stanton, Domna C. "Difference on Trial." *The Poetics of Gender*. Ed. Nancy Miller. Columbia UP, 1986. 157–82.

Stewart, J. G. *Jane Ellen Harrison*: *A Portrait from Letters*. London: Merlin, 1959.

Swift, Jonathan. *Complete Poems*. Ed. Pat Rogers. New Haven: Yale UP, 1983.

Swinburne, Algernon. *Selected Poems*. Ed. Edward Shanks. London: Macmillan, 1950.

Sword, Helen. "Leda and the Modernists." *Proceedings of the Modern Language Asssociation* 107.2 (1992): 305–18.

Symonds, John. *Madame Blavatsky*: *Medium and Magician*. London: Oldhams P, 1959.

Symons, Arthur. *Knave of Hearts*: 1894–1908. London: Heinemann, 1913.

Taylor, Anne Robinson. *Male Novelists and their Female Voices*: *Literary Masquerades*. Troy, NY.: Whitston, 1981.

Thuente, Mary Helen. "The Folklore of Irish Nationalism." *Perspectives on Irish Nationalism*. Ed. Thomas E. Hachey and Lawrence J. McCaffery. Lexington: U of Kentucky P, 1990. 42–60.

W. B. Yeats and Irish Folklore. Totowa, NJ: Gill, 1980.

Tickner, Lisa. *The Spectacle of Women*: *Imagery of the Suffrage Campaign* 1907–14. Chicago: U of Chicago P, 1988.

To-morrow 1.1 (August, 1924).

Toomey, Deirdre. "*Bards of the Gael and Gall*: An Uncollected Review by Yeats in *The Illustrated London News*." *Yeats Annual* 5 (1987): 203–11.

"Labyrinths: Yeats and Maud Gonne." *Yeats and Women*. Ed. Deirdre Toomey. *Yeats Annual* (A Special Number) 9 (1991): 95–131.

"The Unwilling Persephone." *Yeats Annual*, forthcoming.

"'Worst Part of Life': Yeats's Horoscopes for Olivia Shakespear." *Yeats Annual* 6 (1988): 222–26.

Torchiana, Donald T. "'Among School Children' and the Education of the Irish Spirit." *In Excited Reverie*: *A Centenary Tribute to W. B. Yeats*. Ed. A. Norman Jeffares and K. G. W. Cross. New York: Macmillan, 1965. 123–50.

W.B.Yeats and Georgian Ireland. Evanston: Northwestern UP, 1966.

Tuchman, Maurice. "Hidden Meanings in Abstract Art." *The Spiritual in Art*: *Abstract Painting* 1890–1985. Los Angeles: Abbeville P, 1986. 17–61.

Van Duyn, Mona. *To See, To Take*. New York: Athaneum, 1970.

Vickers, Nancy J. "Diana Described: Scattered Woman and Scattered Rhyme." *Writing and Sexual Difference*. Ed. Elizabeth Abel. Chicago: U of Chicago P, 1982. 95–109.

Votes for Women, London, 1910.

Waller, Edmund. *Poems*. Ed. G. Thorn Drury. 1893. New York: Greenwood, 1968.

Ward, Margaret. *Maud Gonne: Ireland's Joan of Arc*. London: Pandora, 1990.
The Missing Sex: Putting Women into Irish History. Dublin: Attic P, 1991.
Unmanageable Revolutionaries: Women and Irish Nationalism. London: Pluto, 1983.

Warner, Marina. *Alone of All Her Sex: The Myth and the Cult of the Virgin Mary*. 2nd ed. New York: Vintage, 1983.

Webster, Brenda. *Yeats: A Psychoanalytic Study*. London: Macmillan, 1974.

Whitaker, Thomas R. *Swan and Shadow: Yeats's Dialogue with History*. Chapel Hill: U of North Carolina P, 1964.

Whyte, J. H. *Church and State in Modern Ireland* 1923–1970. New York: Barnes and Noble, 1971.

Wills, Clair. "Mothers and Strangers." Unpublished paper, Gender and Colonialism Conference, Galway, 1992.
"Upsetting the Public: Carnival, Hysteria and Women's Texts." *Bakhtin and Cultural Theory*. Ed. Ken Hirschkop and David Shepherd. Manchester: Manchester UP, 1989. 130–51.

Wilson, F. A. C. *W. B. Yeats and Tradition*. London: Gollancz, 1958.

Woolf, Virginia. *The Diary of Virginia Woolf*. Ed. Anne Olivier Bell. 5 vols. London: Hogarth P, 1977–84.
The Letters of Virginia Woolf. Ed. Nigel Nicolson and Joanne Trautmann. 6 vols. New York: Harcourt Brace Jovanovich, 1975–80.
"Mr. Bennett and Mrs. Brown." *The Captain's Death Bed and Other Essays*. New York: Harcourt, 1950. 94–119.
A Room of One's Own. Harmondsworth: Penguin, 1945.
Three Guineas. New York: Harcourt, 1966.
To the Lighthouse. Harmondsworth: Penguin, 1964.

Wordsworth, William. *The Poetical Works*. Ed. E. de Selincourt. 2nd ed. Oxford: Clarendon P, 1952.

Yeats, W. B. *Ah, Sweet Dancer: W. B. Yeats: Margot Ruddock: A Correspondence*. Ed. Roger McHugh. New York: Macmillan, 1970.
Autobiographies. London: Macmillan, 1955.
The Collected Letters: Volume 1, 1865–1895. Ed. John Kelly. Oxford: Clarendon P, 1986.
A Critical Edition of Yeats's A Vision (1925). Ed. George Mills Harper and Walter Kelly Hood. London: Macmillan, 1978.
Essays and Introductions. London: Macmillan, 1961.
Explorations. Sel. Mrs. W. B. Yeats. New York: Collier, 1962.
John Sherman and Dhoya. Ed. Richard J. Finneran. Detroit: Wayne State UP, 1969.
The Letters. Ed. Allan Wade. London: Hart Davis, 1954.
Letters on Poetry to Dorothy Wellesley. Ed. Dorothy Wellesley. London: Oxford UP, 1964.

Memoirs: Autobiography-First Draft and Journal. Ed. Denis Donoghue. London: Macmillan, 1972.

"Modern Ireland: An Address to American Audiences, 1932–33." *Massachussetts Review* 5.2 (1963–64): 256–68.

Mythologies. 1959. New York: Collier, 1969.

The Poems Revised. Ed. Richard J. Finneran. New York: Macmillan, 1989.

The Secret Rose, Stories by W. B. Yeats: A Variorum Edition. Ed. Philip L. Marcus, Warwick Gould, and Michael J. Sidnell. 2nd edn, London: Macmillan, 1992.

The Senate Speeches. Ed. Donald R. Pearse. London: Faber, 1961.

The Speckled Bird. Ed. W. H. O'Donnell. 2 vols. Dublin: Cuala Press, 1973.

A Tower of Polished Black Stones: Early Versions of The Shadowy Waters. Ed. David R. Clark and George Mayhew. Dublin: Dolmen P, 1971.

Uncollected Prose. Ed. John P. Frayne and Colton Johnson. 2 vols. New York: Columbia UP, 1970.

The Variorum Edition of the Plays. Ed. Russell Alspach, assisted by Catherine C. Alspach. New York: Macmillan, 1966.

The Variorum Edition of the Poems. Ed. Peter Allt and Russell Alspach. New York: Macmillan, 1957.

A Vision. 2nd ed. London: Macmillan, 1962.

W. B. Yeats and T. Sturge Moore: Their Correspondence, 1901–1937. Ed. Ursula Bridge. London: Routledge, 1953.

Yeats's Vision Papers. Ed. George Mills Harper, assisted by Mary Jane Harper. 3 vols. Iowa City: U of Iowa P, 1992.

Yeats, W. B., ed. *A Book of Irish Verse.* London: Methuen, 1895.

ed. *Fairy and Folk Tales of Ireland.* New York: Macmillan, 1983.

ed. *The Oxford Book of Modern Verse: 1892–1935.* New York: Oxford UP, 1936.

and F. R. Higgins, eds. *Broadsides.* Dublin: Cuala P, 1935.

Index

abjection, 221, 230, 240
  of male lover, 4, 5, 25–26, 29, 34, 35–36,
    55, 85, 73, 109
  of woman, 44, 116
abortion, 152, 228
Adam, Villiers de l'Isle: *Axel*, 47–48, 53, 96,
  97
Adorno, Theodor, 2, 3, 73, 104
AE (George Russell), 143, 173, 248
Aeschylus: *Oresteia*, 161–62, 272
aisling, 59–60, 61, 62–63, 66, 67, 174,
  237
Amazon, 70, 77, 81, 82, 282
androgyny, 12, 13, 15, 256, 263, 269,
  270–71
Anglo-Irish, the, 123–24, 138, 144, 148–50,
  186, 244
Aoife, 77, 78, 81, 282
Aphrodite, 41, 89, 91–92, 131, 135–36
apocalypse, 52–54, 60, 119, 139, 259
apostrophe, 198–99, 267
Aquinas, St. Thomas, 195–96
Arabian Nights, 27, 106, 109, 114
Arensburg and Kimball, 173, 178, 235
Aristophanes, 181, 192, 218
Aristotle, 93, 197
Armstrong, Laura, 14–15
Armstrong, Tim, 274
Arnold, Matthew, 66, 67
  "Study of Celtic Literature," 61
asceticism, 27, 102, 185, 187, 194, 196, 198,
  200–01, 207, 252, 254, 259, 260, 278
Athena, 88, 267, 272
aubade, 218–19
Auden, W. H., 142, 165, 249, 261
Auerbach, Nina, 32
Augustine, St., 239–40

Bakhtin, Mikhail, 148–50, 177, 228–30,
  232–37, 241–43
  The Dialogic Imagination, 234

Rabelais and His World, 229, 243
ballad, 2, 65–66, 165–84, 206, 215, 227,
  233–35, 261–62, 274–79, 285
  nationalist, 16, 60, 66, 166–67, 172
  street-ballad, 140, 165, 167, 168
  transmitted by women, 182, 204–05
Barrington, Margaret: "Colour," 148
Barthes, Roland, 159
Bataille, Georges, 43, 44, 45, 47, 52, 239,
  240, 241
Baudelaire, Charles, 43, 45, 220
Beatrice of Die, 28
Beatrice Portinari, 29–32, 46, 63, 79
Beeton, Isabella, 210
Berger, John, 4, 88, 153, 212
Besant, Annie, 39, 40, 74
Bhagavad Gita, 38, 39
binary oppositions, 5–6, 95, 149, 196, 197,
  207, 208, 239, 243, 253, 271
Blake, William, 37, 231, 240, 254
  "The Mental Traveller," 221
Blavatsky, Helena Petrovna, 36, 37–40, 41,
  254
  Isis Unveiled, 37
  The Secret Doctrine, 252
blazon, 5, 160, 237
blood sacrifice, patriotic, 54, 56–57, 66–70,
  121, 125–29, 134, 174, 231, 238
Bloom, Harold, 250, 259
Blueshirts, 246, 247
Bolsheviks, 130, 139, 229
Boone, Joseph, 204
"Boyne Water," 277
Bradshaw, David, 279
Brehon Laws, 55, 75, 194
Brigid, 55, 75
Brittan, Arthur, 247, 255
Brooks, Cleanth, 195
Brown, Laura, 164
Buddhism, 37, 38, 252
Burke, Edmund, 236

Index